Nation Against Nation

Nation Against Nation

WHAT HAPPENED TO THE U.N. DREAM
AND WHAT THE U.S. CAN
DO ABOUT IT

Thomas M. Franck

New York   Oxford

OXFORD UNIVERSITY PRESS

1985

Oxford University Press

Oxford London New York Toronto
Delhi Bombay Calcutta Madras Karachi
Kuala Lumpur Singapore Hong Kong Tokyo
Nairobi Dar es Salaam Cape Town
Melbourne Auckland

and associated companies in
Beirut Berlin Ibadan Mexico City Nicosia

Published by Oxford University Press, Inc.,
200 Madison Avenue, New York, New York 10016

Library of Congress Cataloging in Publication Data
Franck, Thomas M.
Nation against nation.
Bibliography: p.
Includes index.
1. United Nations.
2. United Nations—United
States.
I. Title.
JX1977.F694 1985   341.23   84-25393
ISBN 0-19-503587-9

Printing (last digit): 9 8 7 6 5 4 3 2 1

Printed in the United States of America

To

SHEILA BIDDLE

"better lo'ed ye canna be"

Acknowledgments

Ecclesiastes tells us (xii, 1):

*"Of making many books there
is no end;
and much study is a weariness
of the flesh."*

This is a fair description of the scholar's lot, particularly in the halls of academe. Yet, this book has been a joy to write, despite the fact that it expresses some decent measure of anguish and anger at the failure of the U.N. dream. The joy was due to the conditions under which this book was written. The Guggenheim Foundation's grant, a sabbatical leave granted by the N.Y.U. Law School and sabbatical stipend supplemented by the N.Y.U. Law Center Foundation facilitated an extraordinary and, indeed, for me unprecedented luxury: sixteen continuous months of undisturbed concentration on one subject. At the U.N., where I had previously worked, concentration comes in 40-second modules, monitored by the hyperactive telephone. The opportunity to pursue tangled skeins of logic, following threads of ideas wherever they might lead, is the scholar's and teacher's delight and I am grateful for its wonderfully recuperative effect.

I am also grateful to the N.Y.U. Center for International Studies for organizing meetings with informed critics while the manuscript was at the draft stage. The Center also funded research assistance through its Junior Fellows program. Particularly helpful were Dean Norman Redlich and Associate Dean John L. Peschel in scheduling my classes, on my return to teaching, so as to facilitate long weekends in which to complete my writing and, otherwise, running interference when administrative and other chores threatened to nibble to death the scholarly urge.

An important reason for my joy in the writing of this book was the quality of personal support from those who worked with me. My assistant, Mrs. Rochelle

Fenchel, did not merely type this manuscript, repeatedly and with great care, but made many important suggestions while performing invaluable editorial functions. Her interest in, and enthusiasm for, this project was a stimulus and constant reminder of the high aspirations with which we had embarked on it.

Five Junior Fellows not only did historic and bibliographic research but actively participated in interviewing numerous sources in New York, Washington, Geneva, and elsewhere. All of them, a most unusual group of young lawyers—Robert C. Treuhold, Margaret N. O'Malley, Jerome M. Lehrman, Troy Alexander, and Kevin W. Quigley—constantly stimulated me with perceptive but unobtrusive suggestions and criticisms.

A substantial number of diplomats, scholars, and U.N. officials have read parts of this manuscript. Herbert Reis, the redoubtable lawyer and conscience of the U.S. delegation to the U.N. for thirteen years, took the time to make important suggestions throughout. Assistant Secretary-General George L. Sherry read several chapters, as did my friends and former ambassadors to the U.N., Theodor Meron and Tommy Koh. Judith Friedlaender read the entire manuscript with great sensitivity. I am deeply grateful to them and to many others it seems best to leave unmentioned. They are not responsible, of course, either for my mistakes of fact or for my personal deductions and conclusions; but their unstinting and solicitous encouragement did measurably improve the quality of my work, as also the ethos in which it was performed.

This is my fourth book for Oxford University Press, which speaks eloquently of the high regard I have for my editors, Leona Capeless and Sheldon Meyer.

New York   T.M.F.
December 1984

Contents

Nation Against Nation

Introduction

*Why do the nations so furiously
rage together?
Why do the people imagine a vain
thing?*

Psalms II, 1.

There are two principal tasks for which the United Nations was established and on which it ultimately must be judged. *First*, there is the task of mitigating, or better resolving, disputes and keeping peace between states when interests clash. *Second*, there is the task of mobilizing the international community to act collectively to deter, or, if that fails, to resist aggression by one state against another. As Secretary-General Kurt Waldheim put it, "the most important tasks of the United Nations are to prevent military conflict between its members and to settle international disputes."[1] Both are essential to the U.N.'s mission of preserving succeeding generations from the scourge of evermore dangerous war.

Certainly, the United Nations family of organizations has taken on myriad other assignments, from facilitating the delivery of mail between nations to the eradication of hunger and malaria. In some of these tasks it has been remarkably successful. In others it is marking time, filling pages and conference halls while providing makework employment for bureaucrats. Yet, all these specialized activities for the amelioration of the human condition presume that there will continue to be a human condition to ameliorate. Unless nations, armed to the teeth both conventionally and unconventionally, resolve their conflicts peacefully and decisively deter aggression, the presumption of a continuing human condition may well prove unwarranted.

It is therefore appropriate and necessary to judge the U.N. by its capacity to fulfill these two principal tasks: not to indulge a misologous aversion to international organization, but to ensure that, if the U.N. is indeed a failure, it will either be put right or that the people of the United States understand that in the dangerous matter of international security, they must rely on themselves rather than on a false hope.

Not that mankind currently has all its eggs in the U.N.'s basket. Naturally, Secretaries-General have long tended to insist, as Kurt Waldheim did as recently as 1982, that, when it comes to human survivability, "the United Nations, with all its weaknesses, represents the best available structure for this purpose."[2] But it is no secret, as a candid senior U.N. official, an American, recently pointed out, that "international institutions are not the sole or, indeed, the principal framework of the international system as it now stands. That system, a system of sovereign states, has another scaffolding—one in which security has to be provided for, as the case may be, by individual and collective self-defence . . . The North Atlantic Alliance and the Warsaw Pact are two major components of this system. . . ." He adds that "the balance of deterrence between the two superpowers . . . is a central element of international security in the nuclear age . . . ."[3]

The current tendency is to discount the U.N. as a peace-preserving tool. The large bronze sculpture outside U.N. headquarters in New York shows a sword being beaten into a plowshare. That remains an unfulfilled aspiration. Worse, the U.N. is no longer even regarded as a propitious forum within which to pursue such hopes. It is increasingly accepted—certainly in Washington and Moscow, but also in Paris, Peking, New Delhi, and Riyadh—that conflicts between states are more likely to be resolved by direct bilateral negotiations than in the chambers of the U.N. Similarly, it is conventional wisdom that states, in the first instance, must rely for security on their own military power and on the deterrent might of regional, ideological, racial, or religious alliances. Only the weakest handful of mini-states, because they have no alternative, now think of the U.N. as their best protection against aggression and other breaches of their tranquility.

Secretaries-General are apt to ask in anguish why this should be so. The incumbent, Javier Pérez de Cuéllar, in his first annual report to the General Assembly, called for an examination "with the utmost frankness" of "the reasons for the reluctance of parties to some conflicts to . . . use the machinery of the United Nations."[4] Such an examination is long overdue, even if it yields little that is not already obvious or, at least, easily deducible from an abundance of data.

Unfortunately, instead of addressing the question seriously, the tendency on the part of Secretaries-General and other senior U.N. officials is to blame the member states, and the "Big Powers" in particular, for lacking the political resolve to use the machinery established by the Charter to alleviate conflicts. Secretary-General Waldheim, in particular, was given to delivering Kantian lectures on the dangers of this lack of socio-political "will."[5] But governments, or at least some of them, are responsible trustees of the national interest and cannot be expected to substitute a romantic "will" to achieve world order for sober nomistic prudence.

Superficially, there would appear to be a *circulo inextricabilis* here: the U.N. does not work because nations do not use it because they think it cannot work. Secretary-General Waldheim has summoned states to break out of the defeatist circle with "positive thinking."[6] If that were all there is to it, nations do indeed merely need a good, stiff dose of *willen*.[7] But there may be more, much more.

Supporters of the U.N., not merely its critics, need to face these additional, more serious obstacles with clarity and frankness; and not primarily with optimism. If it is defeatist to think negatively in situations fraught with opportunities, it is Pollyanna-ish to think positively about situations that are more appropriate to despair. As the old saying goes: "If you are able to keep your head when all those around you are losing theirs, you may not understand the situation." If the U.N. is afflicted with defects that outweigh its capacity for good, then a member's failure to use it does not cause that failure, but merely *recognizes* it in a realistic fashion. As even Waldheim acknowledged, a shift in the behavior of governments in the direction of a habitual deference to the U.N. can only be expected when there is "a general belief that such a transition not only serves the long-term interest of all Governments but is essential to a reasonably secure and civilized future for the human race."[8] But is such a general belief likely, and would it be rational?

§ **1** §

Great Expectations

Baselines of Expectation

Even in an era which has seen extraordinary changes in public attitudes—
toward family, church, sex, dress, and entertainment—it is still surprising that
there should have been such a sea-change in the way the American public
regards the United Nations.

Yet, disenchantment there certainly is. And this is not a phenomenon limited to those liberals of New York or Los Angeles who once formed an
important part of the pro-U.N. constituency, many of whom, because Jewish,
have become alienated by the predominantly anti-Israeli positions taken in
resolutions of the General Assembly. Traveling widely and speaking around
this country as director of research at UNITAR, the U.N.'s "think tank," I was
struck by the prevalence of the mood of disillusion and disappointment, frequently bordering on anger, manifest across the spectrum of geographic, social,
ethnic, and religious groupings.

This impression cannot be rebutted by reference to public opinion polls
demonstrating continued support for selected U.N. activities such as help to
developing countries, the eradication of malaria, or the useful activities of the
World Bank and the International Postal Union. The American public is
sophisticated enough to know that these praiseworthy activities are carried out
by agencies that are largely independent of the principal political institutions of
the U.N. When the laity think of the United Nations, they have in mind the
organs which deal with highly visible political disputes: the Security Council,

the Secretariat, and especially the General Assembly. If they are particularly knowledgeable about the subject, they may also include the Economic and Social Council (ECOSOC) and the Human Rights Commission, which is not a principal organ, but a "subsidiary" of ECOSOC.

That the public's imagination should so narrowly comprehend the United Nations in terms of its primarily political organs is, of course, part of the trouble; some of the less controversial service institutions related to the organization, mostly called "agencies"—the United Nations International Children's Emergency Fund (UNICEF) is an example—do useful work for which much credit is due. But the organs which deal with the big political disputes—the General Assembly, the Security Council, and the Secretariat—are the essential core of the system. Between World Wars I and II the United States belonged to some specialized agencies, such as the International Labour Organization, even while refusing to join the League of Nations. Even now, we could continue to belong to the best of the functional bodies such as the World Health Organization and the World Food Programme, even if we decided to withdraw from the U.N. itself because the initiatives of the core political organs no longer coincided with the U.S. national interest.

Such a tactical withdrawal has now become thinkable precisely because of the disappointment that informs current American attitudes toward the U.N.'s political and executive organs. While it may be argued that the organization today is less venal than is currently perceived, it is also much less effective than we had hoped in 1945. And its ineffectiveness has become almost a virtue when so many of the initiatives, particularly of the General Assembly, are direct assaults against the national interest of the Western World and against democratic values.

Consciously or unconsciously, it is against the baseline of 1945 expectations and aspirations that current U.N. performance is measured. The hopes and expectations born in San Francisco in 1945, and which continued to be nourished during the first decade of the organization's existence while the United States and its allies exercised substantial influence over its political organs, may have died in the hearts of the American public but appear to linger in our collective memory.

Naturally, what Americans think about the U.N. today is at least in part conditioned by the expectations fixed in the formative years. If those expectations were exaggerated, then the subsequent fall in public esteem might also be exaggerated.

The Overselling of the U.N.

The campaign for U.S. entry into the new organization to ensure postwar peace was surely one of the most dramatic examples of hard-sell huckstering in twentieth-century American politics, comparable to the fanfare and high hopes that accompanied the launching of the "War on Poverty" in the late 1960s. Government officials, eminent citizens, public interest groups, newspapers, and members of Congress of both parties participated in an unprecedented effort to "sell" the Charter, which had just been signed in San Francisco. No doubt to a considerable extent, this campaign, partly spontaneous, partly orchestrated by the Truman administration, was spurred by memories of the unexpected defeat in the Senate of the Treaty of Versailles, to which the Covenant of the League of Nations was attached. That event, in 1920, kept the U.S. from joining the U.N.'s predecessor.

Yet, given the fact that the Gallup poll, in July 1945, was showing a 20-1 plurality in favor of the U.N. treaty,[1] it is surprising that the selling campaign was not a bit more restrained. Imagine the opening days of the San Francisco Conference at which the U.N. Charter was put in final form—April 21 and 22, 1945—being designated as days of prayer by a Laymen's Movement whose chairman, Wallace C. Steers, solemnly called for "the largest mass outpouring in history of the soul of man in search of God's help."[2] United in this nationwide effort were such disparate but important groups as the United Farmers, the Congress of Industrial Organizations, the National Association of Manufacturers, the American Legion, the Association of American Colleges, the National Retail Dry Goods Association, and even the Mutual Broadcasting Company.

Government officials—some recruited especially for the purpose, others summoned out of retirement—fanned out across the country to "preach the word." Former President Herbert Hoover emerged from the shadows to describe the San Francisco Conference as the "most fateful conference in all American history" and predicted that during its "fleeting moments the future of mankind may be molded for the next hundred years."[3] The ordinarily tight-lipped former Secretary of State Cordell Hull, speaking from his hospital bed, let it be known that the U.N. held the key to "the fulfillment of humanity's highest aspirations and the very survival of our civilization."[4]

Government officials criss-crossed the country like zealous circuit-riders. The State Department sent the distinguished international lawyer, Professor Clyde Eagleton, to enlist the public support of the nation's attorneys in a series of speeches to bar associations in seven key regional cities.[5] By influencing targeted sections of the public, the Truman administration was trying to influence Congress, in particular the Senate, which had to deliver a two-thirds majority in favor of the Charter before the U.S. could join the U.N. So prevalent did these practices become that Senator Robert A. Taft of Ohio, who ended up voting for the Charter, complained that the government was being turned into "a vast public-pressure group to destroy our constitutional processes." Illegal lobbying by the government, he charged, was being conducted on such a scale "as to destroy the whole legislative process of intelligent consideration."[6]

Yet, members of Congress scarcely needed convincing. They were as united as the public in their enthusiasm for the Charter, and their hyperbole exceeded anything generated by the executive branch. The chairman of the Senate Foreign Relations Committee, Senator Tom Connally of Texas, welcomed the San Francisco Charter as "the greatest document of its kind that has ever been formulated."[7] His counterpart across the Hill, Congressman Sol Bloom of New York, celebrated "this new magna carta of peace and security for mankind" which would be "a turning point in the history of civilization."[8] The senior Republican on his committee, Representative Charles A. Eaton of New Jersey, agreed that "this Charter is the most hopeful and important document in the history of world statesmanship" and "the greatest and most hopeful public event in history." He foresaw "inexorable tides of destiny" carrying us "towards a golden age of freedom, justice, peace and social well-being."[9]

Think of it: "The greatest event in history." Superlatives were thicker than lobbyists' hides on Capitol Hill. In the privacy of the Senate Foreign Relations Committee's executive session, before the treaty was reported to the Senate for consideration, one might have expected to encounter some skepticism and reserve. Instead, everyone agreed with Senator Walter F. George of Georgia that the Charter was "perhaps the most important foreign-policy step that this Nation has taken in all of its whole history."[10] In public, Senator John L. McClellan of Arkansas declared that the U.N. Charter was "possibly the most momentous document ever produced by man,"[11] an excess echoed by Senator Scott W. Lucas of Illinois.[12] Senator Alben Barkley of Kentucky, soon to become Vice President of the United States, thought the Charter would "take its place alongside the Magna Carta, the Declaration of Independence, the Constitution of the United States, Lincoln's Gettysburg Address and his Second Inaugural Address as one of the great documents of human history."[13] Others thought the Charter would usher in "a new era in the history of mankind"[14] (Senator Albert W. Hawkes from New Jersey), and had "grown from the prayers and prophesies of Isaiah and Micah"[15] (Senator Claude Pepper from Florida).

If there were doubts, very few expressed them. Among them were Senator Burnet R. Maybank of South Carolina, who warned his colleagues that a "product, an idea, or a plan that is over sold starts under a handicap."[16] Such skeptics were labeled "peace criminals" by Francis J. Myers, senator from Pennsylvania.[17]

In their unbounded enthusiasm for the new organization, senators were undoubtedly influenced by an unprecedented coalition of private organizations and public-interest groups united to exert pressure for U.S. participation. These included the National Federation of Woman's Clubs, the National Council of Women, the American Association for the United Nations, the National Board of the YWCA, the National Council of Jewish Women, the National Women's Trade Union League, the National Federation of Business and Professional Women's Clubs, the American Federation of Labor and the Congress of Industrial Organizations, and the National Association for the Advancement of Colored People. (After W.E.B. Du Bois had testified for the NAACP before the Senate Foreign Relations Committee, its chairman, Senator Connally, reported to his colleagues that he "was a well-educated colored man who expressed high views about public affairs."[18])

If the Senate voted to approve the Charter, predicted Livingston Hartley, director of the Washington office of the American Association for the United Nations, American security would be "strengthened," American leadership would be "enhanced," power politics would be "limited," Germany would be "kept powerless," armament costs would be "declining," taxes would be "decreasing," and democracy abroad would be "growing." On the other hand, if the Charter were defeated, American security would be "endangered," American leadership would be "reduced," power politics would be "unlimited," Germany would "regain power," armament costs would be "continuing heavy," taxes would be "continuing high," and democracy abroad would be "declining."[19] Looking at the world of the 1980s through the prism of Hartley's vision, one might deduce that the United States had *not* joined the United Nations. We did join, but it did not make the difference Hartley and others promised.

Arrayed against the powerful organizations mentioned above were but a handful of groups and individuals, mostly insignificant or crackpot. One opponent testified that she had heard from impeccable sources that the Duke of Windsor had been promised the Secretary-Generalship of the new organization, thus to become king of the world.[20]

A large majority of the country's daily newspapers were almost as lyrical as the Senators and the organizations. Those urging speedy ratification included the *New York Times, New York Herald Tribune, Washington Post, Washington Star, Baltimore Sun, Pittsburgh Post-Gazette, Christian Science Monitor, Philadelphia Inquirer, Detroit Free Press, Des Moines Register, St. Louis Post-Dispatch, Cleveland Plain Dealer, Cincinnati Enquirer, New Orleans Times-Picayune, Louisville Courier-Journal, Miami Herald, Milwaukee Journal, Nashville Tennessean, Minneapolis Star Journal, Atlanta Constitution, San Francisco Chronicle, Omaha World Herald, Raleigh News and Observer,* and *Chattanooga News Free Press.* While the media exhibited somewhat more caution than the solons about hailing the arrival of the millennium, they were no less emphatic about the desirability of full U.S. participation. As the *New York Times* put it, "it is now or never for this country."[21] The *New York Daily News* and the curmudgeonly *Chicago Daily Tribune* stood almost alone, the latter grumbling, "If we have peace for a time, it will not be because of the operation of the clumsy and self-defeating international mechanism outlined in the Charter but rather because none of the great nations chooses to start a war."[22]

The "Guilt Trip"

The cosmic overselling of the U.N., in part, was merely an effort to ensure that there would be no repetition of the Senate's unexpected failure to ratify

the Treaty of Versailles after World War I, which had its roots in the determination of certain senators to keep the U.S. out of the League of Nations.
The imagined, as well as the real, consequences of America's spurning of the
League were conjured up again and again to silence those inclined to point
out weaknesses in the plans for its successor. The Senate's rejection of the
League, it was argued, had paralyzed the organization and thereby almost
assured World War II. This was at best unproven, and quite probably untrue,
although U.S. failure to join the League may have contributed somewhat to
the breakdown of the international system in the 1930s, which led to World
War II.[23] More likely, however, the League failed because those states that
did belong simply did not have the will to resist acts of aggression that did not
touch them directly. As the distinguished British diplomat and political historian Evan Luard has pointed out, they never accepted that "aggression on the
other side of the world, or even on the other side of Europe, was so immediately a 'matter of concern' as to make involvement in war to defeat it obliga-
tory." Had the League members lived up to their collective security commitments, "Japan would not have invaded Manchuria, Italy would not have
attacked Ethiopia, Germany would not have invaded the Rhineland, Czechoslovakia or Poland."[24]

There is no reason to believe that, had the United States been a member, the
nations of the League would have behaved otherwise or perceived their self-
interest differently. Nor is it likely that the United States, as a member of the
League, would have responded to Germany, Italy, or Japan any differently than
did the other powers, or than it did as a non-member.

Nevertheless, guilt is an effective weapon. Senator Connally kicked off the
Senate debate on Charter ratification by reminding his colleagues of the Senate's 1919 rejection of Woodrow Wilson's "exalted vision," adding that "the
failure of the United States to ratify the League of Nations Covenant enfeebled
the League" and had "rendered it impotent . . . doomed to failure from its
inception."[25] Senator Harley M. Kilgore of West Virginia thought our absence
from the League "set the stage for this war."[26] Senator Lucas warned that the
"world still remembers what the Senate failed to do when the League of
Nations was before it for ratification. It still looks upon this legislative body
with doubt and skepticism and well it might, in view of what happened twenty-
five years ago."[27] But, added Senator McClellan, a "dispensation of providence, as it were," had given his colleagues "the opportunity to rectify that
mistake and to redeem the respect and prestige of this body in the graces of
Almighty God and in the esteem of the world."[28]

In executive session the members of the Senate Foreign Relations Committee took exactly the same position, concerning themselves almost exclusively
with preventing testimony by what the chairman, Senator Connally, referred
to as "nuts" who might run away with the proceedings.[29] There appears to
have been general agreement with Rhode Island Senator Theodore Francis

Green's expression of "fear" that "the same situation may develop as it did in connection with the League of Nations. There, there were some outspoken opponents. They used dilatory tactics, and then they had recourse to reservations which seemed fair unto themselves, and they got stronger and stronger as time went by, with the net result of the failure of ratification."[30] In the end, it was decided to limit hearings to ten days, exclude those Senator Carl A. Hatch of New Jersey called "crackpots"[31] and give the public a "big show" (Senator Connally)[32] under carefully controlled circumstances that would ensure against the unexpected.

Outside Congress, similar tactics were used, by interest groups and the media. The Committee on World Order of the Unitarian Laymen's League told Congress: "It all adds up to this: Whether there is to be a World War No. 3 is up to you."[33] The *St. Louis Post-Dispatch* of June 26, 1945, urged that President Truman be given the opportunity "to tell Marshal Stalin and Prime Minister Churchill that we have not repeated our 1919 mistake," while the *Louisville Courier-Journal* of June 17, 1945, argued that: "Our unhappy record of the past demands rather that we be among the first to ratify this document."[34] The *Chattanooga News Free Press* warned: "Let the Senate politicians beware of meddling with this document, as they did the last."[35]

While the tactic evident in these ploys is perfectly understandable, the overemphasis on the life-and-death difference between U.S. abstention from joining, and participation in, an international organization could not but have created false expectations among those who believed the rhetoric. If, by staying out of the League, America had ensured its failure, then, it seemed to follow, by entering fully and enthusiastically into the U.N., America could ensure its success. When reality later caused the collapse of this simplism it also fractured the faith of those still trapped inside.

The "Ego Trip"

Another theme in the selling campaign was sounded by Clyde Eagleton of the State Department. "No greater opportunity for leadership was ever given to any people," he said, "than is now offered the American people."[36] Greater than the imperium of Rome, of Britain, and of the Mogul emperors? No one was rude enough to ask.

What distinguishes the "ego trip" from the "guilt trip" is that there was plenty of evidence to sustain our sense of preeminence. The *Miami Herald* was immodest but right in asserting, "What has been accomplished in San Francisco has been largely the handiwork of the United States representation."[37] Senator McClellan put it more bluntly: "We occupy an eminent position of strength, of power, and of opportunity for world leadership. The eyes of the world are now upon the United States. . . ." By speedily ratifying the Charter "we shall reaffirm and enhance our position of leadership among the nations of the world."[38]

It was not fantasy, not then. The United States *did* lead the world in planning the new international peacekeeping system. As early as April 1940 State Department officials were circulating option papers outlining machinery for collective security and economic development. Some of these ideas became the core of the Charter.[39] Only the United States came with detailed proposals to the Dumbarton Oaks conference in August 1944. These "Essential Points in the Charter of the International Organization" became the first draft, by default, since the Soviet Union and United Kingdom had only prepared a few ideas in very general terms.[40] Although important concessions were later made to the Soviet Union regarding the "double veto" and separate membership for Byelorussia and the Ukraine, in most matters "it was the U.S. view which ultimately prevailed."[41]

Thus, Senator Howard A. Smith of New Jersey was not altogether wrong in stating: "I am supporting this new policy in international affairs, because a despairing, chaotic world is crying for the positive, constructive, dynamic leadership of America."[42] When the war is over, he said, the U.S. will emerge "not only the strongest nation in the world, but as the one nation whose philosophy of freedom of opportunity has made us the beacon light of hope for the despairing millions of depressed people in all corners of the earth." U.S. participation in the new organization is "going to mean so much to the world" because "the people of the United Nations . . . are looking to us for leadership."[43] His views were endorsed by most of his colleagues.

Senator Edwin C. Johnson of Colorado thought it "our plain duty to assume such leadership with confidence and determination,"[44] while Senator Arthur Vandenberg of Michigan heard the trumpet calling America "to assume the moral leadership of a better world in which we have fought our way to glorious eminence."[45]

And, initially, we *were* preeminent in the U.N. During the first decade of its operation, the U.S. first paid 40 percent and then one-third of the organization's budget. U.S. views almost invariably prevailed in the General Assembly, even when they were frustrated by Soviet vetoes in the Security Council. Senator Thomas C. Hart of Connecticut was not far from the mark when he prophesied, on July 25, 1945, that the U.S. would be "the essential cog in the international organization."[46]

Yet, as historic periods of international preeminence go, this one was short-lived. Almost from the beginning the policies of Argentina, Brazil, Burma, Egypt, India, Indonesia, and Mexico gave notice that a "third world" existed with interests identical with neither those of the United States nor those of the Soviet Union. What could not have been anticipated in 1945 was the mercurial speed with which the Belgian, British, Dutch, and French empires declined, producing a hundred new "third world" states, almost none of which looked to the U.S. for leadership. The U.S. national ego was not prepared for this.

The inevitable disappointment of the American public at the evaporation of U.S. preeminence was the greater because Washington had favored and even aided rapid decolonization. Even during the war, President Franklin D. Roosevelt had tried to persuade the recalcitrant British to extend the U.N.'s new Trusteeship system to include not only former "enemy territories" but *all* colonies and dependencies, in order to speed the process. By that process, the U.S. believed, new states would be born which would share its political values and make common cause with the liberal democracies. And, indeed, most of the new nations did start out with institutions of democratic government—elective legislatures, written constitutions, bills of rights, provisions for judicial review—to which the U.S. could readily relate. The keener was its disappointment when these nations did not seem to respond. Most of them rapidly shed their hand-me-down robes of parliamentary democracy and donned authoritarian armor. As quickly, they distanced themselves from the West in forums of multilateral diplomacy.

By 1970 the United States no longer had much in common with the sociopolitical systems of many of the countries that comprised the new Third World majority in the U.N. And even those countries that retained Western-style democratic forms were found voting as often with the Soviets as with the U.S. Washington had encountered the law of the preeminence of economic interests. So, for that matter, had Moscow when communist China turned against the Soviet Union, proving that there is more in common between two indigents, one of whom is a communist, than between two communists, one of whom is an indigent.

Again, however, measuring the reality of the United Nations today, against the baseline of U.S. expectations in 1945, there is reason for intense disappointment. Their imaginations charged by the rhetoric, Americans expected to assume the leadership of a broken, impoverished, but hopeful world looking to them to lead the way to salvation. Rarely, in so short a time, have aspirations suffered so steep a decline.

The "Consanguinity Trip"

Closely related to the "ego trip," which emphasized the U.S. destiny to lead, was another argument, also heavily relied upon to win over the American public. The institutions created at San Francisco, according to this line, are a natural organic outgrowth of America's own cherished institutions and fundamental instruments of government. In the words of Senator Homer Ferguson of Michigan, the unique genius of the American people extends not only to "science, technology, and industry" but applies equally to "political innovation" and "the art of government." It is therefore only natural that we should show the way toward a new global system.[47]

It was easy to believe that the U.N. Charter was "ours" not merely in draftsmanship but in spirit and in content. "I believe," said San Francisco delegate John Foster Dulles, that the Charter "can be a greater Magna Carta."[48] The concessions wrung by England's barons from King John are not exactly part of American history, but as the previous references to the Magna Carta would imply, the oak of the U.S. Constitution is often seen by American lawyers and legislators as having grown from a British acorn. The U.N., by the same token, would grow from an American acorn. Such horticultural analogies abounded: Secretary of State Edward R. Stettinius, Jr., in a letter to President Truman, on June 26, 1945, spoke of the proposed Security Council, General Assembly, Economic and Social Council, and International Court of Justice as "vines and trees" transplanted from our soil to "unfamiliar environments" where they would flourish, even though it would be necessary "to cut them back and prune them" for their journey from "the world of individual and group relations to the world of international relations."[49]

In this imagined reality—that the U.N. Charter was a sort of extension of the U.S. Constitution—three important misconceptions operated. First, since the world organization was being built in large part to American national specifications, it would be America's privilege to guide those less familiar with it. Second, and closely related, was the misconception that this new international constitution, so closely related to that of the U.S., was bound to evolve—as had its progenitor—into a more perfect instrument. Third, and perhaps most important, was the misconception that the Charter, like the U.S. Constitution, would become the fundamental law of society, determining and umpiring basic power relationships. As in American national life, so in the life of the U.N. all the players, regardless of their short-term interests, would recognize the overriding importance of obeying the "rules of the game."

With hindsight, these are known misconceptions. In 1945 leaders of public opinion vouched for their validity. At the final plenary session of the San Francisco Conference, President Harry S. Truman emphasized the comparability of the U.S. Constitution and the U.N. Charter:

> The Constitution of my country came from a Convention which—like this one—was made up of delegates with many different views. Like this Charter, our Constitution came from a free and sometimes bitter exchange of conflicting opinions. When it was adopted, no one regarded it as a perfect document. But it grew and developed and expanded. And upon it there was built a bigger, a better, a more perfect union.
>
> This Charter, like our own Constitution, will be expanded and improved as time goes on.[50]

Employing the shaky analogy quite specifically, Truman foresaw the rapid drafting "of an international bill of rights, acceptable to all the nations involved. That bill of rights will be as much a part of international life as our own Bill of Rights is a part of our Constitution."[51]

In the Senate, Leverett Saltonstall of Massachusetts recalled his state's progress from colonial town meeting through Continental Congress to federalism, and now, with "the ratification of this Charter we take another step forward, a perfectly logical step on a path still untrod, but with a beckoning horizon towards which it clearly leads."[52]

Indeed, the spirit of '76 was everywhere evident in the Congress of '45. Congressman Bloom thought that the Charter was "conceived in the same spirit" as the Declaration of Independence and the Constitution. It, too, would "develop, in the years to come, into something more nearly perfect, in the same manner that our own Constitution has evolved throughout the years of our existence as a Nation."[53] Senator McClellan saw at San Francisco "the same spirit that imbued our forefathers in 1776."[54] Few could resist the founding fathers' role. Senator Connally actually brought the chamber to its feet, cheering, when he implored:

> Let us rise to our lofty destiny. Let us be among the architects of a structure more marvelous than one built of steel and stone. Let us create a temple of law and reason and justice and peace to serve the peoples of the world.
>
> The world charter for peace is knocking at the doors of the Senate. We shall not turn it away.
>
> There come ringing down through a century and a half the inspired words of Washington as he stood before the Constitutional Convention of 1787 and blessed the new Republic that was being launched upon the earth. Washington said: "Let us raise a standard to which the wise and the honest can repair; the event is in the hands of God."[55]

Connally's Republican counterpart, Vandenberg, chose another model: "I think," he said, "that I now know rather intimately what was in Benjamin Franklin's soul when, at the end of the American Constitutional Convention in 1787, he put his signature to that immortal document."[56]

Many others developed the theme. A young Senator J. William Fulbright from Arkansas thought the Charter was like the Articles of Confederation. "It will be a fatal error," he said, "if we do not follow the example of our founding fathers and be prepared and willing to strengthen this organization."[57] Senator Joseph H. Ball of Minnesota agreed enthusiastically: "I think we are still prepared to go considerably further in granting specific authority and power to an international organization than does the Charter before us."[58] Senator Alexander Wiley of Wisconsin, too, was reminded that after the American Revolution "we tried the idea of a loose union of States under the Articles of Confederation. That experiment did not work." Now we were about to embark on a similar adventure globally. Drawing on our national experience, he said, Americans "must fulfill the great promise of Isaiah: 'I create new heavens and a new earth.' "[59]

Institution vs. Process

Not every member saw visions of these dazzling chimera. Even Senator Vandenberg felt compelled, at one point in the ratification debate, to warn his colleagues that "the flag stays on the dome of the Capitol."[60] Nevertheless, it often seemed as if the U.N. flag was about to be hoisted over the Congress, or the U.S. flag over U.N. headquarters. In any event, to many Americans the two seemed almost indistinguishable.

As noted, the false analogy between the U.S. Constitution and its institutions of government and the new instruments being created at San Francisco led sober people to voice unrealistic expectations: that the U.S. was destined to lead the U.N., that the U.N. would generate continuous creative growth and organic adaption, and that its rules would be obeyed. The analogy gave rise to another, even more fundamental expectation that proved to be fundamentally misleading. The U.S. Constitution does not merely recite rules of conduct. It establishes *institutions* of great vitality. Americans tend to think of these institutions justifiably, as having a corporeal reality separate and above the personal qualities, views, and interests of those who inhabit them. When they began to liken the Charter to the U.S. Constitution, the General Assembly to Congress, and the International Court to the U.S. Supreme Court, they set them up to be measured by those uniquely American expectations; and inevitably, by that standard, the U.N. has disappointed Americans.

With some historical justification, Americans believe that their Constitution, the supreme law of the land, has inhibited and redirected the conduct of Presidents, cabinet members, legislators, and ordinary citizens. To the surprise of most non-Americans, it actually does modify political behavior. The President's lawyers and those of the Congress do not merely cite parts of that document to each other as justification for self-interested conduct. They also cite the Constitution to their principals, warning them that they may not do certain things. Such advice is usually, if not always, heeded.

Nor is our faith limited to the Constitution alone. Historic experience also leads us to believe that a person with what appears to be modest intellectual endowments, such as Harry S. Truman, can be transformed to greatness by entering the precincts of the White House, another institution exerting a power of its own over its inhabitants. Americans were not altogether surprised when Earl Warren, a conservative attorney general and governor of California, suspected of racism toward the state's Japanese-Americans, became a great liberal emancipator of racial minorities upon donning the Chief Justice's robes.

Admittedly, this anthropomorphic, magical view of institutions is not confined to Americans. It was solemnly said, at least until the last decade of the nineteenth century, that the British monarch could do no wrong in his official capacity, although, in private, he might be a scoundrel, a law-breaker, and a sinner. There are other examples, although only a few survive the current age of acerbic skepticism. Some Catholics still believe that the institution of the Church transforms its bishops and priests, when they act in an ecclesiastical capacity, into instruments of God's will—whatever their private condition of grace. More remarkable is the continued willingness of American law to protect officers of a corporation by placing them behind a corporate veil, which often cannot be pierced in order to attach personal liability to individuals for their acts on behalf of the corporation.

Americans, more than most people, still tend to imbue their most important institutions—the Constitution, presidency, judiciary, church, and corporation—with quasi-magical powers. They believe those institutions have qualities that transform those who inhabit them. (I once heard Judge Kenneth Keating of New York admonish an audience of lawyers that theirs was a priestly calling, for "most Americans believe that our courts act under divine guidance." A practitioner whispered in my ear: "He's misunderstood. The public is saying: God only knows what those judges are doing!"). Thus it is that in 1945 Americans believed they were creating another such quasi-magical institution endowed with the capacity to bring a better life to all those who truly believed in it and gave it their trust.

The U.N. Charter established "the strongest war-prevention agency in history" in the opinion of the *Philadelphia Inquirer*.[61] Yet surely, it did nothing of the sort. It was endowed with no powers of its own to prevent war. The Charter merely bestowed on the five senior members (Great Britain, China, France, the Soviet Union, and the United States) the capacity—if they were unanimous and had help from others—to use the Security Council to require the negotiation of a dispute and, if negotiations failed, the imposition of a settlement. While this was an advance, on paper, over the League of Nations, it was a far cry from being "the one bulwark which exists between our civilization and future wars," which was how the leader of a national coalition of women's groups, organized to push the Charter through Congress, characterized the U.N.[62] It did not seem to be understood or to matter that at that very moment the Soviet Union was enslaving Eastern Europe, Ethiopia practising feudal oligarchy, or South Africa behaving toward blacks in a manner almost as racist as that of the Nazis just defeated in war. Somehow, Americans believed, the institution would transform its members.

To understand that this was not a universal perception, even in 1945, one need only consider the spare words of Lord Halifax, acting chairman of the British delegation at San Francisco:

> Here in San Francisco we have seen but the beginnings of a long and challenging endeavour. And there is a sense in which what we have done here is less important than what we have learnt here. We have learnt to know one another better; to argue with patience; to differ with respect; and at all times to pay honour to sincerity. . . . Time alone can show whether the house that we have tried to build rests upon

shifting sand, or, as I firmly hope, upon solid rock, to stand as shield and shelter against every storm.[63]

Halifax, like most delegates at San Francisco, saw that Conference primarily as an experience in global negotiation, requiring tact, sincerity, determination, and patience. Only secondarily did he see it as an institution-building endeavor, and then merely to the extent of creating a shelter—which might or might not survive the inevitable storms ahead—in which the difficult and problematic exercise of multilateral diplomacy might become an ongoing, rather than occasional pastime.

In sharp contrast, President Truman, in opening the San Francisco Conference, stressed that its purpose was to "provide the machinery which will make future peace not only possible but certain."[64] How odd, to believe that—in a world of nuclear power and rampant sovereignty—any "machinery" could make peace "certain." Secretary of State Edward Stettinius spoke of "creating at last a world organization which would be endowed with the power and the will this time truly to maintain the peace."[65]

It matters whether one perceives that at San Francisco an institution was created, or only a forum for negotiations. If the United Nations is indeed an institution, endowed with properties comparable to those of the fundamental institutions of the United States, then the U.N. itself must inevitably bear a share of responsibility for failure. If it was meant to be a transforming institution, it has failed; nations have not been transformed in the course of using it. There is no magic but only a collection of states doing what they have always done: pursuing interests perceived nationally, not from any common perspective.

If, on the other hand, the United Nations Charter is primarily an ordinary treaty establishing a global conference and crisis center, with a permanent staff and infrastructure, where nations may gather at short notice to discuss whatever subjects are of current concern, and where staff may sometimes add constructive proposals, then failure—aside from a leaking roof, or inaccurate translation of documents, or an unimaginative staff—must be, primarily, the fault of the states that inhabit the institution and not of the institution itself.

Only a few Americans seemed to understand at the time. William Green, the president of the American Federation of Labor, did point out that the Charter "only makes possible national cooperation in development of a human agency through which nations may meet together, discuss common problems, and work out methods of dealing with them. This procedure we in the labor movement call collective bargaining."[66] Senator Connally, far more typically, argued that we were joining "an agency of tremendous influence and power" which states had "invested with authority, if necessary, to preserve or restore international peace. . . . a star in the night . . . a gleaming beacon."[67] Senator Warren R. Austin of Vermont, soon to become the chief U.S. delegate to the

U.N., rejoiced that the General Assembly had been given "jurisdiction over the general welfare of the peoples of the earth."[68]

These misperceptions invariably drew on wretchedly misleading constitutional parallels. Senator Lister Hill of Alabama insisted that the U.N. would function just like Congress. The members might "sharply disagree," the debate might become "intense and bitter," but the member nations, like the members of Congress, would be content to know that "they may lose on some decisions, win on others. But . . . win or lose . . ." the stability of the U.N. itself would be everyone's "greatest asset."[69] The center would hold.

Ignoring the Storm Signals

Admittedly, this analysis benefits from hindsight, and it is therefore ungracious to pillory those whose splendid illusions carried the day. But the illusions, however splendid, were of least in part self-induced, even willful. The United States should have known better. Although the San Francisco Conference's staged events received more than adequate coverage, its private crises did not. The result was a failure to apprehend the stormy future, which was clearly foreshadowed by the in-fighting in the Conference's committees and at backstage confrontations. Thus the *Omaha World Herald* blithely rhapsodized that "some day historians will decide that the signing of the Charter at San Francisco, was the greatest milestone in the history of mankind,"[70] and Representative Eaton, the ranking House Republican at San Francisco, came back to report that the Conference had laid "the foundations of a new world civilization."[71] Senator Harold H. Burton of Ohio concluded that it would lead nations to the practice of "the Golden Rule among men and a recognition of the common brotherhood of man under the common fatherhood of God."[72] That would surely have been news to the U.S.S.R.'s foreign minister, Vyacheslav Molotov. In reality, the conference had seen a series of clashes which correctly foretold, for those who wished to know, just how confrontational the politics of the new organization were going to be. Americans, overwhelmingly, did not want to know. Instead, they preferred to bask in a warm miasma of groundless good feeling. This sort of wishful thinking obscured the fairly clear view from San Francisco of troubles ahead, of rocky intervals, stalemate, and threats of disintegration.

For some time before going to San Francisco, the Soviet Union had known perfectly well that it would be hopelessly outnumbered in any one-state–one-vote arrangement that would prevail in the proposed "parliamentary" body, the General Assembly. It had therefore determined, sensibly from its perspective, that the important issues affecting Russia's national interest—particularly questions of international security—must either be outside the U.N.'s purview, or, at worst, be handled in the Security Council, where Moscow could wield a veto. Consistent with this perfectly realistic analysis, delegate Andrei Gromyko went to the brink, again and again, to ensure his country the widest latitude in the use of the veto, not only in situations involving the potential collective use of force by the U.N., but in such lesser matters as setting up procedures for peaceful adjustment of a dispute. The Soviets knew that the way to prevent a rout is to prevent small defeats.

While it was urged, before and at San Francisco, that parties to a dispute be required to abstain from voting on resolutions invoking collective measures, the Soviets were deeply opposed. They thought, again correctly, that this would deprive them of their veto in the very situations where they might need it most. And on these matters, despite a modicum of compromise, Moscow prevailed.[73] It did so by repeatedly taking the conference to the edge of disintegration.

So, too, with Moscow's demand for multiple memberships for itself, to help equalize the numerical disadvantage of the communist world in comparison with the West. Stalin decided to aim high. He insisted on separate membership for each of his sixteen Soviet republics. Eventually, after intense and acrimonious haggling, he settled for three separate seats for the U.S.S.R., Byelorussia, and the Ukraine. It was pure fakery. The latter two were considerably less independent than any American state, and everyone knew it. But it was a reasonable price to pay for Soviet participation.

An even more intense dispute at San Francisco centered on the question of Polish representation. At Yalta, there had been a fragile compromise in the dispute over the composition of the postwar Polish government. Rival exile regimes were stationed in London and Lublin under the auspices, respectively, of the West and Russia. They had advanced mutually exclusive claims. The Yalta Agreement provided that a new Polish government be formed to represent the Polish people as a whole, implying it should be a synthesis of both exile groups. The situation was something of a watershed. It was the first of the many times that Americans deluded themselves into thinking that a dispute between East and West over the destiny of a nation could be resolved by creating a coalition government embracing communists and non-communists. The British, who even then knew better, were sufficiently concerned about Poland's future to propose postponement of the San Francisco Conference rather than risk endorsement of a one-sided solution imposed by Moscow. Washington, however, would not brook delay, not even after Stalin, abandoning all pretense at compromise, arrested the emissaries of the London Polish government who had come to Moscow to work out a coalition, and, instead, entered into a treaty of "mutual assistance" with the puppet Polish communist regime the Russians had set up at Lublin.[74]

At San Francisco, for a few days, it looked as if the conference would collapse under the weight of the Polish events. But, in an action which foreshadowed the future role of the U.N. in disputes between the superpowers, delegates soon agreed on a meaningless Belgian motion, one affirming the pious hope that a new and representative Polish government would soon be formed and would then send suitable delegates to San Francisco.[75] Again, everyone knew better. It was the beginning of the U.N.'s role as the lyrical voice of hypocrisy.

If these disputes had been sensitively monitored, it would have been intimated that, at the very least, the national interests of the wartime Allies would not continue to coincide in peacetime. Such monitoring, in turn, would have warned us that there were storms ahead for an organization built to run on Big Five unanimity. To have admitted this openly need not have led to rejection of the Charter by Congress, where pro-U.N. sentiment was unassailable. It might, however, have made for more modest expectations, which would have served the U.N. better. Such, however, was not the order of the day. "What you have accomplished in San Francisco," President Truman told the delegates at their final plenary session, "shows how well . . . lessons of military and economic cooperation have been learned."[76] "The spirit of cooperation," editorialized the *Milwaukee Journal* of June 26, 1945, "the will to work together, the determination to build a world security organization . . . have been present all through the arduous stage in San Francisco."[77] Returning from the conference, Congressman Bloom reported that the Big Powers had remained "joined in an unbreakable chain of unity."[78] And Senator Vandenberg, while referring to "violent controversy at the outset," spoke reassuringly of experiencing "the mutual understanding which is inevitable when men sit at a common council table and honestly explore their differences." The happy result was that they "never failed to agree."[79]

Americans, alas, wanted—and still want—desperately to discover simple, inexpensive formulas for assuring a quiet world in which they can enjoy in peace the fruits of their—for the most part—well-gotten gains. Isolationism, interventionism, the United Nations, all were at times plausible, simplistic answers to the complex, perhaps unanswerable questions. In 1945, much of the world outside America was either in ruins or darkness. The problem of envy and animosity was simply evaded. Asked what would happen if the permanent members failed to agree on action in the face of aggression, Secretary of State Stettinius answered that "we should not be too deeply concerned with the kind of question Franklin Roosevelt always characterized as 'iffy'."[80] The problem was about as iffy as Haley's comet! Testifying before the Senate, he added, "I believe the five major nations proved at San Francisco beyond the shadow of a doubt that they can work successfully and in unity with each other and with the other United Nations under this Charter."[81] It was a lovely little pipe dream, and Senator Connally embraced it gladly. The "mere existence of the veto," he said, "does not mean that it will be used frequently . . . a compelling world opinion . . . would make it very difficult for a single member of the Security Council alone to veto the peaceful settlement of a dispute."[82]

Only delegate Harold Stassen, briefly on leave from the Pacific Third Fleet, expressed prescient concern. In a letter to Stettinius he urged a greater effort to get Russia to agree to limit the veto to situations where force was proposed to be used directly against one of the five permanent members of the Security Council. Otherwise, he indicated, the veto would become the organization's "Achilles' heel," leading to the "autocracy of a single nation." He foresaw accurately "a tendency for each permanent seat nation to accumulate a group of smaller satellite nations which will rely on the veto power of the permanent seat" to protect their interests.[83]

No understanding of present attitudes of Americans toward the U.N. can be achieved without taking into account the utterly false premises on which the Charter was based, and then sold to the public. Even the clear-eyed Franklin D. Roosevelt, while rather skeptical about the role smaller nations could play, was convinced that the new organization would work, imposing peace in a world disarmed and supervised by the Big Powers, which he privately referred to as the "four big policemen." Could Russia be trusted to work in peacetime harmony? "We have got to trust someone," he told Clark Eichelberger, the head of what was to become the United Nations Association.[84]

It was left to an occasional cynic to get it right. Senator Burton K. Wheeler of Montana said of the U.N.: "it is the only alternative we have, and in the faint hope that it will do some good, I am going to vote for it." But he added, "I am inclined to think, to be perfectly frank, that when we ratify this Charter we are saying to Russia: 'You can do practically anything you want with those countries over there.' "[85]

And Senator Henrik Shipstead of Minnesota, who with Senator William Langer of North Dakota cast the only votes against ratification, probably came closest to the truth, although his colleagues regarded him as something of a crank on the issue:

> Mr. President, we are told we must be realists to understand this Charter, that since it would be unrealistic to expect the strong to admit any sanctions against the misuse of their strength, the hope of peace rests upon the continuing accord of America, Britain, and Russia. But if this is the case, what is the Charter really for? Specifically against whom is this mighty structure of the United Nations, elaborated at San Francisco, directed? Who among the small and weak nations is so wicked . . .? Is it Switzerland, or Sweden, Ireland, or some other little country . . .?[86]

He added: "The question at issue is whether this Charter is real or 'phony': whether it is in truth an instrument to serve international peace and justice, or a cynical imposture bred by hypocrisy out of power politics."[87]

While the correct answer may well be "neither," Shipstead's cranky cynicism now sounds like refreshing candor in the midst of so much exaggerated optimism. And, given the organization's actual track record, Wheeler and Shipstead may have served it better than Connally and Vandenberg in their effort to reduce to realistic scale the inflated expectations of the U.S. public.

Inflated expectations, when they are—inevitably—disappointed, tend to degenerate into backlash. The problem, perhaps, is endemic to our system of government. To secure its Congressional support, a new venture too often is touted as the complete answer to an entire basket of disparate, complex, and perhaps essentially insoluble problems. In modern political public-relations terms, a program cannot be presented as a mere amelioration, "better than nothing," or the least of the evils. It must be oversold to have a chance in Congress. The public demands elixirs; the system is geared to provide them. Yet, the very technique of overselling, needed to ensure that a proposal gets a chance at life, also ensures that it will ultimately be judged a failure and, perhaps, even repealed.

§ 2 §

Happy and Misleading Auguries

Six incidents in the early history of the organization for a time sustained an aura of unrealistic optimism: the Soviet retreat from Azerbaijan, the establishing of the United Nations Truce Supervisory Organization (UNTSO) in the Middle East, the negotiated end to the Berlin blockade, the U.N.'s collective action in Korea, the enactment by the General Assembly of the Acheson Plan, and the establishment of the United Nations Emergency Force after the British, French, and Israeli invasion of Egypt in 1956.

Azerbaijan

In 1942, the British occupied the south of Iran, and the Soviet Union the north, including the region of Azerbaijan, to prevent the nation's rich oil resources' falling to the Nazis. This harsh necessity was somewhat disguised by the two Allied powers' entering into a treaty with the Shah which pretended that Allied troops were in the country with his permission and promised their withdrawal within six months of the war's end. Meanwhile, the Iranian government was guaranteed freedom of movement throughout the realm. In September 1945 the victorious British and Soviets agreed to pull out by the following March. Moscow honored these intentions only in the breach.

While in Azerbaijan, the Soviet authorities had quietly fostered a leftist provincial government opposed to the Shah. Armed by Moscow, it demanded autonomy for the region. In November 1945 the Shah tried to exercise his freedom of movement by sending his militia to re-establish control. He was blocked by Moscow, which claimed that the troops would provoke conflict with

the local Tudeh (communist) forces. On January 19, 1946, the Shah's government sent a complaint to the Security Council. It demanded that the Kremlin
stop its support of the secessionists.[1] The Azerbaijan crisis, the U.N.'s first, was
under way.

Evacuation day, March 2, came and went. Russia's troops remained firmly
in place. Thereupon, Iran's ambassador to the U.N., Hussein Ala—who appeared at times to be acting more under the influence of Dean Acheson and
the U.S. Department of State than on Teheran's instructions[2]—approached
U.N. Secretary-General Trygve Lie about convening the Security Council for
the first time under Article 35(1) of the Charter. (This permits the Council to
investigate and recommend terms for settling peaceably any "situation" or
"dispute" between members (see below, Chapter 9).) Lie was cold to the proposal. He thought that "open disagreements openly arrived at are not necessarily preferable to processes of diplomacy of a more discreet and effective
character."[3] Ignoring Lie's advice, Iran persisted. The U.S. urged it on, sus-
pecting that the U.S.S.R. was about to add military invasion to political subversion. When the decision to go to the U.N. was made, U.S. Secretary of
State James Byrnes exulted: "Now we'll give it to them with both barrels."[4]

Beginning on March 25, the Council devoted several heated sessions to the
issue. Russia's Andrei Gromyko—then, as now, the bloodless semaphorist of
Soviet intentions—told the members there was absolutely nothing to discuss;
the matter would be resolved through bilateral negotiations between Iran and
the Kremlin. He then walked out.

With the Soviet representative absent, the Security Council on March 29
agreed to a proposal of U.S. Secretary of State James Byrnes. The proposal
planted the U.N. squarely in the middle of the dispute by asking the Secretary-
General—in the circumlocution of diplomacy—to obtain fuller information
from Teheran and Moscow "about the status of their negotiations" and to
"ascertain Soviet intentions" regarding troop withdrawal.

The Secretary-General made inquiries in Moscow and Teheran. Five days
later, he reported that Russia appeared ready to withdraw its troops within six
weeks. The Council then decided to postpone further discussion until May 6.
It asked the parties to report back at that time as to whether the withdrawal had
been completed. In the meantime, the Council occupied itself with an arcane
legal wrangle over whether the item should be deleted from the agenda or
merely suspended. The U.S. insisted on the latter course as a way of keeping
pressure on Moscow, a symbolic move deeply resented by the Soviets.

To Washington's surprise, the Russians withdrew from Iran near the May
deadline, after extracting an agreement from Teheran that envisaged a semi-
autonomous government in Azerbaijan. There was also a commitment to establish a joint Iranian-Soviet oil company which would exploit the region's
petroleum resources. Once Russian troops had left, however, the Shah and the
Iranian parliament, safe behind the U.S. nuclear monopoly, promptly repudi-

ated both conditions. In December the Shah's forces reoccupied Azerbaijan, ousting the leftist provincial administration. Moscow, itself often quite relaxed about the need to honor international commitments, made dire threatening noises but ultimately, in the face of counter-threats from Washington and London, chose discretion over valor. The Azerbaijan crisis was over.

When the issue had first presented itself to the U.N., the Security Council had seemed incapable of decisive action. The "UN will die in its infancy of inefficiency and ineffectiveness," Secretary Byrnes had fulminated in the first of many predictions of the organization's imminent demise.[5] Now it was time to apportion the credit. Byrnes concluded that the Russian pull-out was "proof of the strength and effectiveness of the United Nations in helping those countries which truly desire independence."[6] Others thought that Moscow simply acted in misplaced reliance on the agreement with Teheran.[7] Dean Acheson, with U.S. Ambassador George V. Allen in Teheran, attributed Soviet complacence to two-fisted U.S. support for Iran.[8] A fourth view, advanced by the Secretary-General,[9] gave full credit to his own behind-the-scenes role as tactful mediator and fact-finder. All four theories, to some degree, are plausible; indeed, the truth probably encompassed an element of each. In international politics, events tend to have ambiguous and multiple causes. While failure is a waif, success has many fathers.

The Azerbaijan crisis, however, demonstrated that while the new organization could play a part in solving crises, it also had an awesome capacity itself to become part of the problem. In this instance, the Security Council's agenda had become an important, though symbolic, issue. Throughout, the Soviet Union professed itself deeply angered by the inscription and retention of the question of Azerbaijan on the agenda, especially after Moscow had pledged to evacuate its troops by May 6. At that point, even Teheran had instructed its U.N. representative to withdraw the complaint. It was the U.S. which nevertheless, had insisted on keeping the item before the Council. In the spirit of the emerging cold war we prevailed, over the opposition of *both* parties to the dispute and also of the Secretary-General. The agenda thus became the focus of a procedural dispute and a source of aggravated friction between Washington and Moscow, one that continued to sour relations for some time after the last Soviet soldier had been withdrawn.[10]

The lesson is one subsequently demonstrated over and over, in the practice of various U.N. organs: open, symbolic, public diplomacy conducted "on the record" has serious disadvantages for the pursuit of peace. It conduces to the striking of poses and the taking of rigid positions that seem to take on a metaphysical reality of their own and from which it may be difficult to disengage. The crisis also demonstrated another aspect of institutionalized crisis-management: its tendency to transform random events into pregnant precedents, forcing states to react with an eye not only on an event's immediate consequences but also on its long-range potential impact on hypothetical future interactions. Since institutional diplomacy, by definition, is a continuing "game," the players feel, rightly, that they cannot treat each "play" as a discrete event but need to watch the potential effect on the players' subsequent moves. The "agenda question" became both a matter of symbol and precedent. At best, this awareness of the precedential element in any diplomatic episode may promote predictability and develop "the rule of law" in international relations. At worst, it can complicate the resolution of a crisis merely by making it bear an additional burden of predicting and preempting the outcome of disputes that have not yet arisen. It is as if a busy pedestrian, asked directions by a stranger, were to take into account, before answering, the inhibiting possibility that, by being helpful, he might open himself to a flood of inquiries from other passersby. On a street, this fear is probably unrealistic. Not so in an institutionalized framework for interaction. Whatever happens once, however gratuitously, is quite likely to recur, almost as if by right. In diplomacy the parties' present positions are thus conditioned by future expectations; diplomacy conducted in a permanent, highly visible, multilateral institution, such as the U.N., inevitably maximizes this tendency.

The United Nations Truce Supervisory Organization in the Middle East

In the political sphere, what the U.N. has done best is organize international truce observation teams and related peacekeeping forces. After this had been done once, a pattern was set, which has largely subsisted to the present day.

The United Nations did not invent the multinational force. Its predecessor, the League of Nations, had already accomplished a "conspicuous success"[11] in sending military units to the Saar in 1935. But the U.N. has made this sort of thing its specialty, beginning with the crisis surrounding the creation of the State of Israel in 1947–48.

In November 1947 the General Assembly had voted to partition Britain's expiring Palestinian mandate, replacing it with loosely linked Jewish and Arab states.[12] The decision was not welcomed by the Arabs and, as the date for partition approached, there was increasing violence. To try to conciliate, the Security Council established a Truce Commission for Palestine[13] composed of representatives of Belgium, France, and the United States. Its efforts proved futile. On May 14, as the mandate was about to end, the Assembly asked Count F. Bernadotte, the head of the Swedish Red Cross, to try his hand at mediation.[14]

By this time, however, war had broken out between Jews and Arabs. On May 18, three days after the end of the mandate, amidst a massive Arab invasion of the new State of Israel, the Security Council was convened. A violent week later, this organ adopted a resolution calling for a four-week cease-fire to be supervised by the mediator and the Truce Commission.[15] The Council established a team of 63 American, Belgian, French, and Swedish military observers to oversee the cease-fire. Surprisingly, the warring parties agreed.

After a month of inconclusive U.N. mediation, fighting resumed and the fragile truce fell apart. On July 15, the Council sternly "ordered" a new cease-fire.[16] Three days later, the combatants once again complied. Still, intermittent fighting continued, with Count Bernadotte himself soon falling victim to terrorist assassins. He was succeeded by a senior American official of the Secretariat, Assistant-Secretary-General Ralph Bunche. An augmented corps of truce observers was organized—the U.N. Truce Supervision Organization (UNTSO)—under the command of General Riley of the U.S. Marine Corps.

While the bloodshed continued, Bunche began to have some success. On November 16 the Council authorized him to organize direct armistice negotiations between the parties,[17] and on January 6, 1949, the governments of Egypt and Israel agreed on yet another cease-fire. With Bunche chairing, they began to discuss an armistice, a condition halfway up the negotiating ladder from cease-fire to peace. It was successfully concluded six weeks later and signed February 24 on Rhodes.

As the armistice came into effect, the number of UNTSO observers was again increased, this time to 700. Their expanded task was to observe and maintain the armistice and periodically report back to the Council.[18] This was the basis for Israeli-Egyptian relations until the renewed fighting of 1956. It was a significant triumph for the mediating skill of Bunche and redounded to the credit of the Secretary-General and the Secretariat. The world bureaucracy had successfully assumed an independent institutional peacekeeping and problem-solving role, which seemed to justify the high hopes and aspirations of 1945.

The prestige of the Security Council, on balance, was also enhanced. On the negative side, it had dithered away the months before partition, even though war was entirely predictable. On the positive side, once war did break out, its disparate members somehow managed to get together to demand—and get—first a cease-fire, then an armistice. The Security Council, once it had spoken, was actually obeyed. This was due, in part, to the fact that the Middle East crisis was not then enveloped by the aura of the cold war, as was the case with the confrontation over Azerbaijan. Also, in 1948–49, the Soviets and the United States were still united in their determination to establish and protect an Israeli state. Thus the world actually caught an enticing glimpse of what might have been had the wartime alliance survived to build the peace.

But the U.N.'s handling of the crisis, although superficially successful, laid the groundwork for future troubles, again partly due to the role of symbols in its operations. To a large extent, in practice, the U.N. Mideast presence was a Western and, particularly, an American one. Assistant-Secretary Ralph Bunche, General Riley, and many of the UNTSO personnel were American. None came from a socialist state, a circumstance bitterly denounced by the Soviets, the more so as, abjuring their frequent role as troublemaker, they had

supported the resolutions which had made the U.N. peacekeeping role possible
in the first place. In due course, this identification of the U.N. with specifically
U.S. interests led to trouble during the Korean War and, most seriously, in the
Congolese civil war.

Another problem was that the U.N.'s intervention, in effect if not intent, was
not as neutral as it first seemed. The Council's call for a cease-fire did not
really come until after the Arabs had been defeated by Israel. Had the call
come earlier, it would certainly not have been heeded. Thus began what some
observers see as a tendency on the part of the organization, manifest in one
Mideast crisis after another, to stand aside until the Arabs appear to be losing,
whereupon a U.N. presence is interposed to spare the vanquished from having
to accept defeat. In this sense, the U.N. has become a force not for peace but
for stalemate.

This is not all bad. The U.N.'s call for an end to hostilities had provided the
losing side with a public reason to stop fighting without losing face. Nevertheless, the arrival of the U.N.'s blue berets created a new "temporary" status
quo—"truce stranger than friction," as one scholar has called it[19]—that made
it unnecessary for the combatants to make those psychological and territorial
adjustments that alone could have prevented a later resumption of fighting.

The Berlin Blockade

Similarly ambiguous was the role of the U.N. in connection with the Berlin
crisis of 1948. That began when the British and Americans, later joined by the
French, concluded that the Soviet Union was not going to honor its commitment to participate in creating a united democratic Germany. The response
was to "go it alone," to unite the three Western zones of occupation in building the West German Federal Republic.

An early step, announced in June 1948, was to issue a common West
German currency. Moscow responded by harassing Allied rail and highway
traffic passing through the Soviet zone into the Western-controlled sector of
Berlin. On June 23 the Soviets announced the establishment of their own East
German mark, validating it for East Germany but also for all Berlin, which had
a separate status as a nominally united city under joint four-power control. The
Western allies then also authorized use of their new currency in Berlin. Tit for
tat, the war of the currencies had begun.

Given the desolate state of the Soviet and East German economies, it was an
unequal conflict. But the three Western occupiers were not invulnerable. All
their land and water traffic to Berlin had to go via the Soviet zone. Moscow
now ordered it halted. The West considered asserting its transit rights with the
help of an armored column, but wisely chose to respond with a spectacularly
successful airlift, which kept the two and one-half million West Berliners, as

well as British, French, and U.S. troops, amply supplied, even during the difficult winter of 1948–49.

The crisis abated as suddenly as it had begun. On January 27, 1949, without any prior diplomatic signal, Marshal Joseph Stalin, in written answers to four written questions, told J. Kingsberry Smith, the European manager of the International News Service, that a settlement was possible. The conditions Stalin set were significantly inconsequential. Most importantly, he did not even call on the West to withdraw the currency that had triggered the confrontation. Informal negotiations followed at the U.N. between the U.S.'s ambassador Philip Jessup and the U.S.S.R.'s ambassador Yakov A. Malik, the Soviet permanent delegate and deputy foreign minister. These quickly led to an agreement announced on May 12.[20]

Once again, the paternity of this "success" was ambiguous. Several parts of the U.N. had been involved. At the outset of the crisis, it was the West that had convened the Security Council. The Soviets reacted to U.S. charges by denying the Council's jurisdiction. When a resolution was introduced, Moscow vetoed it. Its delegates then refused to participate in further debates, sitting stonily through several Council meetings. The meetings proved futile. The General Assembly labored mightily, bringing forth on November 3 a mouse of a resolution which meekly "appealed to the Great Powers to renew efforts to compose differences and establish lasting peace."[21] Behind the scenes, strenuous personal efforts at mediation were undertaken by the Argentinian president of the Security Council, Foreign Minister Juan Atilio Bramuglia, and, rather at cross-purposes, by Secretary-General Lie.

To what extent did some of these various U.N. activities contribute to ending the crisis? To put it another way: why did the Soviets suddenly decide to end the blockade? Oxford historian and former British delegate to the U.N. Evan Luard recognized "a considerable coup for U.N. diplomacy." It was Secretary-General Lie, Luard contends, who brought the U.S. and Soviet delegates to the point of quiet negotiations under his chairmanship.[22] Understandably, this was also Lie's view.[23] Dean Acheson did not agree, attributing Stalin's policy reversal solely to Western power and tenacity. But Acheson grudgingly grants the U.N. a different utility. "We concluded," he wrote, "that a highly secret, casual approach to the Russians could better be made by [Ambassador] Jessup at the United Nations than through the embassy in Moscow or by the Department to the Russian Embassy. Fewer persons would be involved and those who were—Philip Jessup and Soviet Ambassador . . . Malik—could act in purely personal and unofficial capacities. So it was agreed that Jessup when next he saw Malik should ask, as a matter of personal curiosity, whether the omission of any reference to the monetary reform in the Stalin answers was significant."[24] With studied casualness, Jessup posed the question on February 15, as he and Malik were strolling into a meeting of the Security Council. Malik replied that he did not know, but would find out. A month later he told Jessup that the omission had been deliberate.

The American asked seemingly spontaneous follow-up questions, to which Malik secured new answers. And so it went.

To the satisfaction of both sides, the U.N. provided a setting for very quiet, informal diplomacy—itself an unusual use of that very public forum. In this way, each could measure the intentions of the other without having to pay the diplomatic price for initiating negotiations. When the Russians eventually offered to lift the blockade in return for a face-saving *quid pro quo*—a convening of the Council of Foreign Ministers of the occupying powers—they already knew that the West would accept.[25]

Used in this way, the U.N. proved a useful forum. Its mere existence conduced to a negotiated settlement. On the other hand, the efforts of third parties to become honest brokers did not help. Dr. Bramuglia and other "neutrals" in the Security Council concerned themselves with devising compromises that focused on the currency issue, which turned out to be a decoy, easily forgotten by the Russians once they were ready to settle. The Secretary-General's efforts to mediate were equally unsuccessful. While he understood that the real dispute was not about West or East German marks, but, rather, about the future of Berlin and the *de facto* partition of Germany, his efforts, too, were directed at resolving the currency issue.[26] Lie modestly admits in his memoirs that his role in the real negotiations, those between ambassadors Malik and Jessup, was limited to hosting one evening meeting at his Forest Hills home.[27]

Some observers go much further in discounting the U.N. role. Once "Joseph Stalin had decided that the Berlin adventure was a failure," political scientists Yeselson and Gaglione write, "he would have had no problem of communication through any embassy or a direct approach to the White House." Thus, "the fact that diplomats at the United Nations were involved is meaningless."[28] It is their contention that the issue was brought before the U.N. by the West only to create a credible case for going to war if necessary.

Even this harsh judgment, however, acknowledges the utility of the U.N. for building a public record. The Soviet Union had to be convinced of the West's determination not to be forced out of West Berlin, and the U.N. provided a "bully pulpit" from which to give precise meaning to the airlift and to warn of the consequences of further Soviet measures. Yeselson and Gaglione also a bit too readily discounted the personal and "environmental" factors in diplomacy. Informal relations between our permanent delegates and others, built over a long period of continuous interaction, while sometimes promoting mutual contempt, more often lead to a grudging admiration and a more effective ability to communicate views and to weigh what is being communicated by the other side. It is also much easier for U.S. and Soviet ambassadors to have "unstructured" encounters in the halls of U.N. headquarters than anywhere in Washington or Moscow.

Still, the record does not support the view that U.N. initiatives—those of the

Security Council, of the "neutrals" in the General Assembly, or of the Secretariat—significantly affected the progress or the outcome of this crisis. The Berlin blockade was fostered by Soviet perceptions of national interest. In pursuit of that perception, the Kremlin did not hesitate to use unilateral force. The U.N. could neither prevent nor reverse Russia's gamble. What mattered in the end was Western strength. At some point, Stalin recognized that the blockade had become counterproductive, for it gave the West a highly visible cause in which to demonstrate unity and military-technical superiority.

Yet Dean Acheson, no admirer of the U.N., deliberately chose it as his forum for quiet diplomacy. This worked because the other members, after some preliminary efforts at mediation, modestly withdrew to the sidelines. So did Trygve Lie. The U.N. became a useful place to negotiate precisely because it was willing to be a passive conference center. The members resisted the natural urge to intrude, to pass resolutions, to mediate, and to make judgments.

It is Luard's conclusion that "the fact that it was the U.N. which in this case laid on the successful negotiations did much to enhance its faltering prestige. At last, it was felt, the new organization was doing exactly what it was set up to do: settling disputes between the major powers and averting the dangers of war."[29] This may be giving the organization more credit than the facts support, but there is no harm in that, except to the extent false expectations are thereby kept alive. And there is a benefit to be recognized. Once again, it was probably easier for one side to retreat before a show of power by the other when the retreat could be disguised as deference to the U.N. The same U.N. smokescreen had helped facilitate Russia's retreat from Azerbaijan, and the Arabs' acceptance of a Mideast cease-fire in the war with Israel. Also, Luard is clearly right in concluding that the crisis showed that the U.N. had potential as a place for private negotiation.

That this potential has rarely been realized in superpower disputes, however, is due to many factors. One, alas, is that in subsequent years the membership seldom again mustered the benevolent reticence displayed during the Berlin crisis.

The Korean War

In Korea, as in Iran and Germany, wartime commitments to postwar cooperation had quickly turned to cold-war animosities and the partition of a nation straddling the boundary between East and West. In August 1945 the Japanese, who had ruled Korea since 1910, surrendered to U.S. forces in the area south of the 38th parallel. North of that line, they surrendered to the Red Army. At a Moscow meeting of foreign ministers in December 1945 there was agreement in principle to establish a unified military government for Korea, with the U.S., France, Britain, and the Soviet Union joining in a transitional trusteeship until the nation was readied for independence. What was agreed in principle soon proved inapplicable in practice. The 38th parallel hardened into a *de facto* boundary between two separate Korean nations.[30]

In 1947 the U.S. delegation to the General Assembly, led by Secretary of State George Marshall, took up the question of Korean reunification. Over strenuous Soviet opposition the Assembly's Western majority passed a resolution that called for nationwide elections on March 31, 1948, supervised by a nine-member United Nations Temporary Commission on Korea. The Ukraine, named to represent the socialist states on the commission, refused to serve. An Indian representative, K. P. S. Menon, became chairman. Failing even to gain access to, let alone cooperation from, North Korea, the commission contented itself with observing elections on May 10 in South Korea. These produced a government headed by Syngman Rhee. Unobserved by the Commission, the North held its own version of an election on August 25.

Prodded by the U.S., the General Assembly next declared the government in Seoul to be the freely elected and lawful government of all Korea. It reconstituted the temporary commission as the United Nations Commission for the Unification and Rehabilitation of Korea (UNCURK) and asked it to promote peaceful reunification.[31] Meanwhile, with surrogates planted in Seoul in the South and Pyongyang in the North, the Americans and the Soviets began to withdraw their forces from Korea. Their departure unleashed increasingly serious border skirmishes all along the 38th parallel. UNCURK was no more successful than its predecessor in engaging the North in dialogue. Nevertheless, in 1949 the General Assembly expanded UNCURK's role to include placing observers along the increasingly troubled border. They were thus positioned to report authoritatively on the events of June 25, 1950, when the North Korean army rolled into the South, and so the U.N. system was not bogged down—as so often before and after—by a dispute about the facts.

This should be understood in the context of U.N. politics. When the North attacked, UNCURK observers were asleep in their Seoul hotel rooms, not on patrol along the border. They got their earliest information from U.S. embassy intelligence officers. Still, Seoul being just south of the frontier, they were *there*, and they formed an independent judgment which was relayed to the Security Council by the Secretary-General. The morning dispatch by the *New York Times* may have been more complete, perhaps even more reliable, but a report by a U.N. fact-finding team had a very special power to influence the thinking and conduct of the U.N. member nations.

When the North attacked, the U.S.'s ambassador Ernest Gross, on instructions from Dean Acheson,[32] awakened the Secretary-General at 3:00 a.m. on the 25th with a formal request for the convening of the Security Council. At 2:00 p.m. the Council got down to business. The Secretary-General had the Council president recognize him first. He said:[33]

> The report received by me from the Commission, as well as reports from other sources in Korea, make it plain that military actions have been undertaken by North Korean forces. These actions are a direct violation of . . . the principles of the Charter. The present situation is a serious one and is a threat to international peace. The Security Council is, in my opinion, the competent organ to deal with it. I consider it the clear duty of the Security Council to take steps necessary to re-establish peace in that area.

By his statement, the Secretary-General had effectively preempted the usual frustrating debates over questions of fact and law. Such decisive intervention against the aggressor, however, took the Secretary-General out of contention as a mediator. It was a price Lie paid deliberately, for he perceived these events not as an ordinary dispute to be mediated but as a direct military challenge to the U.N.'s system of collective security.

Few Secretaries-General since have been willing to see a situation in such clear-cut black-and-whites. In part, they may hope for reelection, which requires the assent of the requisite majority of the General Assembly and of the Security Council, including all five permanent members. More often, it reflects a desire to keep open the Secretary-General's options as conciliator and mediator between the parties to a dispute. By taking sides, Lie facilitated prompt action by the Security Council, but he also became unacceptable to the Soviet Union as umpire and, indeed, as Secretary-General.

Beyond making his unvarnished report on the events of June 25, the Secretary-General played another important behind-the-scenes role. A few hours before the Council meeting, he effectively lobbied the delegates of India, Egypt, and Norway, who lacked instructions from their governments. "I believe I may say without risking any offense," Trygve Lie later wrote, "that my views probably influenced the Indian delegation, as well as the delegate of Egypt, Mahmoud Fawzi Bey, to vote in favor of the resolution which was adopted that Sunday afternoon."[34] Moscow soon demonstrated that Lie was quite wrong about not having given offense.

Lie's sacrifice of his neutrality would not have produced action by the Security Council except for another odd circumstance. This was the absence of two governments, those of Peking and Moscow, either of which would have vetoed the initiatives the Council took. Peking's absence was the result of successful U.S. maneuvers that allowed the defeated Nationalist regime to retain the Chinese seat after it had been routed from the mainland to Taiwan. As for the Soviets, in January 1950, in what turned out to be a misguided maneuver, they had walked out of the Security Council in protest against the exclusion of the Peking regime.

It is only in the light of all these circumstances that one can understand the ability of the Security Council, on June 25, to adopt the U.S.-sponsored resolution in so rapid and decisive a manner. It did so by a vote of 9 to 0, with

Yugoslavia, rather bravely, defying Stalin with an abstention.[35] The resolution noted "with grave concern the armed attack upon the Republic of Korea by forces from North Korea" and called for the "immediate cessation of hostilities," while directing the authorities of North Korea "to withdraw forthwith their armed forces to the 38th parallel." It also instructed UNCURK to report on developments while calling on "all Members to render every assistance to the United Nations in the execution of this resolution and to refrain from giving assistance to the North Korean authorities."[36]

The next day, reports from Korea indicated that the South Korean forces, surprised and underarmed, were in disarray. Defeat appeared imminent. In these circumstances, President Truman made his decision to dispatch U.S. forces at once. The move was strongly supported by Trygve Lie.[37] The Secretary-General, like Truman, had hoped that, before the U.S. committed its troops, the Security Council would authorize that step. However, this was frustrated when the representatives of India and Egypt again failed to get instructions from their governments and the Council's meeting had to be postponed. Even the following day, June 27, only a bare majority of seven of the eleven members could be mustered to pass a resolution calling on all states to "furnish such assistance to the Republic of Korea as may be necessary to repel the armed attack and to restore international peace and security in the area."[38] The Indian and Egyptian instructions still not having arrived, their delegates did not participate in the voting.

Technically, the U.S. decision to send troops preceded the Council's request. However, Trygve Lie states: "I, for one, welcomed the United States' initiative,"[39] since the military situation was desperate and private consultations had already established that there was a Council majority for the resolution even without India and Egypt. (The Indians eventually received instructions to vote in favor of the resolution, while the Egyptians were instructed to abstain.)

Narrow as the majority was, the Security Council, for the first time, had authorized collective action to resist international aggression—the very thing for which the U.N. had been established. But collective action had only been made possible by Soviet and Chinese nonparticipation. This was pure serendipity. On June 27, Lie had attended a luncheon with both Soviet Ambassador Malik and U.S. Ambassador Gross. As they got to the dessert and coffee, he remarked to Malik that he was about to set off for a meeting of the Security Council. "Won't you join us?" he asked. "The interests of your country would seem to me to call for your presence."

Malik shook his head no. On the way out, Gross whispered in Lie's ear: "Think what would have happened if he had accepted your invitation."[40] In that event, Lie's strategy,[41] as well as that of the U.S. government,[42] would have been to take the issue directly to the General Assembly. Since the Council's resolutions of June 25 and 27 "recommended"—that is, did not *order*— states to help the South Koreans, and since the Charter also gives the Assembly broad powers to "recommend" action, the Secretary-General was of the opinion that the resolutions could have passed equally well in either body. Later, when the Soviets came back to block the Council, this strategy was reactivated, giving rise to intense and enduring controversy, continuing, in one context or another, to the present.

On July 7, with the Soviets still absent, the Security Council put the finishing touch on its collective security initiative by passing a resolution that asked members to provide "military forces and other assistance" for a "unified command under the United States" and authorized to use the blue and white United Nations flag.[43] Luard concludes that this was a "classic example" of the U.N. performing as intended.[44]

The Secretary-General cabled all members to ask what assistance they were prepared to commit.[45] Twenty-two countries volunteered; of these, 15 were accepted. That number would probably have been greater had the Unified Command not insisted, for purposes of efficiency, that national contributions be made at batallion strength at least.[46]

This resolution and the response to it, was the Council's final action on Korea. The Soviets, at last comprehending the folly of their boycott, returned to block all further action. By then, however, activity had moved decisively from the diplomatic to the military stage. On September 15, General MacArthur landed at Inchon, and, briefly, the tables were turned on the North. Then China entered the conflict and defeated U.N. forces at the Yalu River separating Korea from Manchuria. Later, U.N. forces regrouped and were able to create a stalemate near the 38th parallel, roughly where the fighting had begun.

That stalemate eventually dictated the terms of the Armistice Agreement of 1953. By the end of the war, Korea had not been unified. But then reunification had not been the original purpose of the U.N.'s response to North Korea's aggression. After the success at Inchon,[47] the U.N. raised its sights, but shortly thereafter lowered them again when Chinese entry into the conflict made outright victory impossible. But for the U.N. to have fought the Chinese and North Koreans to a stalemate that denied them conquest of the South was itself a considerable accomplishment.

It has been argued that, even in this instance of U.N. collective security in operation, there was considerably less than met the eye. As noted, the Council had been able to act only because of the absence of the Soviets and Chinese communists, an exigency that never happened again. And, it has been observed, those collective measures under the U.N. flag were not really initiated by the "U.N." but by the "U.S." In this view, the organization merely served to legitimize a U.S. initiative, one that was never seriously influenced by considerations of multilateralism.[48] Trygve Lie, while an enthusiastic supporter of the U.N. in Korea, concedes that he was "concerned with the 'solo' role . . . assumed by the United States."[49] He made various proposals to Washington for setting up a genuine joint command and a real "international brigade" but received little encouragement. Washington's preference for holding all the cards, Lie thought, "no doubt contributed to the tendency of the Members to let Washington assume most of the responsibility for the fighting."[50]

If the U.N. military role was limited, its diplomatic contribution was more so. Although the Secretary-General and various groups of delegates, formal committees, and informal caucuses at one time or another tried to involve themselves in the negotiating process, they were able to contribute nothing. The Chinese, in particular, were unwilling to have the U.N. or the Secretary-General play any sort of mediating role so long as the organization excluded Peking and remained a party to the war.

The fighting continued sporadically for as long as either side saw any possibility of winning. When, after a protracted period of stalemate, Ambassador Malik signaled the Soviets' willingness to have their North Korean surrogates negotiate an end to the fighting, he did so in a U.N. radio broadcast. But this did not make the U.N. the vehicle for negotiations. These took place on the battlefield between the military commanders.

Even if the United Nations was important to the resolution of the Korean conflict only in a rather limited sense, that conflict was very important to the U.N. The crisis eventually prompted a significant shift in responsibility for collective security from the Security Council to the General Assembly. This occurred when, after the Inchon landing, United Nations forces appeared to have routed the North. New instructions were needed as General Douglas MacArthur's army neared the 38th parallel. But, with the Russians back at the circular table, instructions could not come from the veto-bound Council.

Washington wanted to pursue the remnants of the Northern army beyond the 38th parallel, despite serious misgivings among allies with contingents under MacArthur's command. On October 7, 1950, at U.S. insistence, the General Assembly authorized the pursuit of the aggressor into its own territory. The resolution passed on that date by a vote of 47 to 5, with seven abstentions, approving "[a]ll appropriate steps . . . to ensure stability throughout Korea . . . including the holding of elections, under the auspices of the United Nations, for the establishment of a unified, independent and democratic government in the sovereign State of Korea . . ." also authorized the U.N. forces to occupy as much of Korea "as necessary for achieving the objectives specified . . . ."[51] Dean Acheson thought that this "might be construed to mean something more than the prevention of a new attack."[52]

This new and wider mandate for the U.N. force replaced the earlier one spelled out in the Security Council resolution of June 25, which had only called for pushing North Korean forces back to the 38th parallel. Whatever its tactical wisdom, the resolution of October 7 had the most far-reaching implications for the distribution of functions and powers within the U.N.: the Assembly had been used to circumvent the Council. This was fully understood by

Secretary-General Lie, who declared himself elated at the ability of the organization to neutralize obstacles: "This was Korea, not Manchuria"; he wrote; "this was the United Nations, not the League of Nations."[53] To make sure that this was not an isolated victory, Washington, with the Secretary-General's support, persuaded the Assembly to establish simplified procedures for convening that body to sidestep the Council in future.

Uniting for Peace

The British had not been nearly as enthusiastic as Trygve Lie. Wiser heads at the Foreign Office had correctly prophesied, in a warning to the U.S. Department of State, that any move to increase the power of the General Assembly would present dangers to the West once its majority gave way before the surge of new nations being created in Africa and Asia.[54] Acheson disagreed, arguing that "present difficulties outweighed possible future ones, and we pressed on."[55] The U.S. proceeded at full speed to secure the Assembly's adoption of what became known as the Uniting for Peace resolution, or Acheson Plan. Acheson personally introduced it, claiming it would increase the effectiveness of the United Nations against aggression. He urged the Assembly not to allow the Soviet veto to render the organization impotent. In good lawyerly fashion he argued that articles 10, 11, and 14 of the Charter made the Assembly the Council's partner in wielding "authority and responsibility for matters affecting international peace."[56] The U.S.'s ambassador Benjamin Cohen added the uniquely American argument that the U.N. should follow our Supreme Court's practice of construing the Constitution flexibly, allowing the system to invent new ways of overcoming unanticipated difficulties without formal amendment of the basic compact. He cited the invention of the Presidential "executive agreement" as an example of how the U.S. had worked around the awkward constitutional requirement of a two-thirds Senatorial majority for the ratification of treaties, and urged the undoubtedly bemused Assembly delegates to study the creative U.S. Supreme Court decision in *McCulloch v. Maryland*. There the Justices had inferred from the Constitution's enumerated federal powers certain additional "implied" powers not spelled out in the text.[57]

Advocates of the Acheson Plan pointed out that it meticulously adhered to the fundamental difference between the powers of the General Assembly—which may only *recommend* collective action—and those of the Security Council—which may *order* member states to participate in enforcing collective security. Even so, the Uniting for Peace resolution does envisage circumstances in which the Assembly, convened on 24 hours' notice after a veto in the Council, would step in to organize the collective use of force against an aggressor. Such was certainly not the intent of the drafters at San Francisco. Article 10 allows the Assembly to discuss "any questions or any matters within the scope of the present Charter" and "make recommendations to the Members" except when the matter is being considered by the Security Council. But this is qualified by article 11, which says that when the issue relates "to the maintenance of peace and security" and "action is necessary," the matter "shall be referred to the Security Council." U.S. Ambassador Ernest Gross has rightly written that the effect of the Acheson Plan is to transfer to the Assembly "major, rather than merely 'residual . . .' " authority "in relation to peace and security."[58]

Eventually, the International Court declared, in effect, that the Acheson Plan was a lawful interpretation of the Charter.[59] Although the Uniting for Peace resolution had formalized the new rules, they had been evolving almost from the first, when it became clear that optimistic prophecies about Soviet restraint in using the veto were wrong. In 1946, the first Assembly had called on members to implement diplomatic sanctions against Franco's Spain,[60] after the sanctions had drawn a veto in the Council. In 1949, in response to another veto, the Assembly had asked its members to embargo military supplies for communist guerrillas in Greece.[61] Even the Assembly's resolution of October 7, 1950, redefining the mission of U.N. forces in Korea, antedated the Acheson Plan.

Each of these steps was taken at the urging of the United States. Was the U.S. being prudent in the pursuit of its national interest? It can be argued that it might not really have mattered. Once the new nations got control of the Assembly, they would certainly have tried to expand its role even if the West had not already done so. This demurrer, however, is not entirely persuasive. If the U.S. had not broken ranks with the other permanent members of the Security Council, it is doubtful whether the small nations, no matter how numerous, could themselves have brought about so major a shift in responsibility to the Assembly. That shift, we now know, ended up weakening the position of the U.S. in the U.N. even more than that of Russia.

The episode dramatizes two odd, seemingly contradictory tendencies in our policy toward the U.N. One is not to take the U.N. seriously enough; the other is to take it too seriously. The former tendency is personified in Secretary Acheson, who was airily nonchalant about sacrificing our long-term interests in the organization to achieve short-run tactical gains, partly because he did not believe the U.N. had long-term prospects. The latter tendency is apparent in the exaggerated reactions of U.N. boosters. McGeorge Bundy, in editing the Acheson papers, commented that Uniting for Peace was "certainly the most important development in the application of the Charter since it was signed at San Francisco in 1945." In this view, the resolution was a large step toward a new world order. Bundy felt that "just as the United States has led the way in circumventing the Soviet veto, *it has weakened its own veto*; to the degree that this clause of the 'Uniting for Peace' Resolution becomes effective, the basic authority of the United Nations in organizing collective action against aggression now rests with any two-thirds of its members. This is a measure of the degree to which the United States Government is prepared to entrust itself to the weight of the indefinable but important force called world opinion."[62]

It is highly unlikely that this is what Acheson had in mind. Yet, even the editors of the *New York Times* drew satisfaction from the thought that the Assembly was now to be "*the* principal organ of this world organization" and would "assume executive functions" that previously "were supposed to be left to the Security Council."[63] When Uniting for Peace was adopted on November 3, 1950,[64] by a handy 40-to-5 (with 12 abstentions, including India and Argentina),[65] the *New York Times* thought the U.N. had reached a "turning point as an instrument for the suppression of aggression."[66] It was a case of new illusions compounding the old.

The Suez Crisis

The U.N.'s subsequent role in resolving the Suez Canal "crisis" appeared to confirm the *New York Times*'s optimistic view. It seemed the organization, at last, had come to fulfill the highest expectations of 1945, and that the transfer of power to the General Assembly was the vehicle for its redemption.

The Israeli, British, and French invasion of Egypt, late in 1956, led to the formation of the United Nations Emergency Force (UNEF). Unlike U.N. contingents in Korea, UNEF was not created to repel an ongoing breach of the peace with a collective use of armed might, but as a legion of peacekeepers to oversee a decision of the combatants to disengage. Unlike the Korean force, UNEF was genuinely international, commanded by an officer appointed on the initiative of the Secretary-General. It deliberately excluded contributions from any of the Big Five. Instead, UNEF was made up of small units from a broad assortment of states. Although related conceptually to the small observer groups in Palestine and Kashmir, it was far larger: the first truly international militia. Even more important, UNEF was authorized not by the Security Council, but by the General Assembly acting on the basis of the Uniting for Peace resolution.

The Suez crisis began when Egypt's President Gamal Abdel Nasser nationalized the Suez Canal Company on July 26, 1956. After inconclusive negotiations to establish international guarantees for unfettered use of the Canal, Israel attacked Egypt on October 29. The next day a prearranged British and French ultimatum demanded that Egypt and Israel both withdraw from the area of the Canal. When Egypt demurred, British aircraft stationed in Cyprus began bombing Egyptian targets. On November 5 British and French paratroops were dropped near Port Said.

British and French vetoes effectively immobilized the Security Council,[67] but not the Soviets, who began threatening direct retaliation against London and Paris. In a message to President Eisenhower made public on November 5, Soviet Premier Nikolai A. Bulganin warned that his country possessed "all modern types of arms, including atomic and hydrogen weapons." In a concurrent message to British Prime Minister Anthony Eden, Bulganin made this unprecedented threat more explicit, asking how England would feel "if she herself had been attacked by more powerful states possessing every kind of modern destructive weapon?" He boasted that his country need not even send a navy or air force to the coasts of Britain, but could use "other means, such as rocket technique." The letter ended with a pledge "to crush the aggressors."[68] In addition, Moscow began to recruit thousands of "volunteers" for deployment to Egypt.[69] Demonstrating that this threat was being taken seriously, NATO's Supreme Allied Commander, General Alfred M. Gruenther, responded that if the Russians were to use missiles against Britain and France, then "just as day follows night" the West would retaliate and the Soviet Union would be destroyed.[70]

With matters approaching this dangerous pass, the Yugoslav member of the Security Council, specifically invoking the Uniting for Peace resolution, introduced a resolution to convene an Emergency Session of the General Assembly.[71] Since the resolution was procedural, the negative British and French votes did not constitute a veto. The Soviets, who had bitterly opposed the Acheson Plan, now voted with the U.S. to implement it.[72]

After much behind-the-scenes maneuvering—in which Canada's foreign minister Lester B. Pearson[73] and Secretary-General Dag Hammarskjold[74] played leading roles—an agreement was reached. British, French, and—somewhat later—Israeli forces were to withdraw from the Canal and be replaced by UNEF.[75] A few weeks later, the Assembly authorized UNEF "to assist in achieving situations conducive to the maintenance of peaceful conditions in the area" and gave the Secretary-General wide discretion "to take steps to carry out these measures."[76] Hammarskjold negotiated personally with President Nasser to create the agreed framework for UNEF's operations in Egypt,[77] which was duly approved by the Assembly.[78]

At its zenith the UNEF force, with contingents from ten nations chosen by the Secretary-General after consulting with Egypt, consisted of some 6000 officers and men.[79] Stationed along the Egyptian side of the armistice line, the force became a major factor in preventing the renewal of fedayeen raids from Egypt into Israel and in maintaining peace along that previously afflicted boundary. Not only did the Suez crisis further enhance the peacekeeping and conflict-resolving role of the General Assembly, but it also thrust forward Hammarskjold, whose skill in setting up UNEF earned him the respect of world leaders, including President Eisenhower and Secretary of State Dulles.[80]

The Suez crisis thus confirmed the United Nations in its most fruitful line of endeavor: the stationing of international peacekeeping forces between mutually hostile antagonists at that crucial moment in a dispute when both sides perceive disengagement as preferable to continued hostilities. Success, in this instance, paved the way for more such "solutions." When the Lebanese government, two

years later, accused the Egyptian-Syrian union of massive illegal and unprovoked intervention, it was natural that the Security Council should respond
with a call on the Secretary-General to deploy another observer group "to
ensure that there is no illegal infiltration of personnel or supply of arms or
other matériel across the Lebanese borders."[81] The deployment failed to solve
the problem, and U.S. Marines were landed, precipitating yet another Middle
East crisis. But after the Security Council was deadlocked, the Assembly again
stepped forward, authorizing the Secretary-General to make such "practical
arrangements" as would "adequately help in upholding the purpose and principles of the Charter" while facilitating the withdrawal of U.S. forces.[82] These
arrangements consisted of expanding the Lebanon observer force to almost 600
men.[83] It played a significant role in speeding U.S. withdrawal and in stabilizing, for a time, Lebanon's eastern border.

The success of UNEF can best be measured by the frequency with which,
with appropriate modifications, it has been imitated. However, it must be
noted that the Suez episode was unusual in one major respect: the United
States and the Soviet Union were on the same side. With those forces arrayed
together in opposition, it was virtually certain that the Israeli-British-French
military initiative would fail. Once that failure was evident, the General Assembly became a convenient context within which to achieve the inevitable.
The Assembly ensured that the vacuum created by British, French, and Israeli
troop withdrawal would not be filled by Russian (or U.S.) military intervention.
The Assembly's action also diluted the U.S. role in frustrating three of our
closest allies. It enabled the British and French governments to pretend that the
objectives of their intervention had been achieved because UNEF would now
assume responsibility for the security of the Canal. Once again, the organization was able to serve as a smokescreen behind which losers could appear
undefeated and altruistic.

On the negative side, the decision of the U.S. to help enforce the U.N.'s
rules against Britain, France, and Israel, three of its closest allies, at the very
time the Soviets were leading their own allies in a punitive expedition of
aggression against Hungary, cannot but have had serious costs for America's
alliance. There seemed still to be, in Washington, a dangerous confusion
between the U.N. system as the U.S. wished it to be, and the harsher realities.

Summary

The crises in Azerbaijan, Palestine, Berlin, Korea, and Suez were thus, in a
sense, all instances in which the United Nations could be seen, by those of
optimistic disposition, to have played the role for which it was intended, or an
equally acceptable part. In the Azerbaijan crisis, the pressure of public attention focused by the Security Council may have helped persuade the Soviets to
withdraw. During the Berlin crisis the Council provided the facilities for quiet

diplomacy between East and West. The Korean War demonstrated the potential of collective security under the aegis of the Council and of U.N. fact-finding. Twice, in 1948–49 and in 1956, the Secretary-General had demonstrated his ability to promote truces in the Middle East. The Uniting for Peace Resolution could be read as reviving in the General Assembly, the organization's capacity for decisive action, even in the face of the veto.

Those of a more pessimistic bent, on the contrary, would see each case as essentially unique—a fluke—and Uniting for Peace as a tactical disaster. They would also detect the signs of danger in the very public diplomacy encouraged by the U.N. system: the posturing, and the preoccupation with symbolic behavior, procedure, and precedent.

Yet, the appearance of success in each of these cases was manifest. Against this backdrop of limited, but not necessarily negligible, U.N. effectiveness will be seen, later on, the many failures of its system, when blatant aggression was met only by stasis, or worse.

§ 3 §

Et Tu, Nehru

Introduction to Reality

A few instances of apparent success do not necessarily make an effective new international system. While during its inceptive years the U.N. may occasionally have succeeded in applying its principles and procedures, the successes tended to be serendipitous; the failures, fundamental. Still, passionately held illusions die hard. Collective illusions, in which individual misperceptions are reinforced by the group, die harder. Societal illusions emerging from the ashes of war, and purchased with blood, die hardest, and most painfully. The fervently hopeful illusions with which American society—after the years of war—girded itself for participation in the new global system launched at San Francisco have never quite been laid to rest. Even before the first pen stood poised to subscribe the U.N. Charter, however, other events were beginning to lance our illusions. After the first two decades, some persisted, but those who continued to cherish them were perhaps idealistic, but also naive.

Unfortunately, as the wishful thoughts proved false, they were often replaced not by hard realism but by new fantasies destined to bring their own disappointments. Among the optimistic beliefs which were proven false during the first two decades of the U.N. were the following: nations had replaced the use of force with the rule of law; members' military self-reliance had been made obsolete by the new arrangements for collective security; and self-interest would be redefined by each state to give priority to the cooperative nurturing of a new, more peaceful, and just international system in which everyone would have an equal stake.

Instead, it rapidly became clear that:

- Most states which had the power to expand their territory or spheres of influence preferred to advance their national self-interest through such expansion even at the cost of crippling the fledgling system established at San Francisco;
- Many new nations born after San Francisco were no better "socialized," in this respect, than were the older powers of Europe and North America. Indeed, the era of old-fashioned, narrowly conceived nationalism, far from ending at San Francisco, was entering a new and most virulent phase;
- Startling new developments in the technology of war—from blitzkrieg to atomic weapons—made obsolete many of the new principles and procedures of collective security even before they could be tested;
- The system of global wardenship entrusted to the wartime Big Five—who were collectively charged with guarding the peace as they had defeated the Axis—quickly gave way to a system of rival power blocs that sheltered lawbreakers, permitting even modestly endowed states to engage in aggressive acts under the sponsorship of a superpower;
- The U.N., initially believed by many Americans to be a significant, independent actor on the world stage and not merely a place to house and service diplomatic negotiations, was soon shown to be incapable of transforming the perspective, let alone the behavior, of its member states.

U.N. Norms Pertaining to the Use of Force

The Charter of the United Nations deals with many issues, from decolonization to the privileges and immunities of the organization's senior officials. Its most important provision, however, in article 2(4), states:

> All Members shall refrain in their international relations from the threat or use of force against the territorial integrity or political independence of any state, or in any other manner inconsistent with the Purposes of the United Nations.

Not only are states obliged to refrain from the use of force, except in self-defense,[1] but they must undertake to seek to resolve any dispute with another state by negotiation or other peaceful means.[2] Where the parties to a dispute fail to resolve it amicably on their own, both the Security Council[3] and the General Assembly[4] may make recommendations, either procedural or substantive, to help achieve a settlement. If those recommendations are not heeded, or fail to produce the intended result, the Security Council may make binding decisions and back them up by the use of diplomatic and economic[5] or even military[6] sanctions, if necessary deploying armed forces which member states "undertake to make available to the Security Council, on its call . . ."[7] (see below, Chapter 9).

Obviously, the Charter envisages a system of global collective security that is far from toothless. Its sanctions ought to deter any state that, in a fit of national self-interest, might prefer old-fashioned force to peaceful negotiations.

Unfortunately, it was soon seen that the elegant system did not work for a number of reasons, which, in retrospect, seem self-evident. In the first place, the procedure requires the convening of deliberative bodies, which are to debate, vote, and make recommendations or decisions. This process is simply too slow to catch up with the changes that can be imposed by technologically sophisticated aggression long before the U.N.'s cumbersome political bodies can be convened, the disputed facts ascertained, procedural objections met, a resolution drafted and passed by a majority, and its intent implemented. The U.N.'s two principal organs for political deliberation—the Council and the Assembly—together constitute a particularly complicated, highly fragmented pseudo-parliament, suffering all the lugubrious delays of real parliamentary institutions but enjoying little of their redeeming power: ultimately to enforce its own commands. The U.N. has been able to act only when there is no serious objection. This makes it useless, especially when faced with the threat of such highly mechanized forces as were first demonstrated in 1940 by Germany's *Blitzkrieg* that destroyed France's Maginot Line, and which are now appropriately considered "conventional." When such forces are aggressively deployed, the principles of the U.N. demand a collective response, but the procedures—except in the fortuitous case of Korea—are unable to generate action in time, or at all.

True, in some instances the U.N. has responded more quickly than did the League of Nations. In 1932 the League dispatched the Lytton Commission to discover the facts concerning an alleged Japanese invasion of Manchuria. By the time the Commission, traveling by train and boat, had reached the site of the conflict, the Japanese had completed their conquest.[8] Although the Suez crisis (described in Chapter 2) showed a U.N. considerably more agile than that, like the League it is still too slow to preempt most aggressors, which continue to move more rapidly than the organization. The forty years since San Francisco have brought a few innovations to the U.N., such as the Uniting for Peace procedures, but at the same time technology has also revolutionized the pace of aggressive warfare.

Oddly, India, despite congenitally idealistic rhetoric, probably did the most, through recurrent aggressive behavior, to demonstrate the organization's impotence.

Hyderabad

The Hyderabad issue arose after Britain granted independence to the Dominion of India and to Pakistan on August 15, 1947. These two new nations, the former predominantly Hindu and the latter overwhelmingly Muslim, divided between them the inheritance of what had been British India. However, the British Labour government had appeared to indicate, somewhat ambiguously, that the several Princely States of India—technically not part of "British India" but under the protection of the British raj—would "be entirely free to choose whether to associate with one or other of the Dominion Governments or to stand alone."[9] Taking this invitation seriously, the Nizam, or princely ruler, of Hyderabad, in June 1947 publicly announced that, at least initially, he would join neither India nor Pakistan but would see how things developed. As it turned out, they developed very badly.

Hyderabad's 82,000 square miles lie at the very center of India. In 1948 they supported, after a fashion, more than sixteen million inhabitants. While 81 percent were Hindu, the 13 percent who were Muslim included the Nizam, the top echelons of the bureaucracy, the police, and the military. Their sympathies, dictated by religion rather than geography, lay entirely with Pakistan.

Immediately after India achieved independence, relations between Hyderabad and the government at New Delhi became strained, with the latter insisting that the Nizam organize a plebiscite and accede to the Indian Union. In return for Hyderabad's relinquishing control over foreign affairs, defense, and communications, India offered a measure of local autonomy. The Nizam refused, contending that, with the end of British rule, his Princely State automatically resumed its precolonial status of complete independence. He offered a form of loose association between equals, but no accession.[10]

On November 27, 1947, Hyderabad and India signed a one-year Standstill Agreement, which purported to continue between Hyderabad and India "all agreements and administrative arrangements as to matters of common concern, including External Affairs, Defence and Communications" which had previously existed between Great Britain and the Nizam, without prejudice to any long-term solution the two countries might meanwhile work out. The agreement denied India the right to send in troops but provided for arbitration of disputes.[11]

Even as the negotiations required by the agreement became mired, the situation in Hyderabad itself was polarizing. Communists "liberated" some 2000 villages in the Tilangana region. Militant rightist Moslems of the Razakar movement terrorized Hindu villages, looting and molesting without hindrance from the police.[12] The Nizam, richest of the subcontinent's princely rulers, further antagonized India by advancing a large loan to India's archenemy, Pakistan.

During 1948 relations continued to deteriorate, negotiations broke up, and India imposed an economic blockade. Border incursions became frequent. Correctly perceiving his state much the weaker party, the Nizam appealed to the United Nations on August 21.[13] The request was circulated to the members but was not even considered at the Council's August 30 meeting.

In another cable of September 12, the government of Hyderabad predicted an imminent invasion and "earnestly" requested the help of the Security Council.[14] The invasion began the following day. When the Council was convened on the 16th—three days later—it did not—as it was perfectly empowered to do—set up a small committee of its members to fly to the area to investigate. Neither did it authorize investigation or mediation by the Secretary-General. It did not even call upon the parties to cease firing and refrain from unilateral actions that would violate the Charter. The U.S. considered sponsoring such a call but concluded that, in view of the rapid Indian advance, such a step was "not practicable" and would "seriously jeopardize" relations with New Delhi.[15] Instead, the members treated themselves to a lengthy scholarly debate, about whether, under British, Indian, and Hyderabadi constitutional law and practice, a quarrel between India and Hyderabad constituted an "international" dispute.

The Indians, of course, argued that Hyderabad was geographically, ethnically, and legally a part of India and that it had never been, and had not now become, an independent state. In a sense, all this did matter. If Hyderabad was not a "state" in international law, it was not covered by the Charter and could not apply for the protection of the Security Council. The debate on this "threshhold" question may have been unavoidable, and to this day its erudition fascinates law students. However, undisputably there was a real threat to the peace. And even if Hyderabad was not a "state," it was clearly also not yet a part of India. As Secretary of State Marshall had cabled the U.S. delegation to the U.N. on September 1, "It would be futile to have extended debate on the question of whether or not Hyderabad is a 'state' within the meaning of article 35(2). It is clear from the known facts that a dispute exists and that Hyderabad is a party to that dispute."[16] Nevertheless, instead of concerning itself with the substance of the dispute without prejudice to the procedural question, the Council focused on procedure. It thereby made itself as irrelevant to Hyderabad as the Council of Trent. Nothing happening at the U.N. had any practical effect on India, Hyderabad, or world peace.

This was not solely a failure of the rules of the game. Clearly, India preferred an immobilized U.N.. It asked for—and got—an adjournment of five days "to present documents." By that time, the occupation was complete. Britain, which, in a sense, had created the problem by its partition formula, professed embarrassment and clearly preferred the matter kept out of the U.N.. The U.S., trying to save both U.N. principles and its friendly relations with the Nehru government, resisted criticizing India but urged New Delhi to propose a U.N.-supervised plebiscite in Hyderabad on the grounds that India's "objectives would be more fully appreciated if subjected to moral scrutiny of [the] world."[17] Meanwhile, the Security Council continued its fruitless line of debate, while the Nizam's largely ceremonial militiamen surrendered or were killed.[18] Although Pakistan attempted to keep the issue on the agenda, world interest soon wandered to more pressing matters. By September 20, the hapless Nizam, now a captive of the Indian military, instructed his representative to the U.N. to withdraw his complaint,[19] and most Council members thought it best to let the matter drop.

Evening up past scores, Hindus in the next weeks massacred 50,000 Muslims.[20] Nevertheless, U.S. Ambassador Howard Donovan, in New Delhi, cabled the secretary of state that any effort by the U.S. to keep the issue before the U.N. would "seriously, if not irreparably" damage relations with India, driving that country to "become more closely associated with [the] USSR."[21] For the same reason, he strenuously urged that the idea of pushing for an internationally supervised plebiscite be abandoned.[22] Despite Secretary Marshall's fear that this would "create [a] dangerous precedent by encouraging [the] use of force by aggressive states,"[23] the New Delhi embassy's *Realpolitik* prevailed. It was but the first of many instances of conflict between those engaged in bilateral and multilateral diplomacy. Then, as in most subsequent instances, the bilateral interests took precedence. A year later, on November 24, 1949, the Nizam formally embraced India's new constitution.[24]

Thus ended that opportunity for the U.N. to prevent a breach of world peace. Its legacy is an indecisive debate on what constitutes a "state" and a precedent for the proposition that, once aggression has succeeded, the victor can force the vanquished to drop its complaint—a proposition subsequently applied with considerable success in lightning invasions of Guatemala, Hungary, and Czechoslovakia. In none of these instances was the U.N. able to act before the complainant vanished. The lesson is best stated in Shakespeare's *Macbeth*: "If it were done—when 'tis done—then 'twere well it were done quickly."

True, the Hyderabad complaint presented special difficulties for the U.N. because the "standing" of the complainant was open to question. But, as we shall demonstrate, forty years of practice support the conclusion that *every* crisis presents "special" difficulties, which appear as questions of law or questions of fact. Is the complainant a sovereign state? Is force being used to commit aggression or only in self-defense? Is the use of force "proportional" to the provocation? Are troops being assembled on a border in an "aggressive" manner? Have irregular forces been allowed by one country to infiltrate another? Is one country smuggling arms to insurgents in another? These questions can be dealt with crisis by crisis, but crises are not the best times to invent the machinery necessary to obtain authoritative answers quickly. As long as the U.N. has no speedy, automatic stand-by procedures for providing such answers, it will continue to squander time in inconclusive debate.

It would not be difficult to devise speedy and fair fact-finding and law-deciding procedures. The Secretary-General could be asked to investigate and report on virtually any issue of fact in forty-eight hours. To that end, he could have his personal representatives in strategic listening posts around the world. A chamber of three International Court judges convened by the Court's president could hear and decide a preliminary jurisdictional question (e.g., "Is the complainant a state?") in two or three days. Meanwhile, the Security Council could go on tackling the substantive issue, withholding action until the preliminary legal questions have been resolved.

Evidently, what is missing is not the means but the desire to act. In the Hyderabad case, New Delhi knew well how to exploit the cold war to its own advantage by playing off the superpowers against each other. In the end, Washington and London were more concerned with preventing a pro-Moscow "tilt" by India than with implementing the Charter's prohibition on the unilateral use of force. As a result of that choice, and many subsequent ones confirming the same priorities, nations in the 1980s are back almost where they were in 1939. They must look for their security to their own military power and to useful alliances. There is no collective security to be had from the U.N. Perhaps India did not so much undermine the U.N. system as simply publicize the emperor's nakedness.

Kashmir

Hyderabad had been the second largest of the Princely States of British India. Kashmir, the largest, was almost its mirror image. The Maharaja of Kashmir was a Hindu, governing a population that was 80 percent Muslim. Like the Nizam, the ruler of Kashmir chose to join neither India nor Pakistan. Also, like his Hyderabad counterpart, he sought to protect his position by repressing the majority. But, because Kashmir is on the border between India and Pakistan, its potential for setting off a major conflict was substantially greater.

That potential was soon realized. By September 1947 some of Kashmir's Muslims, near the Pakistani border, had begun to revolt. They were supported by an invasion of Pathan tribesmen from Pakistan. On October 24 the Maharaja appealed to India for help and, two days later, signed an agreement acceding to the Indian Union. New Delhi responded by occupying two-thirds of the state, with Pakistani tribal forces holding the other third.

In the case of Hyderabad (and the nearly identical case of Junagadh in Western India), India had successfully used force to support the Hindu majority against a Muslim ruler, citing the U.N. Charter's right of self-determination. In Kashmir, Indian forces supported a Hindu ruler against a Muslim majority, citing the partition agreement to support the right of the prince, not the people, to choose. These seeming inconsistencies led to a perfectly consistent result: India got what it wanted by force of arms.

Pakistan complained to the Security Council about the denial of Muslim self-determination in Kashmir. New Delhi replied that the ruler of Kashmir had chosen to join India, and the question was now a purely domestic one. While Prime Minister Nehru did offer to hold a referendum in Kashmir under international auspices at some unspecified later date, nothing of the sort ever took place.

This time the U.N. appeared to act more energetically, although only after months of debate and delay. In response to the Pakistani complaint, the Council passed a resolution on January 20, 1948, establishing a five-nation team to investigate the facts and to attempt to mediate the dispute.[25] This required the cooperation of both parties. The U.N. Commission on India and Pakistan (UNCIP) consisted of the United States, Belgium, and Colombia (nominated by the Secretary-General), Czechoslovakia, (nominated by India), and Argentina (nominated by Pakistan). A Security Council resolution of April 21 set out the modalities for conducting a referendum under UNCIP auspices.[26] That proved impractical, as fighting again intensified between Indian and Pakistani forces. Instead, the Commission concentrated on arranging a cease-fire, which came about, at last, on January 1, 1949. Then, on January 5, the Commission adopted a plan for an UNCIP-supervised plebiscite.[27]

The haggling of Pakistan and India over how to implement that plan left UNCIP to concentrate on demarcating the cease-fire line and positioning observers along it. Although the plebiscite was never held, U.N. observers stayed on. The cease-fire line became the permanent boundary, modified by sporadic renewal of fighting. UNCIP was later augmented by a United Nations Mission Observers Group for India and Pakistan (UNMOGIP), but the task did not change: to freeze the conflict at the point where aggressiveness was overcome by fatigue.

UNMOGIP has played a useful role in preventing an accidental rekindling of the fires of war. However, to observe a truce brought about primarily by the fatigue of the combatants is not the same as to provide collective security against the unilateral use of force. In Kashmir the unilateral use of aggressive force was neither prevented nor reversed by the U.N. The principle of self-determination was not implemented. Unable to achieve these goals, the U.N. system had to settle for the lesser custodial role. The nature of that lesser role, however, should be understood because it was an accurate portent of the U.N.'s limited future political impact on international conflict. The events in Hyderabad and Kashmir had demonstrated that the U.N.:

- *could not* stop aggression unless the parties, because of the victory of one side, or a stalemate, were ready to stop fighting.
- *could not* compel a member to adhere to fundamental principles (self-determination, nonaggression) when those principles were perceived by the member to conflict with its national goals.
- *could* police a stalemate, making it more difficult to resume fighting, but, by stabilizing the situation, also making it less likely that the parties would engage in serious negotiations.
- *could* serve as an excuse for leaders of hostile states not to resume fighting in response to radical domestic political pressures.

The Hyderabad and Kashmir crises also demonstrated that the use of force in the national interest had not been abolished by the strokes of many pens at San Francisco. Evidently force was not only a bad, and resilient, habit of a few old "imperialistic" superpowers, but had also become a feature of the foreign policies of the new nations born in the idealistic glow of postwar decolonization. This was brought into sharper focus by the Indian invasion of Goa in December 1961.

Goa

France and Portugal, as well as Britain, had colonized parts of India. After the British had granted independence, France voluntarily surrendered its bits and pieces, of which Pondicherry was the largest. Bidden to do likewise, the Portuguese dictator, Antonio de Oliveira Salazar, resolutely refused. He asserted that Goa and the other Portuguese enclaves, having been Portuguese for almost 450 years, were an integral part of the Portuguese nation.

After more than a decade of seeking, but failing, to engage Portugal in negotiations leading to the peaceful transfer of the enclaves, India began a military buildup on their borders. It also sent masses of peaceful but provocative satyagraha ("soul force") marchers across the border, some of whom were killed by jittery Portuguese gunners.

On December 8, 1961, the government in Lisbon informed the president of the Security Council that some 30,000 Indian troops were massing and that Indian naval units, including five frigates, a cruiser, and an aircraft carrier, were approaching Goa's territorial waters.[28]

The conflict was scarcely between equals. The population of Goa, in 1961, stood at 650,000. Most of it consisted of ethnic Indians who were Portuguese citizens. Lisbon's supply lines stretched thousands of parlous miles across states such as Egypt, militantly sympathetic to India. Under the circumstances, the obduracy of the aging Portuguese dictator is difficult to comprehend.

A letter to the president of the Security Council on December 11 from the government of Portugal complained that "Indian armed forces have multiplied violations of the Portuguese frontier and air space in an attitude of clear provocation."[29] India's reply did not deny the charge but, instead, complained of "repression and brutality" and "total denial of civil liberties."[30] Such "foreign domination and the repressive nature of the regime, continue to be constant irritants to the people of India."[31]

Portugal's ambassador Vasco Vieira Garin denied that the enclaves were "colonies" and insisted that they were as Portuguese as Lisbon itself. He also denied the charge of repression, but added that "even if those accusations were well grounded, that fact would not give the Indian Union any particular rights, unless the Government of the Indian Union attributes to itself special duties to supervise international society and assume prerogatives over the administration of other countries."[32]

As matters rapidly moved to a climax, the Portuguese proposed that independent international observers be sent immediately to the "Indo-Portuguese" frontier to determine responsibility for "provocations" and "violations of frontier." It added: "The Portuguese Government does not see any reason why the Indian Government, which apparently places itself in the position of a victim, should fear to accept an impartial observation of the facts."[33] As noted, however, the U.N., as a practical matter, had only been able to position such observers with the agreement of both antagonists. In this instance, India had no intention of allowing international observers to freeze a *status quo* which it intended to change.

During the next days, both President Kennedy and Secretary-General U Thant sent messages to Prime Minister Nehru urging him not to use force.[34] U Thant, in identical notes to Nehru and to Salazar, urged "immediate negotiations with a view to achieving an early solution to the problem."[35] The following day, December 18, complaining of "a full-scale unprovoked armed attack," Portugal requested an immediate meeting of the Security Council "to put a stop to the condemnable act of aggression."[36]

The Security Council met at 3:00 p.m. the same day with the ambassador of the United Arab Republic, Omar Loutfi, in the chair. His country had already barred Portuguese planes and vessels from its air and sea space. Other members of the Council, besides the Big Five, were Ceylon, Chile, Ecuador, Liberia, and Turkey. It was not a promising lineup for Lisbon. "The eyes of the world are focused on you," Ambassador Garin told the Council, and demanded "the obvious decision, condemnation of the Indian Union," and measures to ensure "the immediate withdrawal from the whole of Portuguese territory of Indian forces."[37]

The United States position, much different from what it was in 1948, was stated with remarkable personal intensity by Ambassador Adlai Stevenson. India, he said, "is led by a man whom I regard as a friend, who has been a lifelong disciple of one of the world's great saints of peace, whom many have looked upon as an apostle of non-violence."[38]

Stevenson went on to assert that

> the winds of change . . . must not be allowed to become the bugles of war. . . . Let it be perfectly clear what is at stake here; it is the question of the use of armed force by one State against another. . . . The fabric of peace is fragile, and our peace-making machinery has today suffered another blow. If it is to survive, if the United Nations is not to die as ignoble a death as the League of Nations, we cannot condone the use of force in this instance and thus pave the way for forceful solutions of other disputes which exist in Latin America, in Africa, in Asia and in Europe. In a world as interdependent as ours, the possible results of such a trend are too grievous to contemplate. . . . This body cannot apply a double standard with regard to the

principle of resort to force. . . . There is not one law for one part of the world and another law for the rest of the world; there is one law for the whole world and it is the duty of this Council to uphold it.[39]

Of the Indian minister of defense, Krishna Menon—who had advocated and planned the attack—Stevenson, with less charity, said that he was "well known in these halls for his advice on matters of peace and his tireless enjoinders to everyone else to seek the way of compromise."[40]

As the debate droned on in the Security Council, it soon became apparent that no action could be expected from that body. There were spirited polemics about the status of Goa, as there had been about Hyderabad. Ambassador Jha of India insisted that "it must be realized that this is a colonial question. It is a question of getting rid of the last vestiges of colonialism in India."[41] Goa, he said, was "an inseparable part of India—and it must come back to India. The people of Goa must join their country in freedom and democracy."[42] The territory had been illegally occupied by conquest, and the fact that Portuguese occupation had lasted for 450 years was "of no consequence because, during nearly 425 or 430 years of that period we really had no chance to do anything because we were under colonial domination ourselves."[43] Colonialism was "no longer acceptable. It is the European concept and it must die."[44] Any action against colonialism was justified and could be considered aggression, because it merely reinforced "the tide of world history" and because colonialism itself is permanent aggression.[45]

The "double standard" charge advanced by Stevenson was countered not by India but by Soviet Ambassador Zorin. What about the landing of United States forces in Lebanon in 1958, he asked, or the covert Bay of Pigs operation against Cuba in 1961?[46]

In the atmosphere of mutual recrimination, two speakers in the Security Council debate, Ambassador Benites Vinueza of Ecuador and Ambassador Tingfu Tsiang of China, seemed to understand that both disputants were guilty of violating fundamental norms of the Charter: Portugal, by denying the populace self-determination; and India, by taking the law into its own hands. "Colonialism is an evil," Tsiang said, "but war is even a greater evil. Every warmaker has declared his particular war just, righteous or even holy."[47] The "use of force is not lawful, even in defence of the lawfulness of a given case."[48] While the Portuguese were illegally perpetuating "historical vestiges of a colonial past," that injustice should not be rectified by another. In the circumstances, neither "historical possession nor violent possession should prevail, but the freely expressed wishes of the inhabitants of the disputed territories."[49] Similarly, Ecuador's ambassador called for the dispute to be settled "according to the principle of self-determination."[50]

That suggestion, however, was unacceptable to Portugal and India, for one of the few issues on which both could agree was that the future of Goa was no business of the Goans. "How can there be self-determination by an Indian in order to say that he is part of India?"[51] asked Ambassador Jha. The Portuguese ambassador in Washington, Pedro Theotonio Pereira, when asked whether his country would now be willing to permit a plebiscite, said: "For many centuries, we have had a feeling of friendship for the people of Goa. No plebiscite could compare with this. The people of Goa have the rights of all Portuguese citizens."[52] In other words, no.

As the December 18th debate drew to an inconclusive close, the U.S., Britain, France, and Turkey introduced a resolution which deplored the use of force by India and called for an immediate cessation of hostilities and the withdrawal of Indian forces to positions prevailing before December 17.[53] This resolution received seven votes in favor of adoption and four against. Opposed were Ceylon, Liberia, the United Arab Republic, and the U.S.S.R. The Soviet vote constituted a veto, so the resolution was rejected.[54]

In commenting on the result, Ambassador Stevenson said:

> I believe that I am the only representative at this table who was present at the birth of the United Nations. Tonight we are witnessing the first act in a drama which could end with the death of the Organization. The League of Nations died, I remind you, when its members no longer resisted the use of aggressive force. . . . I find the attitude of some other members of the Council profoundly disturbing and ominous because we have witnessed tonight an effort to rewrite the Charter, to sanction the use of force in international relations when it suits one's own purposes. This approach can only lead to chaos and to the disintegration of the United Nations.[55]

Reporting to President Kennedy on the conclusion of the sixteenth session of the General Assembly, Stevenson again alluded to the "dangerous tendency of nations to apply one law in one part of the world toward one group of states, and a different law to others."[56]

The Security Council vote and debate had demonstrated that India had two lines of support. The first was the Soviet veto, behind which it was safe from any adverse decision. The second was the support of the Non-Aligned Movement (NAM), represented by the Council votes of Ceylon and the United Arab Republic. By their refusal to "blow the whistle" on a fellow member of the growing anti-colonialist grouping, these countries had signaled that it would be useless to take the case to the General Assembly, where the veto does not apply but where a two-thirds majority is required to pass a resolution. Although the U.S. had originally intended to invoke the Uniting for Peace procedure to summon the Assembly and circumvent the Soviet veto, an informal poll by Ambassador Stevenson of African and Asian delegates the day after the Council vote quickly confirmed that they were not disposed to permit any criticism of the Indian action.[57] By 1961 Afro-Asians already constituted about half the Assembly's membership. Uniting for Peace had become "their" weapon rather than ours.

Two days after the end of the Security Council's indecisive debate, the occupation of Portuguese India was completed. The disillusionment to which Adlai Stevenson had given vent in the Council debate was widely echoed in the U.S. media. In one week the *New York Times* carried four editorials condemning India's "inexcusable,"[58] "unjustifiable"[59] aggression which had "undermined"[60] the U.N. The editors called for "more reliance on Western strength and less reliance" on the organization.[61] Columnist Arthur Krock chided Washington for being soft on the NAMs in not taking the case to the Assembly.[62] Across the nation, newspapers large and small echoed these reproaches. The *Omaha World Herald* damned "the bankrupt and tottering" U.N. and added that "the Goa affair had exposed the true nature" of its decline.[63] The San Francisco *News-Call Bulletin* thought that December 18 might well come to be mourned as the date of the U.N.'s expiration.[64] In the view of the *Atlanta Constitution*, the U.N. "chartered to draw the fang of force, was . . . clubbed to its knees by the sudden violence of India."[65] The *Providence Journal* mourned the "disappearance of the dream that the U.N. might provide universal collective security" and added that "as to the major international conflicts of our time, the activities of the U.N. have become largely irrelevant."[66] The tiny *Grand Junction Daily Sentinel* (of Nebraska) proclaimed that "Nehru . . . may well have laid down the final straw which breaks the U.N. back."[67]

In the Senate, Connecticut's Thomas Dodd said that the American people "are disturbed by the failure of the United Nations to take any action to prevent or condemn India's attack on Goa" and added "people are beginning to ask themselves whether the United Nations is worth saving" since, in the light of India's aggression, "this dream lies shattered."[68]

Of course, there were other voices. Unnamed State Department officials were quoted as having said that Americans, rather than withdraw from the U.N. in despair, "must learn to look on the U.N. as another place for politics—in this case international politics. Like all political instruments, . . . it is imperfect and unwieldy, and its uses are limited. But those uses can be very important in the pursuit of some national objectives which cannot be pursued as effectively, if at all, by any other means."[69] The speaker, however, did not specify the uses for which the organization could be very important. Preventing aggression was clearly not one of them.

The Goa crisis reinforced the growing public impression in the U.S. that the organization could not act, even against a middle-sized aggressor, in situations favoring a quick victory. It also demonstrated that the NAMs' standards of international conduct would be no "higher" than those of older nations, and that, in their own interest, they too could be counted on to immobilize the U.N.

The NAMs had joined the world forum, but they had not written its rules. To be sure, nations such as Ceylon, Liberia, and Egypt did care about the principle of non-use of force, if only because they were weak compared to the superpowers and therefore more likely to be victims than aggressors. They cared about the principle of self-determination; they had passionately pursued its application to themselves, and assigned it value in the currency of their domestic politics. Goa only demonstrated that these principles can be overruled by political facts. India, in 1961, was still the shining knight of the newly independent cabal, while Portugal was a nasty fascist dictatorship. Hard cases make bad law, but offer excellent opportunities for politics.

Why, then, such agonized reaction among Americans?

The repeated aggressive use of force by India in the formative years of the U.N., no doubt, was particularly shocking to persons who confused the idealistic nonviolence of Mahatma Gandhi with the traditional *Realpolitik* of Jaharwalal Nehru. The latter was not creating a nation, he was running one, a difference of some consequence. As prime minister, Nehru simply behaved much the way the leaders of other middle- and super-powers have always behaved when faced with a choice between nationalism and internationalism, between a broad and narrow perspective of self-interest.

Would the U.N. have evolved differently if its new member nations had led the way toward a different international standard of conduct, if they had truly renounced the illegal use of unilateral force for political or economic gain? We will never know; for the older, more powerful nations of the international system were doing nothing during this inceptive period to suggest they were role models for such enlightened altruism.

§ 4 §

"A Rather Good Document"

Whatever hopeful public misperceptions there may have been in the U.S. about the U.N.'s potential for transforming the motivation behind traditional state conduct from narrow national self-interest to an international perspective, they were not shared by the leaders of the Soviet Union. The first Secretary-General of the United Nations, Trygve Lie, in July 1946 asked Marshal Stalin: "Do you not feel . . . that the United Nations Charter is a most reassuring document, full of promise for a world still partially in bondage?" "[T]he United Nations Charter," Stalin replied with equanimity, "is a rather good document."[1]

Stalin plainly had not for one moment considered redefining Soviet self-interest to accommodate the idea that his nation might have a significant stake in the new system of collective security and conflict resolution. That the United States, at first, seemed to make such an accommodation may be attributed to a degree of democratic altruism, native optimism, and, probably, to the fact that, initially, America controlled the system. Even at that, the U.S. began to abandon its commitment to the system some years before we ceased controlling it. The truth is that neither the U.S. nor the Soviets had ever really developed the political commitment to the central idea of the U.N., which would have been necessary to make it work, the sort of commitment, for example, which the constituents of our domestic system have to the U.S. Constitution. That takes not merely political will but reciprocal confidence, rooted in trust that the other side will play by the rules established in the fundamental document if we do. There was little reason for Washington to have such confidence in Joseph Stalin.

Czechoslovakia

By February 22, 1948, Czechoslovak communists had staged a coup, which was followed by the "suicide" of Foreign Minister Jan Masaryk on March 10 and by the death of President Benes. The coup preempted elections in May, when the communists would probably have suffered severe reverses at the polls. Moscow's hand was clearly visible, although the West had overplayed its own by trying to enlist Czechoslovakia in the Marshall Plan after Russia had declared that this would not be tolerated.

The coup succeeded quickly. By the time the Czech ambassador Jan Papanek had complained to the Secretary-General of Soviet interference, a new communist representative was arriving from Prague and Papanek's credentials were revoked. The Security Council did hear Papanek in a personal capacity, but the Soviets vetoed a Chilean resolution that would have established an investigating committee.[2]

By article 1(2) of the U.N. Charter, all states are required to "develop friendly relations among nations based on respect for the principle of equal rights and self-determination of people .. . ." The Soviet-sponsored takeover of Czechoslovakia demonstrated clearly what Stalin had meant in his remark to the Secretary-General. The U.N. Charter was a nice, high-minded document to be used when convenient and forgotten when not.

Guatemala

The U.S. rather quickly decided that it might as well play by the Soviet rules. In June 1954 the U.S. Central Intelligence Agency, in cooperation with neighboring Honduras and Nicaragua, mobilized and equipped an army of exiles to overthrow the elected leftist Guatemalan government of President Arbenz Guzman, whose regime had incurred Washington's displeasure by nationalizing the assets of U.S. companies and accepting deliveries of Polish weapons.

On June 19, Guatemala's minister for external affairs cabled the president of the Security Council requesting "measures . . . to put a stop to the aggression in progress against Guatemala." The telegram charged that expeditionary forces from Honduras and Nicaragua had advanced about fifteen kilometers into Guatemala, and that Guatemala City and the port of San José were being bombed.[3]

The Council was convened that same day to hear the Guatemalan representative ask for the dispatch of "an observation mission . . . as quickly as possible . . . to ask questions, to investigate, and to listen."[4] Instead of acting on this request, the Council, chaired that month by U.S. Ambassador Henry Cabot Lodge, considered a Brazil-Colombia-sponsored resolution referring the Guatemalan complaint to the Organization of American States (OAS), which was defeated by a Soviet veto.[5] Its proponents cited article 52(3) which invites the Council to "encourage the development of pacific settlement of local dis-

putes through . . . regional arrangements or by . . . regional agencies . . ."
But under articles 34, 35, and 39 of the Charter, the Council had the power to
consider any complaint involving a threat to peace, without deferring to any
other agency. The resolution was a transparent effort to consign the dispute to
an unsympathetic forum. The Guatemalan representative was understandably
outraged. "We are faced with an outright act of aggression," he said. "Perhaps
at this very moment when it is being proposed to refer the matter to the
Inter-American Peace Committee for a subsequent report, aircraft are mach-
ine-gunning my country."[6]

Tsarapkin, the Soviet delegate, quite correctly observed that "we know that
Guatemala will be overcome while we refer the question to that organization
and allow it time to discuss and decide upon it. . . . The United States of
America . . . dominates the Organization of American States and bends it and
controls it at will."[7] Ambassador Lodge, however, stoutly maintained that the
matter was none of the Council's business, that "the situation does not involve
aggression but is a revolt of Guatemalans against Guatemalans" and that "the
United States . . . has no connection whatever with what is taking place."[8]

It was our position that, if the U.N. did not defer to the OAS, it would be "a
catastrophe" that would "gravely impair the future effectiveness" of both.[9]
Looking at the Soviet delegate and shaking his finger, Lodge said: "stay out of
this hemisphere and do not try to start your plans and your conspiracies over
here."[10] Although the Council did not adopt the Brazilian-Colombian resolution, the U.S.-led majority was easily able to prevent the U.N. from responding affirmatively to the Guatemalan plea.

Eight years earlier, in 1946, when Iran had complained to the Council of
the continuing Soviet military presence in Azerbaijan (see above, Chapter 2),
the U.S. secretary of state had laid down the proposition that "when a state files
a complaint . . . we must assume that it is filed in good faith and that the
complainant is entitled to a hearing and discussion of his complaint in the
Security Council. . . . [W]e should actively support and speak for an investigation" of any "reasonable" complaint.[11] But with the shoe on the other foot,
Washington abandoned this inconvenient principle.

Following the Council debate, the OAS made a show of organizing a commission of inquiry of the Inter-American Peace Committee to go to Guatemala, Honduras, and Nicaragua. It had not yet ventured forth when the Security Council again convened at Guatemala's request on June 25. Guatemala
was rapidly being overrun. Ambassador Lodge, still in the chair, strongly resisted even adopting an agenda, because that would have allowed the Guatemalan representative to speak. By a vote of 5 to 4, with two abstentions, Lodge
succeeded in getting the Council to refuse even to consider the item,[12] and the
Council stood adjourned.

The government of Guatemala collapsed two days later, three days before the
arrival of the OAS fact-finding group. The new anti-communist regime quickly

withdrew its predecessor's complaint. Once again, a superpower's national interest—narrowly defined to exclude the effect of its conduct on the international system—had led it to use covert force to deny the right of a small state to assert its independence. In the process, the U.N.'s collective-security machinery had been exposed as absurdly inadequate.

It was clearly a distortion of the intent of the drafters, to employ article 52 to block Security Council investigation of Guatemala's complaint. At San Francisco, U.S. delegate John Foster Dulles had stated the correct interpretation: the U.N. would be "given the first opportunity to maintain peace everywhere, using presumably regional organizations which it is invited to do but not absolutely compelled to do."[13] Secretary Stettinius had told the Security Council in January 1946: "I wish to make it very clear that the United States Government believes that any Member country of the United Nations which makes a complaint has a right to be heard at this table."[14] Eight years later, the U.S.'s Guatemalan strategy had turned this on its head by giving the regional organization the first (and, in practice, only) say. Expedient hypocrisy had replaced principled rhetoric. It had become clear, too, that both superpowers were becoming adept at suppressing dissonant voices in their respective spheres of influence.

Hungary

In 1956, two years after the Guatemalan episode, the Soviets reciprocated. In doing so, they did not even deem it necessary any longer to operate in clandestine fashion, as they had in Czechoslovakia in 1948. Carefully echoing the U.S. rhetoric at the time of the Guatemalan episode, the Kremlin took the position that its invasion of Hungary was merely another instance of a regional dispute, which was being handled effectively under the Warsaw Pact and was therefore outside U.N. jurisdiction.[15]

On October 27, 1956, France, the U.K., and the U.S. had written to the President of the Security Council drawing his attention to "the situation created by the action of foreign military forces in Hungary in violently repressing the rights of the Hungarian people" and requesting Council consideration of "[t]he situation in Hungary."[16] A day later, by a procedural vote of 9 to 1 (U.S.S.R.), with one abstention (Yugoslavia), the Council agreed to discuss the problem, beginning a debate that lasted until November 4. While fighting continued to rage in Budapest, Soviet ambassador Arkady Sobolev blandly reassured the Council that the "situation in Hungary does not warrant this emergency meeting . . ." and that "Soviet troops . . . had been brought in at the request of the Government of Hungary" to assist in combating a counter-revolutionary uprising. He assured the delegates that these forces had already been "withdrawn from Budapest at the request of the Government of Hungary."[17] But even as Sobolev was speaking, new Soviet forces were invading.[18] Premier Imre Nagy of

Hungary desperately appealed for help, first to the Council,[19] then to the General Assembly.[20]

On November 3 the United States presented a resolution to the Council which called on the U.S.S.R. "to desist forthwith from any form of intervention" in Hungary, to "cease the introduction of additional armed forces into Hungary and to withdraw all of its forces without delay." Affirming the right of the Hungarian people to a "government responsive to its national aspirations" it requested the Secretary-General to provide humanitarian emergency supplies as soon as possible.[21]

As so often before and since, the debate quickly bogged down in a dispute over the facts. Yugoslavia's ambassador Brilej contended, against all evidence, that delicate negotiations were in progress between the Hungarian government and the Kremlin, which "should not be hampered" by further public discussion.[22] Ambassador Sobolev said that he could "confirm that such negotiations are going on."[23]

On Sunday, November 4, the Council reconvened at 3:00 a.m., with Budapest in flames. Recalling Sobolev's reassurances of the previous day, Lodge accused him of a "total lack of candour" and "indifference to human suffering."[24] The Soviet representative responded that the "so-called Government of Hungary headed by Imre Nagy" had come to power as a result of Western subversive activities and had "openly adopted a reactionary and fascist policy." The invasion was merely an expression of "the legitimate concern for the fate of the Hungarian workers" by "the people of the Soviet Union, Poland, Romania, Czechoslovakia and Yugoslavia." It was a local dispute being resolved by the regional organization of fraternal socialist states. Under the circumstances, said Sobolev, it "is quite plain that this question in no way concerns the United Nations."[25]

At the conclusion of the Soviet statement, the U.S.-sponsored resolution was put to a vote, receiving nine votes in favor, with one against (U.S.S.R.). The Yugoslav representative abstained, claiming he had been unable to contact his government for instructions.[26]

With that, Ambassador Lodge immediately moved to call an emergency special session of the General Assembly under the Uniting for Peace procedure.[27] This was adopted by a vote of 10 to 1 at 5:25 a.m.[28]

The second emergency special session of the General Assembly convened immediately. Its delegates gathered even as the first special session, dealing with the British, French, and Israeli attack on Egypt, was still grappling with the creation of a United Nations Emergency Force to interpose itself, ensure a cease-fire, and achieve the withdrawal of British and French forces from the Suez Canal area (see above, Chapter 2). Unfortunately, the second session could not repeat the success of the first, for Russia was a far more tough-minded aggressor than Britain, France, and Israel.

When the delegates arrived, they encountered a U.S. draft resolution which was almost identical to the one first vetoed in the Security Council. An additional paragraph requested the Secretary-General to send observers to Hungary to investigate the facts and report them at the earliest moment to the Assembly.[29] By that time, however, the facts had changed. Soviet forces had occupied the Parliament building in Budapest and arrested Premier Nagy and other members of his government. The newly installed prime minister, Janos Kadar, immediately cabled the Secretary-General that, "Imre Nagy's request to the United Nations . . . cannot be considered as . . . emanating from Hungary as a State."[30] Once again the complaint was resolved by the eradication of the complainant.

With that, it was all over but the shouting. As in the cases of Hyderabad, Czechoslovakia, and Guatemala, aggression against Hungary had moved with a speed that left the U.N. behind in a cloud of aimless rhetoric. The U.N.'s procedures were only a minor cause of the organization's impotence. It was by now becoming clear that a superpower, reacting to challenge in its own backyard, would not be dissuaded by U.N. principles, the Charter, or by resolutions passed or vetoed. Everyone knew that Russia could be stopped on the Danube by nothing less than an ultimatum from Washington, which would have brought the world to the brink of war. Evidently the American people were not ready to go to war for Hungarian freedom, any more than the League powers had been willing to go to war for Ethiopia, Manchuria, Austria, or Czechoslovakia. For that matter, not any more than the Russians had been willing to go to war for a Marxist Guatemala.

A few spokesmen in the General Assembly did call for collective action to defend Hungary or to interpose a U.N. force between the parties. Ambassador Anibal Olivieri of Argentina said that the U.N. "should come promptly and decisively to the assistance of Hungary so that its struggle for freedom may not be frustrated. Our only watchword must be 'now or never.' The principles at stake are those of self-determination and non-intervention."[31] Canada's external affairs minister Lester Pearson recalled the Assembly's success, the previous day, in establishing the emergency force for the Middle East. "Why," he asked, "should we not now establish a United Nations mission or United Nations supervisory machinery of an appropriate kind for the situation in Hungary?"[32] He must have known all too well the answer to his question.

On Being Neutral to Neutral Principles

A principle is a concept which is neutral in the sense that it applies to any relevant situation, regardless of the parties involved. The world community has not generated many principles that work. The U.N. Charter represents the most ambitious effort in history to establish what almost amounts to a codex of principles to apply to all international relations. One measure of the U.N.'s success or failure is the extent to which the majority of its members have upheld these principles even—perhaps *particularly*—when individual states have reverted to their traditional preference for narrow national self-interest and advantage-taking.

No principle is as fundamental to the system predicated on the U.N. Charter as the prohibition on the use of force by one state against another (article 2(4)). At 8:00 p.m. on November 4 the U.S. resolution on Hungary was adopted by the Assembly in emergency session by a vote of 50 to 8, with 15 abstentions. The majority, more or less automatic in those days, was made up primarily of the states of Western Europe and Latin America. Those voting against the resolution were the nations of Eastern Europe. More significant than either was the list of abstainers: Afghanistan, Burma, Ceylon, Egypt, Finland, India, Indonesia, Iraq, Jordan, Libya, Nepal, Saudi Arabia, Syria, Yemen, and Yugoslavia.[33] The abstentions of Arab states on the U.S.-sponsored resolution, at a time when British, French, and Israeli armies were invading Egypt, was to be expected. Even so, it was inconsistent with the Arabs' insistence that the U.N. enforce the principle of non-intervention in their own case. The abstention of six non-Arab countries of Asia, representing the most populous of the new nations, gave a clear preview of what would happen when the Afro-Asian states came to lead the Assembly with an influx of new members.

Sweden's ambassador Gunnar Jarring, recognized as a friend of the Third World, expressed his country's "regret that quite a few States which on other occasions have stressed emphatically the principle of non-intervention in the internal affairs of other States have seen no reason, when voting on this resolution, to demonstrate this attitude of theirs with regard to the recent events in Hungary."[34] U Pe Kin of Burma lamely explained that his government was "located in a capital far distant from New York, and communication is not easy." However, he added, that even if communications were better, he would probably not have been able to vote for the resolution.[35] Ambassador R.S.S. Gunewardene of Ceylon also told delegates that there is "no telephone service possible from New York to Ceylon," and then added that "self-determination . . . is sometimes a long and arduous process. It all depends on how this self-determination is expressed. I am happy that Hungary has in some form or other expressed its desire for self-determination."[36] What could he have meant? Presumably that he was encouraged that 100,000 Hungarians had been willing to die for freedom. But he, or rather, his government, had not been encouraged enough to vote for a reassertion of Hungary's right to be free.

India's representative, the redoubtable Krishna Menon, scorned simple-minded ruses. "I want to say here and now," he told the Assembly, "that the abstention of my delegation was not due to lack of instructions or any other difficulties."[37] Rather, he explained, he was abstaining because India did not think that the sending of observers would work. It would be an "intervention" in Hungarian domestic affairs and would surely antagonize the Soviet Union, making conditions harder for the Hungarian people. Menon was an old Marxist. While practising law in Britain in the early 1940s, he had been chosen by the Dundee (Scotland) constituency's Labour party to stand for election to Parliament, only to be dropped on orders from Labour party headquarters which regarded him as being too close to the communists.[38] As a practical politician he was well aware of India's dependence on Soviet military supplies and on the protection afforded India by the Soviet veto in the Security Council. To Menon, the Soviets and the Western powers were equally unprincipled practitioners of traditional self-serving nationalistic politics; he saw no reason why India should sacrifice its useful relations with Moscow to defend principles to which the Eastern and Western blocs paid deference only when it suited their purposes.[39]

For years the Hungarian item returned to the Assembly's agenda. More resolutions were passed and, essentially, the same group of countries continued to abstain, thereby ensuring that what might at least have been a formal reaffirmation of principles became little but an exercise in East-West cold war dialectics. In explaining his negative vote on a resolution recommending free elections for Hungary, Ambassador Tjondronegoro Sudjarwo of Indonesia said: "We also support the idea of free elections in Hungary, but, again, let this be their own choice, the choice of the people of Hungary."[40] For the present, he seemed to think, the Hungarians had elected to be invaded and slaughtered.

The Hungarian crisis sent mixed signals to Americans who cared about the organization. It demonstrated once again the ineffectiveness of the Security Council for mobilizing collective security against an aggressor, especially a superpower. On the other hand, the new Uniting for Peace machinery worked smoothly enough, convening an emergency session of the Assembly in a matter of hours and producing a resolution that upheld decency and principle, if by a rather narrowly based majority. But it was plain to see that this resolution, and others on the same subject which followed, did nothing to alter the situation in Hungary. Indeed, the Assembly gave India and other "neutrals" a forum for trading their votes for past and future favors. It could even be argued that the public display of sophistry and indifference for which the Assembly provided a prominent platform only succeeded in lowering the political costs of the Hungarian invasion to Moscow. The refusal of prominent emerging nations, the core of the Third World movement, to take a clear stand received at least as much attention in the U.S. as the votes of those few who did. This made it hard, in the face of such a savage invasion of one member nation by another, to sustain much faith in the brave new world of the U.N. system.

There were also many Americans who wondered why the U.S. had joined the Soviet Union in compelling Israel, Britain, and France to abide by principles to which the USSR so obviously paid no attention whatsoever when its own interests were at stake. A suspicion began to form that U.N. principles were a single-edged sword, a way of cutting down the West's will to defend its self-interest.

Evaluation

The failure of the U.N. to act with respect to Hungary, and the unwillingness of key neutrals, not to mention the communist states, to stand by the principle of non-use of force, must be seen against the backdrop of the organization's success in averting an all-out Middle East war. The first emergency special session of the General Assembly was meeting on the Middle East crisis right alongside the second emergency special session on Hungary. For some observers, the sense of euphoria engendered by the Assembly's deployment of the U.N. Emergency Force to the Middle East balanced the gloom occasioned by its failure to do anything to relieve the plight of Hungary. UNEF arranged for the departure of the British, French, and Israelis from the precincts of the Canal. It eventually established a buffer between Israel and Egypt. It prevented unilateral superpower intervention. That appeared to be quite a lot to have accomplished, and was seen by some members to fulfill the prophesy that the Assembly could take over the role the Charter assigned to the immobilized Security Council.[41]

France's ambassador Louis de Guiringaud, however, did not share this illusion. He pointed to the Assembly's decisiveness in acting to stop his country's use of force in Suez and its minimal impact on Soviet activities in Hungary. He compared the reluctance of some important Third World countries to criticize the invasion of Hungary with their eagerness to criticize Britain, France, and Israel:

> It may be, that, faced with a Power whose tremendous strength is now being used to enslave part of Europe, our Organization is powerless to act. If that is so, we must conclude that the United Nations which was established by those who spent six years fighting the fascist dictatorship, has now become, through the misuse of the worst parliamentary methods, a blind instrument in the hands of those who wish to destroy the free world.[42]

The U.S. evaluation was more mixed. In June 1957 the special committee, established by the General Assembly to examine the situation in Hungary and to monitor compliance with the Assembly resolution, issued its report. Addressing the American Bar Association in July, the U.S. ambassador to the U.N., James J. Wadsworth, expressed the view that it had lit "fires of moral condemnation" all around the world that would "plague the Soviet rulers today and will continue to plague them for years to come."[43] A similar view was expressed by Secretary of State John Foster Dulles, who told the U.S. Committee for the U.N. that the organization's handling of the Hungarian crisis "has made it less likely there will be a recurrence of the evil deeds."[44] In the House of Representatives, Congressman Walter Judd, prominent in the United Nations Association, called the special committee's report "a devastating indictment" and prophesied that this "exposé can give the death blow to Communist propaganda if we exploit it successfully."[45]

On the other hand, there were many in the U.S. who shared de Guiringaud's perspective. Senator Joseph R. McCarthy announced on November 17, 1956, that he would seek reelection in 1959 "to continue the fight to get the United States out of the U.N. and the U.N. out of the United States." Inaccurately but vehemently, he criticized the U.N. for its prompt action on behalf of the "Communist stooge," Egypt's President Nasser, while failing to raise "a single voice" in defense of the Hungarian rebels.[46]

Critics were particularly aroused by "the Bang-Jensen case." Povl Bang-Jensen, a Danish employee of the Secretariat, was named deputy secretary of the Assembly's Special Committee on Hungary. Since the committee was not allowed to visit Hungary, it had to rely for information on other sources, primarily the testimony of refugees. Of the 111 witnesses interviewed, 81 sought anonymity for fear of reprisal against members of their families still in Hungary.[47] Bang-Jensen kept a private list of those interviewed, carrying it on his person, hiding it in hotel rooms and at his home. When the Secretary-General found out about it he asked that it be turned over to the Secretariat for safekeeping. Bang-Jensen refused, arguing that to do so would make it accessible to Soviet and, eventually, Hungarian U.N. officials, who would pass the information along to their governments. It was a rational concern being pursued irrationally. Friends suggested he simply make up 111 fake names and hand that over.[48]

After much administrative in-fighting, involving a Joint Disciplinary Committee, a Special Investigating Committee, and the U.N.'s Administrative Tribunal, a compromise of sorts was worked out. It led to a peculiar little U.N. rooftop ceremony at which the list, in a sealed envelope, was burned in the presence of U.N. officials and of Bang-Jensen. By then, however, he had become a media personality, alienated from the organization for which he worked, and a deeply disturbing embarrassment to the Secretary-General. Hammarskjold, at last, fired him for "grave misconduct," a move upheld by the U.N.'s administrative tribunal. A little less than a year later, his body was found in Alley Pond Park, in Queens, New York, where he had shot himself in the head. This made him a martyr in the eyes of some. Even the moderate *Cleveland Plain Dealer* charged that he had been the victim of a "double doublecross by the Secretary-General."[49]

The case merely symbolized to many Americans a growing awareness of the organization's malaise. The *New York Times* took up Ambassador de Guiringaud's attack, charging the Assembly with practicing a "double standard of international morality in which some nations are required to submit to the United Nations injunctions while others, specifically the Soviet Union, are permitted to defy them without reprisal."[50] Seeking to allay such criticism, Secretary-General Hammarskjold could only muster one of his more disingenuous distinctions. The U.N., he replied, did not use a "double standard" in dealing with the Hungarian and Suez crises; rather, there had been an "unequal measure of compliance" with Assembly directives by the nations involved.[51] That did not satisfy many. Roscoe Drummond, in the *Washington Post*, complained that, when "it comes to taking any meaningful action whatsoever on Hungary, the United Nations General Assembly is now showing all the firmness of a creampuff in a heatwave."[52]

But what could the Assembly have done that it did not do? The *Washington Post* and the *New York Times* had both challenged the Assembly to reject the credentials of the representatives of the Kadar puppets, and, in fact, the Assembly did go some distance in that direction. For several years after 1956 it voted to "reserve its position" on the legitimacy of the Hungarian representation. This action stopped short of barring the Hungarians, but it served as a warning and symbol of disapproval.

An editorial in *Life* on March 4, 1957, created a stir by its new belligerence towards the U.N. *Life*'s editors thought that the U.N. should have flown a group of member-nations' ambassadors, stationed in Vienna, to Hungary "by helicopter" before the Soviet intervention. It then should have backed up that initiative with a "permanent . . . observation force" under the "direct control of the Secretary-General, equipped with its own transport and communications system."[53] By comparison with that proposal, *Life*'s editors found the organization's actual performance appallingly inadequate. But was the proposal realistic? Before November 4 Nagy's revolutionary government had not requested the dispatch of U.N. observers. Without such a request, the Assembly could not have acted. And after November 4 it was too late.

Ambassador Lodge replied to *Life* that the U.N.'s "record is not a sorry one. . . . The steps which the United Nations has taken have played a useful part in preventing deportations; in bringing food to the people of Budapest; in helping 170,000 Hungarian refugees to find new homes; in persuading many Asian and African countries for the first time to vote to condemn the Soviet Union; and in dealing a body blow to communism all over the world." As for a permanent observer force, this would have created many problems. Shrewdly, Lodge concluded: "Someday a situation may arise where we may not permit United Nations observers either."[54]

Despite the positive views expressed by Lodge, Dulles, Wadsworth, and others in the diplomatic establishment, the previous near-unanimity of Americans in public support of the U.N. had clearly become a casualty of the Hungarian invasion. Some criticized the U.N. for engaging in nothing but useless talk, while others praised it for providing a global forum in which aggressive acts, if they could not be stopped, could at least be noted and condemned. The *New York Times* still tended toward the latter position. "It remains true," its editors wrote, "that the U.N. cannot deal with monsters bent on exterminating whole populations. It cannot yet rally avenging angels. But it can command the attention of the entire world. It can provide a forum for the weakest and the most oppressed. It can summon up a demand for righteousness and mercy which in the end will prevail."[55] Henry Hazlitt, an editor of *Newsweek*, took a less benevolent view. "Russia will now be able to secure still more allies," he wrote, "because she has shown that she is willing to take risks to support them. We will be able to secure even fewer dependable allies, because we have not shown willingness to take risks to support them in a crisis."[56] The *Wall Street Journal* thought that the public debate in the General Assembly had mostly demonstrated that "countries newly freed will not protest such a thing as the murder of another people's freedom."[57] A few days later it added: "The U.N. can do nothing about Hungary . . . [i]t cannot even settle the issues in the Middle East. It is not, in short, an institution capable itself of preventing war when nations are determined to have war."[58]

By the winter of 1956, many Americans had come to the conclusion that the United Nations system had been grossly oversold in 1945 and that its utility, if any, was of a far more limited order. These observers did not see the manifestations of Uniting for Peace in the first and second special sessions as a triumph of utilitarian growth, but rather as the product of new illusions about the system. They urged that Washington stop trying to be creative in its uses of the U.N., and instead play down the U.N.'s role in our foreign policy, confining it to modest tasks. In the view of the *Wall Street Journal*, the U.N.'s "recent small successes will be destroyed if statesmen now try to put the U.N. to a test it cannot meet—if people now think that the U.N. is responsible for the peace and therefore fails if it cannot keep it."[59] The *Journal's* columnist, William Henry Chamberlin, came to a more radical conclusion. He wrote: "Instead of wringing their hands over this latest discovery that the dream of a supranational authority capable of eliminating strife and conflict may prove again a mirage, Americans might be better advised to take satisfaction in their new freedom to intervene or remain on the sidelines as their sense of right and their sense of national interest may dictate."[60]

Aftermath: Dominican Republic and Czechoslovakia

Five years later Chamberlin's advice appears to have been taken to heart in Washington. In the 1961 Bay of Pigs operation, the U.S. launched a direct, if botched, attack intended to overthrow the Castro regime in Cuba. When the latter tried to complain to the Security Council, just prior to the outbreak of fighting, the U.S. ambassador successfully reused the argument earlier employed during the Guatemalan crisis: that the complaint must first go to the Organization of American States.[61]

Again, in 1965, when U.S. marines invaded the Dominican Republic to prevent an elected leftist government from taking power, Ambassador Adlai Stevenson told the Council that the U.N. should not become involved since that would only "tend to complicate the activities of the Organization of American States by encouraging concurrent and independent considerations and activities . . . by this Council" at a time "when the regional organization seems to be dealing with the situation effectively."[62]

During the Dominican crisis, Washington took the position that any leftist deviation in the hemisphere, even if produced by democratic elections, constituted an attack to which the other nations of the region could respond by exercising the right of "collective self-defense." Although a right of self-defense is recognized by the Charter solely in response to an "armed attack," the U.S. had earlier, with respect to Cuba, persuaded the OAS to treat "adherence by any member of the Organization . . . to Marxism-Leninism"[63] as an armed attack. While U.S. troops were going ashore, the U.S. State Department's legal adviser asserted an even wider right to use military force anywhere in "our" region in "self-defense" against foreign ideologies.[64]

In less than a decade, between 1956 and 1965, Washington's official attitude to the U.N.'s political organs had shifted from optimistic positivism to negativism and indifference. By 1965 the Non-Aligned Movement, often in concert with the Soviets, could make life arduous for the U.S. even in the Security Council. Faced with a hostile Dominican Republic resolution, the U.S. still could not quite bring itself to cast its first veto, but negotiated, instead, for language expressing "deep concern" and calling for strict observance of a cease-fire. It "invited" the Secretary-General to send an observer and report back to the Council.[65] The U.S. agreed to accept a U.N. presence, significantly more than the Soviets had allowed in Hungary, but saw to it that the observer's function was very limited[66] and of short duration.[67]

Clearly there was now an accelerating downward spiral in member-state conduct. The successful U.S. and OAS intervention in the Dominican Republic was followed by intervention—justified in virtually identical terms[68]—by Moscow and the Warsaw Pact nations against the deviant Dubcek regime which had aspired to "socialism with a human face" in Czechoslovakia. On August 21, 1968, as Warsaw Pact troops poured across the Czech frontier, Canada, Denmark, France, Paraguay, the United Kingdom, and the United States requested an immediate meeting of the Security Council to consider "the present serious situation."[69] The Council met that afternoon to hear Prague's ambassador Jan Muzik, emphasizing that he was acting on his government's "explicit instructions,"[70] read a bitter denunciation of the invasion and make a dramatic appeal for help.[71] In reply, the Soviet ambassador Malik lectured the Council on the right of the socialist "community" to give "fraternal assistance" to the Czech people to prevent their being taken over by antisocialist forces. "We declare," he thundered, "with all our determination that nobody will ever be allowed to wrest so much as a single link from the community of socialist States which has been, is and shall remain an unshakeable bastion against all and any imperialist attacks, conspiracies, provocations . . . ."[72]

When the Council reconvened the next morning, Brazil, Canada, Denmark, the U.K., and the U.S. introduced a resolution affirming Czech sovereignty while condemning the armed intervention of the U.S.S.R. and other Warsaw Pact nations. Calling for the immediate withdrawal of foreign forces, it requested the Secretary-General to "keep the situation under constant review" and report to the Council on compliance.[73] In supporting this resolution, U.S. Ambassador George Ball observed that the "kind of fraternal assistance that the Soviet Union is according to Czechoslovakia is exactly the same kind that Cain gave to Abel."[74] He continued:

> What shocks us all is the low appraisal that the Soviet leadership places on human intelligence. How gullible, how childishly credulous does it think humankind really is? No, the whole world can recognize naked aggression when it sees it and the frantic and frightened leaders of the Soviet Union cannot conceal it or disguise it, for the world has already found them out. It has found them out and it despises and is disgusted by their furtive and fraudulent efforts to drape tyranny with sanctimony and anoint it with piety.[75]

By prevailing U.N. diplomatic standards, this was pretty strong stuff.

As the debate continued, the Algerian representative proposed an adjournment to permit "consultations." Canada's ambassador George Ignatieff replied that this would immobilize the Council, permitting a new Czech regime to withdraw the complaint.[76] Algeria's proposal, although not adopted, had the apparent support not only of Hungary and the Soviets, but also of India and Pakistan.[77] Not all Third World countries were looking away, however. Ambassador Boye of Senegal announced that he would join the sponsors of the resolution condemning the Soviet action. He reported that his government "shares the strong feelings raised throughout the world by the military intervention of the Soviet Union" and "fully associates itself with all initiatives and measures aimed at obtaining the condemnation of this armed intervention."[78]

By the time discussion of the motion to adjourn was over, Ambassador Muzik reported that his nation's leaders had either been interned by the invaders, or had fled.[79] The Soviets, with other Eastern European states, continued to talk. It was a filibuster. "What we are witnessing," Ball said, "is a shameless and shoddy and desperate effort . . . to delay and frustrate the proceedings . . . long enough for a new synthetic Government to send a message or a representative to the Council to ask that the Council not consider the question now before us. . . . We are at a point where we ought to stop talking; we ought to vote; we ought to declare ourselves; we ought to 'come clean' with humanity."[80]

But the Council did not vote. Ambassador Malik, observing that "Mr. Ball's nerves are going to pieces,"[81] spoke twice more that day. George Ball expressed dismay that "this solemn body" was being "turned into a circus" by "grotesque procedural nonsense." If the members allow this to go on, he warned, "we are all accomplices . . . in undermining the dignity of the United Nations."[82] Malik's response was to speak again, for forty minutes, surveying such subjects as the war in Vietnam and U.S. exploitation of Latin America's raw materials, including a statistical survey of U.S. lead, iron, copper, and zinc imports.[83] His discourse ranged over Czech commodity trading, citing statistics on products from cotton to phosphates. He raged at Israeli "aggressors," at the policies of Portugal in Angola and Mozambique, and at those of the South Africans in Namibia. After him came an equally digressive Ambassador Milko Tarabanov of Bulgaria.[84] The need to filibuster was, in one sense, a compliment to the U.N., for Moscow seemed to feel it important to block any condemnatory resolution and, if Malik's larynx held out, to do it by delay rather than by veto. While counting as a technical victory, a veto, even they understood, still constituted a public relations defeat.

When Malik had finally run out of words, the Council president asked whether there were objections to proceeding with the vote. In a brief silence, India's ambassador Gopalaswami Parthasarathi raised his hand. He explained that his delegation could not vote for the resolution because it was not realistic and would not help the Czech people in their present circumstances. Except that it applied to a different country, this was India's 1956 Hungarian speech, phrase for devious phrase. Condemning someone—the Indian could not bring himself even to mention the invader's name—would not help, but merely make matters worse. His delegation would abstain.[85] (Three years later, when India invaded East Pakistan, Moscow repaid the favor by vetoing the Council resolution that called on New Delhi to withdraw.[86])

At last the Council voted. The resolution received ten affirmative votes and two negative ones (Hungary, U.S.S.R.). Algeria, India, and Pakistan abstained.[87]

With that resolution vetoed, Canada immediately introduced another, simply requesting the Secretary-General "to appoint and despatch immediately to Prague a special representative who shall seek the release and ensure the personal safety of the Czechoslovak leaders under detention and who shall report back urgently." Malik spoke again, demanding rhetorically "who drowned the fields, villages and cities of Viet-Nam in blood?" Looking at Ball, he shouted: "Your hands are drenched in blood . . . ."[88] Later the same day, he called Canada's ambassador Ignatieff "the chief mouthpiece . . . of the Anglo-American circles" in "this dirty business of theirs, that is, their interference in the affairs of a socialist country."[89] At 3:55 a.m. on August 23, a bleary-eyed Council adjourned for the night.

When it reconvened, it was treated to two more lengthy, irrelevant *tours d'horizon* by Ambassador Malik, including a discourse on gangsterism in New York.[90] The Council once more adjourned without voting. The next day, Saturday, August 24, the Council reconvened at 11:30 a.m. Ambassador Malik began by reading a telegram from "Comrade Winzer," the East German foreign minister in which he "insisted" on being heard,[91] even though East Germany was not yet a member of the U.N. Malik made four more speeches during that meeting, including one of 45 minutes detailing the history of the German Democratic Republic.[92] A proposal to invite Comrade Winzer to appear was eventually defeated 9 to 2, but with four significant abstentions: Algeria, Brazil, India, and Pakistan.[93] The Council adjourned at 4:15 p.m., after hearing a last desperate appeal from Czechoslovakia's foreign minister Jiri Hajek, who had luckily been out of the country when the invaders rounded up his colleagues.

On Monday, August 26, Czech President Svoboda was carted off to Moscow by the Soviets, and he capitulated. The Council meeting for that day was cancelled. By the next day, Svoboda had agreed to Soviet terms, and the Czech representative requested the deletion of the item from the Council's agenda. His letter wanly pointed out that it had not been Czechoslovakia which had initiated the complaint.

This time, the West did not even bother to try to convene an emergency meeting of the General Assembly under Uniting for Peace, nor was the Czech invasion inscribed in the agenda of the regular session of the General Assembly, convening a few days later. The West knew that further efforts would be in vain, given the indifference of much of the Third World. The message was not lost on the American public. Expressing its "bewilderment and disillusionment" at the "tedious, wrangling sessions" of the Security Council, the *New York Times* questioned the reticent role of Secretary-General U Thant—who had confined himself to urging "utmost restraint"—as well as the indifference of much of the Third World. The newspaper asked: "Are the people and Government of Czechoslovakia less worthy of United Nations protection, passion and concern than those of African or Asian states whose plight in the past has so often produced quick Security Council meetings and vehement UN statements?"[94]

The preponderant African-Asian answer to that question, plainly, was yes. But that should not any longer have occasioned either surprise or shock. The U.S. felt passionately about the Soviet savaging of the Czechs because the latter were Westernized Central Europeans with an historic addiction to parliamentary democracy. The Africans and Asians felt similar passion about the savage treatment of blacks and Indians in South Africa. The U.S. had not shared the Afro-Asian passion, nor they the U.S.'s. The behavior of U.N. members merely reflected that difference in national perceptions and priorities, as well as a lack of commitment to any global principles.

Having asked a realistic question, the *Times*'s editors went on to propose an unrealistic answer: to redeem itself, the U.N. must "force the prompt evacuation of Czechoslovakia by the occupying troops and the restoration of the legal Government of Czechoslovakia to its full freedom of action and sovereignty."

None of this was remotely realizable. The *Times* added that the U.N. "will be judged and deserves to be judged by the effectiveness and vigor—or the lack thereof—with which it acts to secure rectification of a blatant international crime."[95] But the U.S. State Department, advised by Ambassador Ball, had already decided not even to try to interest the General Assembly in the case. It understood the hopelessness of it.

That hopelessness was further underlined by the evident lack of concern of Secretary-General U Thant. Having shortly after the Czech invasion gone out on a limb to propose to the Assembly a resolution calling for a halt in the U.S. bombing of North Vietnam, he replied to a question about his silence on Czechoslovakia: "If the Russians were bombing and napalming the villages of Czechoslovakia, you wait and see what I would have to say." The Secretary-General had abandoned all pretence at being motivated by neutral, global principles and was playing politics. As a representative of a Third World perspective, he placed the Vietnam War high on his agenda, but not Czechoslovakia.

The *Times* attacked that "sophistic double standard," and went on to hope that the Assembly would serve "truly as the 'conscience of mankind.' "[96] Like many liberal, internationalist Americans, the editors of the *Times* still shied away from the obvious conclusion that the General Assembly could not be the "conscience of mankind." If perchance a principle was to be asserted, it would be because national or regional self-interest and the principles of the U.N. Charter happened at the moment to coincide.

That still left open the question whether the West was right in abandoning the field. The dramatic verbal war waged by George Ignatieff, George Ball, and others in the Security Council could have been pursued in the Assembly. Some Third World countries, no one knew exactly how many, did not agree with the self-serving circumlocutions of Algeria, India, and Pakistan in the Council and were prepared to say so. Apparently, too, Moscow had been sufficiently sensitive to criticism in the U.N. to have instructed Ambassador Malik, if necessary, to make a fool of himself in public to disrupt the debate. Perhaps it would have been instructive to have brought that show to the larger stage. Professor Stephen Schwebel (now a judge at the International Court of Justice) wrote at the time that the "failure to inscribe the Czechoslovak situation on the agenda . . . of the General Assembly . . . prejudice[s] the principles of the United Nations Charter and. . . . seems to suggest that, since the Soviet Union has bludgeoned the Czech leaders into an 'agreement,' the world should say no more."[97]

U Thant, in his annual report to the General Assembly, did dwell on the Czechoslovak condition to the extent of stating that he found it "frightening" that "one super-State or the other" should so easily be able to crush a small neighbor at will.[98] It was a redundant remark; his conduct had already shown just how "frightened" he was.

§ 5 §

The End of Innocence

When the Warsaw Pact's tanks rolled into Prague, the American public despaired at the U.N.'s incapacity to be effective. Soon, however, to the more realistic observers its incapacity began to seem rather reassuring.

Even in the 1940s and 1950s, when the rhetoric was filled with high hopes and expectations, and U.S. strategy was to strengthen the U.N., the truth was that we had vacillated between adherence to its basic principles and the pursuit of traditional self-interest—a fact that had been obscured by the U.S.'s ability to manipulate U.N. machinery. Habitual American leadership of the U.N. came to an end in the mid-1960s, leaving in place a system that no longer automatically served U.S. interests. This compelled a reevaluation of American commitment: did the U.S. support the U.N. because it served its national interests—in which case that support might be on the way to becoming an historic anachronism—or did the U.S. support the U.N. system, as it had been saying all along, because the U.N.'s very existence was important to the national interest of all member states?

Such a reevaluation, undertaken honestly, would compel the repudiation of an earlier, idealistic innocence, or, rather, compel a realization that the U.S.'s earlier idealism had been more opportunistic than anyone had cared to admit.

The First U.N. State

As early as 1947, the United Nations had become involved in the bitter dispute between the Netherlands and its huge East Indies colony, then struggling to become independent as Indonesia. As the fighting grew, India, Australia, and the United States brought the issue before the Security Council, demanding in effect that the U.N. promote the decolonization of the Dutch territory. After a bitter debate that deeply divided the U.S. from its Dutch, British, and French allies, a United Nations Commission for Indonesia (UNCI) was established to mediate the dispute.

In part because of UNCI's constructive role, an agreement was worked out during the first days of November, 1949,[1] and on December 27, the Republic of the United States of Indonesia came into being. The parties broke a final deadlock by accepting UNCI's proposal that Western New Guinea, part of the Dutch East Indies but ethnically and demographically far removed from the other islands, should continue for one more year under Dutch rule, during which time its future status would be resolved by further negotiations between the Netherlands and Indonesia.[2]

It did not work as planned. Negotiations bogged down, and Indonesia's President Ahmed Sukarno took several impulsive steps which made a peaceful solution even more difficult: he abolished the federal structure of his new nation, using force to crush separatist movements in the South Moluccas and Sumatra, and dissolved the largely ceremonial union between the Netherlands and Indonesia. Both the federal system and the union had been constitutional devices which, theoretically, should have helped to smooth the way for bringing Western New Guinea together with Indonesia: the federal system, by promoting local autonomy for the distinct, if backward, Papuan people; the union, by retaining a symbolic Dutch responsibility for Papuan advancement.

As the deadlock continued and relations between the Netherlands and Indonesia deteriorated, the Sukarno government, in September 1954, took the dispute to the General Assembly.[3] In an acrimonious public debate, the Indonesians accused the Dutch of reneging on the 1949 agreement, while the Netherlands replied that the Indonesians were demanding not negotiation but capitulation.[4] Dutch representatives argued that the 700,000 Papuans and Pygmies of Western New Guinea were neither racially nor culturally related to the Indonesians. The Hague insisted that it had a duty to help them develop to the point at which they could make an informed decision on their future.[5]

Annually thereafter—for the next six years—the simmering dispute came before the Assembly, generating bitter but indecisive debate. Then in 1961 the Netherlands took a new tack by announcing that it was now ready to allow the inhabitants to decide their own future by plebiscite, and asking the U.N. to administer the territory long enough to organize and conduct the voting.[6]

That proposal, advanced by the Netherlands' C.W.A. Schürmann, was quickly rejected by Indonesia. Jakarta was vehemently supported by India; the government in New Delhi, having decided to seize Goa (see above, Chapter 3), wanted no precedent for an impartial, U.N.-conducted plebiscite. But the Third World, already a decisive voting force in the Assembly, was far from united. Thirteen African states, led by Ambassador Omar Adeel of the Sudan, proposed a draft resolution which emphasized the right of the people of New Guinea to self-determination. Ambassador Issoufou Djermakoye of Niger, also speaking on behalf of the thirteen, said: "What has greatly surprised us in this dispute is that one of the parties is not asking for the opinion of the people of New Guinea. . . . It is for the people of New Guinea themselves to say, in the present circumstances, who is entitled to claim sovereignty over their territory."[7] He then called for a U.N. commission to find out what sort of transitional arrangement the indigenous population would prefer. Indonesia's foreign minister Subandrio, rejecting the idea, accused the thirteen of supporting the colonial powers' "well-known policy of 'divide and rule.' "[8]

The African resolution garnered 53 votes in the Assembly, with 41 against and 9 abstentions—not quite enough for the requisite two-thirds majority. Western Europe, the U.S., Canada, most of Latin America, and the non-Arab African states supported it, while it was opposed by the socialist countries, most of Asia, and the Arab nations.[9]

The *New York Times* opined that "dire consequences"[10] would follow if Jakarta were to succeed in denying self-determination to the people of New Guinea. Nine days later, however, Netherlands Prime Minister Jan Eduard de Quay announced that his government was abandoning its insistence on self-determination as a precondition for new negotiations with Indonesia;[11] whereas Indonesia conceded that it might give "eventual" self-determination to the Papuans if it could run the territory in the meantime.[12] Indonesia promised to "carry out all Dutch aims concerning the interests of the population."[13] Almost everyone knew how much store to set by *that*.

Two circumstances had caused The Hague to buckle. The first, and more important, was the pressure exerted on them by the Kennedy administration, which feared that unless Sukarno were appeased the Indonesian communists would ride to power on the issue. The second was that Indonesian military forces for months had been infiltrating New Guinea,[14] which promised a long jungle war for the Dutch to fight. Washington had made it clear that they would have to do so without American support.

On March 13, the U.S. State Department suggested to the Netherlands and Indonesia that Ellsworth Bunker act as "observer" to accelerate negotiations between the Netherlands and Indonesia.[15] This was clearly an effort to ease the way for Dutch withdrawal, an exercise in American *Realpolitik*. However, at Washington's suggestion, with the agreement of both parties, Bunker emerged in a U.N., rather than a U.S., role, representing the "good offices" of the Secretary-General. By obtaining this U.N. imprimatur for Bunker, Washington was once more promoting U.S. national interests, even while seeming to strengthen the organization.

On April 13, Bunker made his first proposal. It called for a two-year transition period during which Western New Guinea would be under direct U.N. supervision but with a gradual transfer of control to Indonesia. At first, the

Dutch held out for the plebiscite to be conducted while the U.N. was still in charge.[16] Indonesia, however, would have none of that.

In May, with the Dutch and Indonesians still at loggerheads, Indonesia, encouraged by India's forceful "solution" to the Goan problem, invaded Western New Guinea by air and sea. The Dutch requested the Secretary-General to "exhort" Jakarta to refrain from aggression and asked him to send observers to ensure restraint. U Thant, on the advice of his influential Indian Under-Secretary-General, C. V. Narasimhan, did neither, explaining that a more affirmative response "would imply I was taking sides in the controversy."[17]

The *New York Times*'s Arthur Krock commented that, evidently, "if a member of the U.N. engaged in aggression in violation of the Charter won't join his victim in a plea [to the U.N.] . . . it is 'unneutral' for the Secretary-General to heed the plea."[18]

While U Thant's evident Third World bias toward Indonesia was being played out in public, less visible but more effective pressure was being brought to bear on the Netherlands by the Kennedy administration. It was made clear, again, that the U.S. would not bail out the Dutch if they continued to resist Indonesia. On May 27, Bunker produced a new draft paragraph which provided for a "free choice" *after*, not before, Indonesian takeover.[19] Reluctantly, the Dutch caved in.

On July 31, 1962, the final agreement was announced and a pact was signed at the U.N. two weeks later. Under its terms the U.N. would administer the territory from October 1, 1962, transferring responsibility to Indonesia by May 1, 1963. Indonesia, not the U.N., would arrange for the Papuan population to participate in an act of self-determination. But it was not required to do so until the end of 1969, leaving ample time to ensure the "right" outcome. The agreement vaguely provided for some form of U.N. participation in the final event.

Hailing Bunker's success, U Thant noted that the organization would exercise "executive authority" over a territory for the first time. The cost of maintaining 1000 troops in the area for seven months would be split between the Netherlands and Indonesia. Eighteen top posts and 150 other positions would be filled by U.N. personnel during the interim administration.[20]

Through the efforts of the U.S. government and Ambassador Bunker the U.N. found itself projected into a highly visible and entirely new proconsular role. What appeared on the surface a triumph for the international system was in fact an arbitrary disposition of people and territory by power politics reminiscent of the 1878 Congress of Berlin. While Bunker attributed this "historic achievement" to "the parties to the dispute and . . . the United Nations,"[21] The *New York Times*, more prescient, saw the achievement as primarily Bunker's.[22]

On September 21, 1962, the Assembly adopted a resolution that authorized the Secretary-General "to carry out the tasks entrusted to him in the

Agreement."[23] With that, the United Nations Temporary Executive Authority (UNTEA) was born. On the same day, José Rolz Bennett of Guatemala arrived in Hollandia, the capital of Netherlands New Guinea, to replace the departing Dutch governor.[24] The world had conceived and given birth to an international nation.

Neither at the U.N. nor in New Guinea were these events greeted with unmitigated delight. Papuan members of the New Guinea Council spoke to reporters "with sadness and anger."[25] "With frightened heart," said Councillor L. Mofue, "the Papuans called for help but there was no reply . . . . We had to allow ourselves to be bound hand and foot and delivered to the enemy. . . . The Papuan feels like an orphan left alone in a dark forest."[26]

The U.S., by engineering this development, earned the approval of some, but by no means all, of the Non-Aligned. At the Assembly, twelve francophone African countries, together with Haiti and France, abstained in the vote on the resolution approving the agreement and involving the U.N. in its implementation. Speaking for the abstainers, the representative of Dahomey severely criticized the Bunker plan's weak provisions for consulting the Papuans on the ultimate status of their land. "Not once," he emphasized, "do we find in the text any mention of a 'referendum,' the most normal, the most usual and the most objective form of public expression of opinion. . . . In other words, the actual public expression of opinion will be organized entirely by the party which has the greatest interest in the yielding of results that are favourable to it."[27]

In the United States, an ebullient Senator Hubert Humphrey told the U.S. Senate, after handsomely congratulating the Netherlands, Indonesia, and Ambassador Ellsworth Bunker, that they had achieved "a remarkable precedent for the peaceful settlement of colonial issues."[28] He foresaw a bright future. "Having solved what was potentially the most dangerous of the issues separating her from the developed West, Indonesia should encounter no hindrance to peaceful, steady progress in the years ahead."[29] He also foresaw a brighter, busier future for the U.N.

But the truth of the matter—that the U.N. was used to sanitize a calculated U.S. exercise in hard-hearted *Realpolitik*—did not escape entirely unobserved. South Dakota Senator Karl E. Mundt complained that the Kennedy administration "has created a new colonial power."[30] Senator Thomas Dodd of Connecticut and Representative John J. Rhodes of Arizona[31] agreed with Pennsylvania Senator Hugh Scott's description of the event as a "sellout of West New Guinea" and of genuine self-determination.[32] This view was shared by the *New York Times* columnist Arthur Krock, who asked: "how many believe that, after Sukarno has administered West New Guinea for seven years, the promised U.N. plebiscite will bring independence to the Papuan natives, even assuming they still will have the courage to vote for it?"[33] Across the country, observers pointed out that, far from embarking on a brave new venture in international administration, the U.N. was rewarding aggression and giving its assent to a solution imposed from outside the U.N., in disregard of the Charter.[34]

In an eloquent epitaph for self-determination, the Netherlands representative told the General Assembly:[35]

> Of what happened . . . I will say only this: that the Netherlands Government regrets that in this instance no effective remedy was to be found against the use of force, contrary to the obligations of the States under the Charter of the United Nations. As a result, the Netherlands was faced with the choice between fighting in self-defense or resigning itself to transfer of the territory to Indonesia without a previous expression of the will of the population. War would have meant exposing the Papuans and their country to death and destruction and many Dutchmen and Indonesians to the horrors of combat—without even providing a sensible solution to the problem. And so, with a heavy heart, the Netherlands Government decided to agree to the transfer of the territory to Indonesia on the best conditions obtainable for the Papuan population.

On May 1, exactly as agreed, the UNTEA administrator, Djalal Abdoh of Iran, turned over what was now called West Irian to Indonesia. The Pakistani troops of the U.N. Security Force (UNSF) were withdrawn, and the Secretary-General announced that he was appointing six U.N. experts, under the super-vision of Under-Secretary-General Narasimhan, to report at intervals of ap-proximately six months on the implementation of Indonesia's obligation to consult the population on their ultimate political destiny.[36]

After his victory on the Papuan question, Sukarno, far from being sated, sought to annex the neighboring British territories of Sarawak and North Bor-neo, which were preparing to join Malaysia. When that failed to engender support either in Washington or at the U.N., the Indonesian government not only turned sharply anti-American but, for good measure, quit the U.N. and expelled the organization's remaining presence from West Irian. Only after the overthrow of Sukarno in 1966 did Indonesia return to the fold, finally schedul-ing West Irian's "act of free choice" for August 1969. By then, however, the world had other things on its mind, and the U.S., in particular, had become the patron of a more pro-Western Indonesia. Instead of a plebiscite, the "free choice" was put, in public, to some 1025 "specially selected" delegates who dutifully voted (unanimously) in favor of continuing Indonesian rule. They did so by gathering in eight pathetic little "consultative assemblies," where they were subjected to hectoring speeches by officials from Jakarta before being called upon, literally, to stand up for permanent union with Indonesia.[37] A forlorn mini-revolt was easily crushed, and some thousands of Papuans fled to the adjacent Australian-administered part of New Guinea. Even members of the Indonesian government were reported to have admitted, privately, that this consultation was a meaningless formality.[38]

The report by the Secretary-General's representative at this charade, Fernando

Ortiz Sanz, noted that his advice had frequently been rejected, particularly as to holding "one man one vote" elections at least in the urban centers.[39] Altogether, the U.N. was able to witness the selection of only about 20 percent of the members of the consultative assemblies.[40] The U.N. representative's request that all sectors of the population be allowed to participate freely in the consultation was met by the "explanation" that there were no opponents to union, or, if there were, they did not belong to "legally existing political groups or parties" and thus did not deserve to be consulted.[41] Ortiz Sanz tried to appeal to Indonesian President Suharto for a more credible implementation of self-determination, but was not even received by the President until ten days after the completion of the act of free choice, due to the President's "heavy schedule of work."[42] Even after such humiliation, the U.N.'s representative had no qualms about certifying that "an act of free choice has taken place in West Irian in accordance with Indonesian practice."[43] If there was moral indignation at this perversion of the U.N.'s principles, it did not come from Washington.

In November the General Assembly considered, but did not adopt, a Ghanaian proposal which would have required by 1975 another, more democratic act of self-determination.[44] Instead, the Assembly accepted the Ortiz Sanz report "with appreciation,"[45] by a vote of 84 to 0, but with thirty African and Latin American countries abstaining in disgust.[46]

Elsewhere, there was considerable satisfaction. The Asian part of the Non-Aligned Movement (NAM) was pleased that the principle of decolonization once again had been reinforced in its part of the world. Indonesia was pleased to have its occupation rubber-stamped. The Secretary-General felt that his office had met an unprecedented challenge successfully. The U.S. government was satisfied that a backward area of the world, a potential political vacuum, had been delivered for safekeeping to a staunchly anti-communist regime. U.N. machinery had again served U.S. national interests. But it was no occasion for satisfaction, and, besides, for the U.S. the writing of a new order was already on the wall.

The Fiscal Crisis

Washington's policy-planners faced America's loss of control at the U.N. just as they were in the middle of their most ambitious effort to build up the powers of the General Assembly. Quickly, and rather smoothly, gears were thrown into reverse. We decided, at the last moment, to leave bad enough alone. The occasion for this about-face maneuver was a $100 million fiscal crisis which had overtaken the U.N. at about the time UNTEA was being launched. While UNTEA was financed by the parties directly involved—the Dutch and the Indonesians—the much larger and more costly UNEF peacekeeping force in the Sinai and the U.N. Congo Operation (ONUC) were financed from the general revenues of the organization. The Assembly, under U.S. dominance, allocated the expenses of UNEF and ONUC by the same formula as was used to assess the members for other organizational expenses. However, both France and Russia withheld their payments on the ground that UNEF and ONUC were "unconstitutional" usurpations by the Assembly of powers that properly belonged to the Security Council. They brought on the fiscal crisis in a deliberate effort to block the U.S.-initiated shift of power to the Assembly and to prevent the important peacekeeping function from slipping beyond the reach of their veto.

The United States had engineered the procedure that had been used by the Assembly to create UNEF and to operate ONUC in the face of deadlock in the Council. Washington was determined, now, to see that the withholding of funds not become a veto by other means. Article 19 of the Charter was to be the weapon. It provided that a state lose its vote in the Assembly "if the amount of its arrears equals or exceeds the amount of the contributions due from it for the preceding two full years." By the end of 1961 both France and the Soviet Union were approaching that level of default. Both nations insisted, however, that UNEF and ONUC were not proper "expenses of the organization" because they had not been authorized by the Security Council.

U.S. State Department strategists decided to prompt the General Assembly to ask the International Court for an advisory opinion on whether article 19 applied to UNEF and ONUC assessments. A few in the Department wondered whether a judicial decision in its favor would really be in the U.S.'s interest; whether, if it won, the principle thus established might not be used to the U.S.'s disadvantage by the emerging Third World majority in the Assembly. But again, the short-term advantages were thought to outweigh the long-term risks.

By a U.S.-inspired resolution adopted on December 20, 1961, the General Assembly requested the International Court of Justice to give an advisory opinion on whether the "expenditures authorized in [certain] General Assembly resolutions . . . constitute 'expenses of the Organization' within the meaning of article 17, paragraph 2, of the Charter of the United Nations?"[47] This states: "The expenses of the Organization shall be borne by the Members as apportioned by the General Assembly." By a vote of 9 to 5, the Court answered in the affirmative.

In arriving at this conclusion the majority decided that the two peacekeeping operations had been lawfully authorized by the General Assembly. They thus endorsed the legality of the Uniting for Peace resolution. Although article 24 confers on the Security Council "primary responsibility" for the maintenance of international peace and security, the Court said that "while it is the Security Council which, exclusively, may order coercive action, the functions and powers conferred by the Charter on the General Assembly are not confined to discussion."[48] This was exactly the argument Dean Acheson and the State Department lawyers had made a decade earlier in proposing the new procedures. The Assembly, said the Court, has concurrent power "by means of recommendations . . . [to] organize peace-keeping operations" although only "at the request, or with the consent, of the States concerned."[49] Since both UNEF and ONUC were deployed with the permission of the states concerned, and members had merely been invited, but not obliged, to contribute troops, they were lawful exercises of the Assembly's limited power.

The Court then went on to hold that, while members' participation in an Assembly-authorized peacekeeping operation was necessarily voluntary, the same was not true for paying the bills. The Charter, said the majority of judges, gives to the Assembly power to apportion expenses among the members, including "the power to provide for the financing of measures designed to maintain peace and security."[50] In other words, the Assembly cannot compel military participation, but it can compel fiscal participation.

Even more radical was the Court's view that the members must pay the costs assessed by the Assembly even if "the action was taken by the wrong organ" and was "carried out in a manner not in conformity with the division of functions among the several organs which the Charter prescribes."[51] In support of this proposition the Court cited the rule of national law which makes a corporation liable, as to third parties, for certain unauthorized acts of its agents.

With this sweeping advisory opinion, the Court not only endorsed the Acheson Uniting for Peace Plan, but went a good deal further. It opened the door to the effective arrogation of much of the Security Council's power by a vote of two-thirds of the General Assembly. It threatened states that used financial withholding to oppose such arrogation, with the loss of their vote in the Assembly.

If the Washington architects of this appeal to the Court believed their victory would compel the Kremlin and the Quai d'Orsay to rethink their refusal to pay, they had seriously misjudged. Both responded that, Court or no Court, they would not support, with money or otherwise, Assembly-ordained activities that ran counter to their national interest. Nevertheless, prompted by the U.S., the Assembly solemnly voted to adopt the Court's legal opinion.[52] Meanwhile, deficits kept growing, as did the arrears of France and the Soviet Union. A confrontation seemed inevitable. American representatives tended to characterize it as a test of wills between those who supported the principle of legality and the practitioners of narrowly self-interested politics. The U.S. said it was determined to see the Charter upheld at all costs.

But, then, there was no confrontation. As Soviet and French non-payment began to approach the equivalent of two years' assessments, the NAMs, now a majority of the 115 members, temporized. Some urged the Russians and the French to make at least token payments on their debt. Others pleaded with Washington to agree to have the Assembly suspend the operation of article 19. Neither approach produced a workable compromise.

And so it happened that, for the entire 1964 Assembly session, when France and Russia had at last fallen more than two years into arrears, to avoid invoking article 19 all business was transacted without voting. Budgets and resolutions were passed and other actions taken, all by laboriously negotiated consensus. Where no consensus existed, the matter had to be shelved. It seemed surreal to most participants. A few, perhaps the most perspicacious, thought it an eminently satisfactory arrangement and regretted that it could not become the permanent way of life.

What was significant was that the U.S. did not push its campaign to its logical conclusion. At any time during the session, simply by demanding a roll-call vote on any item, Washington could have forced the president of the Assembly to declare the fiscal defaulters ineligible. That we, and our allies, hesitated was due to four considerations. First, we were no longer sure that the bluff would work: France and Russia might simply stop participating in the Assembly rather than be forced to pay. Second, the U.S. delegation was unsure that the Assembly president, Alex Quaison-Sackey of Ghana, would rule to uphold article 19. Third, even if he did, the U.S. was not certain his ruling would be upheld by a majority of the Assembly, in view of the fact that the NAMs needed the help of Russia for their own anti-colonial and anti-South African agenda. Fourth, Washington itself was beginning to wonder whether the Court's decision was really in its interest.

Still, the debts kept piling up. They had now reached $170 million. To ward off insolvency, the Assembly, in the autumn of 1964, established a "representative negotiating group," the Special Committee on Peace Keeping Operations, to see whether a compromise could be worked out to restore the U.N.'s financial health and to devise an agreed formula for financing future peacekeeping operations. Meeting throughout 1965, the committee made little headway. France and the Soviet Union continued to insist that the Security Council, alone, should establish, and determine the financing of, peacekeeping operations. The United States continued to cite the World Court decision. In the words of former Ambassador Ernest Gross, "the purse strings should be held by the most widely representative organ."[53]

In Washington, however, doubts were at last emerging about this "widely representative organ." As the discussion wore on, a subtle softening of the U.S. view became apparent. By summer, the U.S. was willing to consider the idea that the Assembly, in assessing costs of future peacekeeping operations, should take into account any strong political objections which might have been voiced by a permanent member of the Security Council.[54] On August 16, 1965, the U.S. abandoned efforts to champion the power of the Assembly and, in the process, jettisoned the Court's opinion.

This loss of innocence is celebrated in a notable speech by the U.S. ambassador. In announcing the about-face, Arthur Goldberg noted the failure of the Assembly to make the Soviet Union pay or to take away its vote. "[I]f any Member can insist on making an exception to the principle of collective financial responsibility with respect to certain activities of the organization," he said, "the United States reserves the same option to make exceptions if, in our view, strong and compelling reasons exist for doing so."[55] The U.S. had stepped back from the brink, having been saved by the single-minded adherence to national self-interest of the U.S.S.R. and France. Those two nations long ago had realized that their interests sometimes required them to reject the majority's interpretation of a U.N. principle and to block its implementation. The U.S., at last, had decided to make use of some of the same self-protective tactics.

In return for winning the effective "right" not to pay, the Soviets promised to make a "substantial" voluntary contribution to help alleviate the organization's immediate cash-flow problem.[56] The report of the Special Committee on Peace Keeping Operations merely indicated that the General Assembly would once again function normally and that current financial difficulties might now be resolved by voluntary contributions.[57]

The Special Committee succeeded at little else. It was not able to produce guidelines for future peacekeeping operations. But, informal guidelines became evident in the practices of the late '60s and '70s. Under these, new peacekeeping forces are established exclusively on the authority of the Security Council. In practice, unless the Russians insist on voluntary financing, operations are now invariably financed as an assessed but separate part of the U.N. budget on the basis of a formula reflecting the regular assessments, which has the effect of minimizing the contributions required of Third World countries and maximizing that of developed members, especially those occupying permanent places in the Security Council.

The U.S. had lost, after realizing that losing was more in its interest than winning. We had lost not just one fight, but also our innocence. We had learned that, often, the nation's adherence to U.N. principles and to the international perspective had endured only as long as those happened to coincide with our national self-interest. In this, we were being neither more nor less parochial than any other member. It had just taken us a little longer to awaken to reality.

By the mid-'60s the romance between the State Department and the General Assembly, begun with the Acheson Plan in 1950 and peaking at the time of the Court's advisory opinion in 1962 had ended. The U.S. stopped expecting to be able to use the General Assembly to advance its interests and began to think of it, if at all, primarily in terms of damage limitation. As is so often the case, the U.S. pendulum may possibly have swung too far. An exaggerated mood of passivity was already evident in the decision not to use the Assembly in 1968 to arraign the Soviets for their invasion of Czechoslovakia.

The new perception gradually spread from the State Department to Congress and the media. At the beginning of April 1965 George Aiken, the dean of U.S. Senate Republicans, explained to his colleagues that the effort to use article 19 to force the Russians to pay had collapsed "like a punctured balloon," not primarily because of fear of a Soviet withdrawal but because it would have set a precedent contrary to U.S. national interests. "The United States now recognizes," he said, "that if it were in the position of the Russians or the French, it would probably react in the same way." The U.S., as well, was "not willing to have article 19 applied to itself when its vital interests are involved."[58] His remarks were quickly endorsed by the Senate majority leader Mike Mansfield; the *New York Times*, too, applauded this new enlightened self-interest. At the time, it pointed out, member nations with 10 percent of the total population represented in the U.N. which together paid only 5 percent of the budget, could now command the two-thirds majority necessary to adopt any resolution in the General Assembly. "As a result," the *Times*'s editors concluded, "the United States shares the Soviet desire to increase the role of the Security Council, where the major nations possess a veto."[59]

A Self-inflicted Wound

The last vestiges of American innocence were shattered in 1967 by the historic decision of the Secretary-General to withdraw the United Nations Emergency Force (UNEF) from its positions on the Egyptian-Israeli armistice line. (Egypt became the United Arab Republic in 1958 by act of union with Syria. The union was terminated by Syria in 1961, but Egypt continued to be called the United Arab Republic for some years, until the term fell into disuse and was formally abolished in 1971.) The UNEF withdrawal was an action of far-reaching consequence to the U.S. national interest, taken by U Thant without consulting Washington, and it generated the most intense negative American reaction in government, Congress, the media, and the public. For the first time, Americans realized that a powerful, independent Secretary-General need not, as in the past, promote values and interests that coincided with their own. As with the General Assembly, so with the office of Secretary-General, the U.S. had not previously faced up to the possible consequences of a new order in which the U.N. system no longer behaved in a fashion congenial to it.

UNEF had been positioned along the armistice line in November 1956 largely at the insistence of the Eisenhower administration. A U.S.-led General Assembly had approved its creation in order "to assist in achieving situations conducive to the maintenance of peaceful conditions in the area."[60] This multinational army, conceived at the momentary conjunction of U.S. and Soviet self-interest (see above, Chapter 2), functioned well for almost eleven years. The U.N. succeeded in coordinating the activities of autonomous units from Brazil, Canada, Colombia, Denmark, Finland, India, Indonesia, Norway, Sweden, and Yugoslavia. In the Thoreau-like words of Secretary-General Thant: "Each contingent marched according to its own national custom and cadence,"[61] but they were unified at the top by a U.N. command structure.

Above all, UNEF succeeded in putting an end to the provocative infiltration of Israel by Arab fedayeen and created a climate of détente. Under its watchful aegis, Israelis and Egyptians were able to cultivate agricultural land right up to the boundary.

UNEF operated on an open-ended assignment, which required no periodic renewal by the political organs of the system. Then, in May 1967, even more quickly than it had been put into place, the force was withdrawn by the Secretary-General. The United Nations and in particular Secretary-General U Thant and his advisers were held responsible by President Lyndon B. Johnson, by leading members of Congress, and by virtually all U.S. mass media for the hasty withdrawal and the war that followed.

It was a crucial turning point in U.S.–U.N. relations, for the unusually intense criticism came not from right-wing habitual U.N.-baiters, but from the political mainstream, and it was directed not at the conduct of member states of the organization so much as at the system's keeper of the keys, the Secretary-General himself.

Among observers and historians of the U.N. it is still possible to provoke considerable debate as to whether all this criticism was warranted, whether the U.N. machinery had sustained a severe, self-inflicted injury, or whether U Thant had acted appropriately within the constraints imposed on him by the system.[62] U Thant's latter-day stomach ulcer was believed by friends to have been caused by an intense belief that he had been unjustly persecuted because of the incident, particularly by U.S. politicians and the media.

The crisis began on May 16, 1967, when Egyptian army commander Eiz-El-din Mokhtar handed a letter to U.N. commander General Rikhye. It stated that Egyptian troops had advanced around UNEF positions to the Sinai border. U.N. observation posts were thus outflanked and isolated. Mokhtar asked Rikhye "to withdraw all these troops immediately." The communication was authorized by the commanding officer of the armed forces of the United Arab Republic, General M. Fawzy.[63]

On hearing this, the Secretary-General asked to see the Permanent Representative of Egypt immediately. He told the ambassador, first, to inform the Egyptian government that the communication should have come to him from the government of Egypt, not gone from one field commander to another. Second, if Cairo was requesting "temporary withdrawal of UNEF troops from the Line or from parts of it, it would be unacceptable because the purpose of the United Nations Force in Gaza and Sinai is to prevent a recurrence of fighting, and it cannot be asked to stand aside in order to enable the two sides to resume fighting." Third, the Secretary-General said, if "the United Arab Republic [wished] to withdraw the consent which it gave in 1956 for the stationing of UNEF on the territory of the United Arab Republic and in Gaza, it was, of course, entitled to do so. . . . On receipt of such a request, the Secretary-General would order the withdrawal of all UNEF troops from Gaza and Sinai, simultaneously informing the General Assembly of what he was doing and why."[64]

It was this tactic which was later severely criticized. Without consulting either the General Assembly or the Security Council, even before receiving an official communication from the Cairo government, U Thant had conceded Cairo's right to end its consent to the presence of UNEF and committed himself to withdrawing the troops as expeditiously as possible.[65]

On May 18, at 12:00 noon, Thant received a message from the U.A.R. foreign minister informing him that Cairo had "decided to terminate the presence of United Nations Emergency Force from the territory of the United Arab Republic and Gaza Strip" and requesting "the necessary steps be taken for the withdrawal of the Force as soon as possible."[66] U Thant replied the same day: "request will be complied with and I am proceeding to issue instructions for the necessary arrangements to be put in train without delay for the orderly withdrawal of the Force."[67]

At this time the Secretary-General did go through the motions of consultation. Just before handing his reply to the Egyptian Permanent Representative, he met with his advisory committee on UNEF to inform them of the response he had drafted. He also told them that he would be reporting his actions to the General Assembly and Security Council immediately. At the meeting, it was reported, several government representatives suggested that the Secretary-General delay his offer to comply, asking instead for more time to consult with other interested parties, including Israel and the states contributing troops to UNEF. It was also proposed that the reply be delayed until after the Secretary-General could obtain the views of the General Assembly. Thant, however, said that, as he interpreted the relevant resolutions, agreements, and documents establishing UNEF and placing it in Egypt, it was not for the General Assembly to decide what to do in response to Cairo's unambiguous request. He adamantly insisted that he would reply to Cairo that evening and report to the Assembly the next day.[68]

Thant did report on May 18, but merely gave his reasons for what had now become a *fait accompli*. To the Security Council, he observed—rather fatuously—that no "peace-keeping operation can be envisaged as permanent or semi-permanent. Each one must come to an end at some time or another."[69] By June 5 the six-day war had broken out. Some called it U Thant's war.

That the U.N. is not exactly gazelle-like in its response to most crises made the unaccustomed speed with which the Secretary-General responded to the demand for UNEF's withdrawal all the more controversial. In his own defense, Thant made two points. First, he argued, the legal basis for UNEF's presence on Egyptian soil made it clear that it could only remain for as long as the Cairo government consented to its presence. Second, at a practical level, there was no way to keep UNEF in place against the wishes of the vastly superior U.A.R. forces.

In support of the legal argument, it was said that UNEF had been created by the General Assembly under the Uniting for Peace resolution. Since such General Assembly actions are limited by the Charter to "recommendations" and are not mandatory, Egypt could not be bound to play host to the international force against its will.[70] Any delay, Thant argued, would be "putting in question the sovereign authority of the Government of the United Arab Republic within its own territory."[71]

There is ample evidence, however, that the Secretary-General need not have acted as he did and, in any event, that he need not have acted quite so expeditiously. After Secretary-General Hammarskjold had flown to Egypt in 1956 to negotiate the presence of UNEF with President Nasser, he reported to the Assembly that ". . . the United Nations, understanding this to correspond to the wishes of the Government of Egypt, reaffirms its willingness to maintain UNEF until its task is completed."[72] In an *aide-mémoire* prepared by Hammarskjold on August 5, 1957, the Secretary-General had recorded that, as a result of seven hours of discussion on November 17 with President Nasser, it had been agreed that the stationing of UNEF until its "task is completed" meant that the troops would remain until *both* Egypt and the U.N. agreed that they should leave.[73] On February 26, 1957, Hammarskjold further stated that, prior to withdrawal of the Force, "an indicated procedure would be for the Secretary-General to inform the Advisory Committee of the UNEF, which would determine whether the matter should be brought to the attention of the Assembly."[74]

The U.S. ambassador Ernest Gross, recalling in 1967 his personal involvement in the 1956 negotiations which had installed UNEF, concluded that it had at that time been the understanding of Hammarskjold and Nasser that whether or not "the task" was, in fact, completed "would be a question which would have to be submitted to interpretation by the Assembly."[75] In the retrospective view of Egypt's legal expert and sometime ambassador to the U.N., Nabil El-Araby, the procedure agreed to in 1956 was as follows: "Egypt's request for the withdrawal of UNEF should be discussed in the Advisory Committee, which is empowered, at its discretion, to convene the General Assembly. If the Assembly should object to the withdrawal, it is submitted that Egypt's 1956 good faith commitment would obligate the Egyptian Government not to act contrary to the wishes of the Assembly."[76]

If these interpretations of the relevant legal documents by leading U.S. and Egyptian authorities are correct, U Thant had considerably more room for maneuver than he chose to employ. At a minimum, he could have postponed the drafting of his note of compliance with Egypt's demand until after thorough study of the options by the advisory committee. That could have taken a while, during which other negotiations might have been set in motion. Or he could have asked the committee to support the view that the task of UNEF had not been completed—a view he apparently did hold—and might then have proposed that the committee arrange to convene the Assembly to advise him, and, perhaps, to mediate between the views of his office and those of the U.A.R. Any of these approaches, at the very least, would have justified delay, which might have prevented the outbreak of war. These observations take on a greater validity if it is true—as Ambassador El-Araby believes—that while Nasser may have been maneuvering to impress the Syrians, who were taunting him for hiding behind UNEF's skirts, he did not intend to attack Israel.[77]

On the other hand, in practice the Secretary-General may not have had much room to maneuver. Troops which had been positioned to stand between the Israeli-Egyptian lines had suddenly found themselves *behind* the Egyptian forces, where they could do no good, but could easily come to harm.[78] Most persuasive is the Secretary-General's admission to the Security Council that "if the [Egyptian] request were not promptly complied with, the Force would quickly disintegrate due to the withdrawal of individual contingents."[79] The Egyptian government did not make its move on May 16 without the complicity of two governments that had provided contingents for UNEF. When Egyptian troops made their surprise deployment around U.N. lines, they did so in the areas occupied by forces of India and Yugoslavia. Had the three nations concerned not acted in some premeditated fashion, the possibilities of accidental conflict would have been enormous.

Such complicity, while a violation of the rules, was not unusual. Commenting on "weaknesses in the authority of the [U.N.] Force Commander," U Thant had already reported that "most contingents in a United Nations force maintain direct communications with their home countries. These are supposed to be used only for domestic and national administrative matters. When, however, as does happen, they are used for direct communications with the home Government on matters which are strictly within the authority of the [U.N.] Force Commander or at times even on political matters, misunderstandings and confusion are very likely to arise" leading to "difficulty . . . in maintaining [UNEF] unity and morale and even in its proper use and deployment."[80]

Further light was shed by India's permanent representative, Ambassador Parthasarathi, when he made known his government's decision that "Indian troops could not remain part of UNEF without the United Arab Republic's approval."[81] Both India and Yugoslavia appear to have informed the Secretary-General that, were he to attempt to delay the withdrawal of the Force by taking the issue to the General Assembly, they would unilaterally withdraw their men. Rather than see his "army" fall apart publicly, Thant chose the path of least resistance.

Even if the logistical explanation exculpates the Secretary-General, it does the U.N. system little credit. Rather, it points to the inherent frailty in the concept of an international force as established by the voluntary contribution of national contingents. As long as the national interest of the participating state coincides with the purposes of the U.N. presence, all is well. When this is no longer the case, however, the national contingent may simply be withdrawn, or may threaten withdrawal as a way to influence a change in the U.N.'s interpretation of its mission. Worse, a national contingent may simply pursue its national interest under the U.N. flag. In the Congo (now Zaire) in the early 1960s, blue berets of one nation sometimes battled and killed blue berets of another in the streets of Leopoldville (now Kinshasa). The neutrality of certain national contingents of the U.N. force in Lebanon (UNIFIL) in recent years has been strenuously challenged by Israel, which claimed to have evidence of their "tilt" toward the Palestine Liberation Organization.

On the other hand, this problem of "tilt" should not be exaggerated. Forces of many countries—particularly Canadian, Fijian, Irish, Latin American, and Scandinavian—have served the U.N. as faithful buffers in more than a dozen peacekeeping operations. It can even be argued that the one political function the U.N. has discharged with reasonable success is the supervision of disengagement between warring forces that have wearied, even if only temporarily, of conflict. That U.N. forces have been more broadly based than, for example, the French-Italian-American force placed in Lebanon in 1982 also accounts for the fact that the former has been distinctly more successful than the latter in avoiding outright attack by the combatants.

Understandably, however, an appreciation of this U.N. function did not fill the air in May 1967, at least not in the U.S. President Johnson professed himself "dismayed at the hurried withdrawal of the United Nations Emergency Force . . . . without action by either the General Assembly or the Security Council."[82] In the Senate, Jacob Javits castigated the Secretary-General for "moving too fast."[83] Senator Burke Hickenlooper was less circumspect: "What was the purpose of putting U.N. forces in the Gaza Strip," he asked, "if it were not to keep the peace . . . ? Now when the peace is really threatened, Mr. [*sic*] U Thant takes off down through the woods like a frightened rabbit."[84] Senator Hugh Scott spoke of the Secretary-General's having "capitulated" and acted "beyond his authority."[85] Scott wondered "if the United Nations will survive the action of its Secretary General."[86] Senator Everett Dirksen charged that "the United Nations Emergency Force has slipped out like a thief in the night,"[87] while Senator Robert Byrd thought it "regrettable" that Thant had acted "so hastily and without consulting."[88] Senator Wayne Morse charged that "U Thant . . . did not have the slightest justification . . . to . . . agree to have those forces withdrawn; he is not the United Nations."[89]

In the view of Senator Henry Jackson the Secretary-General had "violated all canons of courage, good sense and responsibility"[90] and Senator Thomas Dodd addressed Thant in the words of Oliver Cromwell to the Long Parliament: "You have tarried too long for the little good you have done. In God's name, go!"[91] In the House of Representatives, the rhetoric was even more abusive. Congressman Howard W. Pollock, who wondered whether the Secretary-General had been motivated by "sheer stupidity" or actual malevolent design, saw his behavior as "the end of a dream."[92]

Writing in the *New York Times*, C. L. Sulzberger said that "U Thant used his international prestige with the objectivity of a spurned lover and the dynamism of a noodle" and accused him of having encouraged war.[93] The *Wall Street Journal* quoted a U.N. diplomat's assessment of Thant as "a tower of jelly."[94]

According to some who knew him, this unprecedented chorus of criticism wounded U Thant, and he took to lashing back at his critics in public.[95] He firmly believed that the intensity of American attacks on him was a reaction to his homilies in favor of a negotiated peace in Vietnam, more than to his withdrawal of UNEF. The then-incumbent U.S. ambassador, Francis T. P. Plimpton, remarked that the Secretary-General "has been more severely criticized than the facts justify. On the other hand, he has reacted more vigorously to it than he should have."[96]

But the keenest observation may have been that of the editors of the *Wall Street Journal*. "A good share of the trouble arises . . ." they wrote, because the "UN's proponents have too loudly insisted it is the world's shining hope; the present gloom is the inevitable backlash of the previous euphoria."[97]

§ **6** §

His Sisters and
His Cousins and His Aunts:
The United Nations
Civil Service

Disillusion was not to be the exclusive lot of member states. The international civil servants who constitute the core of the organization, the Secretariat—who distinguish the U.N. from a mere conference facility—have also had to adjust to realities quite different from the sanguine illusions spelled out in the Charter. Their disillusionment was all the more painful because the ideal of a truly impartial, dedicated civil service had been within the organization's grasp and then slipped away.

Hankey v. Drummond

With the special exception of the Vatican Curia, before 1920 there really were no such creatures as "international civil servants." According to Francis Paul Walters, former Deputy Secretary-General of the League of Nations, "Nothing like an international civil service had ever existed; and amongst those who claimed authority in administrative problems it was taken for granted that such a body could never be united, loyal and efficient."[1]

The idea of a truly international civil service, which would owe its loyalty exclusively to the global system it was administering, was put into practice by the first Secretary-General of the League of Nations, Sir Eric Drummond, who was chosen for the post by agreement among the principal delegations at the Paris Peace Conference in 1919. Robert Rhodes James claims that the idea of an impartial civil service serving the global community "was the transference to an international environment of an essentially British concept of the disinterested official."[2]

The choice of Drummond appears to have been something of a fluke, since the negotiators had first agreed to offer the post to Sir Maurice Hankey, who had developed the War Cabinet secretariat in Britain and "had become in fact, though not in name, the Secretary-General of the Peace Conference," a post in which he had demonstrated a remarkable talent for efficient administration.[3]

Hankey had gone to the trouble of drawing up a plan for the office of Secretary-General and an outline of the secretariat that would assist him. He proposed that the Secretary-General should preside over a cabinet composed of nine National Secretaries, one from each nation represented on the Council of the League, who would be assisted by their own staffs recruited from their respective countries. The National Secretaries would take turns being Secretary to the Council.

After considering the offer, Hankey eventually declined it. Much later, he confided to Lord Halifax that he never really believed in "either the League or Collective Security."[4] The post was then offered to Drummond, a nineteen-year veteran of the British Foreign Office, who had been a delegate to the Peace Conference, and was a friend of Arthur Balfour and Robert Cecil and much admired by President Woodrow Wilson's confidant, Colonel Edward House.[5]

Drummond set out to create "a secretariat international alike in its structure, its spirit, and its personnel" which, Walters justifiably concludes, "was without doubt one of the most important events in the history of international politics—important not only in itself, but as the indisputable proof of possibilities which had hitherto been confidently denied."[6] In retrospect, Walters judges the experiment a success. "Taken as a whole," he says, "its members, drawn from over thirty countries, differing in language, religion, and training, worked together in a spirit of friendship and devotion. They developed a corporate sense, a pride in the record and reputation of their service, not inferior to any that can be found in the best of national institutions. Never again can it be maintained that an international civil service is bound to be a failure."[7]

So well established was this radical proposition by the time the United Nations was being conceived, that Drummond's ideals were largely incorporated in successive drafts of the Charter, primarily at the suggestion of the United States. While many provisions of the League Covenant were simply carried over into the U.N. Charter, there was a deliberate effort to strengthen the hand of the Secretary-General. Whereas the Covenant required that nominations to senior posts be approved by the Council, the Charter permits the Secretary-General to make all his own appointments.[8]

In San Francisco the United States, assisted by parallel proposals from Canada and New Zealand, had little difficulty in having the Conference accept a statement outlining the inviolate character of the Secretariat. This became article 100 of the Charter, which provides:

1. In the performance of their duties the Secretary-General and the staff shall not seek or receive instructions from any government or from any other authority external to the Organization. They shall refrain from any action which might reflect on their position as international officials responsible only to the Organization.
2. Each Member of the United Nations undertakes to respect the exclusively international character of the responsibilities of the Secretary-General and the staff and not to seek to influence them in the discharge of their responsibilities.

Also, at San Francisco a number of states thought it important to include in the Charter some basic provisions regarding the recruitment of staff. Consequently, article 101 provides that the "staff shall be appointed by the Secretary-General under regulations established by the General Assembly" and that the "paramount consideration in the employment of the staff . . . shall be the necessity of securing the highest standards of efficiency, competence, and integrity. Due regard shall be paid to the importance of recruiting the staff on as wide a geographical basis as possible."

When article 101 was presented by the drafting subcommittee to the full committee on June 4, 1945, the Soviet and Ukrainian delegates made an effort to have it deleted. Their stated reason was that it concerned minor technical details which would burden the Charter with unnecessary trivia. In fact, however, the Soviets did not then, and have not since, agreed with the three important points contained in article 101: that the Secretary-General should be solely responsible for the selection of staff, that regulations for employment should be established by the General Assembly, and that the "paramount" factor in recruitment should be the pursuit of "highest standards" with geographical distribution a secondary factor.[9]

A proposal submitted to the San Francisco Conference by the United States, United Kingdom, Soviet Union, and China would have provided that the Secretary-General be assisted by four deputies who, like the Secretary, were to be elected by the General Assembly on the recommendation of the Security Council for a period of three years.[10] After strenuous opposition led by Canada, this proposal was defeated by a majority which insisted on the authority of the Secretary-General to appoint, free from the control of the political organs, even the most senior officials of the Secretariat.[11]

So Drummond's vision was plainly shared by most at San Francisco and found its way, clearly and succinctly, into the language of the Charter. Although all five of the U.N. Secretaries-General have publicly subscribed to the vision of a truly international civil service, and have violated it to varying degrees in private, its most eloquent exponent was the second holder of the office, Dag Hammarskjold. In a widely noted speech at Oxford, just a few months before his death at Ndola (in what is now Zambia) in September 1961,[12] Hammarskjold warned against attempts to politicize the international civil service, asserting that compromise with such effort "might well prove to be the Munich of international cooperation" and that this "may be no less dangerous than to compromise with principles regarding the rights of a nation. In both cases the price to be paid may be peace."[13]

Recalling Nikita Khrushchev's statement in an interview with Walter Lippmann—that, while there may be neutral countries there can be no neutral men—Hammarskjold eloquently and tenaciously defended the feasibility of a neutral civil service carrying out its functions in accordance with the principles laid down in the Charter and by relevant resolutions of the organization. In Hammarskjold's view, it really came down to personal integrity and freedom from undue pressures.[14]

The Secretary-General was not preaching: he was defending himself. On September 23, 1960, Khrushchev had told a startled General Assembly that the Secretary-General and his staff, as lackeys of the colonialists, "have been doing their dirty work in the Congo." (A U.N. force there was trying to contain a civil war and restrain unilateral foreign intervention.) Abuses of the chief administrative office of the U.N. had reached the point, he said, where the office "should be abolished."[15] In its place, he proposed an executive consisting of three persons representing, respectively, the West, the socialist states, and the non-aligned.

While this "troika" never quite left the starting gate, the General Assembly, at about the same time, received a report of a Committee of Experts established by the Assembly in 1959 to review the activities and organization of the Secretariat.[16] The Soviet member of this committee restated his country's preference for the troika, of course. But more damaging was the "compromise" proposed by experts from Egypt, Ghana, and India, which called for creating three new posts of Deputy Secretary-General. The occupants were to serve for one term only, supervising the work of the Secretariat from the highest level and reflecting "the main political trends in the world today."[17] It was, in fact, a "sub-troika."

Hammarskjold thought that this would infringe on the responsibilities of the Secretary-General, was contrary to the Charter, and could lead to "breakdown and retrogression."[18] The sub-troika was not instituted.

The International Court of Justice and the U.N. Secretariat

Powerful assistance in the fight against politicization had been provided by the other "impartial" branch of the U.N., the International Court of Justice. In two remarkably creative and well-reasoned opinions, in 1949 and 1954, a large majority of the World Court had sided emphatically with the Drummond-Hammarskjold vision of an autonomous Secretariat.

The first opinion concerned the death of Count Folke Bernadotte, on September 17, 1948, in Jerusalem at the hands of Israeli terrorist assassins. The

U.N. mediator had been directing neutral military observers stationed along the Israeli-Arab lines. In international law, since the murder had occurred in Israel, Israeli authorities might have become liable to pay damages for failing to protect Bernadotte. But liable to whom? As the victim was of Swedish nationality, customary international law decreed that it was up to Sweden to pursue the claim. Bernadotte's death provoked the General Assembly into asking the International Court to render an advisory opinion on the following legal question:

> In the event of an agent of the United Nations in the performance of his duties suffering injury in circumstances involving the responsibility of a State, has the United Nations as an Organization, the capacity to bring an international claim against the responsible . . . government with a view to obtaining the reparation due in respect of damage caused (a) to the United Nations, (b) to the victim or the persons entitled through him?

The Court unanimously held that the U.N. was indeed entitled to bring an action for reparations in respect of damage caused to the organization by the loss of the services of its employee.[19] By a vote of 11 to 4, the Court also decided that the U.N. could bring an international claim against the responsible government to obtain reparations due to the injured individual or his survivors.[20]

The result may sound obvious, but in the convoluted world of international law it was nothing of the sort. The U.N. Charter and the Statute of the International Court say nothing whatsoever about the capacity of the U.N. to bring such a legal claim. In traditional international law, only *states* may be claimants against other states, since it would be beneath the dignity of a government to deal with something less than another government. Nevertheless, the judges thought that the U.N.'s capacity to pursue a claim must be implied from the role the Charter assigns to the Secretariat. While they had not confused the United Nations with a sovereign state, the judges did believe that the organization was intended to have whatever legal attributes of sovereignty might be needed to discharge its onerous new responsibilities.

In the Court's view, the U.N.:

> is at present the supreme type of international organization, and it could not carry out the intentions of its founders if it was devoid of international personality. It must be acknowledged that its members, by entrusting certain functions to it, with the attendant duties and responsibilities, have clothed it with the competence required to enable those functions to be effectively discharged.
>
> Accordingly, the Court has come to the conclusion that the Organization is an international person. That is not the same thing as saying that it is a state . . . .[21]

In other words, when the organization is injured, it has the right to claim damages in its own name. "It cannot be supported that in such an event all the

Members of the Organization, save the defendant State must combine to bring a claim."[22]

With these words, the Court decided that the U.N. had a distinct legal identity—separate, that is, from the sum of its members. Such separate identity was necessary in order to protect the organization's integrity and independence. This part of the decision was reached unanimously by the judges.

The second part of the question—could the U.N. put forward a claim for personal damage done to Bernadotte and his family—proved more difficult. As noted, citizens are traditionally protected by their national governments. When a Swedish citizen is killed in Jerusalem, allegedly because of the failure of Israeli authorities to offer him adequate protection, his survivors' claim in international law would ordinarily be pursued by the government of Sweden against the government of Israel. The Court, however, thought that new law was necessary to cover the case of an international civil servant injured in the course of his duties to the U.N. In the words of the majority:

> Under international law, the Organization must be deemed to have those powers which, though not expressly provided in the Charter, are conferred upon it by necessary implication as being essential to the performance of its duties . . . .
>
> . . . To ensure the independence of the agent, and, consequently, the independent action of the Organization itself, it is essential that in performing his duties he need not have to rely on any other protection than that of the Organization. . . . In particular, he should not have to rely on the protection of his own State. If he had to rely on that State, his independence might well be compromised, contrary to the principle applied by Article 100 of the Charter. And lastly, it is essential that— whether the agent belongs to a powerful or a weak State; to one more affected or less affected by the complications of international life; to one in sympathy or not in sympathy with the mission of the agent—he should know that in the performance of his duties he is under the protection of the Organization.[23]

With that, the judges had deliberately broken the exclusive fiduciary relationship between a citizen and his state in those cases where the citizen is working for the international organization. This the judges believed to be the intent and spirit of the Charter, regarding both those provisions creating the Secretariat and those assigning important, and potentially dangerous, functions to the organization to be executed by staff. International civil servants, thereafter, were to look to the Secretary-General, not to their governments, to protect them and safeguard their interests.

In 1954 the Court was asked for another advisory opinion pertaining to the rights of members of the Secretariat. In this instance, a number of employees of the organization, having been dismissed by the Secretary-General at the insistent urging of the United States in the thrall of McCarthyism, brought in the U.N. Administrative Tribunal an action for wrongful discharge. They won and were awarded compensation, which the Secretary-General felt obliged to pay. However, led by the U.S. delegation, which was being prodded by Congress, the majority of the General Assembly was about to refuse to vote the budgetary appropriation necessary to make the payment. Before doing so, however, the Assembly asked the Court to advise it whether it, the Assembly, had "the right on any grounds to refuse to give effect to an award of compensation made by the [Administrative] Tribunal in favor of a staff member of the United Nations whose contract of services had been terminated without his assent."[24] By a vote of 9 to 3, the Court held that the General Assembly has no such right to refuse on any ground.[25]

This decision is important, because it had been argued that the General Assembly is all-powerful when it comes to budgetary matters, and that it may use its budgetary power in any way that the majority sees fit. Moreover, it had been asserted that since the Assembly had created the Administrative Tribunal and had enacted the staff regulations, it retained the ultimate authority to change the rules of the game.

The Court, however, was firmly of the opposite opinion. It held that the "General Assembly itself, in view of its composition and functions, could hardly act as a judicial organ" in determining whether a civil servant's claim was justified. The finality of awards of the Tribunal "was essential to ensure the efficient working of the Secretariat, and to give effect to the paramount consideration of securing the highest standards of efficiency, competence and integrity."[26] Thus, "the assignment of the budgetary function to the General Assembly cannot be regarded as conferring upon it the right to refuse to give effect to the obligation arising out of an award of the Administrative Tribunal."[27] The Charter gives the General Assembly, in respect of the Secretariat, "a power to make regulations, but not a power to adjudicate upon, or otherwise deal with, particular instances."[28] With that, the ICJ in effect interpreted into the Charter a provision similar to the U.S. Constitution's ban on bills of attainder.

In other words, the Court recognized the rights of international civil servants to carry out their administrative duties with appropriate independence and integrity, as against attempts by member states to use the power of the purse to punish them. It is not insignificant that the U.S. judge was one of the four dissenting in the first opinion, and one of the three dissenting in the second.

McCarthyism and the U.N. Secretariat

The issue raised in the second advisory opinion had come to a head because Washington politicians had insisted that U.S. nationals working for the U.N. be above suspicion of pro-communist sympathies. Under-Secretary-General Brian Urquhart, a British citizen, has remarked that, while the Russians never really accepted the idea of an independent international civil service, "it was the spirit of McCarthyism in the United States that constituted the first major challenge"[29] to the survival of Drummond's ideal.

The last year of Trygve Lie's stewardship, 1952, saw the hunt for subversives in the U.S. government extend to the U.N. Secretariat. In May 1952 the McCarran Subcommittee of the Senate Judiciary Committee began its inquiries into disloyalty among U.S. citizens employed in the international civil service. Hearings were held in New York in October and November, at which international officials of U.S. nationality were required to testify. On December 2, 1952, a U.S. federal grand jury, although giving no names and issuing no indictments, publicly concluded that there was "infiltration into the U.N. of an overwhelmingly large group of disloyal U.S. citizens."[30]

Secretary of State Dean Acheson's reaction to all this was to negotiate with the Secretary-General an understanding that any U.S. citizen being considered for employment by the Secretariat would first be subject to U.S. security clearance. Acheson seems not to have excruciated much about this debasing of the ideal of an international civil service, since he had never seriously entertained the ideal in the first place.[31] (Acheson's views on the U.N. got progressively odder. Fifteen years later—mercifully no longer secretary of state—he railed against its persecution of that "weak white nation," Ian Smith's Rhodesia.[32])

On January 2, 1953, the Senate Internal Security Subcommittee published a list of thirty-eight names of U.S. members of the Secretariat who, it was implied, had communist affiliations.[33] According to Urquhart, at that time twenty-seven of these persons were no longer employed by the U.N.[34]

In an effort to deflect some of these attacks, Secretary-General Lie had appointed a committee of three jurists—American, Belgian, and British—to advise on how to deal with the problems being created for him by the U.S. investigations.[35] Their report, published in January 1953, stated, in effect, that those refusing to answer questions concerning their activities should not be continued in U.N. employment.[36] Lie had already got rid of staff members holding temporary contracts with the organization who had invoked the Fifth Amendment. On December 5, after receiving the still unpublished opinion of the jurists, he took the further step of dismissing those staff members with permanent contracts who had sought the constitutional protection against self-incrimination.[37]

Twenty-one of the dismissed American staff members, all of whom had invoked the Fifth Amendment, brought suit against the Secretary-General—by this time Lie had been succeeded by Hammarskjold—and on August 21 the Administrative Tribunal found in favor of eleven of them, awarding compensation to seven and ordering the reinstatement of four.[38]

Although the new Secretary-General thought it impolitic to reinstate the four, he did offer them compensation.[39] This compromise pleased no one. It demoralized the staff, which wanted the four reinstated, and equally antagonized those in Congress who did not want U.S. tax dollars used to buy off "Reds." The latter succeeded in getting a resolution through both houses of

Congress which provided that no funds appropriated for the U.S. contribution to the U.N. could be used to pay the approximately $189,000 in compensation due those wrongly dismissed.[40] The U.S. delegation to the U.N., by that time headed by Henry Cabot Lodge, although having little stomach for the fight, was left with no choice but to oppose the budgetary item making funds available for payment. On December 9 the item was temporarily deferred while the Assembly consulted the International Court.[41] We have already noted that the Court, in a landmark opinion, took the position that the Assembly was obliged to vote the money owed. Nevertheless, to ease the way for U.S. compliance, Hammarskjold proposed that funds for compensation be taken from an income-tax-like assessment regularly levied on all U.N. staff in lieu of national taxes. This proposal secured general, if grudging, acceptance.[42]

The case of the dismissed Americans, however, was merely the tip of the iceberg. On January 9, 1953, just before leaving office, President Truman, pursuant to the understanding negotiated by Acheson, had issued Executive Order 10422, concerning loyalty procedures for employees.[43] This order provides that the U.S. government (the International Organizations Employees Loyalty Board) would henceforth provide the Secretary-General with information on all U.S. candidates for employment. Hammarskjold, negotiating through Lodge and advised by former U.S. ambassador Ernest Gross, was able to obtain a modification to the effect that information provided would be factual only and that conclusions as to a candidate's eligibility would be purely "advisory."[44] In practice, however, there is no evidence that any Secretary-General has actually appointed U.S. nationals about whom the Loyalty Board has made a negative recommendation. In his comprehensive study of the Secretariat, Professor Theodor Meron has observed that "this might suggest that the advisory determinations were in fact decisive, which would amount to infringement of Articles 100 and 101 of the Charter (except, of course, in case that all the derogatory determinations were based on convincing findings of facts, which also demonstrated unsuitability under the Charter standards for appointments)."[45]

Fortunately, the problem has diminished with the change in U.S. public attitudes. In 1977 the Department of State said that no negative determinations as to a potential employee's loyalty had been forwarded to the Secretariat since 1966.[46] President Truman's Executive Order 10422, which had required a "full field" investigation of U.S. employees at the U.N., was eventually replaced by President Gerald Ford's Executive Order 11890 of December 10, 1975, which requires a less onerous "national agency check." Nevertheless, the investigations are still routinely conducted, an "anachronism and an invasion of privacy that survived the McCarthy period."[47] As Shirley Hazzard has observed, "The most significant aspect of the clearance requirement . . . does not lie in the exceptional circumstance of a candidate whose suitability may be contested between the Secretariat and the national agency, but in the pervasive and repressive atmosphere created by such a condition, and in the debilitating conformity it implies and imposes among the majority of the approved."[48] That was and remains true. Moreover, a recent study suggests that there may be moves afoot to revive the earlier, McCarthy-era types of investigation.[49]

The ameliorations in U.S. policy toward the Secretariat should not cause us to forget the dismal situation that prevailed in the early 1950s. In January 1953, as the Eisenhower administration came into office, it asked the Federal Bureau of Investigation to check all U.S. citizens then employed in the Secretariat. Astonishing as it may seem in retrospect, Secretary-General Lie permitted the FBI to set up shop in the U.N. building, explaining that it was for the convenience of the large number of personnel who were to be interrogated and fingerprinted. To the harassed civil servants the presence of the FBI in their "extraterritorial" enclave was a dreary symbol of the capitulation of Drummond to Hankey. Once in the *sanctum*, the FBI proceeded as if on home ground. On June 20 an American agent in plainclothes attempted to take a demonstrator away from U.N. guards in the public gallery. Hammarskjold protested. On another occasion, a senior U.N. official was subjected to a detailed questioning on his relations with various people and his views about communism. Hammarskjold instructed his staff to limit their replies, when interviewed by the FBI, to questions concerning criminal activity only—a category broad enough, however, to cover any political advocacy prohibited by U.S. law, including laws later held to be unconstitutional.[50]

In November 1953, in a letter to the U.S. ambassador Wadsworth, the Secretary-General asked for the removal of the FBI from U.N. headquarters.[51] Yet, by June 1954 the investigations had still not ended. Ralph Bunche, the senior American official in the Secretariat and recent winner of the Nobel Peace Prize for his role in bringing peace to the Middle East, was confronted by professional informers during Loyalty Board hearings.[52] In reply to press questions, Hammarskjold could only waffle: "On the present legal basis which we have in this house, I do not in any way feel concerned."[53] Yet he most certainly was.

Summarizing these events in his memoirs, Dean Acheson, who had been secretary of state for much of the worst period, wrote: "The result was highly unfavorable opinion of the United Nations in the United States and of the United States in the United Nations."[54] This conclusion, however, reflects his idiosyncratic aversion to the U.N. rather than indignation at the way it was being humiliated by U.S. demagogues. "If I needed confirmation," he wrote, "of my opposition to having the U.N. headquarters in New York—which I did not—we had plenty of it during the autumn of 1952."[55]

The Socialists and the Secretariat

The United States, as usual, was not the most egregious but only the most blatant in its undermining of the Charter. This blatancy derives, in part, from inconsistency. States which had never accepted the Drummond vision of an independent civil service could not be expected to behave supportively toward a secretariat attempting to invent its independence. But when agents of the U.S. government, which so recently had proclaimed the coming of the golden age of international organization, began snooping around U.N. headquarters and even at the organization's European offices in Geneva, the staff's confounded expectations turned to general demoralization, a condition from which it has never fully recovered.

The U.S. way of undermining the Secretariat, like much else, is singularly raucous and visible. Russia, too, produced Chairman Khrushchev, who banged his shoe on the Assembly podium. But, generally speaking, the Soviets have acted more like insidious termites than like clowns.

By sheer persistence, and latterly aided by the Third World acting out of a different set of motives, the Soviet Union and other socialist countries have gradually been able to stand the Charter—with its high-minded provisions for an international civil service—on its head. While the Charter states that the staff "shall not seek or receive instructions from any government or from any other authority external to the Organization,"[56] the socialist countries have made their members of the Secretariat unabashed agents of government. For the provision of the Charter stating that the "staff shall be appointed by the Secretary-General,"[57] they have substituted the practice of influencing, and in many cases effectively controlling, who is appointed, how long they serve, whether or not they are promoted, and when their service is terminated. In place of the rule that employment of staff shall be determined on the basis of "the highest standards of efficiency, competence, and integrity" with, secondarily, "due regard" being paid to "the importance of recruiting the staff on as wide a geographical basis as possible,"[58] they have substituted the working rule that certain posts belong to specific countries and may be filled only by its nationals, and that *where* a candidate is from is substantially more important than his or her professional qualifications.

Even as the United States was conducting its witch-hunt in the halls of the Secretariat, the U.S.S.R. "withdrew recognition" from Secretary-General Trygve Lie because of his support for collective U.N. action in Korea. Having once demonstrated the impossibility of Lie's carrying on in the post of Secretary-General over the active hostility of the Soviet Union, Moscow decided to teach the same lesson to his successor, Dag Hammarskjold. The pressure began when the U.N.'s operation in the Congo—which had initially operated to favor Patrice Lumumba, Moscow's candidate in that civil-war-torn country—began to produce results unfavorable to Soviet aspirations.

"We do not, and cannot, place confidence in Mr. Hammarskjold," Chairman Khrushchev had stated. "If he himself cannot muster the courage to resign in, let us say, a chivalrous way, we shall draw the inevitable conclusions from the situation."[59] After such attacks, Hammarskjold, like Lie ten years before, found himself the principal spokesman for the idea of an active Secretary-Generalship, but also the object of a debilitating Soviet boycott.[60] The stasis ended only with Hammarskjold's violent air-crash death in 1961 in Northern Rhodesia (now Zambia), on his way to the war in Katanga.

On the other hand, the Secretary-General's death created a second opportunity for the Soviets to renew their call for a "troika." Modifying Khrushchev's earlier demand for a civil service headed by three Secretaries-General, the U.S.S.R. now indicated its willingness to accept a single, neutral chief executive, providing he were bound to act in a spirit of concert with a cabinet based on the troika principle.[61] In this demand, Moscow was able to capitalize on the fact that, already in 1946, there had been an "understanding" between Secretary-General Trygve Lie and the permanent members of the Security Council to the effect that each of these five states would be entitled to one post at the second-highest level[62] (at that time called Assistant Secretary-General upgraded in 1954 to Under-Secretary).

Eventually, this dispute was settled by an agreement to allow the new man, U Thant, to appoint as many persons to his second echelon "as he sees fit," with the understanding that they would include the three major "tendencies"— Communist, Free Market Democratic, and Neutral. Thant agreed to consult with these Under-Secretaries regularly "in a spirit of mutual understanding." This compromise, while it averted the establishment of a formal troika, nevertheless suggested that the Secretary-General would thereafter be limited to some undefined extent by the need to secure the agreement of deputies named to represent the interests of the major forces in the world. He was given a command different from, and palpably less than, that of his predecessor.

Moscow's interest in the Secretariat has by no means been confined solely to the top post. Its objectives—and, to varying degrees, those of the other socialist states—extend to all echelons and departments of the Secretariat. Those objectives can be stated as follows:

1. to ensure that the Soviet Union and other Socialist states occupy approximately one-third of the professional positions in the Secretariat.
2. to ensure that these positions are filled by persons proposed by Government, rather than through direct, or competitive, recruitment by the U.N.
3. to prevent the creation of a career international civil service and to ensure that Soviet citizens be limited to serving a five-(exceptionally eight-) year contract, after which they are to be recycled back home, with some possibility of serving a second term later.
4. to ensure that Soviet citizens serving in the Secretariat act as representatives,

directly serving Soviet interests in the U.N. and, to some extent, representing U.N. interests in Soviet circles.

5. to secure specific important, and even semi-important, posts as the hereditary right of Soviet citizens, to be passed along from one incumbent to the next.

The Soviet Union and its satellites have not been entirely successful in the pursuit of all five objectives, but the consequences of their efforts on the Secretariat have been little short of devastating, in effect replacing the Drummond-Hammarskjold vision with a distorted version of the concept advanced by Hankey. Hankey had been thinking of a multinational civil service composed of a few dozen professional staff, certainly not of the 50,000 international civil servants working in the family of organizations making up the U.N. system, nor even of the core Secretariat's professional staff which currently numbers 4,338, supported by 11,500 clerks, secretaries, and assistants in general services or related technical, administrative, and clerical posts.[63]

The Soviet attitude was most clearly expressed by A. Roshchin, the Soviet member of the Committee of Experts, which reported in 1961. Roshchin's view in effect extended the "troika" concept to the Secretariat as a whole, seeking the vertical allocation of all posts in accordance with parity among the three basic groups of states.[64] He strongly denounced the concept of a "permanent civil service" and argued that professional appointments should be made only on temporary contracts.

While the Soviet position may have since mellowed slightly as to "post parity," the opposition to career service remains unabated. In the words of James Jonah of Sierra Leone, until 1982 an Assistant Secretary-General with responsibility for personnel matters,

> from the inception of the United Nations one group of States, namely the Soviet Union and the other socialist countries, have not accepted the concept of a career service for the Secretariat. For these States it was preferable to have an intergovernmental Secretariat to which nationals of each Member State would be assigned for brief periods and after which they would return to their own country's service.[65]

Quite properly, members of the U.N. career civil service, as well as of some delegations to the U.N., have serious doubts about the professional motivation of persons working at the U.N. for only a few years, most of whom have been seconded to the international service from government employment, to which they return after a brief interval in New York or Geneva. It is widely believed, Jonah has reported, that such staff, "no matter how high minded, may find it difficult to refuse instructions from their Governments and thus be subject to penalties for showing allegiance to an international secretariat."[66] For many years, secretaries-general operated on the principle that no more than 25 percent of the professional staff should be employed on fixed-term (contract) appointments, and the rest should be career servants. By 1975, however, 38.4 percent of professionals held fixed-term contracts.[67] What is more important is the rapid acceleration of this trend which began in the mid-seventies. Thus, between July 1, 1974, and June 30, 1975, of 298 recruits to professional posts, 254 were given non-career appointments.[68] That trend continues today.

Suspicion of the loyalty to the international system of fixed-term employees' on short contracts is accentuated because these appointments are effectively bestowed by the employee's government rather than by the Secretary-General. Long after Senator Joseph McCarthy's demise, and after U.S. loyalty probes had waned from the obstreperous to the perfunctory, the socialist countries have continued to insist on pre-selecting those of their citizens who may be employed by the U.N. In this, they have set an example which is happily followed by the new authoritarian regimes of the Third World.

The Soviet Union has successfully impressed on the Secretary-General that its citizens cannot be approached directly for posts at the U.N. As vacancies arise, the Foreign Ministry nominates candidates. Usually, they give a perfunctory nod in the direction of the Secretary-General's powers of recruitment designated in the Charter by putting forward two or three candidates. But the U.N.'s choice is narrowly confined to this preselected group.[69] When my predecessor at UNITAR (United Nations Institute for Training and Research) went to Moscow to interview candidates presented by the Government for a vacant senior post, two of the "candidates" pleaded not to be chosen since they did not want their careers interrupted by short-term service in New York.

The Polish government has underscored its adherence to the same principle by arresting, subjecting to secret military trial, and imprisoning Alicja Wesolowska, a Polish member of the Secretariat who had the temerity to obtain a professional staff position on her own initiative.[70] Although the staffer was charged with "anti-state activity," not improper recruitment, the U.N. staff has viewed such penalization with alarm. The U.N. staff association chided both the Secretary-General and the Polish government, noting that her arbitrary arrest, and trial in secret without U.N. presence before a Polish military tribunal, violates not only the Charter but also the Convention on the Privileges and Immunities of the United Nations and the International Covenant on Civil and Political Rights. The Secretary-General has also been faulted for having failed to guarantee "minimal standards of justice and due process" to staff members, "let alone their functional immunity . . . when they work in the service of the Organization." The member states were asked: "Can the United Nations have any moral authority in promoting human rights throughout the world if it proves incapable of protecting and safeguarding the rights of its own staff members?"[71]

Only after she had served almost five years in prison did Polish authorities accede to the direct appeal of Secretary-General Pérez de Cuéllar for the release of Wesolowska. The case plainly manifests the socialist countries' firm belief that their nationals in the Secretariat should fulfill a patriotic function and serve the national interest. A recent study rightly concludes that there "is every reason to believe that the Soviet Government continues to exercise strict control over its nationals in the Secretariat."[72]

It is not an altogether bad thing for U.N. civil servants to have good connections with the government of their nationality. The Secretary-General and other senior U.N. officials can benefit from utilizing their more trustworthy subordinates as emissaries to sound out home governments on a proposed initiative, obtaining their support—or, at least, a benevolent demurrer—before launching a potentially controversial activity. In 1980, in my capacity as UNITAR's director of research, before undertaking an anonymous attitude survey designed to elicit the opinions of U.N. delegates toward various U.N. issues and problems, I used my Soviet deputy to get an informal reaction from his nation's ambassador to this unprecedented project. When that elicited a threat on the ambassador's part to kill it, I took the matter up with a senior Soviet official in the Secretariat who neutralized Moscow's opposition by working out an informal agreement that the project could go forward so long as the Soviet delegation did not have to participate.

But only in exceptional cases is this the way the system works. Much more often, the influencing is done by the member state exerting hidden pressure on the Secretariat through its nationals. While working at UNITAR, I initially took the precaution of having a national of another country with me on visits to my own (U.S.) mission, precisely to demonstrate that I was not being instructed. Once it became apparent that no one else was adhering to this supposedly traditional practice, I also abandoned it, but still kept my visits to the mission down to about a dozen—either purely social, or to solicit financial contributions—in two and one-half years.

My Soviet deputy, however, far from having any such fastidious concern, openly boasted of his close contacts with his country's mission to which he reported at about 4:00 p.m. daily. He used these contacts primarily to advance his own career strategy and to curry favor with the Soviet hierarchy. On one occasion I was considering sending another Soviet citizen, a senior U.N. professional working in a different department, on a mission to Moscow for which he was better qualified than my deputy. The deputy, on hearing this, shortly returned from his mission with the news that "If you send _____ to Moscow, I can assure you that he will not return." On another occasion, he threatened severe reprisals against a colleague in Moscow who had proposed coming to New York to discuss a project under way in the Soviet Union which was sponsored by my unit. Such requests, my deputy explained, may not be initiated by a Soviet citizen, but only by the appropriate Soviet high official. Again, the message was that "_____ is in very serious trouble" for approaching the U.N. on his own, rather than through "channels."

In many instances, the deputy, in opposing a course of action being considered by our department, claimed to be speaking for the Soviet ambassador. Sometimes this had an authentic ring. More often, he was bluffing to get his own way in a bureaucratic dispute of no interest to his government. Several times I was able to confirm this by checking with other, more senior, Soviet employees, particularly those with K.G.B. credentials (who were generally the best informed and least careerist). The point, however, is that my Soviet deputy always thought of himself as working on instruction from his government, and he made this abundantly clear to the entire department, even when, on occasion, it happened to be untrue.

Writing of such matters, Assistant Secretary-General James Jonah has said:

> Obviously, if the independence of the Secretariat is in question, it will be difficult to expect Governments to entrust to the Secretariat anything of major significance to the Member States. . . .
>
> It is indeed regrettable that developments in the international civil service over the decades has brought about this concern about its independence. . . . The fact remains that few Governments truly take seriously the independence of the international civil service.[73]

Another clear indication of the Soviet vision of a multinational civil service is the fact that its professional staff members are required to contribute back to the Soviet Government a part of their salary determined by a formula which seeks to equalize the (higher) U.N. salary and the remuneration the same person would be receiving in the service of the Soviet Union. This is an insidious practice, but it has its non-Soviet counterpart. At the other end of the spectrum, certain more affluent countries have actually been paying a subsidy to their citizens to work for the U.N., a subvention topping their U.N. salary. Such supplementary payments, made by Japan and a few others, have been the subject of protest by the Secretariat.[74] During my service (1980–82), the government of Japan provided unusually generous funding for a temporary professional post, named a candidate (he happened to be well qualified), and despite my objection to any uncompetitive appointment secured the post for him at an excessively high professional grade. While such direct subventions can be rationalized as necessary to entice highly qualified persons to accept short-term U.N. employment, James Jonah has observed that "there is no doubt" that such practices "increase the dependence of staff members who may well feel that such payments can be withheld if the government so desires."[75] They also demoralize the rest of the staff and discourage unsponsored applicants.

The Soviet undermining of the Secretariat is particularly acute when combined with Moscow's insistence that all its nationals serve only on short, fixed-term contracts. As Jonah has pointed out, this means that program managers are reluctant to accept them and they "are viewed with less trust by their own colleagues."[76]

By now all the major contributors to the U.N. budget tend to regard certain top-level posts as theirs by inheritance, to be passed from one of their nationals to the next. If they cannot inherit a post, they at least feel entitled to trade off a position being vacated for another of equal importance. Among the poorer countries, certain important posts are considered to be inheritable within the region. This practice has recently been commended by the General Assembly at the instance of the Non-Aligned majority,[77] with the ritualistic—but contra-dictory—reaffirmation that "no post should be considered the exclusive pre-serve of any Member State, or group of States."[78]

Third World Countries and the Secretariat

Although for quite different reasons, the burgeoning NAM membership of the United Nations has actively supported the effort to transform the Secretariat from the vision of Drummond to that of Hankey.

The vast majority of the new nations of Africa, Asia, the Caribbean, and the South Pacific came into existence after 1956, when the United Nations Secre-tariat had already completed a decade of basic staffing. The new countries have therefore had to adopt dismantling tactics, a sort of global affirmative action, to secure what they consider a fair share of staff posts. The two most important of these tactics happen to coincide with the vision of the Soviet Union. The new states have insisted on reversing the Charter's prescription for recruitment by emphasizing the importance of geographic distribution over "objective" mea-sures of merit. They have also pressed for a larger proportion of fixed-term contracts as opposed to career appointments. The latter preference reflects the new nations' natural concern that posts not be tied to lifetime appointees at a stage in the Third World's development when they have relatively few eligible candidates and can ill-afford to spare their most competent administrators and technicians for protracted international service.

In the tug-of-war between these states and the West—which prefers to see an international civil service recruited primarily on the principle of merit, and for lifetime careers—the trend since 1960 has gone against the West. This may well have been an inevitable corrective to what had gone before. In 1947, after the first wave of hurried hirings, thirteen nations, nine of them from what are now NATO states, occupied 721 of 902 posts in the professional and higher grades not requiring special language qualifications.[79] This was bound to create trouble, and did. As far back as 1921, at the League of Nations, an Indian delegate had proposed a national quota system to redress the imbalance between Europeans and others in the Secretariat.[80] Although his suggestion was not accepted, the pressures in this direction at the U.N. have become much greater with the passage of time and the creation of a hundred new member states.

In September 1948 Secretary-General Trygve Lie, recognizing that geographic distribution had been badly served, proposed a formula that would permit the establishment of "desirable ranges" for each nationality, the number of posts within the range to be based on each member's assessed contribution to the United Nations budget. He chose this standard because the scale of assessed contributions was, at that time, itself based on a number of relevant variables, the most important being gross national income, but with modifications for population and other factors (see below, Chapter 13); the desirable numbers of posts, once established, were further modified by ceilings and floors. Lie concluded that, since U.N. assessments were fixed in relation to a combination of pertinent criteria, it would be reasonable to use these to establish quotas while permitting flexible upward and downward variations of 25 percent.[81] Finally, he proposed that no country be regarded as overrepresented if the number of its nationals serving in the Secretariat was less than four.

While this was acceptable in 1948,[82] it was not a formula that would satisfy an organization in which a hundred new members, almost all of them assessed at the minimum rate, were soon to demand positions of influence. This was not merely a question of "jobs for the boys." It reflected a shrewd understanding of the subtle interaction between policy making and policy administration. Senior, and even middle level, Secretariat staff do influence the way in which Security Council and General Assembly resolutions are carried out. For example, my unit was requested by the General Assembly to convene a conference of experts on racism and apartheid. In organizing this meeting in Geneva, and in chairing it, I took the position that, while the Assembly and some other U.N. meetings had linked Zionism with racism, it would not be appropriate for this particular meeting to do so, since the Assembly had not specifically made the link in the resolution which mandated this conference. Before the meeting convened, I discussed this rationale informally with key participants, pointing out that we would probably never reach the main questions of racism and apartheid if we tried to deal with the Zionist issue. This was accepted, since few of the experts on South African racial policies at the conference were professionally qualified—or inclined—to discuss the intricacies of the Arab-Israeli dispute. Our agenda was easily adopted. But, an organizer with a different outcome in mind could probably have achieved it.

"Underrepresentation" clearly has wide policy implications, which cannot be ignored. In 1964, five years after the surge of new African states into the U.N., Africans still held only 117 professional staff positions, while Western Europe, with approximately the same population, held 341—almost three times as many.[83]

Secretary-General Hammarskjold had favored a Secretariat composed of 75 percent career staff,[84] a formula endorsed in 1962 by the General Assembly.[85] Even so, he acknowledged the role that fixed-term appointments could play in prompting turnover, which, in turn, could eventually promote better geographical balance as more qualified NAM candidates became available.[86] Under U Thant as Secretary-General the 75/25 proportion of career to contract employment quickly shifted, so that, by 1969, more than 34 percent of the professional staff were on fixed-term contracts.[87] Even the 1975 3-to-2 ratio between career and contract employment will inevitably continue to shift in favor of the latter, as the original intake of career officers, primarily from Western countries, is retired and replaced by persons from the new countries, most of whom can only be spared from national service for a fixed term. After 1970, 80.5 percent of new appointments to professional posts were being made on the basis of fixed-term contracts.[88] This suits the new nations. For different reasons, it suits the Soviets. Unfortunately, it also undermines the credibility of the Secretariat.

The new members have also prevailed in their demand that about one-quarter of places in the professional staff be reserved to raise the minimum number of posts distributed among states solely on the basis of their membership.[89] The merit principle can play only a very diminished role in filling these "reserved" posts. An additional entitlement, based only on population, has further reduced the number of posts in the general pool allocated on the basis of assessed contribution.[90] As more and more particular categories of quota are established, the personal qualifications become increasingly less important than where a candidate is from.

In 1980 the Assembly requested the Secretary-General to calculate new "desirable ranges" utilizing a pool of 3,350 distributable posts, allocating to each member a minimum desirable range based on a midpoint of 7.75 posts, reserving 240 posts for distribution to regions on the basis of population, and assigning all additional posts in future on the basis of 10 percent for population and 45 percent each for membership and for the contribution factor.[91]

Besides altering the bases for determining the desirable ranges of employees from each member, the new members have used their voting majority progressively to amend the guidelines for recruitment. In 1975, in Resolution 3417B(XXX), the Assembly requested the Secretary-General to take all necessary measures to recruit new staff in accordance with the principle of geographic distribution from countries underrepresented or unrepresented in the Secretariat and "in particular from the developing countries." By this terminology, the Assembly has tried to give preference to citizens of underrepresented *developing* countries, over citizens of underrepresented *developed* countries (of which there are a number, most notably Japan). In his recent study, Meron has rightly concluded: "It is clear that despite the ritualistic reaffirmation, from time to time, of the principle of merit, that principle which according to the Charter was to be paramount has been relegated to a secondary position."[92] A recent set of guidelines for recruitment issued by the U.N. Assistant Secretary-General for Personnel Services states that the aim must be to recruit at least two out of every five new professionals from unrepresented or under-represented states, and, in obedience to still another recent resolution of the General Assembly,[93] that two out of five recruits should be women.[94]

While Third World countries have not been as rigorous as the Soviets in establishing procedures that would give them control over the selection of their citizens to fill U.N. posts, they have, instead, for the most part, engaged in vociferous lobbying with the Secretary-General, the director of personnel, and with heads of operating departments, to secure preference for favored candidates. In some instances, this is because diplomats from developing countries may wish to give relatives or cronies an opportunity to spend some potentially beneficial years in New York and in service with the organization. In other instances, a government may be desirous of disposing of inept or troublesome but important persons by interring them in the Secretariat. In many instances, it may simply be an overzealous way of promoting the state's interest by securing an appointment for a well-qualified national.

Whatever the reason, the effect has been profoundly negative. In the words of James Jonah: "Things have gotten to such a dangerous stage that many believe that no position could be obtained within the Secretariat without the application of government pressure."[95] This problem did not suddenly arise in recent years. Commenting on the League of Nations Secretariat, Chester Purves noted the "importunities of delegates . . ." who "try to impose upon the Secretary-General recruits of their own choice, even of their own family" and that they were given to haggling "over details, such as the commencing salaries and promotion of their compatriots."[96]

But in the U.N. things have gotten much worse. The process by which an applicant is appointed now routinely involves his or her country's delegation lobbying other delegations from the region to create an *ad hoc* African, Caribbean, or Latin bloc to exert pressure on the candidate's behalf. The Secretary-General or his subordinates are then faced with an unenunciated but evident threat. To refuse a region's candidate is to jeopardize support in the General Assembly for budgetary items or resolutions necessary to the operations of the department in which the vacancy has arisen. Jonah has also pointed out that regional groups and government are even making recommendations about the promotion, transfer, or assignment of staff members already in the Secretariat.

"It is important that one should dwell a little on the impact on the independence of anyone who secures a position in the Secretariat through such outside interference," he observed. "Unquestionably, it is this practice which has raised the gravest doubts in the minds of many observers, as well as of staff members committed to the international civil service, about the independence and neutrality of the international Secretariat."[97] In fact, the Secretariat has many staffers who, knowing that they do not have the political support necessary for their promotion but also aware that, under staff rules, they cannot be fired, have settled for a career of unproductive vegetation.

While heavy regional pressures tend to be reserved for more senior staff appointments, a sharp-eyed observer can see both the trading of votes in the Fifth (Budgetary) Committee, and the offer and acceptance of voluntary contributions to a U.N. unit, conditioned upon agreement to employ a particular candidate, even at such junior levels as assistant librarian or secretary. This politicization is made easy by the slow progress toward establishing universal examinations for civil service posts.[98] Although the lack of such examinations has been amply deplored by U.N. administrative specialists such as the Joint Inspection Unit[99] and by the Advisory Committee on Administrative and Budgetary Questions,[100] it has proven all but useless to hold meaningful competitive examinations to select a candidate who, because of the Assembly's guidelines and bloc politics, must be a woman agronomist from Burundi.

The staff unions and associations of the U.N. in New York and Geneva, and of U.N.-related institutions in Vienna, Nairobi, Addis Ababa, Santiago, Bangkok, and Beirut have told the General Assembly that its members "have come to believe that a successful career in the United Nations is contingent, above all, on 'contacts,' 'knowing someone,' and having pressure applied on their behalf by members of their national mission to the United Nations." This has become "a source of widespread frustration and disillusionment amongst staff."[101]

Secretary-General Kurt Waldheim, toward the end of his term of office, stated that he was "increasingly concerned at the mounting pressures from all sides to secure jobs, especially at senior levels in the Secretariat." He pleaded with members "to exercise great restraint."[102] Unfortunately, as former U.S. Ambassador Maxwell Finger has pointed out, "Waldheim has not himself stood firmly against [such pressure] in certain important cases where the pressure was heavy."[103] The incumbent, Pérez de Cuéllar, has been demonstrating rather more fortitude from time to time.

Probably no Secretary-General, and certainly no head of department, is likely to have the Masada instinct necessary invariably to resist these sorts of pressures. Since such tactics have apparently become socially acceptable among the majority of members, the only real inhibitor—peer group pressure—is off. The International Civil Service Commission, which was to be the body of independent experts who would serve as watchdogs of standards and procedures, in the opinion of a recent study by a senior U.N. research officer has become politicized, with some members lacking "even . . . a basic notion of what is being discussed." The study concludes that "the experts and neutrals are slowly disappearing" throughout the U.N. system.[104] States, knowing what they are doing to undermine the quality of the Secretariat, assume that such conduct is endemic, and they trust the Secretariat less even as they employ deleterious tactics more.

Oddly, the United States, which early did so much to undermine the independence of the international civil service during the McCarthy era, now is one of the very few countries to distain the unsavory practices by which middle echelon and even lower-level posts are obtained for one's nationals, and by which promotion and retention are gained on their behalf. The U.S. tends to hold aloof, not pushing nearly as much as most, with the result that those posts not specifically "reserved" for the U.S. usually go to others.[105] Although the U.S. pays 25 percent of the U.N.'s budget, its share of professional staff posts has shrunk to 12.6 percent from 14.6 percent a decade earlier, with under-representation being particularly egregious at the important upper-middle policymaking level of Assistant Secretary.[106] As in so many matters pertaining to the U.N., the U.S. appears to be among the few countries remaining in the thrall of the very institutional myths and illusions that earlier it had helped to destroy. Or it may simply have stopped caring enough about the U.N. to bother fighting, on the dangerously false assumption that it does not matter what happens there.

The truth is that it matters a good deal to the U.S. national interest. To defend those interests, American strategists must begin with an accurate assessment of the realities.

The large majority of member states of the U.N. neither understand nor believe in the principle of an independent civil service at any level any more. Certainly, their own governments do not encourage the building of such a service at home. On the contrary, they prefer a lusty mixture of politicization and patronage that produces a bureaucracy serving the interests of the governing political party. This is not a perspective likely to be much influenced by the vision of Sir Eric Drummond.

All this matters a great deal. As Professor Inis Claude has written: "In a very significant sense, the identity of every organization . . . is lodged in its professional staff. Members, stockholders, or citizens may control the organization, but they cannot *be* it; the staff *is* the organization."[107] To the extent that the U.N. is an institution, *more* than the sum total of the nations assembled, *more* than a conference center, it is because of the qualities of the Secretary-General and the Secretariat. If they are able to generate fresh ideas, ascertain facts objectively, mediate tactfully, and administer a truce impartially, they give the U.N. an institutional rationale. If they become a mere aggregation of bureaucrats perceived to be serving the interests of their homelands and careers, then the U.S., too, should fight for its rightful share of positions of influence and back up its more senior members of the Secretariat when they confront colleagues using U.N. machinery to advance the interests of their home governments. This the U.S. now does only rarely and not well.

The portents for preserving the Drummond vision are not good. In 1981, my own department's anonymous survey (see above, this chapter) of diplomats representing their countries at the U.N.—with the Soviets and their satellites abstaining—revealed that 83 percent agreed with the statement that the "independence of the international civil service is increasingly being threatened by political interference"; 69 percent also agreed that "the overall performance of the international civil service had declined substantially in recent years."[108]

These findings are cause for concern but it may be too late to do anything about it. As early as 1971, the U.N.'s investigative Joint Inspection Unit published a critical study of the Secretariat which noted the dissatisfaction of member states and of staff with performance and conditions of employment.[109]

The undeniable deterioration in the Secretariat causes the U.S. to face the same range of choices that ensued from the end of other illusions about the organization: to accept the decline, and adapt the trend to politicization as best it can, to the pursuit of its own narrowly defined national self-interest; to try to live strictly by Charter principles in the hope that others may eventually return to them also; or to leave the organization. This study concludes (see below, Chapter 13) that the U.S. interest would best be served by staying in the U.N., adapting its strategy to the new realities, and fighting to protect its interests. But such an important choice can be made only on the basis of a rigorous evaluation of the circumstances under which the U.S. pursues its interests in respect of other principal components of the U.N. system: the office of the Secretary-General, the Security Council, and the General Assembly.

§ 7 §

The Secretary-General
Invents Himself

Introduction

In the words of Under-Secretary-General Brian Urquhart, "The office of the
secretary-general as a political institution has developed further and more rapidly than other organs of the United Nations."[1]

The other organs have developed little and not well. In the Security Council
the "Big Powers," more often than not, use their Charter-given preeminence to
wage war by other means, blocking collective action while tolerating increasingly high levels of violent state behavior. When the powers do feel a need to
negotiate, they now usually prefer to do it elsewhere than in the Council
chamber (see below, Chapter 9). And in the General Assembly, members of
the Non-Aligned Movement (NAM) regularly disport their numerical preponderance to heighten tensions and hinder dialogue with resolutions that posit
extreme or frivolous goals (see below, Chapters 10 and 11).

The Secretary-General has been more successful, and certainly more con-
structively active, in efforts to resolve conflicts and deter aggression. This role
has been largely self-determined. The Charter does not endow his office with
authority to be a global mediator and troubleshooter, although various incumbents have claimed that these functions are his by implication. (The Preparatory Commission, in its report to the first General Assembly, however, did
foretell the emergence of a mediating function.) Since the other political organs have been largely stymied, his autonomous activism has been justified on
the grounds that an otherwise dangerous void must somehow be filled. That

rationale has been advanced by each of the five Secretaries-General to defend an increasingly visible and active role in international relations.

Precisely because that role is not spelled out by the Charter, it is also not hedged with debilitating limitations and procedural incapacities. In this sense, the Secretary-General has had the freedom to invent himself in the light of the experiences and realities of the postwar world, and has not been hobbled to a bad guess as to what those realities might be. The United States, for the most part, has supported the growth of the office, on the ground that a strong Secretary-General is good for the U.N., and thus for the U.S. This vaguely benevolent assumption about the office of Secretary-General is virtually all that is left of our illusions of 1945. Close scrutiny of it is long overdue.

Design and Invention

The rise of the Secretary-General to a role of considerable eminence, even in the company of heads of important states, is primarily a result of clever incumbents' seizing—sometimes creating—historic opportunities. Even so, the Charter of the U.N., while envisaging nothing so grand as the present office, did point the way. It departs radically from the League of Nations Covenant, elevating and embellishing the role. The Covenant merely provided for the appointment of a Secretary-General and authorized him to recruit the Secretariat.[2] The Charter goes much further, stipulating that the holder of the office may be delegated additional functions by the principal organs of the U.N. system (the General Assembly, the Security Council, the Trusteeship Council, and the Economic and Social Council). It also creates an opportunity for the Secretary-General to influence the organization's agenda and ethos by authorizing him to make an annual report to the General Assembly: a sort of "state of the world" address.[3] In another important innovation, the Charter gives the Secretary-General an independent power to bring "to the attention of the Security Council any matter which in his opinion may threaten the maintenance of international peace and security."[4] Equally significant is the Charter's insistence that the functions of the Secretary-General—like those of the rest of the Secretariat—shall be exercised free from "instructions from any government" and that his "exclusively international" role shall be respected by all members.[5]

The Covenant of the League had in mind a professional civil servant of the British type who operates entirely behind the scenes, serving his political masters, and rarely disclosing views in public. The Charter, by contrast, visualizes a Secretary-General with independent political responsibilities, playing an independent role in defense of the principles and purposes of the Charter. President Roosevelt, as well as other founders—but, certainly, not Marshal Stalin or General de Gaulle—wanted the Secretary-General to be a major and dynamic figure striding the international stage, taking initiatives whenever disputes between states could not be resolved by the disputants themselves.[6]

Intendant of the Charter

It therefore seemed appropriate to choose as the first Secretary-General a bluff, "streetwise" Norwegian politician, labor organizer, and minister, Trygve Lie. It was also inevitable that Lie should take seriously the post's responsibilities and opportunities for growth.

"I am determined," he said, on assuming the office, "that the Secretary-General should be a force for peace."[7] He quickly established both his right to speak out, and his independence, as the voice of "world order." In this he has been followed by each of his successors: Dag Hammarskjold, U Thant, Kurt Waldheim, and Javier Pérez de Cuéllar. These men had varying personal styles—Lie and Hammarskjold were as different as mallet and scalpel—yet they all pursued what they believed to be the mandate of the Charter: to be the *independent* and *active* defender of an international perspective. They pressed hard against this slightly opened door. If none of them saw themselves, exactly, as incipient prime ministers of an emerging world government, that was nevertheless the goal. Maneuvering toward it, they were powered by a sense of global, as opposed to national, self-interest. Since all persons are, in a sense, members of a global as well as a national community of shared interests, the Secretary-General's role was to enunciate the values, concerns, and priorities of that part of our consciousness that acknowledges a higher interdependence. It could not be described as a mean calling.

From this vision it followed that all secretaries-general, although elected by the Security Council and the General Assembly, tended to regard themselves as the executive branch and as co-equals of those bodies. Although each was endowed with different powers and functions, each operated on the basis of authority conferred and protected by the Charter. Article 7 supports that view by listing the Secretariat as a "principal organ"—and articles 97 and 101 make the Secretariat uniquely the Secretary-General's domain.

Rather like prime ministers and presidents, all the secretaries-general also have regarded themselves as holding a sacred trust, not as merely occupying a political office. They have been acutely aware that their conduct in office, the repertory of their practice, would inevitably shape the role. If, for the most part, they could proceed at no more than a snail's pace, then, like a snail, they were at least determined to leave an indelible, shiny trace to mark their progress and guide successors. And they have been determined to pass on to those successors a secretary-generalship enhanced, if possible, but certainly not diminished, in stature and power. Each incumbent has tried to enunciate his record and spell out the historical implications of his more important initiatives, in part to lay a firm foundation for the next master-builder.

While Trygve Lie was little given to thinking, let alone speaking, in terms of political theory and institutional philosophy—staples of Dag Hammarskjold's intellectual diet—he took care to emphasize the essential duality in his unique role: to carry out the lines of policy "laid down in the Charter and determined by decisions of the different relevant organs of the United Nations."[8] The conjunctive "and" in that sentence serves to differentiate two crucially different roles: first, as intendant of the Charter's rules and principles; second, as servant of the organization's members as represented in the U.N. bodies. Each of these roles proceeds from a different base of authority, and the two may not always be completely reconcilable. While each is important, the first has taken precedence in situations of unavoidable conflict.

This view of his office as guardian of the Charter and servant of the other organs immediately became controversial in the context of the Cold War. In 1948, Lie reformulated his understanding of the duality of his role in the gathering context of East-West hostility. "As Secretary-General of the United Nations," he wrote, "I am responsible to the collectivity of the Member States. It is not my business as Secretary-General to assess the rights or the wrongs" in a conflict between members. "The collective judgment of world public opinion can be trusted to do that. But it is my recognized duty to speak for the organization—which includes everybody—when I believe the United Nations to be in danger."[9]

This is a distinction not easy to carry into practice. Speaking for the organization is no simple matter when members, as has happened some 200 times in its forty-year history, are in some stage of war with each other. Trygve Lie, himself, soon became *persona non grata* to the Russians when he publicly championed the collective defense of South Korea against the communist invaders. On the election of his successor, Lie wanly welcomed Dag Hammarskjold to "the most impossible job on this earth."[10]

The new Secretary-General came from a Scandinavian civil service tradition close to the British model. He promised to work quietly behind the scenes, "to assist, so to say from the inside, those who take the decisions which frame history." He would "listen, analyze, and learn to understand fully the forces at work and the interests at stake so that he will be able to give the right advice when the situation calls for it."[11] He would be a "catalyst," even "perhaps an inspirer,"[12] but always off the podium, out of the limelight. Sir Eric Drummond redux.

For a time this low profile seemed to work. Journalists summed up Hammarskjold as "the most charming oyster in the world."[13] In his book *Markings* the Secretary-General spoke of his aspiration for "transparency." By autumn 1957, however, Hammarskjold was telling the Assembly that, while his office should ordinarily be guided by the resolutions of the principal political organs, "I believe that it is in keeping with the philosophy of the Charter that the Secretary-General should be expected to act also without such guidance, should this appear to him necessary in order to help in filling any vacuum that may appear in the systems which the Charter and traditional diplomacy provide for the safeguarding of peace and security."[14] This vacuum theory was to become the office's philosophical linchpin.

By the time he embarked on his second term, Hammarskjold was seeing himself as the "spokesman" for "international order and international conscience." He felt that this role would lift him "above the conflicts that divided the Organization,"[15] but of course it did exactly the opposite, as in the case of his predecessor. He became involved in divisive embroglios and was declared *persona non grata* by the Soviet Union.

While U Thant did not share Hammarskjold's proclivity to theorize about his office, he, too, began with professions of great modesty, but rapidly adopted the same expansive attitude towards his role. Before allowing his name to be considered for a second term, he said: "I do not subscribe to the view that the Secretary-General should be just a chief administrative officer . . . a glorified clerk."[16] As the Vietnam War continued to escalate, he became increasingly active in peace initiatives of his own. These got him into considerable difficulty with Washington, although he suffered nothing comparable to Lie's and Hammarskjold's excoriations by Moscow.

"Two simple considerations are inescapable," Thant said;

> First, the Secretary-General must always be prepared to take an initiative, no matter what the consequences to him or his office may be, if he sincerely believes that it might mean the difference between peace and war. In such a situation the personal prestige of a Secretary-General—and even the position of his office—must be considered to be expendable. The second cardinal consideration must be the maintenance of the Secretary-General's independent position, which alone can give him the freedom to act, without fear or favour in the interests of world peace.[17]

Thant also identified more candidly than any of his predecessors the beacon toward which he was steering: "the United Nations must ultimately develop in the same way as sovereign States have done, and . . . if it is to have a future, it must eventually assume some of the attributes of a State. It must have the right, the power and the means to keep the peace."[18] To this end, he developed the office's role as a podium. He used it with growing intensity to address the peoples of the world over the heads of their governments. In the words of one observer, "in the context of public pronouncements and attitude formation, Thant has gone further than either Lie or Hammarskjold, and of course beyond the wildest dreams of the three League Secretaries-General."[19]

Kurt Waldheim began his term with the ritualistic promise of circumspection. When a Secretary-General is summoned to intervene in a problem, he said, it is "wise to refrain from making too many public statements. These can be easily distorted, sometimes intentionally, and only complicate matters."

Moreover, a Secretary-General should only be involved in disputes at the request of the parties or of the political organs. He "stands a chance only if [he] is wanted" and should never "force himself upon a situation."[20]

Yet, before long, Waldheim begin to assert a right to intervene on his own initiative "especially when massive loss of life and human misery" might otherwise result from a dispute.[21] During the crises in Bangladesh and Kampuchea he asserted an independent authority to act "whenever and wherever large-scale military conflict or civil strife within a State results in massive killings of innocent civilians." In such disasters, he claimed, "unwritten moral responsibility which every Secretary-General bears does not allow him to turn a blind eye when innocent civilian lives are placed in jeopardy on a large scale."[22]

In respect of gross human-rights violations Waldheim took a similar view of his prerogatives. He recognized the tension between the Charter's (article 2, section 7) prohibition of interference in the internal affairs of states, and the moral principles—especially those concerning the sacredness of human life—embodied in the Charter. This conflict, he said, must be resolved in favor of the Secretary-General's right to intervene whenever the problem reaches the threshold of world conscience. Efforts "to alleviate particular problems of human rights by various means . . . are a major and continuous task of the Secretary-General and his staff"[23] and are not limited to relieving the plight of individuals. He claimed the Secretary-General could also "undertake contacts with Governments with a view to discussing the human rights situations in their respective countries" in general,[24] and asserted this right with respect to Vietnamese boat people, Ethiopian and Chilean political prisoners, and others. For this purpose he sent Under-Secretary-General Davidson Nicol to Addis Ababa and (American) Under-Secretary Bradford Morse to Santiago.

Such activism still has its price. Waldheim, accepting his second term, echoed Trygve Lie in declaring that his post "is at the same time one of the most fascinating and one of the most frustrating jobs in the world, encompassing, as it does, the height of human aspiration and the depths of human frailty."[25] That he suffered less than his predecessors for his independence and activism is due not to greater reticence but to the climate of East-West *détente* which prevailed during much of his tenure, to some degree sparing him the necessity of making fatal choices.

Finding a Voice

As a first step in the evolution of the office from one modeled on the role of the British civil servant to one inhabited by the first global statesman, the Secretary-General found a voice with which to speak his own independent views: to delegates, to their governments, and—over the heads of governments—to the peoples of the world.

The Charter specifies only two occasions for exercising the Secretary-General's lyric function. Article 99 permits him to summon the Security Council when peace is in danger, while article 98 authorizes him to report annually to the Assembly. In forty years of practice, however, Secretaries-General have invented a far broader range of options for influencing the political organs, and for setting the global agenda.[26]

At the very first opportunity, during the 1946 Azerbaijan crisis (see above, Chapter 2), Trygve Lie began to intervene in the debates of the Security Council. He sided with the Soviets on several matters, causing Washington to question his right to speak. Lie argued that article 99 of the Charter, by giving him the right to convene the Council, by implication also gave him the right to speak and participate in its meetings, even when not convened by him.[27] "Article 99 is an atomic bomb, . . ." he said. "Why can't I use the smaller rifles?"[28]

The incident made necessary a clarification of the Council's rules of procedure, and it decided to study the matter. The Soviets, grateful for Lie's help, urged the widest possible latitude for the Secretary-General. A rule was drafted which gave him virtually unlimited authority to intercede in the Council's debates.[29] Concurrently, the General Assembly also altered its rules to give him equally broad rights.[30]

When North Korea struck at South Korea in June 1950, the Council was convened at the initiative of the U.S., but Lie asked to speak first. He said that it was "plain that military actions have been undertaken by North Korean forces" and reminded delegates of the "clear duty of the Security Council to take steps necessary to reestablish peace."[31] To support his account of events, he gave the Council fresh information supplied by the U.N. commission stationed in Seoul.[32] Lie's forceful intervention did much to galvanize the Council to adopt the U.N.'s first collective security action (see above, Chapter 2).

After the outbreak of war in the Middle East in 1956, Hammarskjold played an even more catalytic role in getting the U.N. moving. Having heard of the attack over the radio at 9:00 p.m., he immediately contacted the U.S. Mission to prod it into action and offered to convene the Council himself if they did not.[33] The reason for his concern is illustrative of the global perspective. In the Secretary-General's opinion, had the U.S. (or failing that, he himself) not acted immediately, the Council would have been convened by the Soviets, thereby automatically making the issue into an East-West confrontation.[34] When the Council met, he began the debate by laying out the issues of fact and principle. Because he could cite fresh information from General Burns, the commander of the United Nations Truce Supervision Organization (UNTSO) serving on Israel's borders, Hammarskjold was in a position to dispel any doubt as to which party (i.e. Israel) had initiated the hostilities.[35] He even threatened to resign unless "those organs which are charged with the task of upholding the Charter . . . fulfill their task."[36]

When the British and French vetoes stymied the Council, Hammarskjold repeated his forthright call to action in front of the first emergency special session of the General Assembly a few hours later. As one observer has noted: "On the one hand, Hammarskjold was preparing the ground for a strong personal role in the response to the situation; on the other hand, he was warning the members of the United Nations that he would not be content— and might well resign—if he did not have such a role."[37] Certainly he exercised to the fullest his lyrical function, making himself the fulcrum upon which the other actors and ideas were balanced. The gamble paid off, with the General Assembly giving the Secretary-General almost complete discretion to create the first truly international peacekeeping militia.

Hammarskjold played a similarly initiatory role during the early stages of the civil war in Laos. After a visit in 1959 to the capital, Vientiane, he wrote U.S. Secretary of State Christian Herter that he "would be quite willing to play the United Nations card" by which he meant "assuming a personal role in the field."[38] The offer was not taken up; so, when the situation deteriorated and the Laotian government contacted Hammarskjold to request the dispatch of a U.N. peacekeeping force, he asked Egidio Ortona, the Italian president of the Security Council, to convene that body to allow him to make a report.[39] The Secretary-General felt that he could not use article 99, which requires him to allege a threat to international peace and security, "without grossly over-dramatizing and prejudging the situation in Laos."[40] Instead, when the Council convened, it had before it a proposed agenda item entitled "Report by the Secretary-General on the letter received from the Minister for Foreign Affairs of the Royal Government of Laos," which laid out options for Council action. Although the Soviet representatives commented on his "suspicious zeal" and "exaggerated efficiency," they refrained from making an issue of it.[41]

In 1960, at the beginning of the Congo crisis, Hammarskjold finally did invoke article 99. Belgium gave the Congo its independence on July 1, and by July 5 the new nation's black army was in revolt against its white officers. With mutiny and chaos spreading, the Belgian airborne troops still stationed at Kamina began to intervene, claiming they were protecting the white population. Ralph Bunche, who had been representing the Secretary-General at the independence celebrations, attended a hurried meeting of the Congolese cabinet on the afternoon of July 10 and there learned that the new government urgently wanted help from the U.N. He explained what sort of assistance might reasonably be expected and helped the cabinet formulate a request for "technical assistance of a military nature . . . for the twin purposes of national defense and the maintenance of law and order."[42] (This wording was eventually changed to "technical assistance in the field of security administration" at Hammarskjold's suggestion.[43])

Meanwhile the government, in panic, simultaneously approached Washington and President Kwame Nkrumah of Ghana for bilateral military help. Hammarskjold, hearing of this, was horrified. He called Secretary of State Christian Herter to head off any direct involvement by the U.S. and, remarkably, won his promise to act only through U.N. channels. On July 13 Hammarskjold invited the members of the Security Council to lunch. Here he proposed three forms of U.N. action: technical assistance to reconstitute the Congolese forces, the introduction of U.N. troops to take over responsibility for law and order from the Belgian forces, and the shipment of emergency food supplies. Having no instructions from their respective countries, no member of the Council opposed these suggestions. At 8:30 that night, Hammarskjold convened the Security Council under article 99.

When the Council met that evening the Secretary-General made the opening statement. He proposed that the Council authorize him to form a peacekeeping force based on the same principles he had applied during the Suez crisis in 1956. By prearrangement, his suggestions were already incorporated in a resolution produced by Ambassador Mongi Slim of Tunisia, one of Hammarskjold's closest confidants.[44] It passed by a vote of 8 to 0, with three abstentions (China, France, and Great Britain) at 3:25 a.m. on July 14.[45] Had the resolution been vetoed by the Soviet Union, Hammarskjold was prepared to introduce a simplified version of his own.

Of this episode it is fair to say that the Secretary-General essentially wrote the Congolese request, conceived the U.N. response, convened the Council, prompted the resolution by which he was empowered to act, and helped to ensure its adoption. It was the high point of Hammarskjold's—and perhaps any Secretary-General's—powers of initiation.

Subsequent incumbents have chosen to use rather more modestly these broad powers to convene the Security Council and galvanize it into action. U Thant felt himself inhibited from taking the Vietnam War to the Council because the Soviets (and, at first, the U.S.) were opposed and, also, because neither Peking nor Hanoi was represented in the U.N. nor willing to use it as a vehicle for negotiations. Nevertheless, as part of his price for reluctantly accepting a second term, Thant cajoled the Council into stating the members' consensus that they "fully respect his position and his action in bringing basic issues confronting the Organization and disturbing developments in many parts of the world to their notice . . . to which they [will] accord their closest attention."[46]

In 1972 Thant's successor, Secretary-General Kurt Waldheim, took the lead in calling on the General Assembly to examine the question of terrorism and "take appropriate measures to prevent any future acts of violence against innocent people." That problem, he said, was becoming "extraordinarily serious and worrying . . . . It is our duty to act."[47]

During the Cyprus crisis that followed the overthrow of President Makarios on July 15, 1974, Waldheim convened the Council using article 99. At his urging, that body strengthened and reiterated the role of the U.N. peacekeeping force (which the Council had established in 1964 and which continues to this day) and authorized the Secretary-General to try his hand at mediating the dispute between Greek and Turkish Cypriots.[48]

Similarly, on November 25, 1979, the Secretary-General, in a message to the president of the Council, pointed to "the grave situation which has arisen in relations between the United States and Iran" as a result of "the detention of [U.S.] diplomatic personnel, in violation of the relevant international conventions"—a situation that "could have disastrous consequences for the entire world." Building on the Laos precedent, he asked that the Council be convened, not explicitly under article 99 but, rather, "in exercise of my responsibility under the Charter of the United Nations . . . to seek a peaceful solution of the problem in conformity with the principles of justice and international law."[49] When the Council met, it was presented with a resolution which the Secretary-General had co-authored and which called on him to exercise his "good offices"[50] to negotiate a peaceful solution to the crisis.

There are many other ways in which Secretaries-General have learned to speak to the members, trying to influence them to act in accordance with his global perspective. One, which is of particularly subtle utility, is to have his principal legal adviser issue a "legal opinion." This practice was initiated in 1946 by Trygve Lie during the dispute over the prolonged Soviet military presence in Iran.[51] At a certain point in the evolution of that dispute, both Iran and the U.S.S.R. were willing to drop the item from the Security Council's agenda whereas the U.S. was not. The Secretary-General, on his own initiative, presented the Council with a memorandum which, essentially, said that an item could not be kept inscribed unless the Council planned to take some form of action.[52]

In January 1950 Trygve Lie released another legal opinion—prepared by his American legal aide, Abraham Feller, and Dr. Ivan Kerno, a Czech—which stated that when more than one delegation purports to represent the government of a member state, the affected U.N. organs should determine which of the contenders is "in a position to employ the resources and direct the people of the State in fulfillment of the obligations of membership."[53] Its effect was to favor the seating of the Chinese communist delegation.

Later the same year, Lie again expressed a legal opinion, this one drafted by his advisors Abraham Feller and Andrew Cordier. It informed the Security Council that, as a matter of Charter interpretation, the North Korean attack on the South must be construed as "a threat to international peace" and that the Security Council was "the competent organ to deal with it."[54] On September 30, working with Feller and Cordier, Lie issued a legal paper suggesting "terms of settlement of the Korean question" which purported to be based on objectives to be found in the Charter, international law, and past resolutions of the Assembly and Council. These called for a cease-fire on the former boundary between North and South, demilitarization, and free elections throughout Korea under U.N. auspices[55]—objectives considerably more modest than those of Washington.[56]

In 1954, when Washington-backed forces were overthrowing the leftist government of Guatemala, Secretary-General Hammarskjold issued a legal opinion that implicitly rejected the U.S. tactic for preventing Guatemala's complaint being considered by the Security Council (see above, Chapter 4). Examining the "relative jurisdictions of the UN and regional organizations, . . ." the opinion found no basis in law or practice for the proposition that Guatemala must first seek a remedy within the Organization of American States before coming to the U.N. It caused "an uproar in [the] State Department."[57]

The practice of Secretaries-General' intervening in the activities of political organs by injecting legal opinions continues to the present. Some—U Thant and Kurt Waldheim in particular—have preferred to suggest to "friendly" members of various organs that they take the lead in requesting such an advisory opinion. In 1970, acting on such a request by Norway's Edvard Hambro—then president of the General Assembly—Constantin Stavropoulos, the legal counsel, opposed as unlawful an effort in the Assembly to reject the credentials of the South African delegation. Where there is no rival claimant for a country's seat, he argued, such a move would have the effect of denying it the rights and privileges of membership in violation of the procedures established by article 5 of the Charter,[58] which permits suspension only by action of both the Council and the Assembly.

In December 1982 the Secretary-General, learning that he was about to be instructed in an upcoming vote, by a resolution of the General Assembly "to guarantee the safety and security and legal and human rights of the Palestinian refugees,"[59] sent his legal counsel to warn delegates that the U.N. could not lawfully attempt to carry out "sovereign powers" in lands under the control of a state without that country's consent.[60] In this the Secretary-General was seeking to influence delegates about to vote on a matter affecting his role. Over the years, he has become a major independent force in the "legislative" process of the political organs. It has become common practice for him to seek out and consult delegations about proposed courses of action. He is widely regarded as a useful ally by delegates—primarily, but not exclusively, those from small and middle-sized states—when they seek to build a coalition in support of a course of action.

Reciprocally, the Secretary-General has frequently taken the lead in nudging delegates to propose initiatives that support objectives that seemed to him warranted by events. After the invasion of South Korea, Trygve Lie personally drafted the Security Council's second Korean resolution, which gave the U.S. command of the U.N. force.[61] Dag Hammarskjold, with Sweden's ambassador Gunnar Jarring,[62] wrote the resolution of July 5, 1958, which directed the Secretary-General to send an Observation Group to Lebanon to inhibit "illegal infiltration of personnel, arms or other matériel across [its] borders."[63] A month later, as the third emergency session of the General Assembly met to consider the continuing crisis in Lebanon and Jordan, Hammarskjold greeted them with a program of "basic needs for action,"[64] which listed his proposals for ending the impasse. The Assembly then obediently adjourned until August 13, to allow Hammarskjold time to pursue private consultations with Secretary of State Dulles and foreign ministers Gromyko of the U.S.S.R., Lloyd of Britain, Fawzi of Egypt, and Engen of Norway. After progress had been made in these talks, the Secretary-General joined with Hans Engen in drafting the resolution, which noted the willingness of Britain and the United States to withdraw their forces from Lebanon and Jordan, and delegated broad discretion to the Secretary-General to make such practical arrangements as necessary to help give effect to this agreed solution. (Actually, Engen and Hammarskjold drafted the resolution over dinner on Sunday, August 17, before going off to see a play. On the way, they lost their only copy in a taxi and later had to reproduce it from memory.)[65]

The drafting role is often accompanied by what, in other places, would be called lobbying. Speaking of the plan for the partition of Palestine before the General Assembly, Trygve Lie has written that "when approached by the delegations for advice, [I] frankly recommended that they follow the [partition] plan."[66] Evan Luard reports that, even without waiting to be approached, Lie "strongly advised delegates" to back partition and personally advocated the use of an international force to impose it.[67] He also publicly supported the United States when it introduced the "Uniting for Peace" procedure (see, above, Chapter 2), having had a hand in inventing it. In private discussions with delegates the Secretary-General argued vigorously in support of the resolution's utility and legality.[68]

Hammarskjold was a masterful lobbyist. When Ambassador Engen's draft of the Lebanon-Jordan resolution encountered some resistance from the Afro-Asian members of the Assembly, the Secretary-General persuaded the Arab members to meet separately to evolve their own formula to put before the Assembly, and offered to be of help. The next day, on August 21, Foreign Minister Mohamed A. Mahgoub of the Sudan introduced what became known as the "Good Neighbor Resolution" which, despite its new auspices, contained virtually all of the provisions of the Engen-Hammarskjold draft. It was adopted unanimously.[69]

As we have seen, Hammarskjold worked effectively to ensure a properly balanced majority in favor of the Security Council's resolution giving him a virtually free hand in designing the Congo peacekeeping operation.[70] Less than a month later the Security Council passed a resolution proposed by Tunisia and Ceylon but essentially designed and pushed by Hammarskjold, which broadened his mandate and gave him the authority to send U.N. forces into the rebellious province of Katanga.[71]

U Thant, too, engaged in drafting and lobbying. After he and Ralph Bunche concluded intense negotiations with the Indians and Pakistanis, Thant devised the resolution of November 5, 1965, in which the Security Council called on the antagonists to cease fighting and to work out a plan for troop disengagement with the Secretary-General.[72] Secretary-General Waldheim, in addition to proposing and promoting Assembly resolutions on international terrorism, also campaigned actively for Assembly-sponsored agreements to curb the taking of hostages and aerial hijacking.[73]

Occasional rebuffs have not significantly diminished this now-well-established prerogative. While the Secretary-General cannot constantly be telling the political organs what to do, nevertheless, he has a remarkable hoard of political capital on which to draw when the circumstances seem propitious. Such capital can be used to promote adoption of a solution he proposes or to block one he regards as counterproductive. For example, before the opening of the 1983 International Conference on the Question of Palestine in Geneva, Pérez de Cuéllar let it be known privately—but widely—that he could not accept any final declaration that called for establishing a new U.N. agency to work on the problem or for the expulsion of Israel from the organization. Though both options had their advocates, the Secretary-General's wishes carried the day.

It is generally accepted today that the Secretary-General may act as an occasional initiator of United Nations action through his power to convene the Security Council, to set agendas, and to participate in Council and Assembly debates and in the drafting and passing—or rejecting—of resolutions.

The "Bully Pulpit"

Theodore Roosevelt called the presidency of the United States a "bully pulpit." Each Secretary-General, in his own way, has seen his office in somewhat the same way. With considerable prestige and visibility at their disposal, incumbents enjoy the opportunity to influence the way governments and peoples think and act, often by going over the heads of delegates to address constituencies directly.

This practice began in the summer of 1950, when Trygve Lie, armed with a "twenty-year U.N. peace programme," traveled to London, Washington, Paris, and Moscow, obtaining maximum publicity for proposals on atomic energy control, disarmament, a standing peacekeeping force, technical assistance for poor nations, human rights, decolonization, and the development of international law. He advocated bringing excluded states into the organization, advanced ideas for limiting the veto, and urged the holding of periodic Security Council meetings at the heads of government and foreign minister levels.

Some of these ideas were impractical and others were old. None was implemented as a result of Lie's tour, which was widely seen by national leaders and the media as "not a very well-judged initiative."[74] But it did provide an early, dramatic precedent for Secretaries-General to express their own political views and propose far-reaching changes in the global system, even when these are at variance with the views of important member states.

This aspect of the Secretary-General's "lyrical function" has become of increasing importance. At a time when the global system appears to be sliding into serious disorder and its political organs lack all will and courage to take remedial action, the Secretary-General, at least, can try to awaken the peoples and the nations to their plight, emphasizing the growing evidence, to quote the poet W. B. Yeats, that "the centre will not hold" in an increasingly centrifugal world.

Dag Hammarskjold used the "bully pulpit" primarily to defend the independence, impartiality, and activism of his office and of the civil service. When summoning the Council to action during the Suez crisis, and, again, while receiving an honorary degree at Oxford, he used his moments on the world stage to conjure up a vision of something akin to a caretaker administration of technocrats, holding the pass until the nations were ready for global government. The response he got in the West and among some in the Third World was primarily *ad hominem*. He was perceived to incorporate congenial social and political values, and so his radical ideas were damned with faint praise. Only the socialists, who did not embrace his values, objectives, or vision, consistently paid attention to what he was saying, and of course they rejected it completely. They had no intention of permitting the Secretary-General to initiate a global strategy of preventive diplomacy[75] that would make him the arbiter of state conduct.

In most situations, Hammarskjold much preferred "quiet diplomacy" to the "pulpit": "private talk, where you can retreat without any risk of losing face and where you can test out ideas, it being understood as only a testing out of ideas and not a putting forward of proposals."[76] Nevertheless, what he left behind in actions, speeches, reports, and a slender *pensée*, is a legacy that continues to exert significant influence. The "bully pulpit" was not a place he relished, but he used it to extraordinary effect.

By far the most extensive use of the "bully pulpit" was made by U Thant, whose natural proclivities differed from those of Hammarskjold. A journalist and educator by training, who had come to diplomacy in midlife, Thant was not so devoted to "quiet diplomacy" and found it relatively easy to operate in the limelight. This may have been a strategy born of necessity, for the Vietnam War made quiet diplomacy a forlorn hope for the Secretary-General of an organization that had no part to play in resolving that conflict. From 1965 on, Thant appears to have decided to spend more and more of his time in the "bully pulpit," using it, increasingly, to hector the U.S. for its role in the war.

U Thant's concept of independence, like Hammarskjold's, was based on a belief in his office's neutrality. For U Thant, however, neutrality became synonymous with neutralism, and alignment with the non-aligned became an explicit article of faith. He was, as he kept explaining, a man of the Third World. And it was the nations of the Third World that saved his office from the Soviet effort to impose the debilitating concept of a troika. In his acceptance speech, Thant, who had been the Burmese ambassador to the U.N., said: "Most of my colleagues present in this hall know me personally. They know that I come from a relatively small country in Asia. They also know that my country has steadfastly pursued over the years a policy of non-alignment, and friendship for all other nations, whatever their ideologies. In my new role I shall continue to maintain this attitude of objectivity, and to pursue the ideal of universal friendship."[77]

What is one to make of this unwitting paradox? The distinction between "non-alignment" and "alignment with the non-aligned" is difficult to conceptualize but of great practical consequence in carrying out the functions of Secretary-General. In Washington, U Thant was eventually written off as hopelessly committed to a bloc of states with interests frequently inimical to those of the U.S. His commitment became particularly evident from 1965 on, when the Third World's numerical majority became an instrument for achieving a long list of important political and, especially, economic objectives that were determined by those nations' collective self-interest, and non-alignment ceased to be merely a midpoint equidistant between the positions of the East and West.

His successor, Kurt Waldheim, sought to retrench, somewhat as U Thant had first set out to do after Hammarskjold's bitter conflict with the Soviets. Waldheim, like Hammarskjold, strongly preferred quiet diplomacy[78] and was a mediocre communicator. Even so, he learned to use the "bully pulpit" for a sort of universal "consciousness raising." Despite a propensity for working behind the scenes,[79] he sought the "global and national recognition"[80] of problems as an essential first step toward their solution.

Like Trygve Lie, Waldheim did not hesitate to propose good, but premature, ideas as a shock treatment administered to the disoriented global *Gestalt*. He thought the U.N. should send its own ambassadors to member states rather than merely receive envoys from them. It was an idea only Canada thought acceptable. Waldheim insisted that it was "extremely practical."[81]

Much of Waldheim's hortatory capital was expended in public efforts to deal with what he perceived to be the tendency of the organization to inflict serious damage on itself. Tirelessly, he urged the members to concentrate on key issues and stop fragmenting and proliferating their efforts.[82] "Tinkering with the machinery or adding new wings and strange contraptions to the already sufficiently baroque structure is usually only a substitute for action," he lectured delegates. In "the absence of real action" the organization tends to "what I have called institutional escapism—the technique of delaying confrontation with a complex problem by setting up a new international institution to deal with it."[83] He repeatedly protested what he called "institutional inflation"[84] and told

the General Assembly "we have too many gatherings, conferences and sessions
of one sort or another. The result is that fewer and fewer people listen to the
speeches, even among the representatives of Governments, let alone the press
or the public."[85] Along the same lines, he called for a muting of the antagonis-
tic behavior being displayed by representatives of governments in the political
organs because "antagonisms or particular contentious issues" were "dominat-
ing the proceedings of the Organization to the point of jeopardizing long-term
constructive work."[86]

His warnings were increasingly coupled with calls for fiscal restraint. He called
for a "redeployment of resources" and a "rearrangement of priorities" so that
"new activities" would be "financed out of the resources released as a result of the
completion or discontinuation of old activities."[87] This was not popular with the
majority, which contributes virtually nothing to the organization's budget but,
each year, casts its votes for new, and sometimes frivolous, activities.

Beginning with Waldheim, the Secretary-General's pulpit increasingly has
been used to deliver suitably dire jeremiads to an organization heedlessly sliding toward chaos. Waldheim and his successor, Pérez de Cuéllar, have startled
members by openly acknowledging gloom about the U.N. At the very beginning of his first annual report, in 1972, Waldheim noted that "after initial
enthusiasm a great disillusionment set in,"[88] adding that "some of the assump-
tions on which the United Nations was based have proved unfounded" and that
"many of the hopes that were entertained at its birth have been disappointed."
The organization has "proved to be of limited value as an instrument of
collective security."[89] The disappointment, he added, appeared to be most keen
"among some of the founding Members of the Organization."[90] (Waldheim's
and Pérez de Cuéllar's annual reports to the Assembly—the "state of the world"
messages, in effect—were written by Brian Urquhart. Those of U Thant were
written by C. V. Narasimhan, while Dag Hammarskjold invariably wrote his
own.)

Three years later Waldheim returned to this theme, acknowledging "strong
criticism of, or even occasional hostility to, the proceedings of the United
Nations in one or other group of countries." He asked the members to take
note of an ebb tide of falling public expectations and to "be conscious of a
certain feeling of unreality, unjustified though it may be, that many people
experience in viewing our proceedings."[91] At the same time, he cautioned that
impatience does not simplify complex problems and that "there can be no
place for despair, however great the frustration, and, in view of the alternatives,
there can be no excuse for giving up the struggle."[92]

By 1978 Waldheim had become bolder in voicing in public the shortcom-
ings of the organization, in particular its failure "to enforce its decisions. . . .
The practical result has been that some small States no longer turn to the
United Nations as the protector of their sovereign rights."[93] He acknowledged a
lack of confidence in the Security Council's "wisdom, objectivity and capacity

for even-handed and effective action"[94] and noted that the malaise had spread even to the Secretariat. There "is no doubt," he said in 1981, "that . . . the rank and file of the staff is sometimes disillusioned."[95]

Following his predecessor's example, Pérez de Cuéllar began his term by conceding that the U.N. "has been unable to play as effective and decisive a role as the Charter certainly envisaged for it."[96] Warning that the nations "are perilously near to a new international anarchy," he noted that the "process of peaceful settlement of disputes prescribed in the Charter is often brushed aside." Meanwhile, the collective security measures "conceived as a key element of the United Nations system" are "now deemed almost impossible in our divided international community."[97] The Secretary-General admitted to feelings of "deep anxiety at present trends" as the Organization "time after time" is "set aside and rebuffed, for this reason or for that, in situations in which it should, and could, have played an important and constructive role."[98]

Such candor on the part of Secretaries-General—simultaneously refreshing and depressing—is a further manifestation of the office's independence. What Waldheim and Pérez de Cuéllar were telling the world was, quite simply, that states' behavior had fallen to a new level of venality, that they were violating their Charter obligations and thereby endangering human survival. Hammarskjold occasionally, and U Thant frequently, appealed to a populace over the head of its government. But they had tended to take on one, or a few, straying sheep at a time. Waldheim and Pérez de Cuéllar have criticized the member nations collectively, like stern schoolmasters lecturing a disappointing class.

§ 8 §

Filling the Void: Action by the Secretary-General in the Face of Inaction by Everyone Else

The "Black Box"

The Secretary-General has found not only voice but also muscle. He not only proposes action to U.N. organs, member governments, and the global public, he also takes action. This tendency to initiate and implement his own policies has developed, in part through a natural tendency inherent in the executive role to take charge, coupled with the paralysis of the organization's own principal political organs, which have seemed willing to permit power to slip from them to the Secretary-General. In Hammarskjold's day, this acquiescence became known as the "leave it to Dag" syndrome. It might be called the "black box" phenomenon: a term used by scientists to describe a part of a system (the human brain, for example) which is capable of transforming and synthesizing stimuli through a process not fully understood, but which is surmised by comparing input and output.[1]

The office of the Secretary-General has become the black box of the United Nations, into which, for lack of agreement on any particular course of action, the members deposit their most pressing and intractable problems, in the hope that, through the operation of some ineffable but ineluctable process, a solution will emerge. That remedy also has the attraction of allowing members to shift the blame to someone else if anything goes wrong.

These black-box solutions fall into two basic categories. The first charges the Secretary-General to exercise his "good offices": that is, to listen to the parties, search for mutual ground, conciliate, mediate, or even just paper over the differences. Originally conceived as a "mail-box" function, good offices have evolved to the point where they may involve the Secretary-General in designing the forum, procedure, agenda, and outcome of negotiations conducted under his aegis. It may also cause him to seek to enlist states amenable to the parties to a dispute in the task of friendly persuasion. Good offices, however, need not produce an agreed solution. The exercise of good offices, itself, often has a therapeutic effect. All but the most volatile disputes tend to cool down, at least a little, while the Secretary-General is making his rounds.

The second category of the black box—the institution-building mode—takes the form of resolutions charging the Secretary-General to create new peace-making machinery, to separate combatants, to supervise a truce, or to observe the causes and conditions of friction. The Council or Assembly may authorize the machinery, but it is the Secretary-General who is left to design and operate it, usually with little specific guidance. There are, by now, dozens of instances in which the Council and Assembly have resorted to both kinds of black boxes, with successive Secretaries-General welcoming and encouraging recourse to them.

On July 15, 1948, the Security Council passed a resolution which, in effect, authorized the Secretary-General to work out an armistice between Israel and its Arab neighbors. He chose first Count Bernadotte and, after the latter's assassination, Ralph Bunche to represent him. Hurrying back and forth between the Arabs' and the Israelis' hotel rooms on the island of Rhodes, Bunche succeeded in working out a formal armistice agreement which was signed by Israel and Egypt on February 24, 1949. It became the model for similar agreements made by Israel with Lebanon, Jordan, and Syria. Their implementation was entrusted to the United Nations Truce Supervision Organization (UNTSO), while the Israelis and Arabs agreed to work out additional problems through Mixed Armistice Commissions. The effort won Bunche the 1950 Nobel Prize for Peace and launched the good-offices version of the black box into the U.N. repertory.

The black box was soon invoked again. After the end of the Korean War, in July 1953, the Chinese communist government decided to try fifteen captured U.S. airmen on charges of espionage. The U.S. contended that the airmen had engaged only in legitimate combat operations south of the Yalu River, which divides Korea from China. Since Washington did not recognize the Peking regime, its diplomatic options were limited. Several attempts to use friendly intermediaries failed, and the U.S. took the matter to the General Assembly on December 4, 1954. By then, eleven of the fliers, together with two civilians accused of being CIA agents, had already been sentenced to various prison terms ranging from four years to life. But what could the Assembly—a loose confederation of states convening for a few months each year in order to deal with a huge agenda of wants and grievances—do about activities of the Chinese government, whose xenophobia was reinforced by its continued ostracism from that body? Over the opposition of the socialist members, and with seven Afro-Asians abstaining, it passed a resolution on December 10 that condemned the trials as contrary to the prisoner-repatriation provision of the Korean armistice agreement, and that asked the Secretary-General to seek the prisoners' release "by the means most appropriate in his judgment"[2]—a typical invocation of black-box magic.

It was an assignment that a lesser spirit might have turned down. Hammarskjold knew that his predecessor, Trygve Lie, had met with a Peking emissary, General Wu Hsiu-chuan,[3] in an effort to end the Korean War and to "bring the Chinese into amiable contact with the United Nations world."[4] Lie had found his guest totally unresponsive, willing only to discuss U.S. aggression and leaving unceremoniously for the airport in the middle of the talks.

Hammarskjold was anxious to avoid a repetition of that debacle. The Assembly's resolution did not help. He had been consulted during its drafting and urged that it not include any condemnation of Peking, as this would needlessly complicate his assignment.[5] Not only was this advice ignored, but Washington even considered getting someone more reliable—the president of the General Assembly, Eelco van Kleffens of the Netherlands[6]—to talk with Peking.

Once the resolution was passed, Hammarskjold emphasized that it did authorize him to employ "the means most appropriate in his judgment."[7] He had already decided to go to China to see Foreign Minister Chou En-lai, and indicated, in requesting a formal invitation, that "the Secretary-General must, in this case, take on himself a special responsibility." This typical circumlocution, and an absence of any reference to the General Assembly resolution or to its condemnation of Peking, was intended to establish that Hammarskjold was asking to come to China in his capacity as one of the Charter-based organs of the U.N.,[8] and not as an agent of the Assembly. This emphatic differentiation, which became known as the "Peking formula," has become the established practice of Secretaries-General when they seek to distance themselves from the confrontational tone of General Assembly resolutions in an effort to protect their credibility as mediators.

With his advisers, Hammarskjold visited Peking from January 5–11, 1955.[9] He emerged believing that Chou was "the most superior brain" he had so far met in the field of foreign politics.[10] After more contacts through intermediaries, four pilots were released. Peking chose Hammarskjold's fiftieth birthday to announce the release of the eleven remaining captives.[11]

Under-Secretary-General Urquhart reports that "Hammarskjold enormously enjoyed the challenge of the Peking experience. It stimulated in him a new taste and new ideas for using his office and his position to tackle difficult problems."[12] He was uncharacteristically ferocious, with respect to the Peking talks, in not permitting others to share either the task or the limelight. When India's foreign minister Krishna Menon tried to take credit for the release of the four jet pilots, Hammarskjold commented that his interference probably had delayed the release by one or two months. After Sweden's ambassador to Moscow, Rolf Sohlman, took it on himself to visit Peking at a critical juncture, Hammarskjold angrily wrote the head of the Swedish Foreign Office that Sohlman's visit was "an example of political innocence in a state of rare purity."[13] This was not vainglorious defense of ego so much as a determination to see that the credit accrued to the office and reinforced its effectiveness. In this he was not helped by the cult of personality launched by admirers, who credited him with a "labor of Hercules" that demonstrated a "capacity to get positive results even out of the most apparently hopeless situations."[14]

Among delegates the "leave it to Dag" syndrome now became ubiquitous. In the early months of 1956, as tensions in the Middle East escalated, the Security Council asked Hammarskjold to examine the situation and take "any measures" that might reduce tensions.[15] On July 26, after Egypt's President Gamal Nasser nationalized the Suez Canal, the Council quickly yielded its prerogatives to the Secretary-General, who conducted private discussions with the foreign ministers of Britain, France, and Egypt[16] in an effort, unavailing as it turned out, to avoid war.

After the Anglo-French-Israeli invasion of Egypt in October, the black box was again invoked, this time in its institution-building mode. When the emergency special session of the General Assembly met to survey the wreckage, it invited Hammarskjold, on November 4, to submit "within forty-eight hours a plan for the setting up, with the consent of the nations concerned, of an emergency international United Nations Force to secure and supervise the cessation of hostilities."[17] This resolution has been described as "a crucial turning point for the U.N."[18] but was in reality more a triumph for the Secretary-General.

Hammarskjold created a large military force—the United Nations Emergency Force (UNEF)—whose command was under his supervision. The mission of the force was to separate the combatants, supervise their withdrawal to prewar boundaries, and ensure against a resumption of infiltration and other provocative acts. The Charter makes no provision for any such functions, least of all ones authorized by the General Assembly and executed by the Secretary-General. While the father of the resolution, Canada's foreign minister Lester Pearson, had some general notions of what a United Nations peacekeeping force might look like, and although UNTSO already in place in the Middle East provided some further hints, most delegates on November 4 had no idea of what exactly they were voting to establish. Though Hammarskjold asked for, and was given, 48 hours to submit a design, in less than seven hours he reported the basic outline of a structure and a mission.[19] His staff had done most of the groundwork while the delegates were still talking.

Two days later, the Secretary-General was ready with a second and final report on the Emergency Force's structure. It "would be more than an observer corps but in no way a military [occupation] force." It would be of a "temporary nature" and operate under the "authorization" of the Assembly, guided by a small advisory committee of members. Beyond that, "a margin of confidence must be left" to the Secretary-General and the UNEF officers he would appoint.[20] The Assembly enthusiastically agreed.

By November 6, six countries had offered contingents; four days later the first hundred Danes and Norwegians were on their way. After intense negotiations between Hammarskjold and the Egyptian government, UNEF was allowed to enter the war zone on November 14. Arthur Rovine's study reports that this "was a feat of brilliant improvisation, and was so regarded [by] the Assembly."[21] An excellent measure of its success, as we have seen, was that, at this stage, it had the support of both Washington and Moscow.

Success invites replication. Two years later, on July 11, 1958, the Council voted to send an observation group to Lebanon's troubled frontier with Syria. It asked the Secretary-General "to take the necessary steps to that end."[22] Hammarskjold had asked for this blank check.[23] He accepted it with the characteristic observation that the necessary steps had already been taken; the team would leave immediately.[24]

The Council's resolution left it to the Secretary-General to decide on the size, composition, and deployment of the United Nations Observation Group in Lebanon (UNOGIL). It was interpreted by Hammarskjold as also giving him considerable diplomatic leverage, which he used audaciously. He cautioned President Nasser against overplaying his hand, warning that continued infiltration of his agents into Lebanon could erode the consensus that kept UNEF in business.[25] Strong words, those, from an international civil servant to the head of a relatively important member state.

The "black box" continued to be invoked during the incumbency of U Thant. On September 21, 1962, the General Assembly invited Thant to invent a U.N. Temporary Executive Authority (UNTEA) for West New Guinea (see above, Chapter 5).[26] Improvising without guidelines, Thant's aides governed the country for seven months, appointing local councils, writing laws, issuing travel documents, and promoting economic development, public health, and education. The administrators were backed by a multinational contingent of troops and a small airforce.

Next, as violence erupted in Cyprus, the Security Council decided, on March 4, 1964, to authorize UNFICYP (a United Nations Force in Cyprus). Once again composition and size were left to the Secretary-General who was asked to act "in consultation with the governments of Cyprus, Greece, Turkey, and the United Kingdom." He was also given authority to appoint the force commander.[27] Thant quickly put together a contingent of some 7000 soldiers from Austria, Britain, Canada, Finland, Ireland, and Sweden. The Council then asked Thant to "use his best endeavors . . . for the purpose of promoting a peaceful solution and an agreed settlement,"[28] a task which has occupied—and baffled—a succession of two mediators and three Secretaries-General trying to exercise good offices.

With the renewal of hostilities in Kashmir in August 1965, the Council demanded a halt to the fighting and requested the Secretary-General "to exert every possible effort" to obtain a cease-fire.[29] The next morning, Thant left for nine days of talks with Prime Minister Lal Bahadur Shastri of India and President Ayub Khan of Pakistan.[30] At the end of the 1973 Yom Kippur war between Egypt and Israel, the Council empowered Kurt Waldheim to establish the second UNEF to bring about disengagement in the Sinai and, once again, left composition and development to his discretion.[31]

During the 1970s and '80s, in the wars in Cyprus, the Western Sahara, Kampuchea, Namibia, and Afghanistan, as well as in the conflicts between the U.S. and Iran, Iraq and Iran, and Britain and Argentina, Secretaries-General Waldheim and Pérez de Cuéllar have continued to exercise their good offices and to engage in institutional peacemaking on the basis of black box mandates from the political organs. Often, however, the black box has been used only as a last resort, less as an act of faith than of despair. This has led to some unedifying wild goose chases. Responding to the urgings of the Assembly and Council, Waldheim flew to Cyprus in February 1977. So far apart were the warring parties that they could not even agree on whether his plane should land at Lanarca, in the ethnic-Greek sector or at Nicosia airport, which was in the U.N. buffer zone. The Secretary settled that by arriving at one and departing from the other, but this seemed almost to exhaust the parties' capacity for compromise, although they did agree to four guidelines for future negotiations.[32] He continued to try, in negotiations conducted, year after year, in New York, Cyprus, and elsewhere, personally chairing six rounds of talks in two years, all to no avail. The Council's original mandate envisaged negotiations "carried out in a reciprocal spirit of understanding and of moderation,"[33] but that ethos has simply eluded the parties, who have wrangled endlessly from behind the safety of the U.N.'s blue line.[34] By 1981 the Secretary-General's optimistic forecast that "negotiations may now enter a more constructive phase"[35] seemed more quixotic than admirable.

On Being Used

The Cyprus negotiations, and the Secretary-General's role in them, illustrate a problem that has grown out of the black-box phenomenon. As Secretaries-General have engaged in more, and more successful, mediations, their hoard of effectiveness has increased, which, in turn, has increased the demand for their services. This cycle can invoke Parkinson's law, as the Secretary-General's role expands beyond its functionally optimal limits. "Optimal" in this context should be defined qualitatively, not quantitatively. The Secretary-General's hoard of effectiveness grows not in accordance with the number of difficult issues he is called up to resolve, but by the ratio of success to failure.

It is natural for a Secretary-General to want to be involved in global crisis management. Such involvement gives meaning and visibility to his role and is probably more interesting than fending off delegates who are importuning jobs for cousins. Arguably, the international system does need a credibly neutral expediter and troubleshooter. Unfortunately, incautious deployment of a Secretary-General in this role creates problems both for the office and the system. An early example is the role played by Dag Hammarskjold during the Soviet invasion of Hungary in 1956. Once again, the Assembly turned to the black box, asking the Secretary-General to "investigate the situation," to observe events "directly through representatives," and to determine the needs of the Hungarian people for food, medicine, and supplies.[36] He was asked to do all this at the same time he was supposed to be designing UNEF for deployment to the Mideast. Understandably, Hammarskjold failed to alleviate the political situation in Hungary, and not primarily because it was impossible to undertake both initiatives at the same time, but because of Soviet intransigence.

While the Secretary-General cannot be faulted for failing to overcome Moscow's obduracy, he can be charged with a touch of professional hubris. He seemed incapable of recognizing failure. When he announced that he intended to visit Hungary on December 16–18, he was promptly contradicted by Budapest, which called the proposed visit "unsuitable." Undaunted, he continued to insist through all of November that the door was open, that he could still negotiate some kind of amelioration of the situation by meeting with Soviet and Hungarian authorities.[37] Not until mid-December did he concede that his proposed mission was stillborn, although it had been evident for some time that the Hungarian government had been holding out faint hope solely as a way of deflecting criticism.

Perhaps Secretaries-General must run the risk of being exploited in this fashion, because the office perforce runs on a modicum of optimistic delusion. There is less excuse for the Assembly which, as late as December 12, voted yet again to ask Hammarskjold "to take any initiative that he deems helpful."[38] Under the circumstances, this was less a vote of confidence in the miraculous black box than a deliberate shifting of responsibility for failure. The U.N. is adept at playing by the rule formulated by Snoopy, the tennis-playing dog in *Peanuts:* "It matters not whether you win or lose, it's how you lay the blame."

Another illustration is provided by the resolution in which the Assembly authorized Secretary-General Waldheim to resolve the conflict between Morocco and the Polisario, the National Liberation Movement of the Western Sahara. Morocco (with Mauritania) had occupied the Western Sahara in 1975. The Assembly's 1975 resolution recognized the territory's right to self-determination,[39] but another resolution, passed at the same time as part of a political compromise, implicitly recognized the occupation.[40] In the first of these two contradictory actions, the Assembly asked the Secretary-General "to make the necessary arrangements for the supervision of the act of self-determination."[41] After a futile, and rather perfunctory, effort, Waldheim publicly rejected the hopeless assignment,[42] which was surely the right response. The Secretary-General is not a fire department, obliged to answer every alarm. His first responsibility is to preserve the credibility of his office. That, in turn, depends upon incumbents' having and obeying a keen actuarial instinct for when to hoard, and when to spend, their effectiveness.

Sometimes Waldheim seemed to possess this sense, sometimes not. Also in 1975, the Security Council invited him "to send urgently a special representative to East Timor for the purpose of making an on-the-spot assessment of the existing situation and of establishing contact with all the parties in the Territory and all States concerned" in order to ensure the population's right to self-determination.[43] The task was impossible. The Indonesians were firmly in control of the territory they had seized and had no intention of relinquishing it. Although the special representative made the inquiries, he quickly concluded that there was no opening for negotiations, just another diplomatic quagmire. Refusing to be used to create the illusion of diplomatic activity where there was only obduracy, Waldheim quickly abandoned the effort.[44]

On the other hand, the actuarial instinct seemed to fail him in dealings with the revolutionary government of Iran on behalf of the American diplomats taken hostage.[45] Waldheim had taken the lead in convening the Security Council on November 27, 1979, to deal with the seizure of the U.S. Embassy.[46] From the beginning there were portents of failure. The Iranian delegation demanded, and got, a four-day adjournment for the holy days of Tassua and Ashura then failed to appear when the Council reconvened. Asked by the Council to "take all appropriate measures,"[47] the Secretary-General replied that he would proceed "as expeditiously and effectively as possible."[48] Two and a half weeks later he declared himself ready to send a representative to Teheran.[49] Ill-advisedly, the Council, in deciding to ask Waldheim to use his good offices, concomitantly threatened to use collective economic measures against Iran if it did not bargain with the Secretary-General in good faith.[50] In the vote on that resolution, the two socialist and two Muslim states ominously abstained. At that point, Waldheim probably ought to have treated his mission as aborted. In a rather belated effort to invoke the "Peking formula," he let it be known through a spokesman that his trip would be based on the inherent authority of his office, not on the Security Council's resolution. U.S. Secretary of State Cyrus Vance, however, unhelpfully claimed that the projected visit was a triumph of U.S. diplomacy.[51]

Circumstances in Teheran being what they were, it might have made little difference if Waldheim's visit had been authorized by any power but Allah. A spokesman for the Revolutionary Council in Teheran immediately made it clear that no invitation had been, or would be, issued. Next, Pakistan publicly disowned its representative, Agha Shahi, who had made the initial arrangements for the trip.[52] Then, the day after its passage, two countries that had voted for the Security Council resolution—China and Zambia—announced that they were dissociating themselves from it.[53]

"I do not trust this man," was the Ayatollah Khomeini's welcoming message.[54] As his plane landed, Teheran newspapers featured a year-old photograph of the courtly Austrian kissing the hand of the Shah's sister. During a ceremonial visit to a cemetary for victims of the Shah's brutality, the Secretary-General was forced to flee from a mob that rushed his car. It was an unedifying spectacle, to say the least. After three days, and having failed to see the Ayatollah or anyone else who might have been able to open serious negotiations, Waldheim cut short his visit, vowing to "continue to exert" his "best efforts" to find a solution.[55] The Ayatollah, he referred to as "a spiritual leader of great influence"[56]—a characteristically careful choice of words. "I'm glad to be back," the Secretary-General said on his arrival in New York— "especially alive."[57] If Hammarskjold's visit to Peking was a textbook case of effective good offices, Waldheim's Iranian venture enterprise was useful as a classic bad example.

Waldheim made another unsuccessful effort at good offices in connection with the lengthy war between Iran and Iraq. In 1974, those two nations had agreed to ask the Secretary-General to appoint a special representative, Luis Weckmann-Muñoz, to work out an agreement to end an earlier outbreak of violence.[58] In 1980, as fighting erupted again, the Secretary-General named Olof Palme of Sweden to mediate on his behalf. Palme made several trips to the area, but without notable effect.[59] The mediation has continued, off and on, under Pérez de Cuéllar,[60] who, in May 1983, sent a three-man team headed by the Secretary-General's military adviser, Ghana's Brigadier Timothy K. Dibuama. The three, invited to inspect damage in the two warring countries,[61] filed a report that, on the basis of evidence presented by the two governments, devoted twice as many pages to Iranian as to Iraqi cities.[62] Because the document appeared to bring more balm to the Iranians than to the Iraqis, there were high hopes at U.N. headquarters that it would induce the former to let the Secretary-General begin serious peace negotiations. "It can, but I don't think it necessarily does," commented Iran's ambassador Said Rajaie-Khorassani.[63] Once more, the credibility of the black box had been ill-served by groundless optimism.

Similarly, the General Assembly asked the Secretary-General, in 1979, to exercise his good offices to promote democratic choice in Kampuchea and the withdrawal of the occupying Vietnamese forces.[64] On this hopeless venture, Waldheim visited Hanoi and Bangkok in August of 1980. Meanwhile the situation got worse. Tens of thousands began fleeing across the Kampuchea-Thai border. By September 1981 Waldheim reported to the Assembly that he had been unable "to bridge the gap" and that "real progress" was "yet to be made."[65] Waldheim's successor, Pérez de Cuéllar, also admitted in March 1983 that the Kampuchean mission had "not so far met with success."[66]

The Kampuchean good-offices venture illustrates the decline in the mystique of the black box. It warns of the danger that indiscriminate recourse to the Secretary-General's mediating function could bring that office to the same level of ineffectiveness as prevails in the other principal organs of the U.N.

The problem persists. In its resolution on Afghanistan of January 14, 1980,[67] the Assembly began by deploring the Soviet invasion and then requested the Secretary-General to seek a solution through the exercise of good offices. Later, the Assembly asked that he promote "a political solution in accordance with . . . the preservation of [Afghanistan's] territorial sovereignty [and] political independence."[68]

In pursuit of this mandate, Secretary-General Waldheim met in 1980 with the prime minister of India and the president of Pakistan and with their respective foreign ministers. He held discussions with the foreign minister of Afghanistan as well as with the secretary-general of the Organization of the Islamic Conference.[69] In 1981, he designated Javier Pérez de Cuéllar as his personal representative, thereby inadvertently solving the problem not of Afghanistan but of the impending election of a Secretary-General, albeit not in a fashion to Waldheim's liking. In that year the mediator made two exploratory visits to the area.[70]

In 1982 Pérez de Cuéllar, having succeeded Waldheim as Secretary-General, appointed Under-Secretary-General Diego Cordovez of Ecuador to carry on. Beginning in January, Cordovez visited Kabul and Islamabad, the capital of Pakistan, to which country between two and three million Afghan refugees have fled. He also called on Iran, which housed another million Afghans.[71] From Cordovez and others in the U.N. has come a stream of optimistic prognoses, all unwarranted. Discussions at the end of 1982 had "allowed progress to be made in the definition of the contents" of a "comprehensive settlement"[72] and to plan its "effective implementation."[73] Cordovez next reported agreement in principle on four interrelated elements of such a settlement: the withdrawal of foreign troops, non-interference and non-intervention, guarantees of non-interference and non-intervention, and arrangements for the return of the refugees.[74]

Early in 1983, after Pérez de Cuéllar visited the then-new Soviet leader Yuri V. Andropov,[75] the U.N. buzzed with the expectation that Moscow was now genuinely interested in negotiating a withdrawal through the Secretary's good offices.[76] Andropov was glad to play along, telling the media that "with the help of the United Nations and its Secretary-General, Pérez de Cuéllar, we believe we can achieve success on some reasonable basis."[77]

Further U.N. shuttle diplomacy in April, between Pakistan and Afghanistan, led to euphoric U.N. reports that "a comprehensive settlement" had been all but initialed. It would commit the Soviet Union to step-by-step withdrawal, but would also require Pakistan to stop all support, including weapons trans-shipments, to the Afghan resistance movement. The agreement would some-how guarantee that Afghanistan would have a government "friendly" to the Soviet Union, and permit Moscow to retain military advisers in Kabul. The Afghan regime would be "free" to "invite" Soviet forces back in the event of a "military emergency" in Iran or Afghanistan itself.[78]

Those reports proved, at the least, premature. Afghan insurgents, who had never been consulted by the U.N., condemned the "sell out" and charged that the "Soviet Union encourages the impression that a negotiated settlement is in the offing. Such an impression tends to neutralize worldwide criticism of its involvement in Afghanistan. The Russians are buying time on the assumption that they can crush the Afghan resistance."[79]

In the third week of June, an undaunted Diego Cordovez conducted another seven days of talks with high-level Pakistanis and Afghans. Although there was no progress, the Under-Secretary insisted that the momentum toward a peace-ful settlement was continuing.[80] His optimism, admirable as it might have been, raised the question whether, in the Secretary-General's eagerness to be the instrument for a peaceful settlement, his good offices might not have become more used than useful.

Self-authorized Crisis-Ministry

As we have seen, each Secretary-General in succession has devised for himself the role of global mediator. Despite its occasional misuse, the role remains useful when a dispute threatens to disrupt peaceful relations among states and, in particular, when a disagreement seems about to escalate into confrontation between the superpowers.

The function of world mediator and fact-finder has become so important a part of the office that every incumbent has given it top priority. Whenever possible, each has sought to have the role bestowed on him by one of the U.N.'s political organs. When that was not practicable, the Secretary-General usually has taken the precaution of securing an invitation from the parties to a dispute. But on several notable occasions he has become involved without leave from anyone. In those instances the Secretary-General has asserted a general right and duty to act as the organization's guardian of Charter princi-ples. Sometimes he has gotten away with it, other times not. Whatever the substantive results, however, it is by now clearly established that, on its own authority, the office may assume both the role of fact-finder and mediator. Hammarskjold claimed that right in his Oxford speech, which argued that article 99 of the Charter, by implication, gives the Secretary-General "a broad discretion to conduct inquiries and to engage in informed diplomatic activity in regard to matters which 'may threaten international peace and security.' "[81] Subsequent practice has confirmed that claim, even though as Hammarskjold admitted to biographer Joseph Lash, "the founding fathers would be extremely surprised" at how article 99 "had developed chapter and verse."[82]

As early as September 1946, when the Security Council was considering whether to send a commission of inquiry to investigate alleged infiltration across Greece's northern frontier, Trygve Lie announced that his office claimed an independent power of investigation separate from that of the Council: "Just a few words to make clear my own position as Secretary-General, . . . I hope that the Council will understand that the Secretary-General must reserve his right to make such enquiries or investigations as he may think necessary, in order to determine whether or not he should consider bringing any aspect of this matter up to the attention of the Council under the provisions of the Charter."[83] On that occasion, he prudently claimed the right without actually exercising it.

In October 1948, as the Berlin crisis deepened and the Security Council remained deadlocked, Lie again stepped forward with his own detailed solution, based on the introduction of Soviet zone currency into West Berlin simultaneously with the lifting of the blockade.[84] When this was rejected by Washington, he offered to have his Assistant Secretary-General, Russian Arkady Sobolev, and his legal counsel, American Abraham Feller, mediate directly with Moscow and Washington. If agreement on general principles could be reached, he offered to have the Secretariat draft the detailed technical plan to implement it. For a time, it even appeared that Moscow, at least, might be interested. The West, however, was not and by November the effort had plainly failed.[85] Washington, in particular, resented Lie's "counterproductive"[86] efforts, which seemed to undermine the U.S.'s stated refusal to negotiate under the pressure of the Soviet blockade.

Undaunted, the Secretary-General, two years later, tried to use the occasion of the December 1950 visit to U.N. headquarters of General Wu and his Peking delegation to start talks on a settlement of the Korean War. No one had invited him to take this initiative, and it failed. For a few days, however, there were flickers of hope.[87] There were also explicit expressions of annoyance, especially by the U.S. government.

In 1956, after Col. Nasser's nationalization of the Suez Canal, Secretary-General Hammarskjold initiated private discussions between the foreign ministers of Britain, France, and Egypt. At one stage there appears to have been agreement on a formula which would have guaranteed unfettered transit through the Canal as well as other protection for the users.[88] But in pursing these efforts the Secretary-General had overestimated the weight Britain and France attached to Colonel Nasser's pledges. On October 29, just as negotiations were to resume in Geneva, Israeli troops stormed the Sinai. Hammarskjold was "stunned" and "outraged"[89] at what he regarded as "shoddy . . . deception."[90]

Two years later several thousand American marines landed in Lebanon.

Successive U.S. and Japanese proposals for augmenting the U.N. Observer Group in Lebanon (UNOGIL) in order for it to replace the American one, were vetoed by the Soviet Union.[91] Hammarskjold then told the Council that he would act on his own authority "in order to help in filling any vacuum"[92] and "to assist in finding a road away from the dangerous point at which we now find ourselves."[93] He would increase the size of UNOGIL. "Were you to disapprove," he said, "I would, of course, accept the consequences of your judgment."[94]

The Council adjourned without objection, and Hammarskjold promptly increased the force of a few dozen U.N. observers to 636 military personnel supported by ten aircraft and four helicopters, in effect transforming it, on his own authority, into the very peacekeeping force previously vetoed by Moscow.

U.N. Under-Secretary Brian Urquhart later wrote, "Hammarskjold had pushed his powers of independent initiative to a new limit . . . leaving behind him a vacuum of constitutional authorization."[95] However, in the U.N. as in the U.S., constitutional authority is sometimes nothing more than what you can get away with. Hammarskjold's initiative, in this instance, was entirely successful. He thereby established for the Secretary-General a stand-by power to initiate peacekeeping in the face of the Security Council's failure to act.

In the autumn of 1959, the Security Council, in response to a Laotian plea, sent investigators to examine charges of communist infiltration from North Vietnam. That group returned to New York on October 20 and published its report on November 5.[96] Hammarskjold put little faith in the ability of the Council's fact-finding mission to resolve the crisis. One day after its return to New York, he proposed that he go to Laos, an initiative Moscow said it would veto if it were put to the Security Council.[97] Knowing that, the Secretary-General simply decided to proceed without seeking the Council's authorization, after securing a personal invitation from the government of Laos.[98] Before doing so, he wrote each member of the Security Council that he was merely availing himself of the "opportunity to get, at first hand, as complete a picture as possible of conditions and developments in Laos of relevance from the point of view of the general responsibilities of the Secretary-General." He also added that he would probably "with the consent of the Government, temporarily station a personal representative in Vientiane." This he justified on the basis of his "general responsibilities . . . regarding developments which may threaten peace and security," and his administrative authority under the Charter.[99] Ambassador Sobolev characterized this action as one which could "only further complicate the situation."[100]

At times, Hammarskjold's eagerness to mediate a dispute led him to steer the parties away from the political organs of the organization. When Thailand and Cambodia proposed taking a dispute to the Security Council, he quietly urged them to accept, instead, the mediation of his personal representative, Yohan Beck-Friis of Sweden. "You can see how much more effective and smooth working such a technique is than the regular one," he wrote, "which involves all the meetings and debates, and so on."[101]

That sort of attitude inevitably created difficulties not only with Moscow but also with the French. President Charles de Gaulle regarded Hammarskjold as an interloper among world leaders. This became apparent in the crisis that ensued after French troops, on July 21, 1961, occupied the Tunisian city of Bizerte to defend its naval base there, which the Tunisian government had been trying to squeeze out with a land blockade. When the Security Council was convened at Tunisia's request, Hammarskjold took the lead in calling for a resolution demanding a cease-fire and the mutual withdrawal of forces.[102] Such a resolution was passed on the morning of July 22, but with France conspicuously abstaining.[103]

When that resolution had no effect, Tunisia's ambassador Mongi Slim, who was close to Hammarskjold, asked the Secretary-General to send military observers to implement a cease-fire. Hammarskjold thought this would require a new decision by the Council, which would almost certainly be blocked by France. Instead, he suggested that Tunisian President Habib Bourguiba invite him to visit the area to ascertain the facts as a first step to mediation.[104] His presence in the region, he thought, might also help to cool things down.

The invitation arrived on Sunday, July 23, together with news of further fighting in Bizerte. Slim urged the Secretary-General to leave immediately, and he booked passage on the first available flight, one leaving the next morning. With both the French ambassador and his deputy away from New York for the weekend, Hammarskjold was only able to make contact with the latter at 7:00 p.m. the evening before his departure. He gave the French official copies of Bourguiba's invitation and of his acceptance, adding that he would be glad to stop in Paris on his way back from Tunis if the French wished it. The news reached French Foreign Minister Couve de Murville at 1:00 a.m. Paris time. He stolidly replied that he had no message for Mr. Hammarskjold, a response the French representative unwisely concluded that did not need to be passed on to the Secretary-General. In these inauspicious circumstances Hammarskjold left for Tunis to defuse the conflict. In Urquhart's opinion, the Secretary-General seemed oblivious of the low esteem in which he was held by de Gaulle.[105]

Were the circumstances not so serious, Hammarskjold's visit might almost be savored as pure French farce, for General de Gaulle set about teaching the Swede a lesson. After a few days of talks with Bourguiba in Tunis, Hammarskjold became convinced that he should return to make an urgent report and recommendations to the Security Council. But before doing so, he wanted to observe conditions on the French side of the line. He therefore asked the French consul in Tunis to arrange a visit to Bizerte and a meeting with the French commander Admiral Amman. By the next day, having received no reply, the Secretary-General proceeded with his party to Bizerte, having telegraphed his time of arrival to Amman.

The dusty party appeared just outside Bizerte at 3:40 p.m. accompanied by an unsolicited convoy of press vehicles. There the Secretary-General was stopped by French paratroopers and ignominiously ordered from his car. When he protested, the paratroopers replied that they had no way of knowing whether they were in the presence of "le vrai M. Hammarskjold" and searched the diplomat and his party. When the battered procession at last arrived in Bizerte, Admiral Amman conveyed a perfunctory expression of regret at the incident, but—acting under instructions from Paris[106]—firmly refused to meet the Secretary-General. As for stopping in Paris, the French demurred, testily adding that they had already heard from the Tunisians what Hammarskjold had to say.[107]

Neither his visit nor subsequent meetings of the Council and an emergency session of the Assembly helped ease the crisis, which abated only with direct French-Tunisian negotiations and after 600 persons had been killed in the fighting.

The failure of the mission is less remarkable, however, than Hammarskjold's audacity in undertaking it at all, entirely on his own authority and with an invitation from only one of the parties to the dispute. Two years later the new Secretary-General, U Thant, took the initiative in working out an agreement between the parties to the Yemeni civil war. This called for U.N. observers to be posted along a demilitarized zone at the Yemen-Saudi border to prevent infiltration.[108] Without seeking authorization, Thant sent a team of 114 Yugoslavs borrowed from UNEF in the Mideast, augmenting it with fifty personnel borrowed from the Royal Canadian Air Force. It was organized by Major-General von Horn, the chief of staff of UNTSO in Jerusalem.

Although Thant's initiative had the approval of the parties to the conflict, the Soviet Union objected strongly, demanding that the Security Council meet before the force was actually put into place. On June 11, by a vote of 10 to 0, (with the Soviet Union abstaining), the Council authorized Thant "to establish the observation operation as defined by him" and to report back.[109] But at that point, the first observers were already in place.[110]

Despite such episodic displays of audacity, in general Thant preferred to act in a more circumspect manner than his predecessor, avoiding, where possible, confrontations over matters he regarded as primarily theoretical. That this did not mean any significant departure from Hammarskjold's perception of the Secretary-General's powers is indicated by Thant's next initiative in fact-finding and mediating. Almost at the same time that he was "yielding" to the Council on UNYOM (the U.N. Yemen Observation Mission), he acted without the Council's permission to send a team of observers to North Borneo–Sarawak. In response to a request by the parties, the team was to determine whether the British territories wanted to achieve independence in union with the Federation of Malaysia, as asserted by the British and the Malays, or preferred union with the Philippines or Indonesia. This time, the Soviets did not object. A nine-man mission of inquiry found that the people overwhelmingly preferred to join the Malaysian Federation.[111] With that, the crisis, which had reached the brink of war, subsided.

Thant's biggest self-starting initiative began on October 23, 1962, when the Security Council convened in the aftermath of President Kennedy's speech that imposed a "quarantine" to secure the removal of Soviet missiles from Cuba. Three resolutions were proposed—by the United States,[112] by the Soviet Union,[113] and by Ghana and the United Arab Republic[114] for the non-aligned. None stood the slightest chance of being adopted.

Such impasses are a Secretary-General's open door. On the night after the Council's first inconclusive meeting, more than 40 non-aligned nations asked Thant to step in.[115] Twelve francophone African states asked him to propose a standstill: the Soviets to stop all arms shipments and the U.S., simultaneously, to suspend quarantine measures. The U.N. would somehow supervise compliance.[116] Meanwhile, at the open meetings of the Security Council, a chorus of delegates publicly urged Thant to act.[117]

In response, still on October 24, the Secretary-General unveiled his first set of proposals, which closely resembled the francophone African plan. It offered each side some of what it was after. The U.S. was to suspend the quarantine while the U.S.S.R. was to stop shipping arms to Cuba "for a period of two or three weeks." This, he asserted, would ease tensions and allow time for the parties "to meet and discuss with a view to finding a peaceful solution."[118]

The U.S. did not think the proposal was even-handed because it left existing Soviet missiles in place. Rebuffed, Thant tried again, this time asking Chairman Khrushchev "to instruct the Soviet ships already on their way to Cuba to stay away from the interception area for a limited time"[119] and asking President Kennedy, in turn, to do everything possible "to avoid direct confrontation with Soviet ships in the next few days in order to minimize the risk of any untoward incident."[120]

Khrushchev replied to Thant the same day: "We . . . accept your proposal . . . ."[121] So did Kennedy. This was at best a modest success. The Soviet decision to halt its ships on the high seas was primarily a response to Washington's overwhelming strategic advantage in a military confrontation on the doorstep of the Americas. But, for tactical reasons, Washington was more than willing to have U Thant take the credit if that made it easier for Khrushchev to yield.

The standstill on the high seas did not end the Cuban missile crisis. Indeed, the next few days were crucial, since it was clear that Washington had already decided to bomb the Cuban sites to prevent their becoming operational if Moscow did not take them apart and send them back to the Soviet Union. The Security Council met once more, on October 26, generating a dramatic confrontation between Ambassadors Stevenson and Zorin in which the Americans, responding to Soviet denials, produced enlarged photographs of Soviet missiles, taken over Cuba by U.S. reconnaissance planes. But the Council, however

conducive to public posturing, could not serve as the site of serious negotiations. The crisis was managed bilaterally, in exchanges between Khrushchev
and Kennedy. On October 28 the Russian leader signaled his willingness to
dismantle the missile systems.

Thereafter, U Thant emerged once more as a factor. The Khrushchev-
Kennedy agreement of October 28 provided for international verification of the
missiles' removal, in return for an American pledge not to invade Cuba.[122] On
the same day, Thant solicited and accepted an invitation from Castro. He
announced that he would take a few aides to Cuba, including his military
adviser, Brigadier I. J. Rikhye of India, and "leave some of them behind to
continue our common effort towards the peaceful solution of the problem."[123]
Thant thought that Castro had accepted, in principle, the posting of U.N.
observers in Cuba to perform the verification function.[124]

The trip proved an embarrassment. The Cubans refused any form of international inspection. Thant and his entire party returned empty-handed, and the
Kennedy-Khrushchev agreement was then verified unilaterally by U.S. aerial
reconnaissance and naval checks on the high seas. The U.N. played no role,
and the U.S. did not have to promise not to invade Cuba. Once again a
Secretary-General's optimism had caused him to miscalculate. But, with the
crisis over, U.S. and Soviet representatives jointly thanked Thant anyway.[125]

The embarrassing incident underscores the truism that Secretaries-General
are least likely to be successful mediators when the disputants are superpowers.
Thant was more effective when fighting erupted between India and Pakistan
(August 1965 to January 1966). After the Council had called for a cease-fire,[126]
he took the lead in setting up a new observer group, UNIPOM (the United
Nations India-Pakistan Observation Mission) to monitor it. Although the U.N.
already had an observer group (UNMOGIP) along the old truce line in Kash-
mir, the additional force was needed to patrol cease-fire lines in new areas of
conflict stretching from Kashmir along the international boundary to the sea.
Thant, acting on his own authority, sent 90 observers, headed by Major-
General B. F. MacDonald of Canada, and funded UNIPOM with $2 million
from an account for unforeseen peacekeeping contingencies. Although the
Soviet Union complained that this was at variance with the Charter,[127] UNI-
POM remained in existence for almost six months. Moscow may have found
Thant superficially more complaisant than Hammarskjold, but, in the end, he
was equally hard to bridle. As one Soviet diplomat remarked, "convincing Mr.
Thant is like fighting your way through a room full of mashed potatoes."[128]

In 1970 U Thant agreed to mediate the dispute over the future of Bahrain,
on which Britain was about to bestow independence but which was claimed by
Iran. The actual negotiations were undertaken for him by Ralph Bunche, then
already terminally ill. During a period of several months Bunche conducted
exploratory discussions with the representatives of the United Kingdom and
Iran to find an agreed basis for exercising the Secretary-General's "good of-

fices." Eventually, in his last triumph, Bunche found the formula. The government of Iran wrote a letter formally requesting the Secretary-General's intervention and outlining, in general, the form it was to take. This letter was received on March 9, 1970, and transmitted to the British government, which indicated its agreement with the proposed mission and its terms of reference. On March 20, the Secretary-General advised the two governments of his willingness to become involved.[129] He appointed his Director-General in Geneva, Mr. Vittorio Winspeare Guicciardi, to conduct a field inquiry during March and April. Guicciardi, after investigation, reported that the people of Bahrain overwhelmingly preferred independence to union with Iran. His finding was accepted by both adversaries and then endorsed by the Security Council, thus ending the dispute,[130]—or almost. The Soviet Union, not one to let a dangerous precedent slip by, sent a letter to the Secretary-General expressing— albeit in comparatively measured tones—its strong objection to his having assumed the peacemaker's role without a prior mandate from the Security Council.[131] It had no perceptible effect, and was not followed up by Moscow. Despite these objections, the right of Secretaries-General to initiate such peacemaking has gradually become quite firmly established. Dag Hammarskjold's visit to Peking in January 1955 to obtain the release of captive U.S. airmen had been authorized specifically by the General Assembly—although the Secretary-General, even then, had made clear he was proceeding to China on his own authority and not that of the Assembly. Twenty-two years later Kurt Waldheim brought about the release of eight French hostages held by the Saharawi Liberation Movement (Polisario) and personally flew them from Algiers to Paris on Christmas Eve 1977. He neither requested nor received the blessing of either Council or Assembly.[132]

On a much larger scale, Waldheim took a purely personal initiative in convening a 65-nation meeting on Vietnamese refugees and displaced persons on July 20 and 21, 1979, at which he succeeded in more than doubling (from 125,000 to 260,000) the number of resettlement places and eliciting $190 million in new funds for resettlement centers, including two new sites offered by the Philippines and Indonesia. Waldheim also negotiated an agreement with the Vietnamese head of delegation, Deputy Foreign Minister Phan Hien, which committed Hanoi to stop forced departures—at the time running at 65,000 per month—and substitute a more humane system.[133]

Blocked in his Assembly-mandated efforts to negotiate Vietnamese withdrawal from Kampuchea, the Secretary-General, acting entirely on his own, organized a highly successful pledging conference to fund a gigantic relief effort on behalf of Kampuchean refugees. Singapore's respected U.N. ambassador, T. T. B. Koh, has said that "if the Cambodian nation has survived, it is due in no small part to the humanitarian relief operation started by Secretary-General Waldheim."[134]

Timing is an important ingredient in the initiation of the mediator's role.

Another, less successful venture was Waldheim's attempt to bring together the warring governments of Iran and Iraq under the aegis of his special representative, Olof Palme of Sweden.[135] The intervention, however, was both too late (in that fighting was already under way) and too early (in that the parties were not yet exhausted enough to stop). The same could be said of Pérez de Cuéllar's honorable try at mediating the Falkland Islands war of 1982. In that instance, too, he was summoned only after fighting had begun, but before either side was ready to abandon the tools of violence.

The Secretary-General also addressed his efforts to a potentially damaging credentials dispute brewing in the General Assembly. On October 8, 1982, the Arab bloc decided to challenge the legitimacy of the Israeli delegation. In response, Secretary of State George P. Shultz announced that the U.S. would boycott, and withhold funding from, any U.N. body that excluded the Israelis. The Secretary-General quietly pointed out to Arab delegates that the ouster of Israel, among other effects, would terminate the role of the U.N.'s 7000-man peacekeeping force in Lebanon, and cripple the organization's $200 million annual aid program for Palestinian refugees.[136] Two weeks later, the Arab bloc "temporarily" called off its campaign.

Whether effective or not in carrying out these functions in particular instances, Secretaries-General have been completely successful in drawing a line between their role and the role played by the political organs at the behest of member states. Successive incumbents have created for themselves a role that is separate and often different from the expressed intent of some, or even most, members. Secretaries-General have felt justified, at times, in acting on their own to safeguard what they perceived to be minimum standards of world order. By the time the U.N. was preparing to celebrate its fortieth anniversary, there could be little doubt that the only important winner in the intra-institutional power struggle had been the Secretary-General. The General Assembly, surely, could make more noise and the Security Council still occasionally attract the television cameras; but to the limited extent the U.N. was now having any salutary effect on the real world beyond its own compound, it was primarily because of the functions being performed by the Secretary-General.

The Secretary-General as Opponent

As the office of Secretary-General became a repository of a sort of unique ethical autonomy—invented, not planned, by incumbents in the midst of crises, and deriving its content from the incumbent's uniquely global perspective—the U.S. reaction vacillated between satisfaction and benign indifference. The U.N. system had somehow managed to produce what political scientists are pleased to call a new "actor" in world politics, not wholly in the control of the members, or even of the superpowers. While this horrified the Russians, it seems at first not even to have been particularly apparent to the United States. As long as Trygve

Lie was rallying less-than-committed members to the cause of collective security in Korea, the efforts of that activist, ethically autonomous Secretary-General were so thoroughly compatible with U.S. aims that it did everything possible to encourage his aspirations, without realizing that, while his aims coincided with its own in that instance, they derived from a radical view of his office which the U.S. had scarcely considered.

To the extent that the longer-run institutional consequences were considered, Washington comforted itself with the illusion that any Secretary-General would tend to side with the U.S. in major international disputes because his international interest, the global perspective, would ordinarily coincide with the U.S. interest, certainly more often than with that of the Soviet Union.

This sort of reasoning led the U.S. to begin a long campaign to strengthen the office of Secretary-General. When Lie's five-year term ended, the U.S. managed his campaign for reelection over strenuous Soviet opposition. The Charter provides that a successful candidate must have the approval of both Assembly and Council. When the Russians declared they would veto his candidacy, Washington took it as an affront to the independence of the office and announced it would veto anyone else, deadlocking that body. The U.S. then led the way in transferring the dispute to the General Assembly, which it controlled. By resolution of that body, Lie's term was "extended" for another five years.[137] This was certainly a violation of the Charter's intent. But, worse, as the Australian delegation pointed out, it established a far-reaching precedent.[138] This could be used to keep an incumbent in office indefinitely, long after he or she had lost the confidence of one or more of the Big Powers. In the U.S., however, the maneuver was seen as a creative development of the world organization as well as a fitting reward for a brave public servant.

To Moscow, on the other hand, it appeared to be another instance of the tyranny of the majority—the U.S.'s. The Russians thereupon refused all further contact with Lie, even addressing necessary communications to the "Secretariat" and refusing to meet with him under any circumstances. Two years into his second term, Lie resigned.

In taking the lead to save Lie, the U.S. believed it was defending the U.N. ideal. In reality, although most Americans did not then realize it, the U.S. was merely pursuing a rather parochial self-interest. Lie had come to suit its global purposes. Had he not done so, the U.S. would certainly not have gone to so much trouble to bend the perfectly sensible rules of the Charter. Washington also tended to the belief that the interests of a strong Secretary-Generalship would coincide with the national interest of the United States. Before long, it became clear that this identity of interests was, at best, a temporary phenomenon. By the time U Thant became Secretary-General, the office had become every bit as much a thorn in Washington's side as in that of Moscow. He frankly identified his "neutral" office with the "neutralist" bloc at the U.N.

Thant's "bully pulpit" became a platform from which to launch a sustained and fairly effective attack on U.S. policy during the Vietnam War. Senator Barry Goldwater, for one, Thant described as "out of his mind,"[139] a view shared by the Johnson administration, for proposing to use atomic weapons. Soon, however, the areas of disagreement began to expand until Thant was confronting Washington over a broad front. In July he expressed his "strong feeling" that "military methods will not bring about peace in South Vietnam." Instead, he urged a negotiated settlement that could be achieved by reconvening the Geneva Conference, at which the French withdrawal from Indochina had originally been negotiated.[140] On a visit to Rangoon, he again called for a "political solution" rather than a military one.[141] He chose the occasion of an invitation to the White House to propose a resumption of the Geneva Conference. That appeal was resented in Washington.[142] The war in the South was going badly for the U.S. and its South Vietnamese ally, while domestic opposition to the conflict was growing.[143] Thant gave the "doves" a focus and enhanced their credibility.

U.S. relations with Thant deteriorated rapidly after that, as the respective perceptions diverged completely. In an effort to respond to the calls for a negotiated settlement, Washington persuaded Blair Seaborn, a Canadian diplomat and a member of the International Control Commission established by the Geneva Agreement, to find out Hanoi's price for starting discussions. Seaborn carried back from North Vietnam the message that, if the United States wanted an end to hostilities, its military should withdraw from South Vietnam and allow the National Liberation Front (NLF) to take over.[144]

U Thant, meanwhile, acted on different information. He insisted that North Vietnam was ready for negotiations without precondition if the United States would abandon its effort to achieve military victory. While Washington had reason to believe that Hanoi would accept no solution but victory, U Thant, with growing vociferousness, insisted that an independent, non-communist South Vietnam could be had by negotiating. To the extent Americans believed Thant, they tended to oppose the continuation of the war.

The U.S. government and U Thant were on a collision course. This became public knowledge as a result of a dramatic series of events beginning with the aforementioned visit by the Secretary-General to Lyndon Johnson in the summer of 1964. U Thant told Johnson that he could set up the meeting he was urging between representatives of the United States and North Vietnam. He left Washington believing that the President had encouraged him to try and, through the Russians, proceeded to sound out North Vietnam's Ho Chi Minh and then his own government in Rangoon. The Burmese government agreed to provide facilities for the meeting. In early October, Thant informed Adlai Stevenson, the sympathetic U.S. ambassador, that all was ready.

Since secrecy was essential, the offer was communicated orally by Stevenson to Secretary of State Dean Rusk. Washington was cool to the offer, in part because South Vietnam was to be excluded, and also because the military-political tide was running so strongly against South Vietnam, a trend the U.S. government thought it could reverse to create a more favorable bargaining posture. Rusk's skepticism was reinforced by Seaborn's report that negotiations would be fruitless unless the U.S. was ready to surrender. Perhaps an additional factor was the dislike and distrust of Thant which Rusk had developed. The Secretary of State gave a noncommital but essentially negative response, orally, to Stevenson. The Ambassador, who favored the proposed talks, thought Rusk might well change his mind after the November elections and therefore said nothing to Thant.

Weeks passed in silence, and Thant began to feel uneasy. While Stevenson was on vacation, Thant contacted Stevenson's deputies at the U.S. mission, Ambassadors Charles Yost and Francis Plimpton, to find out when a reply might be expected. Neither had heard anything of the project. Yost called Harlan Cleveland, then assistant secretary for international organizations in the State Department. He had not heard of it, either. Cleveland finally reached Stevenson in the Caribbean and, on getting the full story, called Undersecretary of State George Ball, who, in turn, contacted McGeorge Bundy at the White House. Neither Ball nor Bundy were in the picture, either.

By this time, the Secretary-General was beginning to feel deliberately humiliated by the U.S. government. As a former journalist, he knew what to do. A few weeks later, when there was still no word from Washington, the whole story appeared on the front page of the *New York Times*,[145] told from the Secretary-General's perspective. During February and March, an angry U Thant, with the help of his Indian aide, Under-Secretary C. V. Narasimhan, proceeded with the diplomatic equivalent of a media "blitz." At a press conference on February 25 Thant argued passionately for "the political and diplomatic method of discussions and negotiations." Thant cited his native Burma as his model: Confronted with widespread communist insurrection after attaining independence in 1948, Burma had dealt with it as a purely internal matter, without either side's receiving outside help.[146] Thant thought that the lesson was simple: if the U.S. would stop intervening, the problem could be solved among the Vietnamese themselves.

To add weight to his prescription, Thant added a fateful sentence: "I am sure that the great American people, if only they know the true facts and the background to the developments in South Vietnam, will agree with me that further bloodshed is unnecessary."[147] This was not hard to translate. The Secretary-General was accusing the U.S. government of lying to the American people. Washington reacted with cold fury. It was not the first time, and certainly not the last, that the charge had been made. But, coming from the "voice of the global conscience" made it more distressing—and effective. The front page of the *New York Times*, a day later featured a report, inspired by "reliable U.N. sources," that North Vietnam had notified U Thant "it is receptive to his suggestion for informal negotiations on the Vietnam situation."[148] The "if only they knew" statement drew from Rusk the defensive response that "I don't know of any situation anywhere in the world on which the American people have been better informed in more detail."[149] To this the Secretary-General responded with a "clarification" which—deliberately—made matters worse. He stated that although the American public is "the best informed in the world," he doubted that even it receives "fully balanced information" regarding "such factors as the great suffering of the people of Vietnam, the tragic loss of human lives and property, uprooting of society; the attitudes of Asians, which so often are misunderstood in the West; the serious risks and dangers implicit in . . . a war course without political efforts to bring the war to an end."[150]

Why had the U.S. treated the Secretary-General so callously, seemingly going out of its way to goad him into open hostility? The answer, as is so often the case, appears to lie in inadvertence rather than mendacity. Secretary Rusk thought he had turned the offer down. Adlai Stevenson had taken it on himself to cover up the Secretary of State's negativism, hoping for a better response later. President Johnson first learned of Thant's offer from the *New York Times*. He demanded of his White House staff whether the Secretary-General had actually made a viable proposal. According to Chester L. Cooper, who was handed the unenviable task of preparing the reply: "Bundy was away . . . A hasty search of the files turned up only a terse account of Ball's earlier telephone conversation with Bundy—a sketchy 'Did-you-know-that-U Thant-told-Stevenson-that-he-could-set-up-a-meeting-in-Rangoon-with-Hanoi?' This by itself did not seem a very robust initiative, and we told the President so."[151] Armed with this incomplete information, George Reedy, the White House spokesman, responded to a journalist's question with the assertion that there are "no authorized negotiations under way with Mr. Thant or any other government. I am not going into any diplomatic chitchat that may be going forth, or way-out feelers. But authorized or meaningful negotiations—no."[152]

This distinctly unflattering characterization of his efforts as "chitchat" made Thant even madder. On March 9, the *New York Times* carried another detailed front-page story, quoting "information obtained today" to the effect that the Secretary-General had approached six of the seven participants in what he had hoped would be negotiations-about-negotiations. It seemed that Hanoi and everyone else except the United States had accepted.[153] The "source" also disclosed that the Secretary-General, after the fall of the Ngo Dinh Diem government in November 1963, had urged the United States to promote a coalition government in Saigon, including non-communist Vietnamese political exiles willing to negotiate the neutralization of South Vietnam.[154] That initiative, too, had been passed over in silence.

In the U.N.-Washington war being waged on its pages, the *New York Times* chose its side. "The conference that Secretary Thant has recommended," its editors wrote, "may or may not be an answer. It certainly deserves a more sympathetic exploration than it is getting from Washington." The "American people . . . would surely opt for negotiation if the issues—all the issues—were made clear to them. The American public has not been sufficiently informed."[155] The same day, the Secretary-General—somewhat disingenuously given his, and his staff's media blitz—complained that his proposal had generated no response from the U.S. "except through the press."[156]

The entire incident made the Washington administration look rude and bellicose. And the problem created by the incident, or, for that matter, the incident itself, refused to go away. On November 30, 1965, *Look* magazine carried a feature story by correspondent Eric Sevareid that told it all again as if newly revealed. According to Sevareid, Adlai Stevenson, on the night before his death, had poured out his heart to the author about the callous U.S. rejection of Thant's initiative.[157] Sevareid, making it appear like a deathbed confession, recited all the events that had already been fully covered in the *Times* months earlier, and commented dramatically: "I do not know that people have premonitions of their death. Yet, as he talked, the thought flickered through my mind that he was telling me these things out of a sense of urgency that they be known."[158] The *Look* article generated countless news stories, which stated or implied that the U.S. was continuing to fight in Vietnam because the hawks of Washington had refused—and then covered up their refusal of—a perfectly viable peace offer.

By this time, the story began to demonstrate an uncanny capacity for reincarnation. Fully a year later, on November 17, 1966, the *New York Review of Books*, in an article by U.N. correspondent Mario Rossi, told the whole story again, portraying it as a new revelation of malevolent maneuvers by a U.S. government determined to snub opportunities for an honorable peace.[159] It surfaced again in 1968 in a book by David Kraslow and Stuart H. Loory.[160]

In reality, the incident illustrates primarily two rather unsensational points. The first is that the system of communication within the Johnson administration left much to be desired; little undermines public confidence in decision-makers as much as evidence that decisions are being made, or not made, in a miasma of incomplete information. Second, the incident demonstrates that a Secretary-General, if so inclined, can make himself a powerful force in the domestic politics of the United States.

U Thant succeeded in taking his case to the U.S. public over the heads of the government in Washington, and helped to create a perception of the government as both untruthful and belligerent. Unquestionably, that perception was helped by many other factors, including the conduct of the government itself. Whether or not it was valid, the perception became an essential ingredient in the success of the growing anti-war movement. The capacity of Secretaries-General to have so significant an effect—in part, no doubt, because they are located here, in the midst of a uniquely open and diffuse political process—must be taken into account in any serious assessment of the impact of the U.N. on the national interest of the United States.

Such an assessment is prompted not only by the demonstration that the Secretary-General could be a dynamic force in U.S. politics, but also by the more pedestrian fact that his reasoning was dead wrong. He was mistaken in his tenacious belief that the North Vietnamese communists were interested in negotiating some sort of "Burmese"—(neutral, nonaligned, and independent) political solution for the South. Hanoi, from the beginning of its military involvement in South Vietnam, had one unshakable goal: the creation of a unified communist state. It did not settle, and would not have settled, for anything less, whatever short-run deviations it might have seemed to countenance for strategic reasons. When President Johnson, in April 1965, finally did offer "unconditional" negotiations with Hanoi, that offer was firmly rejected as the "bait" of "stupid pirates."[161] By that time, however, Thant had become the captive of his own optimism. Even as Peking's official newspaper, *Jenmin Jih Pao*, was stating unequivocally that Thant would absolutely not be received in China on a proposed mediation mission,[162] the Secretary-General let it be known that he was continuing efforts "in a discreet way to bring about a peaceful solution through personal contact with the parties primarily concerned."[163]

Proclivities of the Office

Why Thant should have remained so optimistic for so long about his ability to mediate the Vietnam War, and should have felt such personal affront at the failure of his efforts to effect a negotiated compromise, is a question which needs to be addressed. Only in this way can one begin to understand the implications of a Secretary-Generalship with significant power to affect the national strategy and interest of the United States.

Admittedly, the answer is partially to be found in the personality of U Thant. But there were also at work certain built-in proclivities of the office. It seems as if *all* Secretaries-General tend to be optimistic about their ability to relieve conflict through personal intervention—whether in the Berlin crisis, the Korean War, the Cuban missile crisis, or in Afghanistan. This is not so surprising; peacemakers, too, want to succeed, and to be seen to succeed. That need to succeed may foster a belief in the probability of success.

U Thant repeatedly demonstrated this in connection with Vietnam. He deluded himself into the belief that South Vietnam had a "Burmese" option, which it did not, certainly not after 1964. By then, the communists knew they could win. Talk of compromise was, at most, a tactic for dividing and demoralizing the enemy. The Secretary-General may even have been misreading the lesson of Burma, which had resisted communist control at least in part because the communists had been defeated by the Burmese army. But the advancing of compromise solutions is also an endemic proclivity of the office. Inevitably, the response of Secretaries-General to cold-war–related civil wars tends to be advocacy of negotiated solutions, leading to a "third way"—a "neutral" coalition of communist and non-communist forces.

U Thant was an avowed "neutralist." But even Dag Hammarskjold had taken the same position. During his stay in Vientiane, in 1959, Hammarskjold volunteered a quite detailed prescription for alleviating the Laotian civil war that centered on forming a neutralist coalition government.[164] As events continued to unravel in Laos, Hammarskjold continued to urge the same formula. In early January 1960, after a conservative faction seized control in Vientiane, he wired his friend, King Savang Vathana, that he hoped "the line of independent neutrality . . . [would] be firmly maintained."[165]

Nowadays secretaries-general are almost inevitably impelled in that direction because the Non-Aligned Movement, a majority of U.N. members, have embraced a similar formula. Not surprisingly, Kurt Waldheim and Pérez de Cuéllar appear to have pursued peace in Afghanistan through "neutralization."

Secretaries-General are not naïve, but they are politically atuned. Ever since Dag Hammarskjold learned to lean on the NAMs for support in the face of Soviet attacks on his policies in the Congo, incumbents have frequently linked the neutrality of their office with the cold-war neutralism of the NAMs. At times, usually in private, they do encourage the NAMs to modify their more extreme positions on such issues as the demand for economic concessions from the industrialized nations and on sanctions against Israel. But these are exceptional demonstrations of the traditional independence of the office. During the Cuban missile crisis as well as in the Vietnam War, U Thant relied upon the support of the NAMs in staking out the Secretary-General's position and giving it the weight of "world conscience." As this reliance has increased, the office has ceased to be solely the "conscience of the world" and has seemed to become, at times, the "conscience" of India, Algeria, Nigeria, and Mexico. This coincidence of perspectives extends over a broad range of issues, as demonstrated when Kurt Waldheim repeatedly spoke for the Southern Hemisphere on economic issues,[166] and fawned over Third World "idealism" and its "constructive middle force" in world affairs.[167] When a Secretary-General, nowadays, criticizes the NAMs publicly, it is regarded as a rare act of courage. Pérez de Cuéllar, however, more than his predecessors, has shown some of this gutsy quality, even to the extent of calling openly on Third World countries to put their economic houses in order before asking for help from the rest of the world.[168]

Even if it is now evident that the interests of the Secretary-General are not—certainly not necessarily—congruent with those of the U.S., it can still be argued that the U.S. definition of self-interest ought to accommodate a prominent world official speaking his or her mind on global issues, whether those opinions are to the U.S.'s liking or not. It is in the long-run interest of world peace to create independent voices that can be heard everywhere. Unfortunately, the voice of the Secretary-General, unlike the biblical turtle, is not heard throughout the land. His principal audience is the people of the Western democracies, and largely those in the United States. Neither communist nations nor the many authoritarian states of the Third World would give a platform or press coverage to the Secretary-General were he to advocate "unacceptable" views on their home "turf."

In countless appearances before American trade unions, congresses, associations, and institutions, U Thant was able to hammer at the theme that a negotiated U.S. withdrawal from South Vietnam and Cambodia would result not in the brutal or genocidal communist victory that eventually occurred, but in a peaceful "neutralist" solution. He was an early and effective propagator of the U.S. public's suspicion that the war was being pursued by callous administrations that lied to suit their bellicose ends.

In Moscow, such incidents are handled differently. In the summer of 1962, when Moscow was agitated about the U.N. role in the Congo, U Thant paid a five-day visit to the Soviet Union. In a talk recorded for use by Moscow radio, he said, "the Russian people do not fully understand the true character of the Congo problem, probably due to the absence of the presentation of the other side of the coin." He added that if the Russian people only had "the means of knowing all the facets of the problem they will certainly revise their opinion of the nature of the United Nations' involvement in the Congo."[169] The statement is almost identical to the one made by Thant in reference to the U.S. public's support of the Vietnamese War, which inspired countless news stories, "disclosures," and shook the credibility of the Johnson administration. In sharp contrast, Thant's remarks were simply not carried on the home service by Radio Moscow, nor were they picked up by Soviet newspapers. His attempt to talk over the spires of the Kremlin directly to the Russian people constituted a non-event.[170]

In evaluating U.S. policy toward the U.N., it is necessary to begin with the recognition that Secretaries-General now have little choice but to advocate positions that reflect values and political considerations likely to be at sharp variance with the national interest of the United States. We should also recognize that, from their "bully pulpit" in New York, they have a substantial opportunity to try to influence U.S. politics and the conduct of American foreign policy. This might not be a cause for concern if Secretaries-General also had the opportunity to affect the domestic politics of the U.N.'s other principal constituents. Unfortunately this, as many with many other things at the U.N., has turned out to be a one-sided development.

Unfulfilled by Unifil: The Security Council in Search of a Role

Powers of the Security Council

The drafters of the U.N. Charter intended the Security Council to be the pivotal organ of the new international system they were devising. It was given almost unlimited power to resolve disputes and resist aggression. What the Charter calls "pacific settlement" is the process by which the Council is to resolve "any dispute, the continuance of which is likely to endanger the maintenance of international peace and security."[1] Even before that stage has been reached, the Charter authorizes the Council to look into any "situation which might lead to international friction or give rise to a dispute"[2] and to take appropriate steps to prevent a dispute or situation from deteriorating into a "threat to the peace, breach of the peace, or act of aggression."[3]

In pursuing pacific settlement, the Council is given tantalizing options. It may call upon the parties to commence "negotiation, enquiry, mediation, conciliation, arbitration, judicial settlement, resort to regional agencies or arrangements, or other peaceful means of their own choice."[4] The Council may make its own investigation to determine whether a dispute or situation is actually likely to endanger peace,[5] and may "recommend appropriate procedures or methods of adjustment" to the parties.[6] It can also "recommend such terms of settlement as it may consider appropriate" if the continuance of the dispute "is in fact likely to endanger the maintenance of international peace and security."[7]

The Council was given the task of organizing collective resistance to aggression, in the aftermath of Europe's experience with appeasement and lack of collective resistance to Hitler's "salami tactics" of expansion. The Charter authorizes the Council to act boldly, taking "action with respect to threats to the peace, breaches of the peace, and acts of aggression" including "complete or partial interruption of economic relations and of rail, sea, air, postal, telegraphic, radio, and other means of communication, and the severance of diplomatic relations"[8] as well as "such action by air, sea, or land forces as may be necessary," including "demonstrations, blockade, and other operations."[9]

The Charter further provides that all members undertake to make armed forces available to the Security Council[10] and to "hold immediately available national air-force contingents for combined international enforcement action."[11] To advise the Security Council on the forces' deployment and strategy, the Charter creates a Military Staff Committee consisting of "the Chiefs of Staff of the permanent members of the Security Council or their representatives."[12]

When dealing with disputes or aggression, the Council may act either by issuing recommendations or by making decisions. The former impose only voluntary obligations, but the latter are legislative in nature, binding all the members who must participate in carrying them out, even including the use of economic or military force.[13]

This grand design for pacific settlement of disputes and collective measures to resist aggression was devised at Dumbarton Oaks and ratified by the general conference of the United Nations at San Francisco with remarkably little disagreement, either among the Big Five or between the Big Five and the other states.[14] Of course, there were tensions. The majority at San Francisco, over U.S. objections, were able to extend the Council mandate to include not only the right to recommend procedures for settling disputes but also to design the actual terms of a settlement.[15] In a compromise, it was agreed that the Council could take measures involving the application of force only if a situation had reached the threshold of an actual "threat to the peace."[16] The small and middle-sized states at San Francisco were also able to ensure, this time over Soviet opposition, that the veto would not apply to the preliminary decision to discuss a problem but only later, when it came to taking action.[17]

Despite Soviet opposition, it was also eventually agreed at San Francisco that a permanent member of the Council that was a party to a dispute would not be allowed to cast a veto against a resolution referring the disputants to means of "pacific settlement."[18] However, opponents of the veto were not able to get the same limit applied to Council decisions to take "collective measures" against a threat to the peace. No permanent members were willing to be governed by majority rule in such decisions. They also argued that it was unrealistic to expect the Council to vote economic or military sanctions against one of them, for that would be tantamount to a declaration of world war.

Still, the Council's powers emerged from San Francisco broad enough to constitute, in theory, a potent force. It seems surprising, in retrospect, that the nations of the world should have agreed to such an extensive—if, as it turned out, illusory—system for settling disputes and for taking collective action against aggression. Only the experience of World War II can explain the willingness of such diverse nations to commit themselves to a system which seemed to call for the surrender of a significant measure of their national sovereignty. In the war, statesmen and peoples had glimpsed both promise of what could be accomplished by nations acting in unison and the horrors that could follow failure to prevent future military conflict.

It is the Big Five's veto that limits the actual use of these, theoretically, wide powers in actual instances. Despite all the argument at San Francisco about its scope, the Charter is surprisingly vague about when the veto can be used. It does not define the circumstances under which a permanent member should be considered a "party to a dispute" so as to be ineligible to veto proposals for its peaceful settlement. In practice, permanent members have simply denied that they are "parties" or that there is a "dispute." Neither the Soviet Union nor the United States, for example, has admitted being a "party" to any of the wars in the Middle East. The Soviet Union has strenuously maintained that it had no "dispute" with Hungary, Czechoslovakia, or Afghanistan at the very times its armies were invading those countries, while the United States denied having a dispute with Guatemala when the CIA was orchestrating the overthrow of the Arbenz regime. All this demonstrates the self-evident but oft-forgotten proposition that a limit on sovereignty cannot be imposed by a principle that each sovereign state is free to interpret for itself.[19]

There are other ambiguities. Article 27(2) of the Charter states that the veto does not apply to decisions by the Council on "procedural" matters, but it does not define what that means, or how the Council is to decide in the event of a difference of opinion. At San Francisco, primarily at the insistence of the Soviet Union, the five permanent members agreed among themselves that a resolution should be regarded as substantive rather than procedural if it proposes to "initiate a chain of events which might, in the end, require the Council under its responsibilities to invoke measures of enforcement. . . . This chain of events begins when the Council decides to make an investigation, or determines that the time has come to call upon states to settle their differences, or makes recommendations to the parties."[20] However, in the event of disagreement about whether a matter is procedural, the veto shall apply to that preliminary question. The effect of this is to create another rule that means—whatever the powers say it means. From the very beginning, the "double veto" was extensively employed by the Soviet Union to block even the most modest proposals. A "double veto" is the vote of a permanent member that has the effect of characterizing a proposed course of action as substantive and therefore subject to the veto.

A Fast Start

Despite this, the early years of the Security Council were not entirely barren. In a sense, the Council could even be said to have gotten off to a fast start. On July 15, 1948, it ordered the Arab states and Israel to "desist from further military action" and the parties obeyed. The Arabs explicitly, if somewhat disingenuously, announced that they would accept the order "because of the threat of sanctions."[21] The Council then sent U.N. truce observers to ensure that the cease-fire was carried out.[22]

Two years later, the Council again acted collectively to resist the North Korean invasion of the South. This semi-success (analyzed in Chapter 2, above) was only possible because of the absence of the Soviet Union from the Council in protest against the exclusion of the Chinese communists. On June 25, 1950, the Council declared that the North was guilty of "a breach of the peace" and ordered communist forces to withdraw back to the thirty-eighth parallel. Members were asked to render every assistance to the South and refrain from helping the North. On July 7, the Security Council established a Unified Military Command under United States direction.[23] It eventually restored the South to an approximation of its pre-aggression boundaries.

These early achievements proved all too exceptional, although there have been a few more examples of the Council's using its "big stick." In particular, the Council imposed extensive economic and military sanctions against the white supremacist government of Rhodesia after the latter had unilaterally declared its independence from Britain;[24] and it has put coercive pressure on South Africa's racist regime by ordering a mandatory worldwide embargo on delivery of arms and military matériel of all kinds.[25] While these sanctions can be evaded, there is no doubt that, in the case of Rhodesia, they compounded life's inconveniences for the regime and added to its psychological sense of isolation. Aside from these instances, the Council has not used its powers to halt breaches of the peace or to resist aggressors. In nearly forty years as the U.N.'s designated policeman, it has mostly been paralyzed by disagreement among the permanent members.

Nevertheless, members of the U.N. continue to regard election to the Council as an important trophy. This is in part because the elections assume some of the qualities of a popularity contest among the non-permanent members. But it is also because the Security Council is perceived as the "big leagues" where lesser states may talk and vote as near-equals of the powerful. Accordingly, on August 31, 1965, after U.N. membership had more than doubled to one hundred fourteen, an amendment to the Charter came into effect which increased the number of places in the Council from eleven to fifteen.[26] With that change, the minimum number of votes required to pass a resolution rose from seven to nine.

Restricting the Veto

As we have seen, the U.S. did not accept the death of its early illusions about the U.N. with stoic resignation, a quality seemingly alien to the U.S. character, but instead sought to reform the institution, to overcome the blockages. The Uniting for Peace resolution, which transferred many of the powers of the blocked Security Council to the General Assembly, was one such reform. Simultaneously, the U.S. tried to impose restrictions on the Soviets' lavish use of the veto.

This could not be done frontally. The Charter is hard to amend. First, two-thirds of the members must vote in the Assembly for an amendment, and then ratify it in accordance with each member's national constitutional process. The ratifying majority must include all the permanent members of the Council. While it was possible to pass an amendment enlarging the size of the Council, it was clear from the beginning that Moscow would block any effort to restrict the veto. The U.S. therefore early embarked on complicated parliamentary maneuvers to achieve indirectly what it could not do directly.

In September 1959 the government of Laos requested the sending of a U.N. emergency force to "halt aggression" by North Vietnam. When the Council met to consider this request, the U.S. proposed that, as a first step, a fact-finding committee investigate the validity of the Laotian complaint. A vote was taken, producing the then-customary majority for a Western proposal, but with the Soviets opposed. Moscow's representative, naturally, assumed that his negative vote constituted a veto. The United States, on the contrary, took the position that merely creating a sub-committee was a procedural decision, and, as such, not vetoable. By prearrangement, the president of the Council, Senor Egidio Ortona of Italy, put the question whether the resolution was procedural. By 10 to 1, the Council voted that it was, and Ortona then ruled that the resolution, being procedural, had been adopted. In not recognizing Moscow's veto in this preliminary question, Ortona—whose country was not a party to the San Francisco Declaration—created a potentially important loophole in the permanent members' veto power.

Secretary-General Hammarskjold had been strongly opposed to this maneuver,[27] arguing that it established a dangerous precedent. However, this was not the first time, but the second, that a permanent member had been prevented from using its "double veto" (to have a proposed action characterized as "substantive" and, therefore, subject to the veto). On a previous occasion, during the Korean War, the Chinese Nationalist representative had voted against a proposal to invite the Chinese communist regime to participate in the Council's discussions about the crisis in the Formosa strait. Since all other members had voted in favor, the president of the Council, Britain's Sir Gladwyn Jebb, declared the resolution carried. When challenged by the outraged

Chinese, Jebb simply submitted his ruling to a vote of confidence, which, under the rules of procedure, is not subject to the veto.[28]

A quarter-century ago, the Chinese and Laotian precedents tended to be seen by U.S. and other Western observers as potentially useful parliamentary devices for keeping the Soviet veto within bounds. There was little inclination, at that juncture, to consider whether it would rebound—whether it was in the long-run interest of the United States to create a way for the majority to limit the use of the veto with the help of a sympathetic Council president. "Sufficient unto the day," our diplomats hoped, "is the evil thereof."

The Council as Conciliator and Policeman

As we have noted, one of the Security Council's principal functions is to make peace between disputants—the "pacific settlement of disputes"—by providing the procedures and facilities for resolving quarrels before they get out of control. On rare occasions, the Council has indeed been the forum in which the members have negotiated guidelines for resolving a global crisis—the best examples are resolutions 242 (of 1967) and 338 (of 1973) on the Middle East—or for ending a war, as in the Council's resolution on the Falklands in 1982.[29] These did not resolve the dispute, but set out the terms on which a negotiated settlement could be achieved or hostilities ended. On the whole, however, the Council has not been a success at the pacific-settlement task. Sadly, the Council's lushly appointed chamber, with its representation of a phoenix rising dramatically from the ashes, has seldom been used for serious negotiations. Even when the Secretary-General has called the Council's attention to a situation evidently approaching the crisis level, the membership has remained paralyzed by dissension.

A dramatic example of this penchant for stasis occurred in 1971, when the Council was faced with a disastrous civil war in the eastern (Bengali) region of Pakistan. Elections in that region had returned a large majority of candidates committed to regional autonomy. Pakistan's rulers—officers drawn mainly from the western region—responded with a campaign to extirpate the separatists. Repression and secessionism grew in ever widening circles of violence, sending millions of refugees into neighboring India. They brought with them chaos, disease, and famine.

These circumstances were well known. It was also known that India had long cherished the dream of breaking up its traditional adversary, Pakistan, into two mutually hostile, weakened states. It took little prescience to see a threat to the peace, precisely of the sort the Security Council was intended to handle. Yet the Council did not meet. New Delhi mobilized, but none of the Council's members called for a meeting. In a memorandum to the Council's president, dated July 20, 1971, the Secretary-General pointed out that the humanitarian disaster was of such magnitude as to create a potential threat to peace, and he called on the Council to play a more forthright role. He alluded to the organization's long experience in sending truce observers and disengagement forces in order to separate adversaries and allow tempers to cool, and emphasized the Council's varied resources for conciliation and persuasion.[30] Still it did nothing.

On November 29, fighting broke out between India and Pakistan, and the Secretary-General, in transmitting information about it, again urgently asked the Council to give serious consideration to the steps it might take. For a start, he proposed calling a cease-fire, then stationing observers along the boundary. Still there was no response.[31] Informal consultations among the members had quickly shown that the Soviets would veto any resolution that might interfere with a rapid Indian military victory.

By December 6, some members—Somalia, Argentina, Burundi, Japan, Nicaragua, and Sierra Leone—introduced a resolution to transfer the matter from the deadlocked Council to the General Assembly under the "Uniting for Peace" formula.[32] A few days later, the Assembly did call on India and Pakistan to return to their previous boundaries, but it was too late. India simply ignored the resolution. On December 12, the question was considered once more by the Council, but India was still safe behind the Soviet veto. The next day, Dacca, the capital of East Pakistan, fell to Indian troops. Pakistan's foreign minister excoriated the Council members: they had failed shamefully, had procrastinated, had shied away from ending aggression, and had denied justice to Pakistan. He ended by announcing that he would not be a party to legalizing aggression, and walked out.

Not until six days later, well after the surrender of the Pakistani army in the eastern province, did the Soviet Union permit the Council to pass a resolution. Even then, the resolution addressed only humanitarian questions of relief and rescue.[33]

That performance must have shattered whatever hopeful illusions were still cherished by small and middle-sized states—that the U.N. could guarantee their safety, either by imposing pacific settlement procedures at an early stage of a dispute or by providing collective security once the dispute had ripened into an armed attack. It was quite clear that, behind the shield of its new treaty of friendship and cooperation with Moscow presciently signed on August 9,[34] India had been free to take whatever actions it wished.

It can be argued that the Council still serves as a sounding board for just causes. The Warsaw Pact powers' invasion of Hungary in 1956 was the occasion for using the Council to publicize the world's outrage. The U.S. used it again in 1983, after the Soviets had shot down a Korean civilian airliner, but it is reluctant to use it in this purely hortatory fashion. During the Vietnam War there was no inclination to use the Council at all. While Nicaragua has indicted the U.S. repeatedly in the Council, the U.S. has failed to counter with formal charges of its own based on Nicaraguan support for insurgents in

El Salvador. Washington now usually prefers to pursue its public advocacy elsewhere, reserving the Council for increasingly infrequent decisions on matters of importance where there is sufficient consensus among the members.

This restraint is not widely shared. In recent years, a sense of futility has led to the inversion of the Council's intended function. Instead of meetings of a small group of leading nations engaged in the serious search for solutions to critical problems, sessions have attracted hordes of delegates, not elected to the Council but customarily accorded the privilege of attending and speaking. Increasingly, the purpose of meetings has not been to take action but, rather, to ventilate grievances and strike attitudes. Thus the Council now tends to be used as a place to let off steam without any serious intent to negotiate a solution. This is too bad; at age forty, what the U.N. least needs is another General Assembly.

Interpositional Peacekeeping

To the extent that the Council has succeeded, it has not been in the two areas assigned to it by the Charter: pacific settlement of disputes, and collective measures to deal with threats to the peace. Instead, it has been in truce observation and in policing the disengagement of warring armies, two "peacekeeping" functions not visualized by the Charter.

The concept of "peacekeeping" logically should include the full range of diplomatic and coercive measures available to the Council for use against violators of the global peace. In U.N. practice and semantics, however, the term has come to be used, in a more specialized sense, to mean the peaceful interpositioning of U.N. personnel, in response to an invitation of the disputants, to oversee an agreed cease-fire.

The key to peacekeeping is the agreement of the disputants to the U.N.'s role. In protracted conflicts, a sense of stalemate, fatigue, or overweening danger may eventually induce the parties to seek respite. At that moment, the U.N. may be able to step in, posting blue-bereted personnel along the line of conflict in such a way as to make it more difficult for enemies to re-engage. The U.N. contingents undertaking such missions are recruited from states acceptable to the parties to the conflict, as well as to the superpowers whose approval is necessary for a mandate from the Security Council. A force may range from a few dozen truce observers to a multinational army of many thousands, supported by civilian staff as well as by air and naval contingents. Its mission may be no more than to keep a look-out for infiltrators and weapons-smugglers. Or it may encompass more, as it did in the Congo, where the U.N. set out to maintain the unity of a country against schismatic factions, ousting foreigners dabbling in the civil war, retraining the national army, rebuilding the economy, and nudging rival politicians to form a government of reconciliation.

The Charter provides no guidance as to how these activities are to be carried out. Article 40 permits the Council, in a dispute, to apply "provisional measures." However, nowhere in the Charter is there any specific authority for the U.N. to use military forces to undertake long-term "peacekeeping" as a provisional measure. In the simple world of the Charter, when fighting breaks out the Council must ultimately decide who started it and then order the community of states to act collectively to punish the initiator. The real world, however, hardly corresponds to this rather Old Testament-like expectation. Instead, the U.N. has found it all but impossible to fix responsibility for initiating a conflict, since, to do so, would require a sorting out of causes and effects as perceived through the lenses of incompatible ideologies. To a Palestinian terrorist, the "cause" of the death of Israeli athletes or schoolchildren is the Israeli military occupation of the West Bank. In such circumstances of divergence the best the U.N. can do is not to fix blame or to punish, but simply from time to time to blow the whistle. Provisional measures have thus themselves become solutions, rather than temporary stop-gaps.

The first large peacekeeping operation, UNEF in the Middle East, established in 1956, was authorized not by the Security Council but by the General Assembly (see above, Chapter 2). The second, and to date largest, was ONUC, the U.N. Operation in the Congo. ONUC was originally authorized by the Security Council but, after Moscow became disenchanted and began to cast its veto, it looked to the Assembly for guidelines and authorization. These two operations brought on a fiscal crisis that nearly crippled the organization. France and the Soviet Union, in particular, refused to pay the costs of activities for which they had not voted and which, they argued, were beyond the scope of the General Assembly. As a result of this dispute (see above, Chapter 5), subsequent peacekeeping operations have been authorized by the Security Council. Indeed, the authorizing of such operations has become the principal constructive function of the Council.

U.N. peacekeeping operations—including truce observation and border patrols—have occurred in Greece, Palestine, Kashmir, Suez and Gaza, Lebanon, Jordan, the Congo (Zaire), West Irian, Yemen, Cyprus, India, Pakistan, and Syria. They are represented by an alphabet soup of strange acronyms: UNYOM (United Nations Yemen Observer Mission) established on June 11, 1963; UNIPOM (United Nations India Pakistan Observer Mission) established by Security Council resolution on September 20, 1965; UNDOF (United Nations Disengagement Observer Force) stationed between the forces of Israel and the Syrian Arab Republic in accordance with an agreement reached on May 31, 1974;[35] and so forth.

To say that the Security Council established most of these peacekeeping forces may be to give the Council more credit than the facts quite sustain. More accurately: the Council has taken the leading role in *authorizing* the establishment of peacekeeping forces. The forces function in accordance with agreements between the parties to the dispute, usually worked out with the active help of one or both superpowers and, sometimes, of the Secretary-General. In few instances was the Council the actual forum in which the agreement to establish a peacekeeping operation was negotiated. The 1964 agreement to establish UNFICYP on Cyprus was reached in negotiations conducted in the precincts of the U.N.—not, of course, in the public sessions of the Council—but, in almost all other instances, the Council has only ratified, legitimated, and multilateralized agreements reached elsewhere. It is not an indispensable function, but neither is it insignificant.

The Security Council, the Superpowers, and UNEF II

A good example of this limited function is provided by the creation of UNEF II (the second United Nations Emergency Force in the Middle East) after the Yom Kippur war of 1973. That conflict began with the Egyptian surprise attack on the East Bank of the Suez Canal on October 6, 1973. As soon as fighting started the U.S. requested a meeting of the Security Council. Four meetings were held between October 8 and 12, but even Washington had no expectations that these would produce results.

The U.N. did serve one useful purpose at this stage. The Secretary-General reported to the Council, on evidence supplied by his truce observer team (UNTSO), that Egypt had struck first.[36] Egypt had asserted the opposite, but so effective was the Secretary-General's report on the facts that the Egyptian government abandoned its version.

Aside from that, the Council had little role to play. As long as the Egyptians were advancing, either their socialist and Third World allies in the Council were unwilling to let the U.N. order a cease-fire, or they demanded an exorbitant price for it. As a cease-fire condition they insisted on complete Israeli withdrawal from the Sinai and all other territories captured in the 1967 fighting, including Gaza and the West Bank.[37]

If the Third World and socialist states were in no mood for a cease-fire while their side was winning, Washington was equally unwilling to have one while its side was losing. Secretary Kissinger, believing the intelligence estimates, was convinced that the Israeli forces would turn the tide within seventy-two hours, a prediction that soon proved too optimistic. He opposed any move, such as a Council-ordered cease-fire "in place," which would ratify the Egyptian gains,[38] and urged Moscow not to propose such an initiative. Because none of the principal parties saw a cease-fire as being in their interest, the U.N. did nothing during the first two bloody weeks of fighting. "The whole point and purpose of the U.N. as an instrument of peace," the *New York Times* editorialized, "is being tested, and once again it is wretchedly failing that test—dissipating its moral force in vapid debate."[39] It looked and sounded even worse on television and radio. When the Council did meet, the seats at the side of the chamber were filled with representatives whose countries were not members of the Secu-

rity Council but who noisily applauded the most virulently anti-Israeli dia-
tribes, leading one delegate to remark that he felt he was "in the middle of a
lynch mob."[40]

After the first five days of frontline slaughter, Secretary-General Kurt Waldheim at last felt compelled to prod the Council. Although he "did not want in
any way to interfere with the efforts of the Security Council, which under the
Charter has the primary responsibility for the maintenance of international
peace and security," nevertheless, in view of the Council's inaction and the
"appalling human losses," he needed to express his profound concern "with the
role of the United Nations in such circumstances. The primary purpose of our
Organization is the maintenance of international peace and security. If we fail
in that role the central point of the Organization's existence is jeopardized." He
urged the members of the Council "to consider once again how the obstacles to
effective and peaceful action can be surmounted and the primary role of the
Council can be reasserted in the interests of peace."[41] But he made no concrete
suggestions, and his appeal produced no action. "It has been another bad week
for the United Nations," the London *Times* reported. "It has been reduced to
the role of a bystander, waiting to see who would win. . . . There was no
prospect of agreement on any form of joint action and even the propaganda
possibilities appeared to have been exhausted for the time being."[42]

Only when Israel's army finally turned the tide of battle, massively reinforced
by a tardy, but ultimately decisive, U.S. airlift, was this impasse broken. Up to
then, the Security Council served primarily to amplify the most exacerbating
rhetoric.

Once the Israelis began to win, however, diplomatic activity picked up. But
not yet in the Council. On October 17, Soviet Premier Kosygin flew to Cairo
for negotiations with President Anwar Sadat. At that point, Israel had captured
substantial additional territory from the Syrians on the northern front and was
beginning to win in the Sinai. Kosygin urged Egypt to salvage what it could of
its earlier advantage. Two days later Kissinger flew to Moscow. Negotiations led
to a U.S.-Soviet "four-point cease-fire plan."[43] On his way back to Washington, Kissinger stopped in Israel to explain it to the Israeli cabinet.

The next day the plan was presented to the Security Council as a "take-it-or-
leave-it" resolution. It was produced only a few hours before the meeting and
had not even been the subject of the customary polite prior "consultations"
between the sponsors and other members. Adopted at 10:00 p.m., it called for
a cease-fire in place "no later than 12 hours after the moment of . . . this
decision"[44] to be followed by negotiations to occur "immediately and concurrently with the cease-fire . . . under appropriate auspices aimed at establishing
a just and durable peace in the Middle East."[45]

Ambassador Huang Hua of China refused to participate in the voting, charging the superpowers with "collusion in the Middle East" and of imposing "the
situation of 'no war, no peace' again on the Arab people."[46] Saudi Ambassador

Jamil M. Baroody fulminated against the history of U.S. treachery, beginning with the "erstwhile haberdasher of Kansas . . ."[47] Harry Truman. Then all the members but China dutifully endorsed the U.S.-Soviet initiative.

This did not end the fighting, and Israeli forces subsequently crossed the Suez Canal for the first time, cutting off the Egyptian Third Army Corps and threatening Cairo. Brezhnev denounced this as "flagrant deceit."[48] One day later, on October 23, the leaders in Moscow and Washington again put their heads together, producing an agreement which surfaced as another Council resolution. It requested the Secretary-General to send "United Nations observers to supervise the observance of the cease-fire."[49] Still the Israeli advance continued. Although Nixon and Kissinger kept in close touch with Brezhnev and Kosygin, assuring them that efforts were being made to curb the Israelis,[50] the situation remained dangerously fluid. On October 24, a desperate Anwar Sadat appealed to the Soviet Union and the United States to send troops to implement the cease-fire.[51] This was followed by a telegram from Brezhnev to Nixon which Kissinger described as "menacing."[52] Washington announced that it would not agree to the dispatch of U.S., much less of Soviet, troops, and would veto any U.N. resolution authorizing them.[53]

Only at this stage of the crisis did something occur which could be seen as a Council initiative, with that body operating as it was intended, a forum for real multilateral diplomacy. Eight Non-Aligned members of the Council announced that they would propose a resolution interposing a new Emergency Force (UNEF II) between Egyptian and Israeli armies.[54] Their draft neither included nor excluded any contributors to the proposed force. Moscow quickly agreed to support the resolution but announced that it would also send troops. With that, Washington placed its military on DefCon III, an "accelerated state of readiness."[55] It also exerted intense pressure on the Egyptian president to withdraw his invitation to Soviet forces.

Sadat agreed,[56] and the Council then adopted the eight-nation resolution authorizing UNEF II[57] after incorporating a proviso that the force "be composed of personnel drawn from States Members of the United Nations except the permanent members of the Security Council."[58] The Council gave the Secretary-General 24 hours in which to draw up guidelines for the composition, financing, and day-to-day command of the force, a task which, previously tackled in the abstract by the General Assembly's Special Committee on Peace Keeping Operations, had proved intractable for over a decade. Now a veteran Secretariat official, George Sherry—an American—was given the assignment and completed it well before the deadline. Soviet Under Secretary General Arkady N. Shevchenko was able to determine that Moscow after years of resistance to such a formula (see Chapter 5, above), suddenly had no objection to the costs of the operation being levied on the basis of the Assembly's regular assessment of contributions by member states to the organization's budget. The next morning Sherry's draft was approved by the Secretary-General and reported to the Council[59] which adopted the new guidelines without objection.[60] However, the force was authorized for only six months, thus satisfying the Russians that the Council, subject to the Soviet veto, would keep it on a short leash.

If this helped secure Soviet cooperation, the U.S. was likewise satisfied that UNEF II would avoid a different pitfall. Its predecessor, UNEF I, had been peremptorily expelled by President Nasser in 1967 (see above, Chapter 5). This time, the U.S. ambassador, John Scali, put on record Washington's understanding that the force could not be withdrawn during any period for which it had been authorized by the Council without that body's specific approval.[61]

In approving the Secretary-General's guidelines, the Council had defined the Secretary-General's role more clearly—and somewhat less broadly—than in previous peacekeeping ventures. Waldheim was required to keep the members fully informed and to submit to the Council for its decision all "matters that might affect the nature or the continued effective functioning" of UNEF II. For the first time it was agreed that "geographic representation" should apply to the composition of the peace force, a requirement which made it necessary to include a Polish contingent.[62]

In all, the operation involved 7000 men and cost $30 million in its first six months. As noted, it was quickly put together by the Secretary-General in consultation with members of the Council. Most important to the operation's success was the Council's adoption of the Secretary-General's draft guidelines on financing, which avoided a fight over allocation of costs such as had marred UNEF I and ONUC. When the Council agreed that UNEF II be funded as general "expenses of the Organization"[63] by the General Assembly under article 17(2) of the Charter, in accordance with a formula weighted to require only minimal contributions by poor countries, this became the model for all future peacekeeping operations.

UNEF II was reauthorized regularly at the request of both Egypt and Israel. It successfully completed its assigned task to the mutual satisfaction of both countries and its presence helped pave the way for the eventual negotiation of a peace treaty. The *New York Times* now "recognized the indispensable role of the maligned and neglected" U.N.[64]

After the first Egyptian-Israeli disengagement agreement was signed on January 18, 1974, at Kilometre 101 on the Cairo-Suez road in the presence of Lieut.-General Ensio Siilasvuo,[65] UNEF II assumed responsibility for inspecting a substantial area between Egyptian and Israeli lines (the "zone of disengagement"), as well as a much larger area between the Egyptian line and the Suez Canal ("area of limited armament and forces") where its task was to ensure strict compliance with the commitment to thin out forces.[66] Both sides agreed that this job, too, was well done, although the Soviets refused to pay their share of the increased cost entailed in this enlarged task. Nevertheless, Secretary-General Waldheim correctly summarized the widely held perception that UNEF II had demonstrated that the United Nations "is still a useful instrument if it is used in the right way."[67]

Problems of Dysfunction: The Uncertain Mandate

ONUC

The Council's function in authorizing peacekeeping operations is likely to be successful if multilateral diplomacy in the Council, or bilateral diplomacy among the superpowers, or a mix of both, has given the peacekeepers a clear mandate. If this is lacking, U.N. peacekeeping can easily become enmeshed in cold war politics.

ONUC, the United Nations Operation in the Congo, is a dramatic example.[68] On June 30, 1960, King Baudouin, at Leopoldville (now Kinshasa), proclaimed the independence of the Republic of the Congo (now Zaire). So swiftly did events move, thereafter, that only two weeks later the U.N. Security Council had adopted its first resolution on the Congo and launched the U.N. on what the Secretary-General called "its biggest single effort."[69] Ralph Bunche, who had come to represent the Secretary-General at independence celebrations, stayed on to preside over an emergency rescue operation.

The first serious violence took the form of tribal rioting on Saturday, July 2, near the towns of Leopoldville and Luluabourg. On Monday, the 4th, police fired on rioters in Coquilhatville, capital of Equateur Province, killing ten and wounding thirteen.

Mutiny broke out in the Congolese army on July 5. Three days later, Prime Minister Lumumba agreed to dismiss all white officers and promoted to general a sergeant, Victor Lundula. Joseph Mobutu, another former non-commissioned officer, was made chief of staff. Panic-stricken whites fled from Leopoldville across the Congo River to Brazzaville, capital of the neighboring Congo Republic.

At the same time, the Belgian government sent 600 additional troops to reinforce the several thousand still stationed at bases retained by Belgium under its treaty of friendship with the Congo. Additional troops were sent to the province of Katanga at the request of its premier, Moise Tshombe, who greeted their arrival by proclaiming secession and demanding admittance to the U.N. A few days later, Belgian paratroop drops were under way throughout the country.

With the new nation literally falling apart, President Kasavubu and Prime Minister Lumumba, on July 12, cabled the Secretary General: "The Government of the Republic of the Congo requests urgent dispatch by the United Nations of military assistance. This request is justified by the dispatch to the Congo of metropolitan Belgian troops in violation of the treaty of friendship." The message accused the Belgian government of having carefully prepared the secession of Katanga "with a view to maintaining a hold on our country" and asked for military aid "to protect the national territory of the Congo against the present external aggression which is a threat to international peace."[70]

Belgium stated that its troops would stay until their task could be assumed by the Congolese themselves. The government of the Congo responded by announcing a "state of war" with Belgium. Quickly, the clouds of East-West confrontation began to gather over the African equator. The Soviet Union charged Belgium with plotting to reoccupy its former colony and accused NATO of complicity. Premier Lumumba and President Kasavubu threatened to seek aid against the Belgians "elsewhere" unless it were immediately forthcoming from the U.N.

It was in this context that the Security Council was convened at the behest of the Secretary-General.[71] Hammarskjold indicated that, if a U.N. force were sent to the Congo, he would avoid becoming a party to internal conflicts. He intended to obtain, in the first place, troops from other countries in Africa and to exclude contributions from any of the permanent members of the Council.[72]

Working through the night, the Security Council adopted a resolution early on the morning of the 14th. It had been introduced by Tunisia, acting in close consultation with the Secretary-General, and passed by a vote of 8 to 0, with China, France, and the United Kingdom abstaining.[73] It called on the government of Belgium "to withdraw their troops from the territory of the Republic of the Congo," but did not authorize the use of force for this or any other purpose. It authorized the Secretary-General to provide technical and military assistance to the government of the Congo in order to help them prepare the national security forces "to meet fully their tasks."[74]

What tasks? To prevent looting and raping? To put down the rebellion in Katanga? To force the Belgians to withdraw? The resolution simply did not say. Different states voting for it in the Security Council would have answered these questions in very disparate ways.

That was how the U.N.'s difficulties began. In order to put together a resolution that would not be vetoed by any of the five permanent members, it was necessary to find wording that would fudge the real issues, leaving them for resolution in a pragmatic, case-by-case fashion. Unfortunately, that the principal parties had quite contrary expectations of the U.N.'s role put the Secretary-General in endless case-by-case dilemmas. Any interpretation satisfactory to Washington was likely to be unsatisfactory to Moscow; one acceptable to Leopoldville was certain to be unacceptable to Brussels.

Shortly after the U.N.'s involvement, a further defect in its mandate appeared, one which could not have been foreseen by the drafters. On September 5, President Kasavubu dismissed Prime Minister Lumumba, charging him with fomenting civil war. The prime minister returned the compliment by announcing the discharge of Kasavubu. President Kasavubu quickly named Joseph Ileo to form a new government, but, before he could assume office, Joseph Mobutu, the chief of staff, announced, on September 14, that the army had taken power and proscribed all political activity by Lumumba, Kasavubu, and for good measure Ileo. Mobutu also ordered the closing of the Soviet and Czechoslovak embassies, which were being helpful to Lumumba. Congolese troops surrounded the ex-prime minister's residence, where ONUC forces were also stationed. The cold war had engulfed the Congo, and with it the fledgling ONUC.

The U.N.'s mandate had authorized the Secretary-General to provide "the Government with . . . military assistance" and to help the "national security forces." But *which* government? That of Lumumba? Kasavubu? Ileo? Mobutu? And whose forces? When the Secretary-General went back to the Security Council for clarification of his mandate, he found that body hopelessly deadlocked. Lumumba had already called on Moscow for direct military intervention and, in response, a fleet of Soviet air transports and technicians as well as Czechoslovak military officers had begun to arrive. President Nkrumah of Ghana sent his friend Lumumba funds and advice even while providing contingents for ONUC. The United States supported President Kasavubu diplomatically, while aiding ONUC logistically. The Belgians, French, and British appeared to be supporting Katangan President Tshombe's right to secede.

Deadlocked by the veto, the Security Council on September 17 voted to summon the Assembly under the Uniting for Peace procedure[75] over strenuous opposition from the Soviet Union and France. When the Assembly began to assume jurisdiction over ONUC, those two states took the position that the entire Congo operation had become illegal.

The rush of political events in the Congo left the U.N. as referee in a game without rules. Having been invited in to achieve a particular purpose—the restoration of law and order and the withdrawal of Belgian troops—ONUC now found itself in the midst of a complex constitutional debacle which threatened to become a civil war of gigantic proportions. The U.N. could not, however, avoid the shift in its role. Secretary-General Hammarskjold's efficiency had quickly promoted it to the largest military and economic factor in the country. There were nearly 20,000 U.N. troops in place. Whether that force was brought to bear on one side or the other was almost always decisive. When it acted, that was decisive, just as when it did not.

That the U.N. operation had become so intensely controversial and evolved in such unanticipated directions was due, in part, to the vagueness of its original mandate and to the insufficiency of that mandate once the cold war and civil war had overtaken events. ONUC's troubles were also due to the fact that the mandate was open-ended. It had been authorized "in consultation with the Government of the Congo" to continue to provide "military assistance" until the government forces were able, "in the opinion of the Government to meet fully their tasks."[76] But, again, *which* government? Thus, ONUC became a sort of "Flying Dutchman"—a ship without port. What is surprising, is that out of it all emerged the relatively cohesive and governable nation of Zaire.

Virtually everyone agreed, however, that ONUC should not be a precedent for future operations.

As we have seen, subsequent peacekeeping efforts were authorized for a specified amount of time, usually for a renewable six-month term. This means that if radical changes of circumstance occurred, within a relatively short period the Security Council would have occasion to decide whether these warrant a change in the operation's mandate. In the absence of agreement, particularly among the permanent members, the operation would terminate automatically, rather than continuing on the sole authority of the Secretary-General.

UNIFIL

Nevertheless, the problem does recur, because operations are still launched without clear mandates. Thus, when Israel, on March 15, 1978, seized a six-mile-wide strip of Lebanon in retaliation for Palestinian raids across its northern frontier, Washington proposed the creation of a United Nations Interim Force in Lebanon (UNIFIL). Brian Urquhart, the Under-Secretary-General with peace-keeping responsibility, opposed the idea as unworkable in the same way ONUC had been. Nevertheless, by a vote of 12 to 0, with the Soviet Union and Czechoslovakia abstaining, and China once again not participating in the vote, the Security Council adopted the U.S. initiative on March 19.[77] The force of 4000 was to "supervise the cessation of hostilities, ensure the peaceful character of the area of operation, control movement and take all measures deemed necessary to assure the effective restoration of Lebanese sovereignty. . . . until the Government of Lebanon assumes its full responsibilities in southern Lebanon."[78] It was authorized for an initial period of six months and its cost of $68 million was to be allocated by the Assembly as an expense of the organization, in accordance with the equitable formula that released most Third World countries from all but minimal contributions.[79]

The Council's passage of the resolution obscured the fact that there was not much agreement on UNIFIL's mission. The representatives of China and Russia immediately stated that, while they had not vetoed the operation, neither would they support or pay for it.[80] The guidelines, too, proved less than helpful. In all, UNIFIL was launched with only an unclear mandate created by a fragile and deliberately imprecise political compromise. In the original draft, the U.S. resolution had explicitly authorized the force to control movement within a demilitarized area and "to prevent the entry of unauthorized armed persons into the zone." That wording was intended to be a clear enunciation of UNIFIL's authority to disarm any PLO units that chose to remain in the South. In the negotiated revision of that test, the phrasing had been dropped in favor of less precise language authorizing UNIFIL to control movement and take measures to help restore Lebanese control.[81] Unfortunately, the government of Lebanon, profoundly weakened by years of civil war, Syrian occupation, and PLO autonomy was in no shape to assume responsibility for pacifying

Southern Lebanon. Instead, the U.N. had to improvise, thereby earning criticism both for tolerating the presence of the pro-Israeli Christian militia of Major Haddad and for negotiating—at the level of an Under-Secretary-General—with the PLO as if it were the government of Southern Lebanon.[82] And, of course, when the Israelis reinvaded Lebanon in 1982, UNIFIL was criticized for failing to stop them, a task for which it had never been envisaged.

UNIFIL, therefore, is a failure except by comparison to any alternative. Despite criticism, it has regularly been extended by the Security Council.[83] On May 3, 1978, its strength was raised from 4000 to 6000 troops.[84] For a brief time, between July 1981 and April 1982, the U.N. was even successful in negotiating and enforcing a complete cease-fire between the PLO and Israel along the boundary patrolled by UNIFIL. The operation was not withdrawn even after it was surrounded by the 1982 Israeli advance, which made its task, by its own admission, "virtually impossible." When its mandate was renewed again, on July 18, 1983, Lebanese Foreign Minister Elie Salem told the Council that UNIFIL had succeeded in "insuring relative peace and stability in the areas under its control."[85] The Soviet Union (with Poland) again abstained, but China, in an about-face, voted in favor of the extension "out of deference to the wishes of Lebanon and to help in creating stability and promote a settlement."[86] The force, at that time, consisted of 5,888 men from Fiji, Finland, France, Ghana, Italy, Ireland, the Netherlands, Norway, Senegal, and Sweden.

Problems of Dysfunction: The Frozen Status Quo

Even a successful U.N. peacekeeping operation is likely to produce a negative concomitant: its very success in defusing a confrontation conduces to stalemate. Examples of this abound, in Kashmir, on the Golan Heights, and, most dramatically, in Cyprus. As early as 1967, the Secretary-General, in his report to the Security Council on the work of the United Nations Peace-Keeping Force in Cyprus (UNFICYP), pointed out that there were no negotiations going on between the parties, despite Council resolutions calling for them, and despite the dangerously high level of tensions. He warned that the parties' excessive confidence in the presence of the U.N. force may well have reduced the sense of urgency needed to prod them into a deliberate search for solutions to the communal problems between Turkish and Greek Cypriots. The Secretary-General added that he wanted the parties to keep in mind that UNFICYP could not be positioned between them indefinitely.[87] (At the time, it consisted of a total of 4,449 military personnel and had already cost the U.N. approximately $70 million in the three years since its inception.[88])

In 1974, the Turkish invasion, following a Greek-sponsored coup on the island, brought about radical changes in that *status quo*, with the invading army occupying approximately one-third of the Republic. UNFICYP, caught in the middle, sustained considerable casualties but was neither authorized nor able to prevent the Greek coup, let alone the Turkish invasion. Just before these events UNFICYP had been reduced to 2,197 personnel[89] for reasons of economy. Now it had to be reinforced by the hurried addition of 2000 men from Denmark, Finland, Canada, Sweden, and Britain.[90] When the foreign ministers of Greece, Turkey, and the United Kingdom, again working outside the context of the Council, reached agreement on a standstill and on the establishment of a security zone between the combatants, to be supervised by UNFICYP, the Security Council obligingly adopted resolutions ratifying the call for a cease-fire and reaffirming the U.N. force's interpositional role.[91] But the Council did not then, or subsequently, move the parties to resume serious negotiations, although it repeatedly urged that these be initiated forthwith, and that their "outcome should not be impeded or prejudged by the acquisition of advantages resulting from military operations . . . ."[92]

That the Council's efforts to achieve negotiations have led nowhere is partly the "fault" of UNFICYP's success in stabilizing the situation of *de facto* partition of the island. The Turkish forces have remained where they were when the cease-fire came into effect, and UNFICYP, in effect, has become, at least in part, another disengagement force patrolling, and thus—inevitably—reinforcing, the new *status quo* imposed by the last round of fighting.

This is an obvious criticism to make of the U.N. presence, and one that is frequently made by the socialist members. With the exception of Yugoslavia, they refuse to contribute financially to UNFICYP. But it is more significant that neither the Turkish nor the Greek Cypriot community wishes to see the force removed. To each side, while the *status quo* is highly unsatisfactory, all but one of the alternatives is worse. That alternative, outright victory over the other side, would be extremely costly and is probably beyond the military capability of either side. The respective governments in Athens, Ankara, and in the two Cypriot communities are realistic enough to know this, but are also politically aware that, were the U.N. not in the way, they would come under irresistible pressure from their own supporters to attempt a military solution. Thus UNFICYP, and other U.N. peacekeepers, also serve as a convenient excuse for governments not to pursue popularity by courting disaster.

Gimbel's or Macy's

The purpose of U.N. peacekeeping is to create disengagements, allow tempers to cool, and keep superpower rivalries at a distance. Sometimes, however, the U.N. is not the vehicle for attaining these objectives.

The Egyptian-Israeli peace treaty of March 26, 1979, negotiated outside the U.N. and reviled by the Assembly,[93] provides that the U.N. be asked to supervise its implementation,[94] but U.S. President Carter assured the signatories that if "the Security Council fails to establish and maintain the arrangements called for in the Treaty, [I would] be prepared to take those steps necessary to ensure the establishment and maintenance of an acceptable alternative multinational force."[95]

In July 1979 the mandate of UNEF II expired and, because of the peace treaty, was not renewed by the Security Council. After a round of consultations with members the president of the Council reported, on May 18, 1981, that no agreement could be reached on establishing a U.N.-sponsored force to monitor the Camp David accords.[96] Moscow had indicated a readiness to veto any such proposal. With that, the parties to the treaty, aided by the U.S., set about creating a new peacekeeping institution, the Multinational Force and Observers (MFO), outside the U.N. framework. MFO consists of troops and observers stationed on both sides of the border to verify compliance with the complex limitations, imposed by the treaty, on the levels of Egyptian and Israeli military presence in four zones (three on the Egyptian side of the border and one on the Israeli side). The new organization also has a naval component charged with patrolling the strategic Strait of Tiran, which is internationalized by the treaty to assure Israel's access to the Gulf of Aqaba.

MFO has been a success, and, therefore, challenges the U.N. in the one area of its evident proficiency. In the careful words of Leamon R. Hunt, who was its first head, MFO "held the promise of finding better ways in an environment relatively free of the accumulated bureaucratic weight and political complexity of an existing organization."[97] During the first year of its operation, it consisted of 2600 personnel from Australia, Colombia, Fiji, France, Italy, the Netherlands, New Zealand, United Kingdom, United States, and Uruguay. Norway provided the commander of the force and several officers. Its budget for fiscal year 1982–83 was $103.5 million, with one-third each being contributed by Egypt, Israel, and the United States. Most of the states providing contingents are absorbing all or part of their cost.[98]

The success of MFO, combined with the general attitude to the U.N. of the U.S. mission under Jeane Kirkpatrick, paved the way for the organization to be bypassed again when an international force had to be sent to the Beirut area after the 1982 Israeli invasion. Although the PLO and, reluctantly, the Soviet Union, were prepared to have the Council authorize a U.N. force to supervise the departure of the Palestinian militia from the Beirut enclave, this option was not pursued. The Israelis expressed strong reservations about the impartiality of a U.N. contingent in that role and the Christian-led Lebanese government preferred to accept French, Italian, and U.S. contingents with British support. Nevertheless, a U.N. presence probably could have been established had the chief U.S. delegate pressed for it within the councils of power in Washington and in negotiations with Lebanon and Israel. According to one State Department source, "Jeane was the one to whom we looked for advocacy of a U.N. role. When she didn't fight for it, nobody did."

It can be argued that a U.N. force could only have been put into Beirut with the sort of hazy compromise mandate that created such problems for ONUC. This cannot be proven or disproven, because the U.S. delegation did not really explore the option. The alternative, however, did not prove to be any bargain. The U.S.-French-Italian-U.K. force in Lebanon left too quickly, then returned after the Shatila camp massacre with an even more uncertain mission, which allied it with one side in a growing civil war. Once it encountered resistance from elements of the population, it was quickly shown to have a shaky political and military foundation. Its all-Western composition also virtually guaranteed the accelerated intrusion of the cold war. As U.S. representatives had gone to great lengths to point out during the 1973 negotiations preceding the establishing of UNEF II, the posting of superpower forces in the region contributes to the very dangers and tensions the force is intended to alleviate. Arguably, a force of neutrals, established by the Security Council and underwritten by all 159 U.N. members, might have fared better and could scarcely have done worse.

The incident may simply serve to suggest that skepticism toward the U.N.'s capabilities, while a healthy antidote to earlier illusions and unwarranted optimism, can also create new harm for the national interest if taken too far. It is not necessarily true that the organization is incapable of doing anything that accords with the national interests of the United States. Some Reagan administration officials, however, appear to believe exactly that. The result, in the Beirut instance, was more flag-draped coffins being flown home on military transports, leading to the disintegration of a fragile national consensus, followed by another unedifying U.S. withdrawal from commitment.

Proposals for Reform

It is argued that if the Security Council worked better, there would be no reason for states to go elsewhere to solve important problems of collective security and peacekeeping. Such non-U.N. collective security machinery as the North Atlantic Treaty Organization and the Warsaw Pact would be unnecessary, as would the non-U.N. institutions for peacekeeping such as the MFO.

There has been no shortage of proposals for improving the working of the Security Council. For more than twenty years, Finland has championed Trygve Lie's original plan to upgrade the Council by having it meet regularly as a committee of foreign ministers, an option actually provided by article 28(2) of the Charter. In 1970 it was decided to try out the idea[99] and, on October 21, a closed session was held, attended by the foreign ministers of Spain, China, Colombia, Finland, France, Nepal, Nicaragua, Poland, U.S.S.R., U.K., U.S., and the deputy foreign minister of Syria. Burundi, Sierra Leone, and Zambia were represented at the usual ambassadorial level. The session began with a *tour d'horizon* by the Secretary-General, followed by what the U.N. press office called an "exchange of views" on current issues affecting international peace and security.[100] In fact, it turned out to be a purely formal ritual, which had been expected to accomplish nothing, and met those expectations. Since foreign ministers of most countries attend part of the annual general debate, the Assembly provides many informal opportunities for consultation. Such meetings are likely to be more productive than a formal session of the Council. It is difficult to imagine a subject that could more profitably be discussed by the foreign ministers of China, the U.S.S.R., and the United States in the presence of the permanent representatives of Burundi and Sierra Leone.

A more functional set of recommendations for improving the Council's utility was made in 1982 by a commission headed by the recurrent Swedish premier, Olof Palme. It recommended limits on the veto: If members in a dispute request the U.N. to send observers, fact-finders, or mediators, the report proposed, no permanent member should veto such a request.[101] One advantage claimed for this proposal is that it could be implemented by a "gentlemen's agreement" between the permanent members, or by an amendment to the Council's rules of procedure, rather than by formal amendment of the Charter.[102] The reaction of the Big Five to the recommendations has been reserved at best. Both superpowers tend to the view that any conflict, anywhere, affects their national interest, and they are reluctant to yield, in advance, any of their special Charter rights.

One American ambassador thought that, while any agreement limiting the veto is highly unlikely, the permanent members may be moving toward a practical accommodation comparable to the one evolving between the U.S. President and Congress in respect of the controversial War Powers Resolution governing the former's discretionary use of the armed forces for the conduct of limited hostilities. He predicted that "the Secretary-General will be free to act on his own in a crisis for a limited number of days; but then he would have to come back to the Council if he wanted to continue those efforts."[103] As indicated in the preceding chapter, something of this sort is probably already within the Secretary-General's implied powers.

Other proposals for improving the functioning of the Council focus on its fact-finding capability. They include the establishment of an "early warning system" and "tripwires" which would jolt the members into action and clarify the issues before a crisis becomes unmanageable. A variant would have the Council authorize the stationing of U.N. "ambassadors" in each member state to engage in activities that include fact-finding, forecasting, and mediation.

Although there is room for such innovations, the search for more fundamental reforms in the workings of the Security Council is not likely to be productive. Oddly, this is not because the present structure of the Council is beyond salvation, but because it is perfectly satisfactory. If the Council is not working, it is not because there is anything seriously wrong with its structure or mandate but because, in a world of sovereign states, its paralysis is an accurate reflection of the intense differences that divide nations. It is not a suitable forum for bilateral negotiations, particularly among the superpowers, because there are too many extraneous actors likely to get in the way. One exception (noted in Chapter 2) occurred over three decades ago, during the Berlin crisis, when the rest of the Council's members stood aside to let the Soviet-U.S. negotiations proceed informally and unobstructed by grandstanding. This has rarely been repeated. When governments are ready for multilateral or inter-bloc negotiations, the Council's informal consultative process is perfectly adequate. And once an agreement has been reached—inside or outside the U.N.—on what to do, the Council provides a workable way to establish credible machinery—good offices, peacekeeping forces, truce observation teams, and fact-finders,—for doing it.

That simply does not happen often enough.

§ 10 §

The General Assembly and the U.S. National Interest

The General Assembly Perceived

Most Americans, when they express views about the United Nations, dwell on the activities of the General Assembly. It is the work of the General Assembly that is usually cited by those who oppose the organization and U.S. participation in it. While the Assembly is probably the least useful major organ of the U.N. system—certainly now, from the perspective of U.S. national interest—the nay-sayers' negativism is ofttimes exaggerated and sometimes downright irrational. The critics tend to exaggerate either the Assembly's importance or its impotence, or sometimes both.

That the Assembly should be so central to the popular perception of the U.N. is at least in part due to its unselfconscious capacity for media hype. The public sessions of the Security Council usually unfold with a somnolent solemnity that defies news-making while its slightly more interesting "informal consultations" are not open to reporters. Only when it tackles a war-threatening crisis does the Council's performance become a media event. The Assembly, on the other hand, seeks—and sometimes holds—the limelight from September to December by staging its annual extravaganza, featuring star turns by batteries of visiting heads of state, supported by a cast of thousands and spiced by ample corridor gossip. Obligingly, it provides amusing and outrageous antics of such colorful eccentrics as Sir Eric Gairy, who, when prime minister of Grenada, regaled the assembled delegates with calls for dialogue with Unidentified Flying Objects and the world of plants. What could provide more irresistible copy, or a better photo "opportunity," than the dance executed in 1971 by the berobed Tanzanian Ambassador Salim Salim to celebrate communist China's defeat of U.S. efforts to exclude it from the Assembly?

Attention-getting, too, is the Assembly's perennial tendency to cast the United States in the role of villain. Speakers, and resolutions, pillory the U.S. for its support of "racist" South Africa and "aggressive" Israel, and blame America for the poverty of the Third World and the sins of multinational corporations. Immoderation is newsworthy in a way reasonableness can but envy.

The popular negative perception, however, is not primarily the fault of the media, which strive for balanced coverage. For example, the General Assembly's criticisms of Israel and of the U.S. role in the Middle East rated 451 column inches in the *New York Times* between January 1, 1980, and January 1, 1983, but that newspaper, in the same period, also devoted 239 column inches to the Assembly's criticism of foreign (i.e., Soviet) forces in Afghanistan. The public impression, nevertheless, is that Israel gets pilloried, while others go scot-free. The first part—that Israel is pilloried—is correct enough; the second part, however—that others get off scot-free—is wrong.

There is much about the Assembly for the American public to dislike. Its "one state, one vote" system equates the 220 million Americans with a few hundred thousand citizens of Iceland or Grenada. At the beginning of 1984, of the 159 member-nations twenty-nine had fewer than one million inhabitants. In part because this system so utterly distorts reality, the Assembly produces huge paper-majorities for resolutions that seem to us, at best, absurd. For example, the U.S., Britain, and France, which between them have given independence to one billion ex-colonials, are verbally battered for not forcing "freedom" on the handful of inhabitants of the Marianas, the Falklands, and the Isle of Mayotte, persons who perversely wish only to remain American, British, or French; meanwhile, not a word is said of the captive nations of Eastern Europe. The Assembly could not find its voice when General Idi Amin terrorized Uganda, nor when the Baha'is and others were murdered by the theocratic dictatorship of Iran. Yet it chastised the U.S. for saving Grenada from its own lethal replica of Amin.

All this may be deplorable, but it is not nearly the whole picture, which is neither purely black nor white, but mottled and gray. From the perspective of the U.S. national interest, the Assembly is part drama, part travesty, part farce, and part tragedy. Only a carefully calibrated image of the Assembly can facilitate accurate conclusions as to whether, when, and how the U.S. should participate in, or disengage from, what we once hoped would become the global marketplace of ideas, the town meeting of the world.

What the Assembly Does

During the thirty-seventh regular annual session in 1982[1] the Assembly approved 430 resolutions and decisions. Given the number and variety of serious problems on this globe, the Assembly's allocation of attention is little short of bizarre. Of the 430, fully forty-one were devoted wholly or partly to criticizing Israel; thirty-five dealt with white domination in Southern Africa; and twenty-six took the form of appeals for help to individual nations facing severe economic, social, or medical needs. Thus, the three overriding preoccupations—Israel, Southern Africa, and disaster-assistance—motivated almost one-quarter (22 percent) of the Assembly's resolutions in 1982. A study by the Heritage Foundation, based on the same year, concluded that the Assembly and its seven main committees devoted over one-third of the delegates' time to debate on the Middle East alone.[2] Psychic energy is also egregiously misallocated. However important the Southern African and Middle Eastern issues may be, they are treated so mordaciously—linking and equating the one with the other, for example[3]—and by so many duplicative committees, that the output numbs rather than arouses. And this simple-minded emphasis on a few topics serves as a screen that keeps the Assembly from addressing other, more widespread problems for which there are no simplistic remedies.

In most instances, the U.S. is heavily outvoted in the Assembly. Of the 157 resolutions, or parts of resolutions, passed by recorded vote in 1982, the United States was on the losing side in all but twenty-four. In 94 instances, we voted against adoption and in thirty-nine we abstained. Indeed, we frequently find ourselves almost completely isolated, without apparent allies, a symbolic condition that justifies genuine alarm. On nineteen resolutions, the U.S. was entirely alone in opposition; and on another eighteen we were joined only by Israel.[4] Nor did these concern only unimportant or tangential issues. We were alone in opposing resolutions on a convention to prohibit the manufacture of chemical and bacteriological weapons,[5] on the promotion of "a new world information and communication order,"[6] and on protection against "products harmful to health and the environment."[7] In all, the United States was on the losing side almost four times as often as on the winning side, and we stood alone, or with Israel only, more often than we found ourselves in the majority.

These statistics appear to confirm the widely held American perception that the Assembly is a cold and hostile place in which to conduct U.S. foreign policy. The world gangs up on the U.S. there. It should be understood, however, that American isolation in the Assembly is the result not only of genuine Third World *animus* against the rich, powerful United States but also of the very firm stand Washington has taken, particularly since the beginning of the Reagan administration, in opposition to the wishes of a majority of states in four important areas. The U.S. has rejected virtually all censure of Israeli and South African policies, firmly opposed the economic demands and claims of entitlement presented by the Third World, and resisted most efforts to increase the U.N. system's range of activity and the size of its budget. Altogether these four areas of confrontation between the U.S. and the Third World—and, indeed, quite often much of the rest of the world—account for most of the instances in which the U.S. finds itself in the minority, and for virtually every case in which it is entirely isolated.

Outside these four large areas, the U.S. tends to be in agreement with, or does not seriously challenge, the views of the Assembly's majority. In 1982, the U.S. enthusiastically joined 105 other members in calling on Vietnamese forces to withdraw from Kampuchea—a resolution vehemently opposed by the Soviet Union, Vietnam, and the other clients of Moscow.[8] The U.S. was with 114 nations in calling for the withdrawal of foreign troops from Afghanistan;[9] and joined the majority to work out ways to avert new flows of refugees[10] and to examine the relation between mass population exoduses and the violations of human rights by governments.[11] On such diverse issues as the improvement of the position of women in public life,[12] the development of a global strategy for drug control,[13] and the prohibition of torture and other cruel, inhuman, or degrading treatment or punishment of prisoners,[14] the U.S. is in substantial agreement with the positions taken by the majority of the Assembly, even though it remains skeptical about the sincerity of many of the states that support these noble aspirations.

The picture is further shaded upon examining another group of resolutions, those adopted without a vote. In 1982 the Assembly took action on 340 resolutions,[15] of which more than half—183—were accepted by consensus. Some were uncontroversial or purely cosmetic, but others represented a good-faith effort to negotiate from divergence to convergence. Indeed, creating consensus has become an increasingly important part of the Assembly's work. This results from a growing, if grudging, awareness on the part of the voting majority that resolutions passed without the support of major powers are likely to achieve nothing. If that glimmering of realism should become conventional wisdom, the Assembly might once again become a serious, productive place for dialogue.

Consensus: The Assembly and U.S. Territories

An example of this is provided by the U.N.'s gingerly handling of the U.S. overseas territories. Three of these—the U.S. Virgin Islands, American Samoa, and Guam—are classified by the U.N. as colonial dependencies. In a separate but related category are the Marianas, Carolines, and Marshall Islands, which are under U.N. supervision but administered by the U.S. as the Pacific Islands Strategic Trust Territory. Finally, there is the special case of the Commonwealth of Puerto Rico.

There has been discussion in the Assembly and its subsidiary organs, and, in the case of Puerto Rico, some real bitterness. But the bottom line is that in no instance has the national interest of the United States actually been undermined by any Assembly action. The socialist countries have repeatedly tried—and failed—to enlist the Third World majority in one or another maneuver against America. In particular, they continue to use the Assembly to impugn

U.S. intentions and to criticize its motives. But they have made few converts and, in failing, have revealed not U.S. isolation but their own.

It is one of history's miracles that half the globe, in less than a quarter-century, has navigated a mainly smooth transition from colony to nationhood. Judge Manfred Lachs, of the International Court of Justice, has observed that "at San Francisco we believed we were setting two objectives on the road to peace: de-colonization and disarmament. We thought that de-colonization would take at least fifty years while disarmament could be achieved in a decade. In fact, it turned out to be exactly the other way around."[16] No doubt the repeated and ringing affirmations of the "right" of self-determination in the U.N. Charter helped establish the climate in which decolonization was able to flourish. If more credit is due to the fatigue of postwar Europe and to the Labour Party of Britain—still, the U.N. also helped, by keeping up a steady drumbeat of inspections and criticism which eventually made the concept of empire universally unfashionable. The colonial powers, in time, resigned themselves to the dictum of Pasha Osmin, spoken at the end of Mozart's *Abduction from the Seraglio:* "If one cannot win someone's heart by one's good deeds, one must then set him free."[17]

In establishing the right of self-determination the General Assembly took the lead, despite strong resistance. In the 1950s and early 1960s, colonialist nations insisted that the Assembly had no authority to set standards, let alone time-tables for implementing self-determination. They rejected demands to report on, and be accountable for, political developments in their dependencies. They denied that the Assembly had jurisdiction to dispatch inspectors and to pass judgment on their performance on the basis of new standards to which they had not agreed.

By the early 1960s, however, this resistance by the colonial powers began to melt, and, by 1968, it had about ceased. Only Portugal continued to insist that colonial governance was an internal matter and no concern of the Assembly's. The others had even accepted in principle the right of the Assembly in "appropriate" instances to send visiting missions to examine their few residual colonies.[18] By 1982 there had been twenty-five such inspections by teams deployed with the consent of Britain, Australia, New Zealand, the United States,[19] France, Spain, and eventually Portugal. These countries also prepared extensive reports to the organization,[20] which were fully debated. Even the chairman of the Assembly's Special Committee on Decolonization, by 1982, was commending the "full co-operation of all the administering Powers."[21]

Since the U.S. had ceased to be a major colonial power by 1947, after the grant of independence to the Philippines, and had long espoused anti-imperialism as an article of political faith, the anti-colonialist stance of the General Assembly was not directly adverse to America's national interest. On the contrary, in this area of U.N. concern the U.S. fared reasonably well, even in the face of efforts by the socialist states to portray the U.S. as an enemy of self-determination. Thus it was Washington which, in 1977, suggested that a visiting mission be sent by the Assembly to inspect the U.S. Virgin Islands dependency.[22] To the surprise of some hard-nosed Washington skeptics, the visiting mission's report and subsequent action by the Assembly were cooperative and non-adversarial, both in tone and content.[23] Since that time, the resolutions passed by the Assembly on this subject invariably satisfy the U.S. and are regularly adopted by consensus.[24]

Equally exemplary has been the Assembly's performance in respect of American Samoa. Washington has reported annually on the progress of Samoa's 30,000 inhabitants, and in 1980 it welcomed a visiting U.N. mission.[25] The Assembly has even commended the "positive attitude of the Government of the United States."[26] The three members of the mission who visited the island for a week in July 1981—Ambassador Abdul G. Koroma of Sierra Leone, Mr. Dasant Vishnu Nevrekar of India, and Mrs. Lenore Sylvia Dorset of Trinidad—faithfully reported[27] the evident "attachment of the people (of Samoa) to the United States"[28] and recorded U.S. accomplishments in medical care, education, and the promotion of self-government. Their report states that the leaders interviewed "expressed their satisfaction with the existing political status of the Territory and their desire to maintain the present relationship with the United States."[29] In turn, U.S. Ambassador William Courtney Sherman has expressed the view that the mission produced "constructive work" and an "excellent report."[30] On the question of Samoa, as on the Virgin Islands, there is no trace of antagonism between the U.S. and the U.N. The Assembly's annual resolutions on this subject have been accurate and non-judgmental, and they pass by consensus.[31]

Somewhat more difficulty has been encountered by the U.S. in connection with the Pacific island dependency of Guam, because it is near Asia and houses an important U.S. military base, from which B-52 bombers had flown to bomb Vietnam and Cambodia. Even so, a fairly acceptable compromise has been worked out. Guam, with a population of about 100,000, has made it abundantly clear to the Assembly's investigators that it wishes to become neither an independent nation nor a state of the union. Through its elected territorial government and its elected delegate to the U.S. House of Representatives in Washington, Guamanians also press the view that the U.S. base must continue and, if possible, be expanded. These are not sentiments that fit the credo of national liberation developed by the Non-Aligned Movement (NAM), and so it is understandable that some states have been tempted to try to embarrass Washington during the Assembly's consideration of the item. The instigators are Moscow's surrogates in the NAM: Angola, Cuba, the Lao People's Democratic Republic, Mozambique, and Vietnam. In 1977 they introduced a confrontational amendment to the proposed "consensus" resolution on Guam. It deplored the presence of military installations on the island, asserting that these would prevent the people from exercising their right of self-determination.[32]

There followed intense behind-the-scenes negotiations between the United States and the moderate majority among the NAMs. As a result, the Non-Aligned bloc refused to rally behind the confrontational proposals, which were withdrawn and replaced by a preambular paragraph which merely states: "that the policy of maintaining military bases and installations in Non-Self-Governing Territories which inhibit the right of self-determination of peoples is incompatible with the relevant resolutions of the United Nations."[33] This formulation was adopted by consensus. The NAMs were able to inject a ritualistic reference to their unifying (if largely unheeded) liturgy of demilitarization. The U.S. was equally able to concur on the ground that its base on Guam, being maintained with evident consent of the people, is not in the category criticized by the resolution.

The following year, the Guam resolution prepared by the Third World majority stated that "military bases could constitute a factor impeding" self-determination.[34] The United States once again felt itself able to go along with this compromise since it only stated a hypothetical contingency ("could"), without passing judgment. This compromise worked until 1981.[35] At that time Cuba chaired the more than 100-member NAM bloc, manipulating the group's often overextended diplomats with considerable skill. The Thirty-sixth Assembly thus found itself presented with a draft resolution on Guam which reflected the proclivities of Havana and Moscow. It stated baldly that "the presence of . . . military bases [on Guam] constitutes a factor impeding the implementation" of self-determination.[36] This language became the subject of intense controversy. An amendment to restore the previously used compromise was offered by Canada, Denmark, Fiji, Japan, New Zealand, Papua New Guinea, Philippines, Samoa, Senegal, and the Solomon Islands.[37] Wisely, the United States had prompted friendly countries of the region to take the lead. They did so to much better effect than had the U.S. been its own advocate. The representative of Fiji pointed out that "the documentation . . . before the Committee did not suggest that those [military] facilities were standing in the way of self-determination."[38] The Sri Lankan representative pointed out that his country, a charter member of the Non-Aligned, had become independent in 1948 while retaining a British military installation on its territory but that "the presence of those bases had in no way impeded the accession of the people of Sri Lanka to independence."[39] With the help of the bulk of Third World nations, the pro-U.S. amendment was carried by a vote of 66 to 41, with 16 abstentions.[40] Those opposed were primarily the socialist countries and their allies, although, notably, joined by Mexico, Nigeria, and India. The next day the usual resolution on Guam was again adopted by consensus.[41]

This compromise has held. The resolutions of 1982[42] and 1983[43] admonish "the administering Power" to "ensure that military bases and installations do

not hinder the population of the Territory from exercising its right to self-determination and independence."[44] Since these words do not suggest that the U.S.
base does in fact hinder self-determination, it is an acceptable compromise
between "theology" and reality. It also demonstrates the usefulness of resolutions used as instruments of negotiation rather than of psychic gratification and
propaganda.

For some, however, confrontation is preferable to consensus.

The Consensus Cracks: Guam and the Pacific Trust Territory

Blocked frontally on Guam, the Soviets in 1982 tried a different tactic. Opening a second front is not a particularly difficult maneuver in the General
Assembly, which works primarily through a forest of standing committees,
special committees, ad hoc committees, subcommittees, and working groups
("closed-ended," and "open-ended"). Since the jurisdictions of these many
jealous fiefdoms inevitably overlap, the same issue can be raised and re-raised
in various forums or in subgroups of the same forum, seeking out the one in
which a sympathetic chairman or an unobservant membership will accept—
probably as part of a "package deal"—a proposition dear to the heart of some
special interest. (Any American who has served at the U.N. could endorse the
observation that the best training for operating in the General Assembly is
probably service in the U.S. Congress.)

In 1982 the issue of Guam—already having been dealt with quite reasonably
a few days earlier by the appropriate subcommittee and then in plenary—was
suddenly reopened by an otherwise innocuous draft resolution adopting the
annual report of the Special Committee on Decolonization. Buried in its
mounds of anti-colonialist platitudes was a call for immediate and unconditional withdrawal of all military bases from colonial territories.[45] While Guam
is not specifically mentioned, this formula, in effect, wiped out the plenary's
carefully negotiated compromise on Guam. The new resolution also went on
to imply that all dependencies must undergo "de-colonization," whether they
want it or not.[46]

This set of propositions was adopted by the Assembly in a vote of 141 to 2,
with 8 abstentions. Its adoption was a tribute to the agile tactical and strategic
maneuvering of the socialist bloc and particularly of their surrogates within the
Non-Aligned Movement. Some left-NAMs enjoy a degree of influence out of
all proportion to their numbers because they work harder and more relentlessly
than the rest. Singapore's doughty ambassador Tommy Koh—at the U.N. until
1984—was probably the only non-communist member of the NAM's inner
circle whose determination and endurance matched those of Cuban delegates
in the Movement. This means, generally, that as midnight comes and goes in
the councils of the NAM and more delegates drift away, the few dedicated
moderates often find themselves hopelessly manipulated.

Having won a partial victory, Moscow's surrogates have employed similar tactics to harass the U.S. in its relations with its Pacific Islands Strategic Trust Territory, consisting of three island groupings captured from the Japanese during World War II: the Marianas, Carolines, and Marshall Islands. These were transferred to the United States under a trusteeship agreement approved unanimously by the Security Council on April 2, 1947.[47] Under its terms, the Pacific islands, with a population of slightly under 50,000, were designated a "strategic" area. According to article 83 of the Charter, all functions of the U.N. relating to such strategic area, including approval of the trusteeship agreement, and its eventual termination, are assigned to the Security Council. The agreement also specifically permits the U.S. to establish naval, military, and air bases and stations and to deploy armed forces in the territory.[48]

In the years since 1947, the United States has slowly encouraged the islands' economic and political development. Despite fleeting efforts to maintain the political unity of the archipelagoes, they have moved in the direction of separate constitutional development reflecting different political interests and geographic factors. By 1984 the Trust Territory had evolved into four separate entities: the Commonwealth of the Northern Marianas, the Republic of the Marshall Islands, the Federated States of Micronesia (Yap, Truk, Ponape, and Kosrae), and Palau. The Northern Marianas, in 1975, chose a form of close constitutional relationship with the United States. The other three units, in a series of elections and plebiscites, have moved toward a modified form of independence in loose association with the United States. In practice, this means that the three will have an agreement under which the U.S. is to perform certain defense and development services for them. As currently under consideration, this relationship will be terminable by either party,[49] although certain functional aspects would survive termination for a fixed term of years.

Negotiations between Washington and the three "Associated States" have been extraordinarily complicated. Each has pursued different priorities. Claims to compensation for past U.S. nuclear testing in the area, as well as demands for military protection and economic aid at fixed levels, have been set off against U.S. interest in military base rights.

Throughout this process the participation of the indigenous population has been carefully monitored by the U.N. Trusteeship Council, which was delegated this task by the Security Council in 1950.[50] While its visiting missions have sometimes criticized the United States for inadequate efforts to develop the local economy, they have consistently confirmed the legitimacy of the results reached by the local electoral process to which every constitutional proposal has been submitted at each stage.

This is not to say that meetings of the Trusteeship Council have been purely romantic interludes for the United States. Petitions from local residents, various human rights organizations, environmentalists, and others have criticized the U.S. for subordinating both the economic and political development of the islands to its own strategic interests. The Soviet Union has given active and vocal support to these charges, which have steadily increased in intensity. Moscow repeatedly alleges that the United States has deliberately encouraged fragmentation so as to better dominate the four regions and perpetuate the U.S. military presence.

Currently these attacks are becoming more serious. Moscow has character-ized as "unlawful"[51] Washington's decision to terminate the Trust after a final plebiscite in each territory and approval of the result by Congress.[52] Although the U.N. Trusteeship Council, dominated by the West[53] and free of the veto, has agreed in principle that the creation of the Commonwealth and three Associated States would fulfill the American obligation under the trusteeship agreement,[54] final authority resides with the Security Council. There, the Soviets have threatened to veto any action to approve the painstakingly negoti-ated arrangements, even if approved by the local population, the U.S. Con-gress, and the U.N. Trusteeship Council.

Specifically, Moscow objects to any arrangements with the three Associated States in which the United States retains responsibility for their security and defense. It also objects to the incorporation of the Northern Marianas into the United States. So far, the U.S. has made no public statement as to what would happen if the Soviet Union were to veto the implementing of the four agree-ments. The U.S. delegation hopes that the issue will not become another cold war skirmish, but, rather, that the Eastern Pacific members of the U.N. will take the lead in modulating the Soviet position. If this fails, then, a member of the U.S. delegation predicts, "we'll just go ahead and implement the agree-ments without U.N. approval, and let the Soviets try to convince the Pacific region to ostracize the Associated States as if they were South African Bantus-tans. They won't succeed."[55]

Meanwhile, however, the Soviet effort at disruption has shifted to the Gen-eral Assembly. It seems not to matter to the majority of the Assembly that, under the terms of both the Charter and the Trusteeship Agreement, it has no jurisdiction over the islands. The Assembly's Special Committee on Decolon-ization (the "Committee of Twenty-four") has simply taken to considering the subject, citing its broad mandate from the Assembly to oversee the implemen-tation of General Assembly Resolution 1514 (XV) of December 14, 1960, which calls for the granting of independence to all colonies. Legally, the Pacific islands are not U.S. colonies, but such fine distinctions do not bother the Committee. Neither has the Special Committee taken to heart the specific provision in the U.N. Charter (article 83) which assigns responsibility for this Trust Territory exclusively to the Security Council. Nowadays, the socialist–Third World coalition is quite as adept at "up-dating" the Charter, case-by-case, as was the U.S. three decades ago when it could still command a majority in the Assembly.

The United States has reacted to the Committee's and Assembly's overreach by refusing to participate in their discussions of the Trust Territory. Washington ritualistically points out that its cooperation is extended to the proper agency, the Trusteeship Council. Nevertheless, the Special Committee has taken to spending three or four days a year "considering" the state of the territory. Since it receives no help from Washington, it has had the Secretariat prepare annual reports on conditions in the islands based on U.S. reports made for use by the Trusteeship Council.[56] The Committee, to which the other major Western nations also do not belong, then makes a number of conclusions and recommendations.[57] These have tended to be superficial and condescending. They regularly "reiterate," for example, that it is "the obligation of the Administering Authority to create such conditions in the Trust Territory as will enable its people to exercise freely and without interference their inalienable right to self-determination and independence."[58]

However, the U.S. has not objected so much to the substance of these recommendations as to the Assembly's jurisdiction.[59] In 1981 the delegations of five nations not themselves exactly paragons of self-determination—Afghanistan, Bulgaria, Cuba, Czechoslovakia, and the Syrian Arab Republic—took matters a step further. Up to that time, the report of the Special Committee, containing reference to many matters other than the Trust Territory, had been presented to the General Assembly for adoption in a catch-all resolution that did not mention the Pacific islands specifically. Now, however, these delegations offered a resolution which, embodying and sharpening the tone of the Special Committee's report, dealt specifically and exclusively with the United States administration of the Pacific islands. When that resolution was taken up in the Fourth Committee, the U.S. representative reacted sharply, expressing serious doubt whether they were acting "out of concern for the peoples of Micronesia."[60] He added that the text "represented a serious, unprecedented, divisive and provocative step."[61] Such confrontational tactics, long employed by the Soviets, worked. The Australian motion to "adjourn" the item was carried by a handsome 71 votes to 30, with 20 abstentions.[62] The largest number of states voting with the U.S. were from Africa, Asia, and, in particular, from the Pacific region, backed by our traditional allies in Western Europe and Latin America. We had thereby demonstrated that Cuba may have captured the Special Committee, but not irretrievably the NAM.

By the following year, 1982, the Special Committee, in addition to expressing its regret at U.S. refusal to cooperate with the Committee, took the significant step of itself preparing a resolution on the Pacific islands for adoption by the Assembly. Its tone, for the obvious reason, was very similar to the five-nation resolution that had been "adjourned" the previous year.[63]

The resolution was routed to the Assembly's Fourth Committee where, on November 16, the chairman stated that, on the basis of his informal consultation with the chairman of the Special Committee as well as with a number of delegations concerned, he recommended that the Fourth Committee "decide not to take any action at the present stage on the draft resolution."[64] This recommendation was adopted by the Assembly's plenary a week later.[65] Once again, the U.S. had succeeded in protecting its national interest by close attention to every aspect of the agenda and the work of each fiefdom, even those in which it chooses not to participate formally. It had negotiated intensively with leading friendly members of the Third World and convinced them of our *bona fides*, early enough to let them "carry the ball" with many of their associates. No one seeing this process in action, below the surface of Assembly events, could doubt that the Third World was not a monolith and that many of its members were open to a serious search for accommodation with the U.S.

Nevertheless, this annual harassment continues.[66] While the U.S. fends off the attackers, a few members of its delegation do permit themselves to wonder aloud whether the victory is worth the trouble. Some conclude that nothing significant would be lost if the United States were defeated on this matter, since the Assembly's action, if it were to pass a resolution on the Marianas, for example, would so obviously be illegal. These critics argue that diplomats' time could be put to better use. Other critics come from the opposite direction. Why not fight the issue head on, they ask? Instead of taking a stand on technical jurisdictional issues, the U.S. should concentrate on the substantive issues, vigorously defending its policies even before the Special Committee, explaining its actions despite the evident hostility of the Committee's skewed membership. Those who favor this strategy point out that the Committee's membership is so overwhelmingly anti-Western in part because leading Western states have chosen not to seek election to it. Even if the U.S. lost in that forum, it is argued, it could reopen the fight under more favorable auspices in the Assembly's Fourth Committee and in the plenary, where all states are represented.

The Case of Puerto Rico

The effort of socialist and left-leaning NAMs to embarrass the United States in its negotiations with the Pacific islands has been replicated in attempts to raise the question of Puerto Rico's alleged colonial status. Here, again, U.S. diplomacy has been successful. Indeed, it is a textbook success that deserves serious study in order to determine whether the winning strategy used in that case can be more widely deployed in connection with other items before the Assembly.

Article 73 of the Charter requires members to give the U.N. regular reports on developments in their colonies. In the organization's first years, Washington annually filed such reports for Puerto Rico. However, in the 1948 general elections Puerto Rican voters overwhelmingly approved a new "Commonwealth" status for the island, and Congress subsequently adopted a compact implementing that decision and authorizing the Puerto Ricans to draft their own constitution. After that constitution, written by an elected convention and ratified by local referendum, was approved by the U.S. Congress, the U.S.

announced that Puerto Rico had ceased to be a colony and had become a self-governing Commonwealth freely associated with the United States.

The Assembly's Committee on Information thereupon decided that this new status "constitutes a mutually agreed association," making it "no longer necessary or appropriate" for Washington "to transmit information" to the U.N.[67] The Assembly ratified this in plenary.[68]

With that, Puerto Rico dropped from the Assembly's agenda for more than a decade. Then, in 1966, the issue was revived by the newly formed Special Committee on Decolonization.[69] The Committee, in effect ignoring the Assembly's 1953 decision, decided to investigate whether Puerto Rico was subject to the Committee's jurisdiction. In April 1967 a working group reported inconclusively. The U.S. warned that a reversal of the 1953 decision would constitute serious interference in its domestic affairs. The Soviet Union, Bulgaria, Poland, and Tanzania replied that Puerto Rico continued to be a dependent territory, pointing to the power of the U.S. Congress, in which Puerto Rico has no vote, to legislate for the island in certain matters. At the end, the Committee decided to adjourn the debate but, ominously, without reaffirming the position taken by the Assembly in 1953.[70]

The issue simmered on the General Assembly's back burner for several more years. Then, on February 9, 1972, Cuba's ambassador,[71] supported by the Marxist Chilean government of Salvador Allende,[72] formally requested the Special Committee to include Puerto Rico on its list of dependent territories. On August 28, by a vote of 12 to 0, with 10 abstentions, the Committee adopted a resolution—sponsored by Iraq, backed by Bulgaria, China, Czechoslovakia, Ecuador, India, Mali, Sierra Leone, Syria, the Soviet Union, Tanzania, and Yugoslavia—which recognized the "inalienable right of the people of Puerto Rico to self-determination and independence," a decision which challenged the 1953 determination that self-determination had already taken place. The Committee instructed its working group to prepare a report on how to implement Puerto Rico's unrealized national rights.[73]

Such a decision by the Special Committee, with only twenty-four members, is not the voice of the Assembly. The twenty-four cannot repeal decisions of the parent body. Nevertheless, the Special Committee's action, along with its other activities, was duly reported to the Assembly, and the report was approved by a large majority (99 to 5, with 23 abstentions).[74] The five negative votes were cast by France, Portugal, South Africa, the United Kingdom, and the United States.

The situation was now quite muddy. Although the 1953 Assembly resolution had not been repealed, neither had it been given effect by a subordinate committee responsible to the Assembly. And the Assembly had done nothing to bring the committee into line. Inch by inch, Washington was losing ground. Puerto Rico had again become a subject for public debate, first in the Special Committee and now in the plenary meetings of the Assembly.

Does any of this matter? Most of the world little noticed, and cared less, that an obscure committee of the powerless talk-shop of the U.N. had arrogated the right to oversee the relationship between the United States and its Common-wealth. But there were consequences. The Special Committee is authorized and well-funded to hold annual hearings. To these now flocked the most radical Marxist-Leninist and pro-independence groups in Puerto Rico. Al-though their policies, at best, had never attracted more than 10 percent of Puerto Rican voters in free and secret elections, those parties now had a global microphone over which to broadcast the most exorbitant allegations. Their mere presence on the world stage gave them a form of legitimacy, their cause almost an aura of historical inevitability. Since the U.S. refused to participate in these hearings, as—except in 1978—did almost all mainstream Puerto Ri-cans, the radicals were free to give reams of uncontradicted testimony to a sympathetic Committee. They began to create a paper record on which were based a string of Special Committee reports and resolutions in which those unrefuted allegations were presented as the truth.

It is a fallacy to assume that no one pays attention to this paper record. Diplomats who know virtually nothing of Puerto Rico read the Special Com-mittee's reports and, if they represent NAMs with a psychological stake in the work of the Committee, they may well believe what is written. Once the Committee has decided what "facts" are real and has reported that to the Assembly, its distortions and half-truths have a way of becoming conventional wisdom. They reappear, buttressed with authoritative U.N. citations, in publi-cations all over the world. No matter how often they are later refuted, these "facts" take on a life of their own and frequently are cited to justify subsequent U.N. activities.

In 1973, the Special Committee—by a vote of 12 to 2, with nine absten-tions—took the campaign a step further. It requested "the Government of the United States of America to refrain from taking any measures which might obstruct the full and free exercise by the [Puerto Rican] people of their inalien-able right of self-determination and independence, as well as of their eco-nomic, social and other rights."[75] This language does not actually accuse the United States of anything. Neither was the Committee's resolution submitted to the Assembly for specific approval, except—again—as part of the annual report. Still, it tended to establish the Committee's right to set standards for Puerto Rico and to criticize the U.S. if they are not implemented.

By 1978 Cuba upped the ante. It proposed to the Decolonization Committee a draft resolution which asserted that Puerto Rico must be free "always" to opt for independence, "notwithstanding" any other decision on its future status at which "the people of Puerto Rico may arrive."[76] They must continue to have the unilateral right "to modify the association through the expression of their will by democratic means"[77]—a formula worked out by Havana with Puerto Rico's anti-statehood sometime-Governor Hernandez Colon. The Cuban draft also demanded that Puerto Rico must be "a country," no matter what status its voters might choose, with "its own representation in the international community and organizations."[78]

Although the U.S. had stopped participating in the work of the Special Committee, it lobbied strenuously against the Cuban draft and secured its rejection. In its place, however, was adopted a resolution containing almost equally objectionable provisions, including an allegation of continuous "persecutions, harassments and repressive measures" against "organizations and persons struggling for independence."[79] That allegation was affirmed by 10 votes with none opposed, but with 12 members abstaining. In retrospect, it seems extraordinary that Washington could not turn those abstentions into negative votes.

The next year the Cuban delegate to the Assembly's plenary session congratulated the Committee for having "wrenched from the cells of imperialism after a quarter of a century" four heroic "political prisoners."[80] He was speaking of the Puerto Rican assassins who had fired on President Truman. In a rather too mild reply, the U.S. called this "inappropriate."[81]

By 1980 the Committee had gone another step, this time *condemning* the "persecution, imprisonment and repressive measures" used by the United States in Puerto Rico.[82] It demanded that the U.S. assist it in collecting "information relative to the persecution, harassment and repression of Puerto Rican patriots"[83] and "terminate all its military activities in Puerto Rico and allow the people of Puerto Rico to live in peace in their own Territory."[84]

It is indicative of the quality of moral discourse in the Special Committee, that the members patiently, perhaps even enthusiastically listened to the speech of Afghanistan's ambassador, Mohammad Farid Zarif, whose government had just been installed with the help of 80,000 invading Soviet troops. "Some of our countries have in the course of their histories experienced dark days of being colonized by this or that repressive exploitative colonial Power," he began. One could see some of the delegates lean forward. Dared Zarif criticize his Soviet mentors? But he continued: "Those of us who have fortunately not passed through such an era can taste the bitterness of those experiences through pondering what their position and their condition would have been if their own peoples and countries had been under colonial domination. . . . " There are few surprises in the Committee on Decolonization.

Safely back on track, Zarif added that the nation of Puerto Rico "has been rudely denied its birthright. Its natural resources have been stolen; its best sons and daughters have been imprisoned and executed; its land has been used for the launching of military provocations against surrounding countries."[85]

Braced by this sort of rhetoric, the Special Committee, in 1981, recommended "that the General Assembly examine the question of Puerto Rico as a separate item at its thirty-seventh session."[86] Up to then, the socialist states had confined their mischief to the Special Committee, where they could have things their own way. Given the mild U.S. response, Cuba was now emboldened to believe it could carry the Assembly's plenary, securing a full-fledged repudiation of U.S. policy. To support his demand, Cuba's ambassador Raul Roa-Kouri drew fully on the "facts" established by the Committee hearings—for example, that U.S. policy had "led to the forced exodus of 2 million people, the largest such human contingent in the history of this hemisphere."[87]

By a vote of 10 to 3, with 10 abstentions, the Special Committee voted to ask the Assembly to inscribe the issue of Puerto Rico on its agenda.[88] This request was tucked away in its annual report to the Assembly, which is invariably accepted by the Assembly but without specifically endorsing any part of it.

The U.S. delegation confidently expected that this practice would be followed, as usual, in 1981. They were wrong. After introducing the report, the Committee's rapporteur, a Syrian, added that approving the annual report would be tantamount to endorsing the recommendation to include Puerto Rico as a separate item in the Assembly's next agenda.[89] Foolishly and unintentionally—his speech had been prepared for him by an excessively candid member of the Secretarial—he thus gave away a clever maneuver intended to catch the United States by surprise. Thus alerted, the U.S. delegation swung into belated action. As one American delegate recalled, "the Committee's tactic was brilliant. It did not call for a vote on the item but merely laid the groundwork for a later interpretation that its adoption constituted a decision to inscribe Puerto Rico in the agenda. We know that the decolonization report is a sacred annual ritual and that it's virtually impossible for any country—particularly for a Western country—to amend it from the floor. Nevertheless, that's what we had to threaten to do. Behind the scenes we raised holy hell with the NAMs."[90]

The U.S. amendment would have specified that approval of the Special Committee's report by the General Assembly did *not* constitute inscription of the Puerto Rican item in the next session's agenda.[91] After intense informal negotiations, the Iraqi president of the General Assembly, Ambassador Ismat Kittani, announced on December 3 that, following "consultations with numerous delegations concerned" he had found agreement that adoption of the Special Committee's report "would not constitute a decision by the General Assembly" to inscribe the item in its agenda.[92]

"We knew that wouldn't stop the Cubans," said U.S. Ambassador William Sherman. "All we accomplished was to force them to bring the item to the Assembly openly, for an up-or-down vote, rather than hiding behind the skirts of the Special Committee's report."[93] And, of course, it gave the United States time to maneuver, to mount its most sophisticated effort to reverse a tide in General Assembly politics.

Winning One

To prepare the way for this confrontation, the socialist states, led by Cuba, redoubled their efforts to create "facts" about the political situation in Puerto

Rico that would set off the NAMs' anti-colonialist reflexes. With leftist governments and organizations subsidizing their travel expenses, radicals packed the
roster of witnesses appearing before the next set of hearings at the Special
Committee, even though they represented the views of no more than the 6.7
percent of Puerto Ricans who had voted for independence at the previous
election.[94] The other 93.3 percent were represented by a lonely trio.

What the Committee heard was strange indeed: that the people of Puerto Rico
wanted the U.N. "to put an end to [their] enslavement and exploitation."[95] The
galleries warmly applauded calls to use "bombs, arms and anything that it takes"
to liberate the "motherland."[96] Onetime anti-Vietnam activist David Dellinger
reported that "Puerto Rico is one of the permanently invaded territories."[97]

The Bulgarian member of the Special Committee waxed rhapsodic about the
"ample evidence supplied to us again this year by the representatives of a broad
spectrum of Puerto Rican political parties and organizations."[98] Witnesses were
subject only to friendly cross-examination and patty-cake rebuttal. Since the
U.S. State Department boycotts the Special Committee, it had to refute the
testimony in face-to-face meetings with individual delegates. The task was now
assigned top priority. Its urgency became fully apparent when, on August 17,
1982, the foreign minister of Cuba formally asked for the inclusion of the
"Question of Puerto Rico" in the agenda of the Thirty-seventh Assembly.[99]
That request was referred to the Assembly's General Committee which has
preliminary responsibility for the agenda. There, Cuba suffered its first defeat
by a vote of 11 to 7, with 8 abstentions. Those voting with the U.S. were:
Austria, Brazil, Canada, France, Haiti, Jamaica, Philippines, Turkey, U.K.,
and Upper Volta. Those voting with Cuba were: Democratic Yemen, Ghana,
Libya, Nicaragua, Poland, and the U.S.S.R.. Eight members—Cyprus, Kuwait, Mali, Nigeria, Qatar, Uganda, Yemen, and Zambia—abstained.[100] It was
an important victory, but only one shot in the campaign.

Next came the vote in plenary. Here the Cuban motion was rejected by 70
votes to 30, with 43 abstentions. Outside the socialist bloc and its penumbra,
it garnered only the votes of Argentina (venting its pique at the United States
for having supported Britain during the Falkland Islands war), Ghana, Iran,
Iraq, Libya, and Venezuela.[101] That final victory, in the words of the U.S.
delegate who had quarterbacked it, "was substantially more decisive than we
had predicted."

What had gone right? In the words of one senior U.S. delegate:

Approximately two-thirds of states are represented at the U.N. by persons who can
determine how to vote on an issue like this one, and who get very few instructions
from home. Influencing them becomes synonymous with influencing the outcome of
the vote. Most people do not understand that many of the delegates neither seek nor
get instructions. A few are so trusted by their own governments that they can usually
commit their country without even having to refer back to the capital. Others are

uninstructed more-or-less by default, because their foreign offices can't stay on top of every U.N. issue. We concentrated on those two categories, making it as clear as possible that the U.S. Government attaches the greatest importance to this issue and would deeply resent—and remember—a vote cast against us. We didn't hesitate to personalize the issue, putting ourselves, our own feelings, on the line. Personal relations matter more than you might think at the U.N.[102]

Another U.S. delegate had a somewhat different theory:

We put out a triple-line whip to all friendly and neutral countries. In practice, this meant that we brought diplomatic weight to bear at all three pressure-points: on their missions in New York through the U.S. mission, on their embassies in Washington through the State Department, and directly on the foreign governments in their national capitals through our ambassadors over there.

All this had been done before, but not with such detailed planning and concerted strategy. The effort was focused first on the 29 members of the General Committee. No stones were left unturned at this stage, rather in the manner of a close vote in Congress. For example, about ten hours before the vote, the U.S. mission found out that the Austrian delegate had been instructed to abstain. That was very bad news, Austria being the bellwether of "friendly" neutrals. If it abstained, so would many of the U.S.'s NAM "friends." "A whole raft of the non-aligned would take it as a signal that it was O.K. to vote against us," one U.S. delegate remarked. "They would conclude that the U.S. didn't really mind." Immediately, a highly placed U.S. representative was dispatched to see his Austrian counterpart. He carried a heavy docket of information on Puerto Rico as well as on the law pertaining to self-determination. "We went to see the Austrian Ambassador here and covered him with paper," he reported. "The Austrians like that; they are very data- and precedent-conscious." Meanwhile, the U.S. State Department contacted Austria's ambassador in Washington. The U.S. official recalled:

We talked angry, we didn't threaten anything specific, nothing bilateral, no squeeze on reciprocal trade, we just let him know that we were going to be extremely unhappy, that this was a matter of utmost importance, not only to us but particularly to members of Congress, that there would be repercussions on Capitol Hill. Next, Mrs. Kirkpatrick placed a call to [Austrian] President Kreisky. He wasn't in, but they asked what it was about and she told them in no uncertain language. After that, it wasn't really necessary for her to talk to him because he would have got the message, if only from the fact that she was calling him personally. We even sent out scouts to find Kurt Waldheim. We finally located him somewhere on the lecture circuit and talked to him about using his communication lines to get through to the Austrian Government, to let them know how strongly we felt.

"Well, something must have worked," the official concluded, "because the Austrian instructions were revised and they voted for us in the General

202 Nation Against Nation

Committee."[103] He added that it "was extremely important for us to win decisively there, because very few of the NAMs will vote against a decolonization resolution, no matter how absurd, or how much they disapprove of its content. But they will vote to uphold the procedural decision of a committee."[104]

This sort of "damn the torpedoes, full speed ahead" diplomatic campaign of the U.S. at the U.N. is more unusual than it ought to be. The U.S. still tends to pursue its goals, too often, with a less determined strategy than might be expected from a democracy in which the domestic politics of lobbying and vote-trading has been raised to the level of a national art. It is sometimes argued that the high amount of turnover at the upper levels of the U.S. delegation, where ambassadorial appointees rarely serve more than a few years, places us at a disadvantage in tactical confrontations with seasoned veterans of foreign missions. More likely, we have simply not marshalled the personnel or brandished the weapons necessary to win, because Washington has been inclined to see U.N. resolutions as mere paper tigers.

Members of the U.S. delegation concede, privately, that we have begun "mobilizing" too late, too far down the U.N.'s "legislative" road; that, for example, the U.S. has been lax in fighting to make our position part of the record emanating from the Special Committee on Decolonization. One U.S. delegate has said:

> I guess that when we walked out of that Committee with the British, years ago, and announced that we were not coming back, we felt that it was so heavily stacked against us that we could never influence its product and were probably better off ignoring it. . . . What we'd really like is to get it abolished. But that seems unlikely, so we ought to rethink our strategy. Perhaps we haven't tried hard enough to refute some of the outrageous things said by the petitioners. For example, we've never gone in for subsidizing the travel of Puerto Ricans who want to speak for the majority position. It's a violation of the Committee rules, of course, but everyone else does it. Or, perhaps we should have tried harder to find ten of the best who would come at their own expense. Even if it doesn't affect the outcome in the Special Committee, the participation of anti-*independistas* would make it harder for the rapporteur to claim that all parts of the island's political spectrum agree with the Committee's preposterous assertions.[105]

In preparation for the 1982 fight in the Assembly, the U.S. State Department did invite San Juan's Mayor Hernan Padilla to join the U.S. delegation. He not only made an extraordinarily eloquent spokesman in debates in plenary session, but proved to be a highly effective lobbyist with Latin American delegations. "Our democratic system does not need the intervention of the international community," he insisted. "We, the Puerto Ricans, and we alone, will decide how and when our political status should be altered. It is our responsibility. It is our right. It is our destiny."[106]

In a few foreign capitals, government ministers expressed anger at the vociferousness with which the local U.S. ambassador had pressed for a "sympathetic understanding" of the U.S. position. Sometimes this involved explicit threats of retaliation in matters such as technical assistance, sales of farm surplus commodities, and military aid. In a few instances, it was reported that the United States threatened to use its nearly decisive weighted vote in the World Bank to oppose loans to recalcitrants. In most cases, however, threats were not spelled out, but were implicit—or thought to be—in the urgent tone used to press the American case. Certainly, Washington has let the impression be formed, from Ouagadougou to Jakarta, that the U.S. no longer pretends to give aid without strings; and that one measure of a potential recipient's aid-worthiness is sensitivity to top U.S. priorities in the General Assembly (see below, Chapter 13).

A senior U.S. diplomat summed it up:

> The vote-gathering operation mounted in respect of Puerto Rico has dramatized the extent to which the U.S. cares about words in U.N. resolutions. We will no longer extend sympathy or credit to states that vote for a resolution aimed at our throat and which then send their ambassador around to assure us that they don't really agree with it but felt bound to maintain bloc solidarity. We have given notice that kicking the U.S. is no longer a cost-free strategy. That may not add to our popularity, but popularity, in a setting like the U.N., is little more than a trap the weak set for the strong. We've fallen into it long enough. Andy Young was the most popular ambassador we ever had in New York. The Third World made him feel he was one of them, and he loved it. But what good did that do the U.S.?

The delegation headed by Jeane Kirkpatrick seems to have taken its strategic guidance from one of its coffee mugs, which says, simply, "No More Mr. Nice Guy!"

Finally, the U.S. delegation, in the Puerto Rican case, did not content itself with a purely defensive strategy. Instead, it fought fire with fire, attacking the government of Cuba for denying its entire population what it alleged Washington was denying the Puerto Ricans. The very concept of self-determination, as adumbrated by the Special Committee, was challenged as essentially racist by Carl Gershman, the U.S. representative in the Assembly's Third Committee, since the concept was only applied to Western colonialists while denials of self-determination were considered unexceptionable whenever the oppressors and the oppressed were of the same race.[107] In these heated exchanges, the message was that the United States intended to take the conceptual fight back to its tormentors. For such a militantly intellectual policy to have full effect, however, Washington would first have to commit substantially greater resources to the battle than are currently available to the overworked delegation. Next, it would have to shed its own conceptually inconsistent double standard in dealing with dictators who are pro- and anti-U.S. (see below, Chapter 12).

Abraham Lincoln, in his 1861 inaugural address, said: "This country, with its institutions, belongs to the people who inhabit it. Whenever they shall grow weary of the existing government, they can exercise their constitutional right of amending, or their revolutionary right to dismember or overthrow it."[108] The U.S. does not sufficiently draw on its own radical tradition. Currently, what needs to be overthrown is the low estate to which diplomacy has fallen in American values. The Assembly affords an opportunity to educate, to state radical native principles, and to stick to them, not least in the symbolic world of paper resolutions and roll-call voting. It should make no difference whether U.S. principles are adopted or rejected. What does matter is the principles with which the U.S. chooses to identify and the cogency with which it makes its case on their behalf: against repression, against aggression, and for fair economic and social opportunity. Here idealism, realism, and self-interest can converge. With a loud clear voice—and policies consistent with what we say— America must ally itself with the reasonable expectations of peoples everywhere and place hypocrites on notice that it will not be put on the defensive in matters pertaining to the aspirations of the human spirit.

§ 11 §

"A Place Where Lies Are Told": Israel Before the General Assembly

Zionism as a Form of Racism

In an Assembly where the U.S. is but one of more than 150 states, there are challenges to the U.S. national interest that have been overcome by compromise and consensus-seeking; others have been contained by exerting concerted tactical pressure in the right places. But there are some challenges that have simply defeated the U.S.

On November 10, 1975, the General Assembly, following the recommendation of its Third Committee, adopted its shortest, and, perhaps, most fateful resolution. In its sole operative paragraph, the Assembly stated flatly that "zionism is a form of racism and racial discrimination."[1] The roll call vote on this determination was 72 to 35, with 32 abstentions. Of those voting in favor, 14 were communist countries,[2] and 36 were countries with Muslim majorities (17 were predominantly Arab states).[3] Of the non-communist Europeans, only Cyprus and Malta supported the resolution: Cyprus because its Christian government needed Arab support against its own Muslim secessionist minority; Malta, in a futile courtship of Libya's surplus billions. Among the nations of the Americas, the resolution garnered help from the two leftist regimes—Cuba and Guyana—and also from Brazil, Mexico, Grenada, and Chile. Among the non-Muslim Asians, the most notable proponent of the resolution was India. The Indian government, that indefatigable advocate of moderation and compromise, had refused to condemn the Soviet invasions of Hungary and Czechoslovakia, in each case preaching the need to avoid harsh, polarizing judgments.[4] Where Israel was concerned, polarization ceased to trouble the Indians.

Numerically, it was not a particularly disastrous defeat for Israel, which was accustomed to losing votes but winning wars. Earlier, on November 10, a proposal by Belgium to adjourn the debate and defer the vote to the following year's session had narrowly been beaten, 67 to 55, with 15 abstentions.[5] That vote had revealed only a minority of members anxious to rush to judgment.

Nevertheless, the resolution passed. And it touched a raw nerve, precisely as intended. The psychological pain was intense, and the Israelis did not try to deny their enemies the satisfaction of seeing it. Ambassador Chaim Herzog rose to remind the Assembly that its vote had come on the very night when, thirty-seven years earlier, Hitler's storm troopers had launched the infamous *Kristallnacht*, the night of the smashed windows, burning synagogues, and desecrated holy books and scrolls. "It was the night," he warned, "which led eventually to the crematoria and gas-chambers." Was the U.N. now embarked on the same bloodied road?[6] Defiantly he stood before the delegates and tore their resolution in two.

U.S. Ambassador Daniel Patrick Moynihan had given top priority to the fight against this resolution. Now, in defeat, he promised that the "day will live in infamy" and predicted that the "terrible lie that has been told here today will have terrible consequences." The word, the very concept of racism, had been distorted—even drained of meaning. People would no longer be stirred by its invocation. The ability of the U.N. to command the moral indignation of mankind had been dissipated. People, he continued, "have already begun to say, that the United Nations is a place where lies are told."[7] He ended by reiterating that the U.S. "does not acknowledge, it will not abide by, it will never acquiesce in this infamous act."[8]

Writing of this afterwards, Moynihan noted that the racism issue "took the Israelis by complete surprise."[9] It simply was not considered credible that the community of "peace loving states" would level such an accusation against the survivors of the Nazi holocaust. Yet there had been warnings. On August 30, at Lima, Peru, the Fifth Summit Conference of the Non-Aligned Movement (NAM) had cobbled together their agenda for the upcoming special session of the General Assembly, a meeting to be convened just before the start of the regular thirtieth session to draw world attention to the economic demands of the Third World. Despite this economic focus—indeed, in a serious distraction from the special session's avowed purpose—the NAM's heads of state agreed to accommodate their Arab colleagues by adopting a paragraph of the meeting's final declaration, which stressed their "struggle against imperialism, colonialism, neocolonialism, racism, Zionism, *apartheid* and any other form of foreign domination."[10]

Even this was not the first tying of Zionism to racism. An earlier linkage had occurred on July 1 of the same year, 1975, at a conference sponsored by the

General Assembly to launch the International Women's Year. Meeting at Mexico City, the conference had adopted a Declaration of Mexico on the Equality of Women and their Contribution to Development and Peace." Zionism would not seem to be a natural target for such a meeting. Yet, among the thirty "principles" in the final declaration—which is invariably drafted by "leading" participants before such a meeting even begins—was the following:

> Women and men together should eliminate colonialism, neo-colonialism, imperialism, foreign domination and occupation, Zionism, *apartheid*, racial discrimination and the acquisition of land by force, since such practices inflicted suffering on women, men and children.[11]

Most Western delegates at Mexico had treated the inclusion of zionism in that litany as an aberration. When it came to approving the Declaration's thirty principles, they looked the other way. Only Israel and the United States voted "no." Some explained that their affirmative vote should not be interpreted as agreement with that characterization of zionism. Nevertheless, the paragraph had not just slipped by as a trivial part of a larger package. It had been adopted by a separate roll call vote: 61 to 23, with 25 abstentions.[12] Clear notice had thus been served, but few chose to heed it. Mexico's Luis Echeverria, who was completing a term as his country's president and assiduously campaigning for the post of U.N. Secretary-General, had rashly lent the prestige of the host government to its adoption. Jews cancelled their Acapulco vacations, but the event went largely unremarked by Western nations.

Not only Israel, but also the U.S. State Department, essentially underestimated the importance of what was happening. Even when the racism-zionism item was inscribed in the agenda of the General Assembly, Washington was slow to sound the alarm. As Moynihan observed, "the disposition in Washington at this time was to dismiss exchanges in the General Assembly as 'mere words.' "[13]

The words, however, were becoming more lethal. A few days into the regular Assembly session, mad President Idi Amin of Uganda, then serving as president of the 46-member Organization of African Unity, received a respectful, even enthusiastic hearing from the delegates. He accused the "Zionists" of having "colonized" the U.S., of monopolizing "all the tools of development and power" including "virtually all the banking institutions, the major manufacturing and processing industries and the major means of communication." U.S. Jews had "turned the CIA into a murder squad to eliminate any form of just resistance anywhere in the world." He ended by calling for "the extinction of Israel as a State."[14]

This time the U.S. reacted. Speaking before a convention of the A.F.L.–C.I.O. in San Francisco a few days later, Ambassador Moynihan warned that the attack on Zionism was really a thinly disguised blow against democracy in general, by corrupt, authoritarian governments in the U.N. To illustrate this larger issue, he added that "it is no accident, I fear, that this 'racist murderer' "—Amin—"is head of the Organization of African Unity. For Israel is a democracy and it is simply the fact that despotisms will seek whatever opportunities come to hand to destroy that which threatens them most, which is democracy."[15] Let there be no mistake, Moynihan added, "democracy is in trouble. There is blood in the water and the sharks grow frenzied."[16]

Moynihan admits that he blundered.[17] The fact was that Idi Amin had not been deliberately chosen to represent his fellow African heads of state. It was his turn to be president of the OAU, that year, as an automatic byproduct of the OAU leaders' having last met in Uganda.[18] Many Africans had privately expressed their embarrassment and dismay at this happenstance. Now Moynihan seemed to be implying that Amin had been chosen to speak for Africa precisely *because* he was a racist murderer.

The importance of the incident can be, and certainly was, both exaggerated and exploited. Yet it did give America's enemies an almost irresistible opening. "I had offended Africa," Moynihan admits. The lesson, he concluded, was that one should not write speeches on airplanes.[19] To put a finer point on it: the lesson is that U.S. delegates cannot hope to be effective in attacking the Assembly's majority for conspiring to lie if they are not absolutely sure of their facts. Often, such errors, or a shortage of relevant facts to prove the case, are simply symptoms of a shortage of skilled research personnel.

The incident occurred just after the Third Committee had approved the resolution but before it reached the plenary session for the final debate and vote. During the interval, several Third World delegates let it be known that they would not have voted for the resolution, or would have opposed it rather than abstaining, had it not been for Moynihan's "provocation." Such assertions are often self-serving, made by those who want to have it both ways. Nevertheless, Britain's ambassador, Ivor Richard, went out of his way to express (again, privately) the view that the U.S. had contributed to its own defeat.

By putting all Africans into a category with Amin, Moynihan had accidentally stumbled over what has since become a cardinal principle of U.S. relations with the NAM in the U.N.: "disaggregation." If it expects ever to win a test of strength in the Assembly, the U.S. must differentiate between members of that bloc, making common cause, whenever possible, with those states that lean toward its views on specific issues. In Africa, for example, sophisticated governments like those of Botswana, Kenya, Nigeria, and Senegal have very little in common with, say, the military dictator of Ethiopia or the bizarre ruler of Libya. Our diplomatic efforts must start from a recognition of those differences, encouraging them to become as manifest in U.N. voting behavior as they are in other aspects of national policies. "Disaggregating" the NAM is never easy. The Movement has considerable power to reward the faithful and punish defectors. The U.S. must take care not to make disaggregation more difficult.

Words, All Words

Ambassador Moynihan may have erred in one particular instance, but he had done so because the pressures were enormous and the passions formidable. On balance, he earned much credit for making the "terrible lie" about Zionism a salient issue of the Thirtieth General Assembly. He focused world attention on the U.N.'s penchant for waging verbal war without the rhetorical equivalent of a Geneva Convention to civilize and modulate conflict. "Today we have drained the word 'racism' of its meaning," he thundered. "And how will the small nations of the world defend themselves, and on what grounds will others be moved to defend and protect them, when the language of human rights, the only language by which the small can be defended, is no longer believed and no longer has a power of its own?"[20]

In warning of these longer-range dangers of the institution's self-debasement, Moynihan was teaching a lesson, the significance of which transcends the considerable importance of what he called the "obscene" Zionism-racism resolution. Words matter, concepts matter, truth matters.

Even so important a lesson, however, can be exaggerated. A thoughtful memorandum to Moynihan written by Charles H. Fairbanks, then a political scientist at Yale (and more recently Deputy Assistant Secretary of State for Human Rights), comes close to overreacting. It argues that, after the "obscene lie," the "charge of racism will eventually become something that people laugh at. To call Zionism a form of racism makes a mockery of the struggle against racism as the emperor Caligula made a mockery of the Roman Senate when he appointed to it his horse." The Assembly's majority had inflicted "the most crippling blow yet dealt in the irreversible decline of the concern with human rights as we know it."[21]

While Fairbanks is right in urging strenuous resistance to the debasement of basic concepts, it is quite as wrong to take words in U.N. resolutions *too* seriously as not to take them seriously enough. Americans, versed in the street politics of a tumultuous democracy, ought not to be overly impressed by the "obscenities" emanating from the General Assembly. There, too, the poor and the powerless use words as their way of inflicting pain on those who always seem to win without ever having to raise their voices. The tactic of "hitting out with words," the attack with "fighting words" are no different in the Assembly than in the inner-city street politics of New York or Detroit. Neither the word "racist" leveled at Israel nor that of "motherfucker" or "pig" thrown around street confrontations is intended to communicate dictionary-precise information. What is intended is psychic damage. What is communicated is rage.

In 1975, a deeply divided, militarily impotent but economically mercurial

Arab world found that it could rally—or buy—the support of enough poor and powerless nations to constitute—with the Soviet bloc—a majority of the Assembly. They chose to use that power to inflict psychic pain. Inadvertently, they also demonstrated once again their extraordinary ineffectiveness as a force in serious world politics. While their tactics, as Fairbanks and Moynihan have warned, do potentially undermine concepts that serve as underpinnings of our civilization, valuable societal concepts tend to be quite resilient. Incest still shocks our social conscience despite the loose street-epithet that debases the concept. Racism, as correctly applied to describe South Africa, can still anger many civilized persons even though the concept has been misapplied, egregiously, to Zionism.

This is not to argue that we should not take seriously the street epithet hurled at us in anger. The lie, repeated and insufficiently refuted, may begin to confound truth. What should be of equal concern, however, is the real message of powerless verbal abuse: both the incoherent anger and the implicit plea for attention.

The United States must take seriously the random malevolence of the General Assembly, but without exaggerating its importance to global politics.

How the Assembly Came To Be Taken Seriously

If the Assembly, controlled in respect of many issues by a coalition of socialist and Third World members, is capable of inflicting psychic pain, we need not wonder how it acquired that institutional capacity. It is the U.S. government, after all, which strove all too successfully to make the Assembly into the flagship of the U.N. system. That was at a time when it led the majority and largely got things its own way. The culmination of U.S. effort came with the passing of the Uniting for Peace resolution[22] in 1951, over the dire warnings of some of our closest allies who correctly foresaw the long-range dangers (see, above, Chapter 2).

U.S. efforts, however, began much earlier—indeed, almost as soon as it was realized that the Soviet veto in the Security Council would paralyze efforts to use U.N. machinery to advance U.S. objectives in the cold war. At first the U.S. set out to increase the powers and functions of the Assembly in connection with the Greek civil war that began almost before the U.N. was born. On December 3, 1946, after Athens complained to the Secretary-General that its northern communist neighbors were supporting the Greek guerrillas,[23] the Security Council set up a Commission of Investigation[24] which traveled to the area between January 30 and May 22[25] but reached few agreed conclusions about the causes of the war. With the U.S. and the Soviets accusing one another, the Council was soon deadlocked.

A less internationalist head of state than Harry Truman might then simply have resorted to taking unilateral initiatives to protect Western interests in

Greece. Instead, the State Department determined that the new organization must be made "relevant." This meant circumventing the deadlocked Security Council. After much debate over tactics and law, Washington decided to seek collective action through the General Assembly, where the Soviet veto could not operate and the U.S. would be able to count on an almost automatic majority.[26] Thus, ten days after the inconclusive Security Council debate on the Commission of Investigation's report, the U.S. brought the question to the Assembly. On October 21, 1947, that body overwhelmingly voted to set up the United Nations Special Committee on the Balkans (UNSCOB).[27]

This had consequences that reached beyond the immediate crisis. The Assembly, conceived as a global town meeting, was suddenly propelled into the business of peacemaking and conflict management. It was a fateful tactical choice, for the U.S. had now demonstrated how the Assembly could intervene, actively, in a dispute between members and, more specifically, in what manner the Assembly could influence the outcome of such a dispute.

The resolution went beyond creating UNSCOB, calling on Albania, Bulgaria, and Yugoslavia not to "furnish aid and assistance to the . . . guerrillas."[28] In promoting UNSCOB, Washington made sure that the Committee would be heavily weighted toward the Western perspective. In addition to the U.S., Australia, Brazil, Nationalist China, France, Mexico, the Netherlands, Pakistan, and Britain were elected. Places were left vacant for Poland and the Soviet Union,[29] but understandably they declined to participate in a body so inhospitable to their interests. The mandate the U.S. arranged for the Committee empowered it to "observe the compliance" of the parties and asked it to report back "as a matter of urgency," even proposing a special session of the Assembly,[30] if necessary.

Eventually, the Committee unanimously blamed the governments of Albania, Bulgaria, and Yugoslavia for providing the guerrillas with "aid and assistance on a large scale."[31] On that evidence, the Assembly called on those states to stop behaving in a fashion "inconsistent with the purposes and principles of the Charter of the United Nations"[32] and asked UNSCOB to continue monitoring "compliance."

UNSCOB operated with "extensive American logistic support"[33] but was primarily funded by the U.N.'s regular budget, which is approved by the General Assembly. This meant that the socialist states were asked to pay for activities to which they strongly objected and which were aimed against them. It was another way of "strengthening" the Assembly's power and circumventing the veto-bound Security Council. This sort of thing continued until December 7, 1951, at which point the Assembly, expressing appreciation for UNSCOB's "invaluable services," authorized its termination.[34]

Valuable or not, UNSCOB did not win the Greek civil war, a victory that was due primarily to increased U.S. military and economic aid to Athens, and to the timely defection of Yugoslavia's President Tito from the Soviet bloc.

Nevertheless, the role of UNSCOB is notable, if not for its effect on the Greek civil war then, certainly, for its impact on the development of the General Assembly. Washington had established the right of the Assembly to take from the Security Council responsibility for laying down normative conditions for ending a dispute between members. The Assembly had successfully asserted the right to conduct on-the-spot investigations and publish reports attributing fault, to demand and monitor compliance, and, generally, to harass the Assembly's outvoted minority.

This was the role the Charter had reserved for the Council. It was a series of U.S. initiatives, beginning with the Greek case and culminating with the Assembly's role in the Congo Operation (see, above, Chapter 9) that inverted the division of functions between the Assembly and the Council; and, of course, this abuse did not cease after the West lost control of the Assembly.

Comes the Nemesis

That the U.S. no longer controls the Assembly does not mean that comparable power now rests elsewhere. The hundred new nations which have joined the U.N. since 1955 have produced neither leadership nor partnership comparable to that which characterized the early period of Western dominance. The Third World nations often do not vote in a solid bloc. The more radical of them can only triumph with socialist support, which, particularly on fiscal and economic matters and power-sharing, is not invariably forthcoming. The NAM coalition that has taken leadership from the U.S. is both fragile and unstable. In respect of some issues, however, its common front has held relatively firm, including issues pertaining to Israel and South Africa.

As to these, the tactics employed reflect those which Washington pioneered in 1946 and enshrined in the Uniting for Peace procedures. When action in the Security Council is blocked (nowadays more often by a U.S. veto than by a veto of the Soviets) the matter is transferred to the General Assembly, where a socialist–Third World majority sets out the norms they deem applicable to resolving the dispute—norms which are always unacceptable to one of the parties—and proceeds to establish heavily biased committees to "oversee" and "implement" them. The costs of these activities are ascribed to the organization's general budget, which, in practice, means that the nations opposed to the Assembly's initiative end up paying for efforts to compel compliance. To those who savor historical nemesis, this is surely a classic example.

That Israel should be the victim of this nemesis, however, is particularly poignant. The Jewish homeland, after all, at least in part, owes its legal existence to a General Assembly resolution of November 29, 1947, authorizing the partitioning of Britain's Palestinian mandate into separate, economically linked Hebrew and Arab states.[35]

Having thus helped give birth to Israel, the Assembly has continued to play an active part. From the beginning, long before the NAM majority became a fact of life, the Assembly has demanded that Israel neutralize Jerusalem and its environs under "effective United Nations control" as originally envisaged by the partition plan, and that Arab refugees "wishing to return to their homes and live at peace with their neighbours should be permitted to do so."[36] It also asked that "compensation should be paid for the property of those choosing not to return."[37]

These demands on Israel, at first, were always linked to progress in Arab-Israeli peace negotiations. Since the Arabs, with the recent exception of Egypt, have refused to make peace, Israel argues that it is absolved from these reciprocal obligations. In the 1956 war the Assembly linked its call on Israel to evacuate the Sinai and return to the previous armistice lines to a call on Egypt to permit unimpeded Israeli navigation through the Suez Canal. Both nations were equally asked to "desist from raids across the armistice lines."[38] Again, after the 1967 war, the Security Council's resolution 242 clearly conditioned its demand for Israeli territorial concessions to reciprocal Arab recognition of Israel's right to secure boundaries.[39]

After that, however, this evenhandedness withered, and soon only Israel, and not the Arabs, was being required to make concessions. This was done by uncoupling demands on Israel from demands on the Arabs and, instead, linking the former to recitals of inherent Palestinian "rights" which Israel was found to be violating. The Assembly's tactics thus shifted from mediation and conflict resolution—a political process involving negotiations culminating in mutual compromise—to the collective assertion of non-negotiable Arab "rights" coupled with confrontational efforts to compel compliance by the Israeli violators. It was a long step backward from the days when the Council and Assembly had sent Count Bernadotte and Ralph Bunche to practice their healing versions of shuttle diplomacy.

In 1968 the Assembly established a three-member Special Committee To Investigate Israeli Practices Affecting the Human Rights of the Population of the Occupied Territories. But even in setting it up the Assembly's resolution concluded that those rights were indeed being violated.[40] A decade later, the Assembly completed its uncoupling of Israeli withdrawal from Arab willingness to make peace. The resolution on the "situation in the Middle East" now "reaffirmed" that "peace and security within recognized and secure boundaries will not be achieved"—and here the disjunction occurs—"until Israel withdraws from all occupied Palestinian and other Arab territories, and until the Palestinian people attains and exercises its inalienable national rights."[41] The previous year's version of this careful legal formula had stated that peace within secure boundaries (Israel's objective) could not be achieved *without* Israel's withdrawal from Arab land, a proposition that still linked the two sets of concessions so as to make each dependent on the other.[42] Now, the Arab concession was no long required *until* after the Israelis had relinquished their occupied territories, so that the failure of the Arabs to make peace could no longer serve as a defense against the Assembly's demands on Israel.

Concurrently, the Assembly began to pass resolutions which characterized the Israeli occupation of the West Bank as "colonialism," a concept of much emotional importance in Third World circles. Next, the Assembly's resolution of November 1970, adopted by 71 votes to 12, with 28 abstentions, for the first time linked the plight of the Palestinians with that of blacks in South Africa.[43] The tactical importance of this linkage cannot be exaggerated. Until the Arab defeat in the six-day war of 1967, Israel had commanded considerable influence in the new nations of Africa, many of which had experienced unpleasant interludes as Arab vassals. New leaders like Julius Nyerere, president of Tanganyika (later Tanzania), identified with the democratic socialist pioneering ethic of zionism and invited the establishment of African kibbutzim with the help of Israeli experts. That altered after the defeat of Egypt in 1967, and the change became firmly established after the further defeat of Egypt in the 1973 war.

The reasons for this are complex and have little to do with the merits of the Arab-Israeli conflict. Africans were aroused, in 1967, when the Sinai, a substantial part of their continent, was occupied by an extra-continental power, and a "white" one, at that. Then, there was the cold war factor. Israel, which had been supported for U.N. membership by both the Soviet Union and the United States, by the 1960s had become heavily dependent on its military alliance with Washington. The Arabs, once considered American clients, had by now qualified as more-or-less bona fide neutrals and, therefore, compatible with the Afro-Asian non-alignment ethic. By the mid-70s, the socialist regime of Israel had been replaced by a rightist one, severing the threads of empathy that had tied the African socialist leaders to Israel. The racial factor, while not explicitly introduced until 1975, also began to play a significant role in converting Africans to the Arab side. As Israel occupied more land populated primarily by Arabs, the Jews were analogized to the white European settlers of Rhodesia and South Africa, denying equal economic, social, and political rights to the inhabitants of the West Bank and Gaza "Bantustans." General Assembly resolutions now regularly condemn the alleged collaboration between South Africa and Israel in political, military, economic, and nuclear activities and demand that Israel stop supporting the South African racist regime.[44] These resolutions ignore the well-documented fact that, while Israel accounts for only two-fifths of one percent of the Republic of South Africa's external commerce,[45] the socialist countries, as also many African and Middle Eastern nations, trade extensively with the Republic. Israel is also regularly reviled for supplying nuclear weapons "capability" to South Africa despite vigorous denials and a telling lack of evidence.[46]

Then, too, there were economics at work. The Arab-led oil cartel had demonstrated the potential fiscal, as well as political, benefits of Third World unity, awakening the hope and pride of all impoverished primary producers.

Meanwhile, the newly wealthy Arab states, many with very small populations incapable of absorbing more than a fraction of their new wealth, were soon outbidding traditional Western foreign assistance programs and reaping commensurate political benefits. Driven to the verge of bankruptcy by the same astronomical oil costs that were disrupting the economies of the West and depressing markets for primary products, developing nations were ill-positioned to resist Arab offers of subsidized oil sales and interest-free development loans just for the sake of friendship with Israel. Finally, many African and, to a lesser extent, Asian states, outraged by what they perceived as Western indifference to their efforts to rally the international community for action against the racist regime of South Africa and, more generally, to alleviate poverty in the Third World, recognized in Israel a vulnerable Western outpost against which to retaliate.

It is against this background that the General Assembly in 1974 voted to invite the Palestine Liberation Organization "to participate in the sessions and the work of the General Assembly in the capacity of observer;"[47]asked the Secretary-General "to establish contacts with the Palestine Liberation Organization;"[48] and pushed the Secretariat to promote Assembly-endorsed PLO goals.[49] In thus politicizing part of the Secretariat, the Third World was redeploying the tactics which already were in use against the colonial powers and South Africa. The following year, in addition to enacting the "Zionism-racism" resolution, the Assembly established the Special Committee on the Exercise of the Inalienable Rights of the Palestinian People, in order to help the "Palestinian people" obtain "independence and sovereignty." The Secretary-General was asked to provide all "necessary facilities."[50] Elected to this committee, on which Western nations refuse to serve, were seven communist nations (Cuba, German Democratic Republic, Hungary, Laos, Romania, the Ukraine, and Yugoslavia), nine left-leaning neutrals (Afghanistan, Cyprus, Guinea, Guyana, India, Madagascar, Mali, Malta, Sierra Leone), and seven others, states every one with a predominantly Muslim population (Indonesia, Malaysia, Nigeria, Pakistan, Senegal, Tunisia, Turkey).[51]

While the Assembly cannot significantly alter the military and economic realities, it can help to generate a climate. In the case of Israel, that climate is now one of unrelenting animosity and confrontation—of siege. Demands on Israel are no longer balanced by demands on the Arabs. Not only does the Assembly no longer call for peace with recognition of Israel's right to exist, it now denounces peace. Instead of praising the Camp David accords between Egypt and Israel, which secured the return of Sinai, the largest occupied territory, the Assembly *condemned* "partial agreements and separate treaties."[52] The vote on that resolution was an astonishing 102 to 17, with 20 abstentions. Guatemala was the only Third World country to vote against it. Even Egypt, at which it was clearly aimed, pathetically sought protective cover by joining with the censorious majority.[53]

Embargoes and Delegitimization

The General Assembly has not contented itself with one-sided condemnations of Israel and demands for asymmetrical concessions to the Palestinians. In recent years it has begun to try to enforce these demands by calls on Assembly members to institute an embargo on Israel that would restrict its military and economic viability. These efforts have gone hand in hand with others to oust Israel from the Assembly, to delegitimize it, and to liquidate the symbols by which the world acknowledges its statehood.

In 1972 the Assembly began to threaten Israel with economic sanctions using the rationale of a 1962 opinion of the Court, obtained at U.S. urging, which had held that the Assembly could engage in such collective actions when the Council was blocked by vetoes, as long as participation is not mandatory (see above, chapter 5). The resolution of that year "invited" all states "to avoid actions, *including actions in the field of aid,* that could constitute recognition" of "changes and measures carried out by Israel in the occupied Arab territories"[54] (italics added) in alleged contravention of the Geneva Conventions of 1949.[55] At about the same time, on the basis of "research" by its Special Committee, the Assembly began condemning Israel for the "pillaging of archaeological and cultural property in the occupied territories" as well as "interference with religious freedom" and "illegal exploitation of the natural wealth, resources and population" of the area.[56] These were charges which, if true, would justify "collective measures," such as economic sanctions and expulsion from the U.N.

During the 1975 session, the threat of sanctions began to be implemented, as the Assembly requested "all States to desist from supplying Israel with any military or economic aid as long as it continues to occupy Arab territories and deny the inalienable national rights of the Palestinian people."[57] Prompted by a report of its Special Committee on Human Rights in the Occupied Territories, the Assembly explicitly found alleged Israeli practices to "constitute grave violations of the Charter,"[58] thereby further laying the groundwork for more serious efforts to apply a broad range of sanctions.

In 1981, even before the Israeli invasion of Lebanon, came an emphatic call from the Assembly for sanctions "to put an end to the flow to Israel of any military, economic and financial resources which would encourage it to pursue its aggressive policies against the Arab countries and the Palestinian people."[59] After the invasion, in the summer of 1982, another emergency session of the General Assembly coupled a renewed call for an end to "military, economic and political" aid to Israel with condemnation of those who continue to "encourage the flow of human resources to Israel,"[60] a formulation that provides justification for Soviet refusal to permit Jewish emigration.

Efforts at the economic destabilization of Israel were pursued in tandem with the objective of diplomatic isolation. In 1979 the Assembly took its first step in the direction of suspending Israel from participation. It voted that Israel "constitute[s] a serious and increasing threat to international peace and security"[61]—words which, in the context of the Charter, virtually demand the offending member's suspension. At the Assembly's emergency session in the summer of 1982, this was reinforced by the finding that Israel "is not a peace-loving Member State" and that it has failed to carry out "its obligations under the Charter,"[62] words evoking article 4 of the Charter, which states that membership in the U.N. "is open to all . . . peace-loving states which accept the obligations contained in the present Charter."

At its next session in 1982, and again in 1983, the Assembly came close to that ultimate decision. In both years, the Iranian delegation took the lead in trying to prevent the Israeli delegation from participating in the Assembly.

In 1983, after the Iranian ambassador had moved to reject the credentials of the Israeli delegation, he was followed at the rostrum first by the representative of India, who charged Israel with "genocide,"[63] and then by Libya's representative, Ali A. Treiki, who called Israel's creation the "most shameful blot on the history of the United Nations" and summoned the members to correct "this deed . . . and drive this Member—if it can be so called—from our Organization."[64] Nevertheless, the effort to reject Israel's credentials was defeated by a Norwegian procedural motion to take no action on the Iranian amendment. That tabling motion carried by 79 votes to 43, with 29 abstentions (including India).[65]

While the effort was not successful, it generated some of the bitterest debate in the memory of Assembly veterans. The PLO accused the "Judeo-Nazi" regime of "genocide" and sought to establish that the present rulers of Israel had themselves "fully participated in the elimination of innocent civilians" during the holocaust in partnership with Hitler. U.S. Ambassador William Sherman has pointed out that such debate, "instead of reflecting efforts to seek new approaches and new language that might bring the various interested parties together in the search for peace . . . can only help to solidify antagonism."[66]

What of the future? On the question of participation, the U.S. has made it clear that if Israel is excluded, it, too, will walk out of the Assembly and this tactic is now mandated by U.S. law (see below, Chapter 13). As for the efforts to berate and chastise the Israelis, tactics are less clear. In the opinion of a senior member of the U.S. delegation:

> We have so little influence now on the annual deluge of resolutions condemning Israel that we no longer even try to get involved in negotiations with their sponsors. The [U.S.] delegation has fallen back to the position that worse is better. The more hysterical and patently absurd the charges against Israel, the less effect they are likely to have on the governments, delegates and populations of all but the most committed members. And it also absolves us of moral ambiguity, making it easier to vote "no" with a clear conscience.[67]

True as this may be, it underestimates the reaction among the American public
to the virulent spectacle staged annually, or more often, by the Assembly.
Obversely, it underestimates the change in the Assembly's climate brought
about by the broad campaign of hate. In 1982, when the charge of racism was
again revived, it generated scarcely a ripple, even when the resolution charged
that "racism and racial discrimination" were systematically pursued in the
occupied territories in the same way as in southern Africa.[68] At best, in the
years since 1974, there had been a steep rise in the world's capacity to tolerate
the U.N.'s untruth. At worst, the untruth was gaining acceptance as conventional wisdom.

Caveat

That things have come to this pass is not simply attributable to a single cause:
not to confrontational Arab tactics, nor even to the mendacity of the majority
of members.

Israel has become the Assembly's "group-victim" in a fashion that hurts the
Assembly's institutional credibility as well as Israel's psychological sensibilities.
Yet, Israel is not blameless. Its national policies have increasingly been shaped
by those of its opponents, mirroring both their absolutism and intractability.
Nor are Israel's interests wholly identical with those of the United States. In the
1982 Assembly debates, the U.S. joined the vast majority in opposing new
settlements on the occupied West Bank. In Washington's opinion, these have
"undermined efforts" toward "constructive" peace negotiations.[69] The U.S.
government has also stated its displeasure at the "illegal" extension of Israeli
law to the Syrian Golan Heights, the deportation of Arab West Bank leaders,
and the rash of crimes committed by Israeli settlers against West Bank Arabs.[70]
In many public statements, the U.S. State Department has made clear that it
genuinely shares the concern among Third World governments for Israeli
expansion and for certain aspects of its treatment of Arabs under occupation.

Although the U.S. has thus joined in some of the criticism of Israel, it
emphatically remains that nation's best U.N. friend. While U.S. help is appreciated, it is also part of Israel's problem. Much of the venomous anger at Israel
which is fashioned in Moscow, Teheran, Tripoli, or Damascus is really directed against the United States and only incidentally at Israel or Israeli policies
in the occupied territories. Israel is widely seen as America's state on the
Jordan, making plausible a tactic of attacking the U.S. through Israel.

That tactic works, in part, because it is able to enlist the support of many
NAM states that have different grievances against the United States. They
resent U.S. refusal to join in cooperative efforts to stabilize world commodity
prices and to utilize the resources of the sea bed for the benefit of the poor. The
nations of Africa and Asia feel humiliated at their inability to ameliorate the
treatment of blacks and Asians by the white regime in Pretoria. They realize

that the South African problem has almost nothing in common with the very considerable, but quite different, problems of the West Bank, or with any other aspect of the Middle East crisis. Nevertheless, many NAM states participate willingly enough in the Arab-socialist tactic of equating Israel with South Africa welcoming any available means of hitting out at the United States (and, to a lesser extent, Western Europe) *through Israel* for Washington's—or London's or Bonn's or Paris's—perceived indifference. Western capital investment in and trade with South Africa, and the perceived unwillingness to "get tough with Pretoria" are seen to sustain the racist regime. Black suffering thus mingles with Arab suffering because the U.S. (or the West) is perceived as the common cause of both. Every time the West, in the Security Council, vetoes another resolution that seeks to impose sanctions on South Africa, the waves of Third World anger pass through Jerusalem on their way from Lagos to Washington. U.S. policy on South Africa, perhaps as much as any Israeli policy, has rallied the Third World to the Arab cause. Israel, while benefitting from U.S. support on Middle Eastern matters, thus pays the diplomatic price for U.S. policy toward South Africa and, more generally, toward the Third World. It is not a simple causal relationship, but then the U.N. is a place of convoluted realities.

Anti-Zionism and the Secretariat

The Assembly's majority has also done its best to achieve an anti-Israeli politicization of the Secretariat. To some extent the attempt has been successful.

The push for sanctions against Israel has been coupled with a drive to secure U.N. diplomatic and material support for the PLO. In 1974, as we have seen, the Assembly recognized the Palestine Liberation Organization as "the representative of the Palestinian people" and invited it to participate in its deliberations.[71] This was done despite the fact that the PLO's 1968 Palestine National Covenant lays claim to all of Israel, rather than merely to the "occupied territories" and, in article 6, bars from citizenship in this Palestine all Jews not living permanently in the territory prior to 1917.[72] The Assembly thus gave its imprimatur to a movement that seeks the destruction of a member state.

In recognizing the PLO, the Assembly also ordered the Secretary-General to "establish contacts" with it "on all matters concerning the question of Palestine." Thus began the Assembly's effort to make the Secretary-General support the PLO's cause. In 1975 it asked him to assist the Assembly's Committee on the Inalienable Rights of the Palestinian People to establish their right to independence and sovereignty. One year later, the Assembly voted to create a Special Unit on Palestinian Rights within the Secretariat to staff the Assembly's Inalienable Rights Committee by preparing pro-PLO publications and giving them "maximum publicity . . . through all appropriate means."[73]

This Special Unit in the Secretariat, although under the titular supervision of an American Under Secretary-General and headed by a comparatively moderate Sri Lankan, has become an in-house tool of the PLO—as its civil servants, suitably recruited with pro-PLO qualifications in mind, are perfectly willing to admit. It faithfully busies itself with organizing pro-PLO conferences and regional seminars, commissioning highly partisan studies,[74] and "cooperating" with the Department of Public Information, itself sharply tilted to the Arab side, to produce films and photographic exhibitions in support of the Palestinian cause.[75]

Professor Julius Stone has rated the unit's subsequent work a "sinister game" and "a deep and wide-ranging threat to the whole international legal order, and to the United Nations itself."[76] In 1978 the Assembly requested the Secretary-General to "ensure" that the U.N.'s Department of Public Information provide "full co-operation" to the Palestine Unit and help it to "perform its tasks" of disseminating the PLO's case globally under U.N. auspices.[77]

In the words of Charles William Maynes, President Carter's Assistant Secretary of State for International Organization Affairs, "there was a concerted effort, by the Arabs . . . to compel the Secretariat to take sides."[78] Maynes concludes that "the United States should . . . be prepared to suspend its membership in bodies where the membership succeeds in directing the institutional machinery to favor one cause over the other."[79] This was not the way we felt when Trygve Lie organized the U.N. to support South Korea's fight against Northern aggression. *Autres temps, autres moeurs.* Congress has now ordered the State Department to subtract from U.S. dues the proportion used for the activities of the Secretariat's Palestine Unit and the Committee on Inalienable Palestinian Rights[80] (see below, Chapter 13).

So far, the U.S. is alone (with Israel) in the withholding of such dues. The objectionable activities, in the words of Israeli Ambassador Yehuda Blum, are still primarily paid for by the "taxpayers in those [Western industrialized] countries which contribute the bulk of the United Nations budget and which have consistently voted against the activities of the Committee."[81] There are indications, however, that other Western states are leaning toward withholding, prodded by the U.S.

In 1979 the Assembly decided that the Unit on Palestinian Rights should be upgraded to the level of a Division and its functions expanded to include the organizing of at least four seminars during the following year, the establishing of closer ties to non-governmental organizations, and the "[m]onitoring of political and other relevant developments affecting the inalienable rights of the Palestinian people"[82]—in other words, explained a U.S. member of the Secretariat, intelligence-gethering. The Assembly also called for the mounting of a "photographic display" at U.N. headquarters by the Department of Public Information to demonstrate to visitors "the grave situation . . . of the Palestinian people."[83]

But it is important to understand the limits as well as the extent, of this tendency. A pro-PLO tilt has not significantly affected the rest of the Secretariat. To be sure, there are persons throughout the U.N. civil service who try to skew the work of their departments to reflect the anti-Israeli policy of their states of nationality. But they are not endemic. (There are also a number of traditional anti-Semites. These can be from anywhere. It was a top Western European Secretariat official who, in 1982, when my department properly made public a study critical of parts of the U.N. system, remonstrated with me for "feeding the voracious hatreds of the worldwide Jewish-controlled media.")

Much more typical is the standard set by the Secretary-General, in parrying Assembly-mandated tasks that are essentially propagandistic. This can best be characterized as "strict compliance," or doing only what is absolutely necessary. In January 1982, for example, the chairman of the Special Committee To Investigate Israeli Practices wrote the Secretary-General to seek his "intervention" with Israel to get it to cooperate with the Committee.[84] A month later, the Secretary-General replied: "a further démarche has now been made. I regret to inform you that we have been advised that the position of the Israeli Government concerning the Special Committee remains unchanged."[85] This exemplifies strict compliance. A Secretary-General, when asked to "intervene," can exercise his good offices, busy himself with quiet diplomacy, even turn to public advocacy. In this instance, he chose to be no more than a post office for the exchange of messages.

When the General Assembly commanded the Secretary-General to undertake a "feasibility study" for a proposed Arab university in Jerusalem,[86] he replied "that it was evident that the actual establishment of the university at Jerusalem was possible only with the agreement and co-operation of the Israeli authorities."[87] With commendable equanimity, he advised the Assembly to focus its efforts on funding graduate fellowships that would help students at the existing Arab universities on the West Bank and Gaza go elsewhere for graduate work not currently available at these institutions.[88] By avoiding the traps of partisanship, the Secretary-General—using such development agencies as UNIDO and UNDP—has been able to carry out training and industrial development projects in the occupied territories[89] for the benefit of the Arab population with the cooperation of the Israeli authorities.

On the issue of anti-Semitism, Pérez de Cuéllar has been reported as telling a group of Jewish leaders that "any kind of what you might call discrimination or unacceptable language" used by delegates during the U.N. debates "is a shame for the organization." He stressed his willingness to use "quiet diplomacy" as a way of curbing further excesses.[90]

Senior members of the Secretariat have taken their lead from the Secretary-General, tilting toward neither Arabs nor Israelis but conforming to the mandates of their professional responsibility. For example, when the Assembly, in 1982, took up an Arab-initiated resolution to have the Secretary-General "issue identification cards to all Palestine refugees and their descendents"[91] and "to undertake effective measures to guarantee the safety and security and legal and human rights of the Palestinian refugees in the occupied territories,"[92] the

Secretary-General went out of his way to emphasize the difficulties and "[e]xtensive financial implications" of issuing the proposed cards.[93] Next, then-legal counsel Professor Eric Suy of Belgium addressed the Special Political Committee of the Assembly to emphasize that under international law[94] "responsibility for ensuring human and other rights within such territories attaches to the occupying Power."[95] He later added that when "international organizations carried out any activity within a given territory, they must do so with the consent and, as necessary, the co-operation of the authorities in effective control of that territory."[96]

Such examples of professionalism challenge Daniel Patrick Moynihan's dire conclusion that the system as a whole has become "profoundly corrupt . . . . infiltrated and near to immobilized" by agents of the Soviet Union, the PLO and like-minded forces.[97] U.S. critics tend sometimes not to see the trees for the forest. Yet the best U.S. approach to the U.N. Secretariat, as also to U.N. delegations, is disaggregation: seeing each individual, each department, unit, or division on its own merits and carefully calibrating the response accordingly. Even Yasushi Akashi, the harried Japanese head of the U.N.'s office of Public Information, required by the Assembly to publicize the PLO cause, remains determined to walk a tightrope between disobeying the Assembly's ukases and destroying the credibility of his unit. Sometimes he needs help to keep his balance. In November 1982, for example, Israel's Ambassador Blum wrote to the Secretary-General expressing his government's "strong objections" to the "tendentious and one-sided approach" of the Secretariat-produced *U.N. Chronicle*. Blum's protest was triggered by a story on page 18 of the October *Chronicle* which carried a photograph of Damur, Lebanon, with a caption asserting that it "had 16,000 people in early June" before the Israeli invasion. "A month later," it said, "only ten people remained in its ruins." The town, however, had been destroyed when the PLO killed hundreds of its Christian inhabitants in the winter of 1976.[98] Blum accused the DPI of using "pejorative" and "misleading" phraseology in reference to Israel and of becoming an agency of "misinformation," a "pliant tool in the hands of those . . . who would exploit the United Nations for their own nefarious end." He demanded that the Secretary-General "instruct the Department . . . to cease forthwith these dubious practices."[99]

No formal response was received, but the vehement protest had its effect. There was a staff shakeup at the *Chronicle*, and instructions were issued requiring more even-handed language. The Israeli mission concluded that the ensuing issues were comparatively "satisfactory."[100]

Such blunt counter-pressure is good for the organization's integrity. It must be exerted whenever an agency which has been established to serve the whole organization and all its members seems in danger of falling captive to a purely partisan perspective. Not enough Westerners at the U.N. are willing to make a fuss. At a 1981 seminar in Moscow run jointly by my U.N. institute (UNI-

TAR) and the Soviet Academy of Science, I found that the Soviet participants were reading papers in which the West was constantly being referred to as "the capitalist exploiters" and "the imperialist powers." In mid-conference I withdrew our department's co-sponsorship of the conference until the authors agreed to substitute such acceptably neutral U.N. terms as "developed capital-exporting industrial nations." Called to account, the Soviets quickly agreed that the terminology was improper, although the dispute was later referred to by a Moscow bureaucrat as my "disruptive cold war behavior."

Eternal vigilance, and even, where necessary, more "disruptive cold war behavior" is needed to preserve the Secretariat's neutrality. This requires a commitment, on the part of delegations and of Western members of the Secretariat to the fine art of making a fuss. The Soviets and some Arab nations never cease trying to project their partisan perspective under the U.N. imprint. Each such effort must be confronted as it happens. In this spirit, both Israel and the U.S. in 1983 lodged strong protests as soon as an exhibition of "Palestinian-struggle posters" was mounted at U.N. headquarters. The exhibition was quickly closed on orders of the Secretary-General.[101]

In these encounters, efforts to keep the Secretariat impartial are quietly cheered on by the majority of its personnel. Whatever their nationality, ability, or competence, none—except, perhaps, the most dedicated Soviets—really wish the Secretariat to become irrelevant. Most U.N. civil servants realize that their relevance depends upon being, and being perceived to be, above the political brawls that have made the General Assembly and Security Council such backwaters of diplomacy. Significantly, the Third World nations that regularly vote with the Arab and socialist states against Israel seem, for the most part, not to have tried to influence their nationals in the Secretariat to use their posts to undermine Israel or to advance the PLO cause.

As long as the U.N.'s civil servants continue to exercise a reasonable degree of independent judgment on Middle Eastern issues, there is cause for hope, for renewed effort, and for a finely calibrated strategy that distinguishes between the various players in that complex game.

§ 12 §

The Double Standard

Introduction

Are the members of the U.N.—in St. Matthew's phrase—"blind guides, which strain at a gnat, and swallow a camel"? (St. Matthew, xxiii, 5.) Ambassador John L. Loeb, Jr., a U.S. alternate delegate in 1983 to the Thirty-eighth General Assembly, spoke for many in and outside the U.S. government when, after the end of the session, he charged, in the *New York Times*, that "for decades, the United Nations has practiced a double standard."[1] Ambassador Jeane Kirkpatrick has elaborated the same point, accusing the organization of being "perverted by politicization in the last decade."[2]

No indictment of the U.N. has been made more frequently or with greater vehemence than that it singles out Western and pro-Western states for obloquy, while ignoring far worse excesses committed by socialist and Third World nations. This charge is partly false, partly true, and partly irrelevant.

Partly False: The Double Standard and Aggression

In response to the U.S. invasion of Grenada, the U.N. General Assembly, on November 2, 1983, invoking cloture to cut debate,[3] deplored U.S. "armed intervention," calling it "a flagrant violation of international law and of the independence, sovereignty and territorial integrity of the State."[4] The vote was 108 in favor to 9 against, with 27 abstentions.[5]

This resolution does not name the United States, specifically, as the culprit; however, it is clear at whom the finger is pointing. The text reaffirms "the sovereign and inalienable right of Grenada freely to determine its own political, economic, and social system, and to develop its international relations without outside intervention, interference, subversion, coercion or threat in any form whatsoever."[6] It calls for "an immediate cessation of the armed intervention and the immediate withdrawal of the foreign troops."[7] Outside of the hard-core socialist bloc and some Third World clients, most states voting for the Grenada resolution seemed to be responding less to the merits of what the U.S. had done than out of deference to the abstract principle at stake, the U.N.'s rule prohibiting any unilateral resort to force except in self-defense (article 2(4) of the Charter). In private exchanges with Americans, many delegates expressed more sympathy than dismay. Off the record there was widespread concurrence that the invasion had probably saved Grenadians from a period of brutal misrule. On the record, however, most neutrals agreed with Sri Lanka's ambassador Ignatius B. Fonseka[8] and Thailand's ambassador Birabhongse Kasemsri[9] that the harm the U.S. was doing to the global system—by violating one of the U.N.'s key principles—far exceeded any good it might be doing in Grenada.

The resolution was widely perceived in the U.S. as evidence of an anti-American bias in the Assembly. Yet, by and large, the Assembly, year after year, has been quite even-handed in criticizing any aggressive use of force, whether by the United States, a socialist country, or a nation of the Third World. Thus, on November 14, 1979, after the Vietnamese invasion of Kampuchea, the Assembly called for "the immediate withdrawal of all foreign forces" and an end to "all acts or threats of aggression and all forms of interference in the internal affairs of States of South-East Asia." It forcefully restated "the right of all peoples to determine their own future free from outside interference."[10] It also called on all states "to refrain from any interference in the internal affairs of Kampuchea in order to enable its people to decide their own future and destiny free from outside interference, subversion or coercion, and to respect scrupulously the sovereignty, territorial integrity and independence of Kampuchea."[11]

The Kampuchea resolution, promoted primarily by China and the non-communist states of the region, was passed by a vote of 91 to 21, with 29 abstentions.[12] In the years since 1978, it has been reiterated by each Assembly with increasing vehemence[13] and growing majorities.[14] The intent and the form of these resolutions are essentially the same as in the Grenadan case. To be sure, the U.S. role in Grenada is not equivalent to the Vietnamese occupation of Kampuchea. For one thing, the U.S. immediately announced that it would withdraw the bulk of its troops within two months, while Hanoi's forces have settled in for what appears to be permanent lodging. However, in voting for the Grenada and Kampuchea resolutions, members did not assert that the two situations were identical, but merely that the principle of non-aggression should have been applied in both cases and should always take priority over other considerations. This may be wise or foolish, but it is not an example of a double standard.

Most states which voted for the Assembly resolutions on Kampuchea also voted for the one on Grenada. A few did not, and it is these few, not the U.N.'s majority, which can be said to apply a double standard. The U.S. is among them. We, and the nations of the Caribbean that joined our military intervention, voted against the Grenada resolution, but voted for those on Kampuchea. Conversely, the Soviet Union and its socialist bloc supported the Grenada resolution but voted solidly against those on Kampuchea. If this is all too predictable, the voting behavior of the Non-Aligned is more interesting. Ten member states—Afghanistan, Angola, Congo, Cuba, Ethiopia, Guyana, Libya, Mozambique, Nicaragua, and Syria—voted for the resolution on Grenada but felt compelled to vote with the Soviets *against* the resolution on Kampuchea. India, characteristically, found no problems voting to criticize the U.S. intervention while conspicuously failing to condemn the Vietnamese occupation of Kampuchea. So did Mexico.[15] Those states thereby stand exposed as purveyors of a double standard, a condition that does not go unnoticed in the U.N. community.

If the conduct of some states attests to *their* double standard, the charge is not applicable to the majority of members. The Assembly's actions in the two cases under discussion, far from proclaiming a double standard, merely throw into bold relief the embarrassment of those members of the so-called Non-Aligned Movement (NAMs) who are compelled publicly to pursue Moscow's line at considerable cost to their global credibility and standing. In an odd sense, it even speaks well of America that its friends seem not to feel a comparable compulsion to toe the line drawn by Washington. None of our Western European allies, for example, voted with us on Grenada.

The U.N.'s activity following the Soviet invasion of Afghanistan on December 27, 1979, falls into the same pattern. The Assembly was convened under the Uniting for Peace resolution[16] (see above, Chapter 2) after a Soviet veto had prevented the Security Council from passing a resolution introduced by six NAMs, although it received thirteen affirmative votes. The Sixth Emergency Special Session met from January 10 to 14, 1980, and adopted a resolution introduced by Pakistan and twenty-one NAM co-sponsors.[17] It *"strongly deplores* the recent armed intervention in Afghanistan" and appeals to "all States to respect the sovereignty, territorial integrity, political independence and non-aligned character of Afghanistan and to refrain from any interference in the internal affairs of that country" while calling for the "immediate, unconditional and total withdrawal of the foreign troops . . . in order to enable its people to determine their own form of government and choose their economic, political and social systems free from outside intervention, subversion, coercion or constraint of any kind whatsoever."[18] The vote was 104 to 18, with 18 abstentions.[19] Once more, Angola, Cuba, Ethiopia, Grenada, and Mozambique were placed in the embarrassing position of having to vote with Moscow against the overwhelming majority of NAMs. India, consistent in its inconsistency, abstained.[20]

Particularly exposed was the Soviet hold over Democratic Yemen, which was the only Muslim country, in 1980, to vote against condemning Moscow's attack on a fellow-Islamic republic.[21]

Other NAMs were implacable in their denunciations of Soviet aggression. Ambassador Falilou Kane of Senegal referred to "a contagious illness. Yesterday it was Kampuchea, today it is Afghanistan—not to mention the wounds which have not yet healed in certain parts of Africa. Who will be the victim tomorrow? . . . a serious blow has been dealt to the theory that the Soviet Union and the socialist countries are the 'natural allies' of non-alignment."[22] Expressing Nigeria's "disappointment and disillusion' " with the Soviet Union, Ambassador B. Akporode Clark said: "We will never subscribe to the use of double standards which lead some States to view identical situations with favour in one set of circumstances and with distaste in another."[23] Singapore's ambassador Tommy Koh added: "[W]e′ must demonstrate our adherence to those principles by applying them uniformly and consistently to all states, whether they be from the West or from the East or from the Non-aligned Movement itself. The actions of the Soviet Union in Afghanistan are, in the view of my delegation, in clear contravention of those principles."[24]

Even socialist Yugoslavia gave its vocal support to the resolution, "recognizing the right of the people of Afghanistan to free and independent development and reaffirming the fundamental principles of the Charter."[25] The foreign minister of Zaire demonstrated that the justifications being given by Moscow in 1980 were textually identical to those advanced for the invasion of Hungary in 1956.[26]

The debate during the emergency session demonstrated, with a few visibly embarrassed exceptions, the continuing importance which most Third World nations attach to the principle of non-intervention and the non-use of force, regardless of the violator's identity. Each regular session of the Assembly, beginning in 1980, has renewed the call for the application of the principle to Afghanistan, in increasingly tough words and with increasingly large majorities.[27]

By 1982 Syria, its defeated armed forces in desperate need for massive resupply by Moscow, felt compelled to vote against that year's Afghanistan resolution.[28] This put it at odds with the "demand for the immediate and total withdrawal of all foreign troops from Afghanistan" issued by the Islamic Conference of Foreign Ministers.[29] But only a few of the Non-Aligned failed to join the chorus of remonstrance.[30] Country after country rose to refute the Soviet version of events and to demonstrate their incredulity and revulsion.

Does this do any good? Does anyone in Moscow listen? Do the men of the Kremlin believe that this annual verbal onslaught represents a real cost to their foreign policy? Or have they long ago concluded that it is all hot air which will dissipate as they consolidate their hold on Afghanistan? The answers to these difficult questions cannot be known with any certainty. What is clear, however, is that NAM delegates rose in large numbers to acknowledge that their nations felt personally threatened by Russia's attack on a Non-Aligned state and that this action exposed as a lie Moscow's aspiration to be considered the champion and natural ally of the NAMs. No double standard can be charged to these courageous members, who had nothing to gain except that their principled conduct keeps alive the badly mauled rule prohibiting the aggressive use of force.

That prohibition has also been undermined by nations of the Third World, indeed, even more frequently than by the superpowers. Chapter 3 and 9, above, catalogue the repeated decisions by India to take the law into its own hands, employing military force to resolve disputes involving Hyderabad, Kashmir, Goa, and Bangladesh. Indonesia has employed force in respect of North Borneo and Sarawak, and West Irian, and more recently to subdue East Timor. Morocco (and to a lesser extent Mauritania) has sought a military solution to the dispute over the Western Sahara. Tanzania sent its army into Uganda to topple Idi Amin; Somalia has used force to "liberate" its ethnic cohorts in Ethiopia; and Iraq has resorted to all-out war with Iran.

Has the Third World's majority stood firm in the defense of pacific principles when its own rank-and-file was implicated? The answer, quite predictably, is that the NAMs have been less steadfast and more divided in their attitude when the violators have been from their own ranks. This is particularly so when force is used, as in Goa, to "extinguish a vestige of colonialism." In those instances the majority has tended to remain quiet, although it is worth recalling Britain's success in obtaining a resolution from the Security Council supporting its position during the Falklands' crisis. That would not have been possible had much of the Third World not agreed that Argentina's aggression was an unacceptable form of "decolonization."[31] In speeches at the Security Council, there were *pro forma* invocations of colonialism's evils.[32] But in the Delegates' Lounge, even most Latin Americans distanced themselves from the "adventurists" of Buenos Aires. Ambassador Munoz Ledo of Mexico stated publicly: "We reject the use of force to settle this or any other conflict."[33] Kenya's ambassador C. G. Maina led an almost unanimous array of African states in condemning Argentina's "naked aggression," adding: "if we bend the principle of decolonization of peoples to look like the redistribution of territories, this Organization is in real trouble."[34]

Why did the Third World accommodate India's invasion of Goa but not Argentina's effort to seize the Falklands? Goa was ruled with an authoritarian hand by the Salazar dictatorship in Lisbon, a government which, because of its more egregious colonial policies in Africa, had become among the world's most unpopular. By contrast, the British by 1982 had divested themselves of virtually their entire empire with considerable grace. India, at least at the time of its Goan invasion, was the recognized and admired leader of the Third World, while Argentina, in the early 1980s, was ruled by a semi-fascist junta. Moreover, up to that point, the junta, although taking its place among the NAMs, conspicuously distanced Argentina from the NAM campaign against South Africa. Of course, such factors made a difference; the U.N. is not the only human institution to interpret principles pragmatically.

For similar pragmatic reasons, the General Assembly and, for that matter, the Security Council did not criticize Tanzania for using force—Dar es Salaam actually pleaded "self-defense" rather unconvincingly—to topple Idi Amin. If ever there was a reason for bending a principle to accommodate realities, this must surely have been it. However, although most members similarly sympathized with India's use of military force to end Pakistan's bloody repression of Bangladesh, the Assembly nevertheless passed a resolution calling on India to withdraw its troops and observe a cease-fire.[35] That resolution passed with a majority of 104 to 11, with 10 abstentions.[36] Only the Soviet bloc could bring itself to vote with New Delhi.

Again, when Morocco occupied the Western Sahara after the termination of Spanish colonial rule, in defiance of the General Assembly's resolution "reaffirming the right of the population . . . to self-determination,"[37] the Assembly reaffirmed "the inalienable right of the people of Spanish Sahara to self-determination" and "its attachment to the principle . . . and its concern to see that principle applied to the inhabitants" under "guarantees" of "free and genuine expression of their will."[38] That rebuke to Morocco was delivered by a vote of 88 to 0, with 41 abstentions.[39] The United States—itself guilty of a double standard in this case—was among the abstainers[40] in a show of friendship for Morocco's pro-Western monarch. Since 1975 the General Assembly and its Special Committee on Decolonization have kept up the pressure, despite Morocco's insistence that the Western Sahara problem has been solved.[41] Annual resolutions are adopted reaffirming the Assembly's previous position.[42]

Pressure has also been exerted on Indonesia in response to its seizure of East Timor on December 7, 1975, just as it was about to get its independence from Portugal. Five days later, by a vote of 72 to 10, with 43 abstentions,[43] the Assembly passed a resolution which "*Strongly deplores* the military intervention of the armed forces of Indonesia in Portuguese Timor" and called for their withdrawal "without delay . . . in order to enable the people of the Territory freely to exercise their right of self-determination and independence."[44] That vote followed no ordinary pattern of alliances. Albania, Australia, Brazil, Cuba, Haiti, Iceland, Pakistan, and the Soviet Union joined in this unprecedented condemnation of a Third World state. India voted with the aggressor. The United States, whose president was in the Indonesian capital of Djakarta on the day of the invasion, abstained. In later Assemblies, the U.S. took to voting with Indonesia against resolutions reiterating the rights of the Timorese people.[45] To Washington, it appeared that the Indonesian invasion had prevented a clique of leftist Portuguese military officers from turning the colony over to FRETILIN, an indigenous Marxist political party. Once again, we voted in accordance with our own double standard, condemning leftist aggressors, but not those we perceive to be our friends. However, some other Western and pro-Western Non-Aligned states voted to sustain the principle of non-aggression, even if it meant criticizing a pro-Western government. Put more broadly, many states define their self-interest to include the upholding of the principle of non-aggression no matter which state violates it. Washington does not, yet our public officials complain loudly about the "outrageous"[46] double standard of those few who voted to criticize our use of force in Grenada but did not criticize Soviet action in Afghanistan.[47]

What is one to make of all this? Certainly not that the majority of the General Assembly lightly disregards principle when it comes to condemning aggression and the unilateral use of force. The record of the United States, in condemning the use of force against Afghanistan and Kampuchea while tolerating violators in the Western Sahara and East Timor, has demonstrated considerably more political opportunism than have the rank-and-file U.N. members. Among the Third World nations, there is enough evenhandedness to account for large majorities that have passed resolutions criticizing aggression equally by the United States, the Soviet Union, India, Morocco, Indonesia, and (in the Security Council) Argentina. If there is a double standard, it usually afflicts only a small proportion of the Third World in any particular case. The traditional alliance subsystems are not reliable guides to actual voting behavior in cases involving unilateral use of force, whether by the U.S., the Soviets, or the NAMs. The superpowers, by contrast, consistently do not vote for the principle but for political self-interest. As heads of alliances, they feel they cannot afford to be principled. As militarily mighty states able to look after their own security, they are not as reliant as the majority on the protection of rules and principles. They can do more or less as they like, and, often, they do. The superpowers, and a few other states that perceive themselves as lions among sheep, value these short-term gains. This could be a very near-sighted view of their national interest if it causes the world to become an ever more unpredictable, violent, and dangerous place. In any event, the double standard is their problem, not that of the Assembly's majority.

The U.S. was able to take advantage of the majority's evenhandedness at the 1983 Assembly when faced with a Nicaraguan draft resolution condemning aggression against that nation. It persuaded the NAMs to change the text to condemn all "acts of aggression against the sovereignty, independence and territorial integrity of the States of the region."[48] Most NAMs fear aggression more even than they fear hunger and poverty. They do what they can to prevent the principle of non-aggression from being debased for purely partisan advantage. This is not because they are more principled than we, but because the principle is so central to any definition of their self-interest.

As is so often the case, the exception to any generalization about the U.N. is the special case of Israel. As has been noted in Chapter 11, the Assembly's majority invariably condemns Israel for deploying military force, but does so without any effort to criticize or inhibit those who use provocative force against it.[49] In 1983, for example, the Assembly condemned "Israel's . . . expansionist and annexationist policies"[50] while uttering no word about the Syrian occupation of large parts of Lebanon. It criticized U.S.-Israeli military cooperation without mentioning the thousands of Soviet military "advisers" operating with Syrian forces. Whatever claim to principled behavior the political organs of the U.N. may have, crumbles to a double standard whenever Israel is on the agenda.

Partly True: The Double Standard and Human Rights

With the rather sizable exception of the Middle East, the U.N.'s aggregate performance—as opposed to that of a few members—cannot be accused of operating on a double standard in dealing with the unilateral use of force. The same cannot be said in the field of human rights, although a bad performance is getting slightly better, particularly if one views the U.N. system as a whole and not merely the performance of the Assembly.

Articles 55 and 56 of the U.N. Charter commit members to take joint and separate action to promote respect for human rights and fundamental freedoms. Other provisions of the Charter set out steps the organization can take to promote this objective.[51] These authorize the Assembly to initiate studies and make recommendations "for the purpose of . . . assisting in the realization of human rights and fundamental freedoms for all without distinction as to race, sex, language, or religion."[52] The promoting of "universal respect for, and observance of, human rights and fundamental freedoms"[53] is assigned to the Assembly and, under its authority, to the Economic and Social Council (ECOSOC).[54]

The Charter thus authorizes the organization to involve itself in drawing up fundamental standards to regulate the way governments behave toward their own populations, and to monitor compliance with those standards. This is a significant advance over the days of the League of Nations. With a few exceptions, the protection of people's rights, before the middle of the twentieth century, was left wholly to the state. A recent Congressional study has noted that the Charter "opens up a new frontier in international law: The formulation of rules of international law directly affecting individuals."[55] Previously, international law had contented itself with fragile efforts to regulate conduct between governments, not between governments and citizenry.

Under the Charter, ECOSOC is authorized to make studies and reports, prepare recommendations and draft conventions for submission to the Assembly, call international conferences, and set up commissions to promote human rights. All this sounds, and was certainly intended to be, hopeful and far-sighted, incorporating an important lesson of World War II: a world in which totalitarianism flourishes behind national boundaries is a war-prone state system. At great expense the world had learned, it seemed, that brutal treatment by a government of its own population is an unusually reliable indicator of its proclivity eventually also to brutalize the populations of other states.

The general counsel of Amnesty International, Nigel S. Rodley, has observed that this lesson has been implemented quite unevenly. While "the UN has been more active and effective in 'promoting' human rights (its norm-creation function)" it is less active and effective when enforcing these rights, i.e., in implementing the norms.[56] A second kind of unevenness comes from the quality of implementation. Here the "double standard" is much in evidence. As the aforementioned Congressional study correctly states: "Violations in some countries are criticized while injustices in others are ignored."[57] Or, as President Jimmy Carter observed, the U.N. procedures "have been used to highlight human rights violations in particular countries to the neglect of violations in others."[58]

The U.N.'s development of human rights principles and norms began with the Assembly's drafting of a Universal Declaration of Human Rights, which was proclaimed on December 10, 1948.[59] Although the Declaration is a non-binding resolution and not a treaty, it has become "the moral touchstone for all claims at the international level that justice has not been done at the national level."[60] It defines as basic human entitlements such rights as those to life, liberty, security of person, freedom of religion, freedom of opinion and expression, freedom of assembly, and self-government through free elections. It proclaims freedom from slavery and torture, the right to a fair trial and to equality before the law, a presumption of innocence, and the right not to be subjected to retroactive laws, freedom of movement within one's state, and freedom to leave and return to it. It postulates rights of asylum abroad, nationality, privacy, family, property, and trade unionism. But it makes no provision for monitoring, let alone enforcing, national compliance with these high-minded principles. Thus began the U.N. tendency to make rapid progress in enunciating desirable standards but little advance in giving them effect.

On December 16, 1966, the General Assembly adopted the International Covenant on Economic, Social and Cultural Rights and the International Covenant on Civil and Political Rights together with its Optional Protocol.[61] After receiving the requisite number of ratifications, these conventions came into force in 1976. The United States has signed both, but not ratified either, although they were submitted to the Senate for approval by President Carter in February, 1978. By the beginning of 1983, 75 countries had ratified or acceded to the International Covenant on Economic, Social and Cultural Rights, and 73 had done so in respect of the International Covenant on Civil and Political Rights. Twenty-eight countries had become parties to the Optional Protocol.

These covenants, unlike the Declaration, are treaties. In legal theory, they are binding on those that accept them. But only about half the international community has done so; and the covenants have huge loopholes, which enable governments to suspend or circumvent many of the enunciated fundamental freedoms on such grounds as national security, territorial integrity, public policy, public morality, and the protection of the rights and reputation of others,[62] and to permit "derogation" on grounds of "public emergency."[63] The Covenant on Economic, Social and Cultural Rights, in addition, frames most of its rights in terms of a national obligation to work toward goals, rather than in terms of vested rights.

The process of enunciating principles, both in the form of treaties and non-binding Assembly resolutions and declarations (the latter are resolutions by another name), continues apace. Vast areas of human suffering and deprivation have been covered: women's rights, children's rights, workers' rights, rights of the disabled and of the mentally retarded, educational rights, and religious rights. Others, such as those relating to the rights of aliens and migrant workers are currently under consideration. The U.N. has also been active in the drafting of principles prohibiting "crimes against humanity," such as genocide (on which a convention was adopted on December 9, 1948)[64] and racial discrimination (on which a declaration was adopted in 1963, followed by a convention in 1965).[65] In 1973 this was followed by the Assembly's adoption of the Convention on the Suppression and Punishment of the Crime of Apartheid.[66] Torture has also received attention, with the adoption, on November 2, 1973, of the Assembly's resolution calling on states to renounce any form of torture and cruel, inhuman, or degrading treatment or punishment.[67] This led eventually to the Declaration on the Protection of All Persons from Being Subjected to Torture and Other Cruel, Inhuman or Degrading Treatment or Punishment,[68] and a draft convention on this subject is now making its way toward adoption. In 1979, the Assembly adopted a Code of Conduct for Law Enforcement Officials.[69] Three years later a resolution was passed that sets forth Principles of Medical Ethics relevant to the role of health personnel, particularly physicians, in the protection of prisoners and detainees against torture and other cruel punishment.[70]

All this activity conduces to the thought that what the U.N. now needs is not more enunciations of high principles, but practical machinery for giving effect to, and monitoring compliance with, those already on the books.[71] In this respect, the organization has been much less effective. Nevertheless, there has been some progress, which is not widely noted. The International Covenant on Civil and Political Rights obliges all parties to submit periodic reports to the Human Rights Committee, a body of eighteen experts elected by the participating states. Reviewing these reports, the experts can pose questions to states' representatives and, in their report to the General Assembly, may make comments on the information thus received. Article 41 of the Covenant also provides that states may make declarations allowing the Committee to receive complaints of violations against them made by other states that have made the same declaration. States accepting the protocol have also agreed to allow individuals residing in states adhering to the Covenant to bring complaints to the Committee. By 1981, the Human Rights Committee had received 147 communications under this optional procedure.[72]

In respect of some of these, the Committee has found that the complaints were justified and that violations had occurred. Fourteen complaints pertained to Uruguay, but—despite the affirmative findings of the Committee, which has no power to give binding decisions, let alone to enforce them—that country did not feel morally compelled to comply with its obligations. Nevertheless, Amnesty International and other human rights groups say it is useful to have their allegations confirmed by the Committee's international experts.[73]

The International Covenant on Economic, Social and Cultural Rights provides even less opportunity for monitoring implementation. That responsibility is left to ECOSOC and is implemented by a working group of fifteen delegates from ratifying countries that examines reports submitted by states under article 16 of the Covenant. The International Labour Organisation (ILO) also reports to ECOSOC on compliance with those articles of the Covenant that fall within its competence.[74]

In addition to the procedures established under the Covenants and applicable only to those states that have volunteered to become parties, the U.N. has established another system for monitoring compliance with human rights principles, a system that can be used in respect of any U.N. member and does not require consent. The system got its start in 1946, when ECOSOC established a Commission on Human Rights, which, one year later, created a Sub-Commission on the Prevention of Discrimination and Protection of Minorities. Without asking, the U.N. began to receive a steady stream of communications—from governments, organizations, and individuals (not excluding cranks)—complaining of serious rights violations. In 1970 ECOSOC authorized the Sub-Commission to create a working group that would review all such communications, including those from individuals, and transmit to the Sub-Commission those that revealed a "consistent pattern of gross . . . violations."[75] The Sub-Commission would consider these and report to the Commission, which would then choose from among three courses of action: to do nothing, to undertake a study of the situation, or to establish an investigating committee. It was an important new venture for the U.N. system.

The ECOSOC resolution is hedged with the proviso that actual investigations, as opposed to studies, may be undertaken only with the express consent of the state concerned and in cooperation with that state.[76] It also protects states by requiring that the procedures shall be secret until such time as the Commission is ready to report on them to ECOSOC.[77] Not until 1979 did the Commission make public one of the cases it was considering, having received authorization from ECOSOC to remove the restrictions on the file of Equatorial Guinea. It then appointed a special rapporteur to study the situation in that country.[78] The rapporteur did investigate the trail of atrocities committed by the regime of Macras Mguema and presented the report to the Commission on February 12, 1980.[79] It was subsequently made public. In 1978 the Commission also approved a study of the Idi Amin regime of Uganda.[80] However, in the case of Equatorial Guinea, the study was authorized on the eve of the offending regime's collapse; and the Uganda study was undertaken only when Amin was already in flight.[81]

These two cases, flawed—to put it mildly—by their timing, nevertheless established that the Commission, if the majority of its members so decide, can investigate gross violations of human rights and can proceed in public. At first this extraordinary procedure was used primarily in connection with the countries of Southern Africa and Chile, but more recently has also been applied in the cases of Bolivia, Kampuchea, El Salvador, Guatemala, Poland, Afghanistan, and Iran.[82]ed852

In addition, the Human Rights Commission may decide to criticize a member's human rights performance even without extensive prior investigation. This was done in 1983 in connection with Kampuchea, a move later endorsed by the General Assembly.[83] The Commission's resolution—passed by a vote of 28 to 9, with 4 abstentions[84]—condemns "the persistent occurrence of gross and flagrant violations of human rights in Kampuchea" and requests the Secretary-General to "monitor" developments and keep the situation "under review."[85] The General Assembly resolution—passed by a vote of 105 to 23, with 19 abstentions[86]—also found a "violation of humanitarian principles."[87]

In the same year the Commission, on the advice of its Sub-Commission, reaffirmed the right of the Afghan people "to determine their own form of government" free of "outside intervention, subversion, coercion or constraint of any kind whatsoever."[88] This was adopted by a vote of 29 to 7, with five abstentions.[89] As noted, the Assembly passed, overwhelmingly a similar resolution,[90] which reaffirms the economic, political, and social rights of the Afghan people,[91] while asking the Secretary-General to make "a report on the situation at the earliest appropriate opportunity."[92] Also in 1983 the Commission publicly expressed deep concern at "the continued reports of widespread violations of human rights and fundamental freedoms in Poland, including the imposition of severe punishments under martial law procedures on numerous persons" as well as "the dissolution of a democratically based trade union movement supported by a majority of Polish workers."[93] In receiving a rather meek report of the situation in Poland prepared by under-Secretary-General Hugo Gobbi for the Secretary-General at the request of the Commission (see below), the members forthrightly deplored "the attitude of the Polish authorities in not co-operating with the Commission on Human Rights over the implementation of its resolution" and reaffirmed the "right of the Polish people to pursue its political, social and cultural development, free from outside interference" while calling on the Polish authorities "to terminate the restrictive measures imposed on the exercise of human rights and fundamental freedoms," particularly the severe prison sentences. The Secretary-General or his representative was also asked to continue to study developments.[94] While the Polish case was therefore given careful attention by the Commission, the same cannot be said for the General Assembly, which simply ignored the problems identified by the organ charged with bringing human rights issues to its attention.

The Human Rights Commission, in 1983, also criticized various Third World states. One resolution expressed *"profound concern* at the continuing grave violations of human rights and fundamental freedoms in the Islamic Republic of Iran," including "evidence of summary and arbitrary executions, torture, detention without trial, religious intolerance and persecution, in particular of the Baha'is, and the lack of an independent judiciary and other recognized safeguards for a fair trial."[95] This was passed by a vote of 17 to 6, with 19 abstentions.[96] However, this resolution, like the one on Poland, was not taken up by the 1983 session of the General Assembly. Other resolutions that could be said to fall under the general heading of "indictments" passed by the 1983 meeting of the Human Rights Commission pertain to East Timor[97] and the Western Sahara.[98] Each was adopted very narrowly. The Assembly that year reiterated the rights of the people in the Western Sahara,[95] but did not take up East Timor.

What does this tell us about a double standard? In 1983 the Human Rights Commission publicly criticized three socialist states: the Soviet Union (in reference to Afghanistan), Vietnam (in reference to Kampuchea), and Poland. It leveled criticism at Iran, Indonesia (in reference to East Timor), and Morocco (in reference to Western Sahara). These indictments must be weighed against the Commission's initiatives against states closely identified with the U.S.: Guatemala, Chile,[101] El Salvador,[102] and Israel.[103] In 1984 the Commission also took up in closed session allegations against Albania, Argentina, Benin, Haiti, Indonesia (East Timor), Malaysia, Pakistan, Philippines, Turkey, and Uruguay,[104] but decided in an open session—by a vote of 17 to 14, with 12 abstentions—to take no further action on Poland.[105] If this does not appear to sustain a generalized charge of "double standard" against the Human Rights Commission—at least not in the last few years—the same cannot be said of the General Assembly. As noted, it wholly overlooked the Commission's initiatives on Iran and Poland, while waxing eloquent in castigating Guatemala, Chile, and El Salvador,[106] not to mention Israel.

When it comes to human rights, the treatment of Israel in both the Commission and the General Assembly, is in a class by itself. In 1983, for example, the Commission, in various resolutions, expressed its deep alarm "that Israel's policy in the occupied territories is based on the so-called 'Homeland' doctrine which envisages a mono-religious (Jewish) State."[107] Israel's policies toward civilians in the occupied territories are characterized as "war crimes and an affront to humanity," while the Israeli authorities are accused of the "arming of settlers . . . to commit acts of violence against Arab civilians."[108] Also contained in resolutions of the Commission were charges that the Israelis, as a matter of policy, practiced the "torture" of persons under detention, pillaged archaeological and cultural property, and interfered with Arab religious freedoms.[109] According to the Commission, Israel systematically practices "repression against cultural and educational institutions, especially universities, in the occupied Palestinian territories" and has been engaged in the "dismantlement" of Arab municipal services.[110]

Many of these determinations of fact began as allegations by the PLO and were subsequently the subject of investigation by various U.N. organs, including the ILO, the World Health Organization (WHO), and the United Nations Educational, Scientific and Cultural Organization (UNESCO). Not untypical of the quality of these fact-finding efforts is a 1979 UNESCO experts' investigation of educational, scientific, and cultural conditions in the occupied West Bank. The experts surprised UNESCO by largely absolving Israel of wrongdoing. Their report was suppressed by the Executive Director, who subsequently appointed a new commissioner, M. Jacqueline Hénin, a French-Arabist, who then produced the condemnatory report needed to satisfy the institutional bias.[111] Such slanted fact-finding generates kindred resolutions. In 1983 the Human Rights Commission found Israel guilty of "the inhuman treatment of the Syrian population" in the Golan Heights[112] and expressed deep alarm at the treatment of persons detained by Israel in Lebanon.[113] These indictments, inevitably, are reiterated in General Assembly resolutions which culminate in a call on members to "suspend economic, financial and technological . . . cooperation with Israel" and to "sever diplomatic, trade and cultural relations" in view of Israel's aggressive policies and persistent violations of human rights.[114]

These very serious measuress voted against Israel for human rights violations contrast with the lack of action against far more serious offenders. The Assembly has never been able to bring itself to address the extirpation of entire populations—some seven to nine million persons—in Burundi, Kampuchea, and Pakistani Bengal. Nor did the mass murders perpetrated by Idi Amin in Uganda and, more recently, by the Ayatollah Khomeini in Iran, bring the U.N. to vote sanctions. Speaking to the Assembly after Idi Amin's overthrow, Uganda's new president, Godfrey L. Binaisa, chided the delegates for their failure to implement the human rights norms. "In light of the clear commitments set out in those provisions of the Charter, our people naturally looked to the United Nations for solidarity and support in their struggle against the fascist dictatorship," he said. "For eight years they cried out in the wilderness for help; unfortunately, their cries seemed to have fallen on deaf ears." Thus the Amin regime "continued with impunity to commit genocide against our people." President Binaisa correctly identified the cause: an unwillingness of the NAMs to allow even the most egregious conduct by a member of the group to create fissures in the bloc's vaunted solidarity. As he put it, "somehow, it is thought to be in bad taste or contrary to diplomatic etiquette to raise matters of violation of human rights by member states within the forums of the United Nations."[115]

Against this background, the avalanche of charges against Israel, even those which have some basis in fact and the many which do not, provide ample justification for charging the human rights components of the system with practising an indecent double standard. But Israel is not the only case in point. While it is superficially true that the Human Rights Commission in 1983 under intense pressure from the West did at last pass a resolution challenging the human rights record of Poland, this was no more than a token beginning toward rectifying the practice of the Commission and, even more, of the General Assembly, which is to lash out hard at pro-Western states engaging in human rights violations while treading as on raw eggs when the alleged violations are those of a socialist or Non-Aligned country.

The resultant double standard is exemplified by comparing the ways the U.N. system has dealt with concurrent human rights complaints against Poland and against Chile. Such an examination quickly demonstrates that the apparent evenhandedness of critical resolutions passed by the Human Rights Commission on both Poland and Chile is but a thin veneer disguising the underlying reality of unequal treatment.[116] The situations in the two countries have much in common. In both, military rulers had established dictatorships after overthrowing civilian governments, ruling repressively, by decree, and prohibiting all political and social movements thought to be inimical to the regime. In both, trade unions were dissolved or curbed. Censorship was imposed on the media, and many leaders in the arts and professions were placed under arrest without trial. Lawyers and clerics who sought to defend those detained were themselves subject to detention or harassment. Reports of torture persisted. Academics—both faculty and students—thought to be less than wholehearted in their support of the new order were dismissed from the universities. While it is possible to disagree about the extent to which each of these practices was prevalent during the early periods of military rule in Chile and in Poland, there is little doubt that they were widely employed by both generals, Pinochet and Jaruzelski, respectively, to bring their nations to heel.

The U.N.'s response to the case of Chile was markedly sharper than to the case of Poland. Almost from the moment the Allende regime was overthrown, the U.N. system has performed as a model of global concern. This is understandable only in terms of the U.N.'s bloc politics. Pinochet, with indirect U.S. help, had overthrown the Marxist regime of Salvador Allende, who had led Chile into the NAM, which therefore felt obligated to scourge the usurper. Poland, in the view of the NAMs, had long been a Soviet preserve, and it thus matters little whether or not Moscow decides to tighten the leash.

On March 1, 1974, the Commission on Human Rights took the highly unusual step of authorizing its chairman to address a cable to the Chilean military authorities expressing the members' concern for the protection of the lives of political prisoners and calling for strict observance of the principles of the United Nations Charter and the International Covenants on Human Rights.[117] ECOSOC, by consensus, quickly seconded that demand.[118] Next, the Sub-Commission on Prevention of Discrimination and Protection of Minorities called for a "study" of Chilean human rights violations,[119] and the General Assembly—charging the Chilean junta with "gross and massive violations," including "the practice of torture" and operating "concentration camps"— demanded the immediate release of all political prisoners and safe conduct out of the country for those who desired it.[120]

In the spring of 1975 the Human Rights Commission set up a working group of five members to inquire into these charges.[121] Although the working group was refused admission to Chile, it was able to report to the 1975 Assembly,[122] which, in turn, expressed *"its profound distress* at the constant flagrant violations of human rights, including the institutionalized practice of torture, cruel, inhuman or degrading treatment or punishment, arbitrary arrest, detention and exile."[123] The Assembly then demanded the release of political prisoners and called for the return of free trade unions and the restoring of intellectual freedom,[124] while reiterating the working group's demand to be allowed entry into Chile to investigate conditions. The vote on this resolution was 95 to 11, with 23 abstentions.[125] The United States, Canada, and all of Western Europe voted for its adoption.

Since then, pressure on Chile has been escalated by the various components of the system.[126] In addition to monitoring events, calling for specific reforms and issuing condemnations, the system has brought pressure on Chile's friends to cut off economic and military aid to the Pinochet regime.[127] The working group, in 1977, conducted hearings in Caracas, Venezuela; Geneva; and New York. Its report is highly critical of arbitrary arrest, detention, and trial; the disappearance of detained persons; torture; the work of the secret police; the expulsion of dissidents from the country; and the condition of intellectual freedom; as well as a lack of cultural, economic, and social rights.[128] The General Assembly, in 1977, used those findings to express its "profound indignation" at the regime's "methods of systematic intimidation, including torture, disappearance of persons for political reasons, arbitrary arrest, detention, exile and deprivation of Chilean nationality."[129] The United States again voted in favor of this resolution, which was adopted by 96 to 14, with 25 abstentions.[130]

When the Chileans decided to permit a visit from the working group in 1978, that mission reported some improvement but attributed it largely to continuing international pressure, and emphasized the continued censorship, and the politically motivated limitations on education and on freedom of association. While admitting that a large number of individuals had been released from prison following the April 1978 amnesty, the report noted a continued concentration of arbitrary power, a lack of judicial impartiality, and an exclusion of much of the population from any right to participate in the government of the country.[131] On the basis of the working group's report, the Assembly in 1978 adopted another detailed resolution listing the transgressions of the Chilean government and the steps it ought to take to bring itself back into conformity with international human rights standards.[132] The Assembly also asked the Commission to select a Special Rapporteur to investigate and report on a regular basis.[133] In response, Abdoulaye da Dieye of Senegal was appointed. Additionally, Felix Ermacora of Austria and Waleed M. Sadi of Jordan were taken on as experts to study the question of the fate of Chile's missing and disappeared persons. The first report of the Special Rapporteur and of the experts went to the General Assembly in November 1979.[134] On the basis of this information, the General Assembly again passed a very detailed resolution criticizing the restrictive practices of the junta.[135] The United States, together with Western Europe, once more supported that resolution.

In the ensuing years, the pattern has been pretty much the same. Critical reports are prepared by the Special Rapporteur and form the basis of resolutions by the Human Rights Commission, ECOSOC, and the General Assembly.[136] What has principally changed, however, is that the Reagan administration's representatives now oppose these annual rites,[137] contending that conditions in Chile, nowadays, are no worse than those obtaining in many other U.N. member states. So long as the U.N. system refuses to take equal cognizance of these other human rights violations, Washington says it will no longer participate in the harassment of Chile. This position can be disputed on tactical grounds, for it abdicates the U.S. role as font of the historic libertarian movement. It was also hotly disputed on moral grounds by the U.N.'s Dutch director of the Human Rights Division, Theo van Boven. "I find it unacceptable,". he said, "that a situation of gross violation of human rights in any country should not be discussed, or action taken thereon, simply because other situations have not been taken up as well."[138] Basic human freedoms, in this view, must be regarded as absolute entitlements, not as a commodity of political exchange.

Still, it is not difficult to empathize with the frustration felt in Washington and in the nation at the selective way the U.N. implements its human rights mandate. Because Pinochet's Chile is ostracized by the NAMs and hated by Moscow, it is not protected by powerful blocs the way Idi Amin was immunized from U.N. criticism. On the contrary, it is an irresistible target. The Assembly regularly condemns Chile's failure to cooperate with U.N. demands[139] and carry out international human rights obligations.[140] Cosmetic political reforms are rebuffed, because "exceptional powers" are still vested in the military[141] and because the "security organs" still operate with impunity and make "clandestine" threats against Chilean human rights advocates.[142] The U.N. rapporteur draws withering attention to the continued existence of military courts,[143] the controls on freedom of thought and expression, the conflict between Church and State,[144] and the controls on trade unions[145] and universities,[146] as well as to the failure of the regime to conquer "recession, unemployment and devaluation of the national currency."[147]

In a sense, the U.N. system's harassment of the Chilean junta is the very model of what an aroused international community can do to discomfit a regime which imposes harsh, repressive measures on its citizenry. Although the system's response is in the form of paper bullets—the Special Rapporteur's investigations, reports by working groups, human rights subcommissions and commissions, and condemnatory resolutions by ECOSOC and the General Assembly—these do exact at least psychic and public-relations costs from the offenders, increasing their pariah-like isolation and making it less acceptable for governments, intellectuals, clerics, and leaders of the professions, even of Western nations, to consort with them.

No effort even remotely comparable, however, has been made by the U.N. system to curb similar abuses in Poland. While the offenses of Pinochet and Jaruzelski are not identical, they are remarkably similar in their prosaic ways. It is therefore striking to compare the report on the Polish situation made at the behest of the Human Rights Commission by Under-Secretary-General Hugo Gobbi.[148] Unlike the acerbic reports of the working group and the Special Rapporteur on Chile, it can best be described as fastidiously solicitous of the feelings of the Polish authorities. Instead of condemning the Poles for their total lack of cooperation—they refused to see or admit Gobbi—he merely mentions that "I did not have the possibility to visit Poland," as if he were a bashful Baedeker, and deduces from this that he "thus was not in a position to verify the allegations" made against the Polish authorities.[149] In Chile's case, refusing entry to U.N. investigators was treated as tantamount to an admission of guilt—which, of course, is a reasonable surmise. Gobbi's report spends as much time explaining why repression was instituted as on the repressive measures themselves. He notes that the government of Poland "introduced martial law on 13 December 1981" because it felt it could thereby avert "a civil war, economic anarchy as well as destabilization of State and social structures." The authorities are quoted as stating "that the restrictions were of a temporary nature and would terminate with the stabilizing of the situation."[150] While the report cites Amnesty International's allegations of ill-treatment of political internees, it takes no position on these or other charges.[151] Regarding the suppression of the Solidarity trade union federation, the report tells its audience only that the government adopted a new law on trade unions, which "gives a new trade union structure to the country, abolishing all the existing organizations, because of the 'political' actions contrary to the statutes of the trade union and to national legislation, undertaken by some of them."[152] This could as well have been written by the regime as by a U.N. investigator.

As in Chile, the military government of Poland has tried to preserve its powers in the guise of partially restored civil rule. The U.N. saw through such cosmetics in Chile, but not in Poland. Reporting that Polish martial law had been suspended on December 18, 1982, the Under-Secretary merely cautions that "some of the provisions introduced by the new law, limiting the capacity to choose new employment, and the provisions modifying articles of the penal code still appear not to be in complete conformity with the provisions of the [Human Rights] Covenants."[153]

Particularly striking is the report's extraordinary conclusion that as "regards allegations concerning the situation of political prisoners, it is not possible to make any evaluation without a verification *in loco* in direct consultation with those concerned and primarily the Polish authorities."[154] Non-cooperation by the Chilean government certainly did not have the same exculpatory effect. Where the Gobbi report emphasized the progress made, the Chilean working group was at pains to contrast token reforms with continued massive repression. Gobbi concluded, a "number of positive steps have been taken by the Government of Poland . . . [which] eliminates most of the rigours of life under martial law," and expressed the hope that "further measures for normalization will be taken."[155]

One year later, the U.N.'s report on the situation in Poland, produced by Gobbi and, on his departure, by Under-Secretary-General Patricio Ruedas, was even softer and more exculpatory. The rapporteur stated the position of the Polish authorities, noted the partial amnesties and new legislation described by the regime, declared himself "impressed by the spirit of moderation evidenced by all members of the Polish Government who met with him and is authorized by the Secretary-General to say that he, too, noted favourably that spirit." The Secretary-General was quoted as being "very encouraged on all fronts" by the situation. The report concludes by hoping that it will contribute "towards the process of healing and reconciliation of Polish society."[156] All this is in sharp contrast to the Chilean rapporteurs, who took it as their task to confront repression and manifest a global conscience.

Anyone comparing the Polish and Chilean reports in the light of the contemporary realities in those two countries could come to no other conclusion than that the United Nations system, when it comes to the monitoring and enforcement of international human rights, clearly applies a double standard, albeit not in every instance nor in every agency.

Partly Irrelevant: The Ethical Significance of the Double Standard

As this book has tried to make clear, the United Nations is a corporate body consisting of sovereign member states, gathered in political organs such as the General Assembly, the Economic and Social Council, and the Security Council, and in subsidiary bodies such as the Human Rights Commission. These political organs, components of the U.N. system, deliberate and act in accordance with the perceived national self-interest of the member states. The outcome may be a "U.N." resolution, but is, in fact, no more than an expression of the collective political will of a multitude of sovereign states. If there is a U.N. "double standard," it is the "double standard" of the *member states* that is to blame.

There is another sense in which the U.N. could be said to have a "double standard." If, for example, the Secretariat were to discriminate in its activities against certain of the members, or if the Secretary-General tilted in the direction of some states' interests and away from the interests of others, or became selectively passive in the discharge of his functions, or if the judges of the International Court of Justice (ICJ) habitually were to decide cases in accordance not with judicial impartiality but with their national biases, then it could truly be said that the U.N. proper—the core of the system—had, indeed, adopted a "double standard." However, while the Secretariat, Secretary-General, and ICJ have all been criticized in this respect, it is not principally they who stand accused. Rather, the principal offenders are the member-states of the political organs, those that define self-interest in such a way as to cut across basic institutional and societal principles. Even the Secretary-General, for all his timidity, has shown more resourcefulness and courage vis-à-vis Poland than did the majority of states in the General Assembly, which has failed to take any public position at all.

To the extent that the "double standard" is practiced by U.N. political bodies, it is because the members speak, vote, and act in accordance with their perceived political self-interest rather than in accordance with the high principles they have themselves enunciated. While such principles do exist in the U.N. Charter and in various U.N. conventions and declarations, they have a tendency to become inconvenient in a crisis and to be overridden by the political concerns of the moment. Thus most states speak, vote, and act in accordance with these "higher" principles only when they coincide with their political interest.

Most states in the U.N. are small and weak. They are more likely to be the victims rather than the perpetrators of aggression; and therefore their perceived national interest usually coincides with any application of the principle that force must not be used to resolve conflicts between nations. The reason a majority of states can usually be found to support a condemnation of the unilateral use of force is that most of the Third World, being weak and vulnerable, believes it to be to their advantage to reinforce the law against aggressive behavior, no matter which state violates it. By contrast, Third World nations are much less committed to human rights principles because their governments, for the most part, do not take human rights very seriously. The tendency is to regard any human rights abuse as negotiable: blocs of votes for or against an offender are traded for past or future favors which often pertain to some quite different area of concern. It must be added that the Third World is by no means alone in not taking human rights seriously.

The "double standard" also comes into play when states interpret the facts of a particular situation to suit their own convenience, ignoring or obfuscating preponderant evidence. Sometimes the *Rashomon* phenomenon operates: differences in culture and perspective can affect the way a fact is perceived. More often, however, disagreement over the facts merely reflects wishful thinking or willful deception, constituting a hypocritical avoidance of the fundamental rules of international conduct—by lying.

The complaint about the "double standard" is an emanation of the sense of fairness. The complainer probably feels that if country A is accused of torturing its political prisoners, and country B is engaged in the same practice, both A and B will be—ought to be—treated similarly. When U.N. organs subject country A to dire threats and dark accusations while ignoring similar conduct by country B, that expectation is frustrated. How an observer of the U.N. reacts to that frustration depends on how seriously the expectation has been entertained. It is arguable that the expectation, being unrealistic, should never have been formed. The political organs of the U.N., after all, are not assemblages of judges or philosophers but of politicians. In all likelihood, the imbalance in the treatment of countries A and B merely signifies that A has fewer friends and less powerful protectors among U.N. members than B. Country B may belong to a more cohesive bloc whose members consistently support one another regardless of the merits. Perhaps fewer members are beholden to country A for past voting or other favors. Country B may hold more IOUs than A. The decision to investigate, or even punish country A for its conduct is, quite simply, treated by many states as a political question addressed by political representatives in a political fashion. It is very little influenced by a concern for equality of treatment, as between A and B. Though members are precedent-conscious in procedural matters, the moral stricture that "likes be treated alike" does not significantly inhibit the political behavior of states in the representative organs of the U.N.

But why should it? The United States is in the minority, even among democracies, let alone among the full complement of states represented at the U.N., in subjecting its political institutions (the Congress, the executive branch) to a requirement that the laws treat all citizens alike, affording them "equal protection of the laws." The United States, moreover, is almost entirely alone in implementing the idea of equal protection by making the political process subject to judicial review—philosophers' justice. It is the court, not politics, that decides whether blacks may be given preference at the universities,[157] and Indians, at the Bureau of Indian Affairs.[158] "Fairness," in the U.S. system, is enforced by a judicial process isolated from politics by the life tenure of judges.

There is no commitment to "equal protection" in the U.N. order of things. At best, fairness is one of the many considerations in a government's decision to vote for or against a resolution. And there is no judiciary to override the political organs of the U.N. when the majority applies principles unequally in accordance with a double standard. In this, however, the U.N. closely resembles the vast majority of its members, including most parliamentary democracies. It is the U.S. which appears to project an unorthodox expectation that the U.N.'s political bodies, like the U.S. government, should act ethically in accordance with philosophically determined principles implementing equal protection. (And even in this, the U.S. is inconsistent, for it itself palpably abandons U.N. principles when these collide with national self-interest.)

Of course, the U.N. does have a court, the International Court of Justice. But at San Francisco the ICJ was explicitly denied the power to impose its views on the political organs by an equivalent of the novel U.S. concepts of judicial review and supremacy. Each U.N. organ was left free to interpret its own mandate, and has done so all along in accordance with political rather than ethical imperatives. The United Nations is not the "conscience of the world" as we were once wont to think, but a highly politicized conference of states. The realistic analogy is not a court, with its majestic concern for principle, but a bazaar, with its emphasis on price and trade.

This makes us uncomfortable and disoriented. We oscillate between the Puritan tradition of upholding right principles even in the face of their abandonment by everyone else, and, at the other end of the pendulum's swing, a desire to shed moral ephemera in favor of a policy of hard-nosed, pragmatic self-interest. What this ignores is that there may be circumstances in which the consistent advocacy and practice of our "moral" principles is defensible in purely strategic terms. Militarily weak nations have a strategic interest in the consistent assertion of the prohibition against the use of force, for example. Perhaps the U.S. has a comparable operational-tactical interest in the consistent pursuit of the principles of human dignity and freedom, not because (or, not *solely* because) that is the ethical position but because the persistent idea of freedom undermines the political authority of repressive regimes which, despite the case of Chile and Guatemala, for the most part are actual or potential enemies of the United States.

The U.N. is not to be faulted for performing as the political body it is. The U.S. may be faulted, however, if it fails to develop an optimal political strategy and to implement it with all the resources at its disposal. The problem is not that Israel, Chile, and El Salvador are pilloried in the Assembly, while Poland, Iran, and Cuba are not. Rather, it is that the Soviet Union has formed a winning political coalition with the Non-Aligned countries on many issues, human rights being only the most salient and galling example. In taking over human rights, they have lifted from the democracies the one subject concerning which Western leadership ought to be nearly unassailable. In other words, the problem is not that politics is paramount, but that we have failed to play political hard-ball.

§ 13 §

Playing Hard-Ball

Taking Initiatives

The balmy days of 1945–60 now seem a distant shore. Then, the United States could command the U.N.'s agenda; nowadays the tendency in Washington is to think of the U.N. as a Venus fly-trap, to be approached warily or, better, not at all. In 1982, when Nicaragua indicted the U.S. before the Security Council for aid to the insurgent *contras,* Jeane Kirkpatrick reportedly urged Washington to let her bring a counter-complaint citing Nicaragua's interference in El Salvador. The Department of State, however, prevailed with its view that the U.S. should take as few initiatives in the U.N. as possible, since no good could be expected to come from there. Yet, even now, occasional U.S. victories—such as in blocking Cuba from raising the Puerto Rican independence issue before the General Assembly (see below, Chapter 10)—suggest that the situation is not hopeless: not, that is, if Washington chooses the right issues and commits sufficient diplomatic and intellectual resources to winning.

Winning in the U.N. is not easy for the U.S. The organization's 1984 membership of 159 states is grouped into blocs, which roughly approximate political parties. The Group of 77 (or Developing Nations bloc) consists of some 120 states. Next largest, and more influential because better organized, is the Non-Aligned Movement which claims 99 members. Also large and often cohesive is the 50-member African Group. The Islamic Conference has 41 member-countries, but is usually divided except on the Palestine question. Lacking in cohesion, too, are the Asian Group (39 members) and the Latin American Group (33 members), both of which have pro-Soviet adherents who actively prevent the groups from taking consensual positions of which Moscow disapproves. The Western European "and Others" Group is smaller (22 members) but acts mostly in concert. The Eastern European Group (11 members) is strained because three members (Albania, Romania, Yugoslavia) often refuse to take their cues from the Kremlin. The Arab Group (21 countries) is usually divided between shifting alliances of radical and moderate regimes. The smallest groups—the five Nordics, the six-member Association of Southeast Asian Countries, and the 10-member European Community—are perhaps the most cohesive.

While the blocs are extremely important in determining many outcomes in the Assembly, they are not invariably decisive. Many states belong to more than one bloc and are subject to influences—their bilateral relations with the U.S., their membership in the British Commonwealth, or their cultural and fiscal ties to France—that are not made manifest in the bloc system.

The United States is both weakened and, in some sense, strengthened by being the only member (with Israel) to belong to no group. On the one hand, operating on its own, Washington cannot expect to muster the automatic support of a bloc of votes; nor can it act as a broker trading promises to deliver a quantity of votes for one set of issues in return for the support of another bloc for resolutions of particular interest to the U.S. It often vainly seeks ways to induce individual members of blocs to vote even their national self-interest when that self-interest coincides with American rather than with bloc policies. A dramatic instance of failure is the Law of the Sea negotiations. During the early days of that conference, in 1974, the United States made generous proposals for global revenue-sharing, to be financed by a levy on mineral resources extracted from the ocean floor beyond a 12-mile zone allocated exclusively to each coastal state. Latin American states, anxious for a wider area of exclusive national control, opposed the offer and were able to carry almost all the Third World states, including many with little or no coastline which would have benefited significantly from the American offer.

On the other hand, by belonging to no group, with its requirements for consensus and log-rolling, Washington is relatively free to pursue a range of U.N. objectives in its own time and fashion. Whether this is sufficient recompense, whether its isolation is truly splendid, remains a subject of dispute among U.S. delegates and experts.

What is beyond dispute is that it is uniquely difficult for the U.S., under present circumstances, to use the U.N. to pursue even a relatively enlightened policy of national self-interest. And yet, in significant instances, this is attainable. The effort deserves to be made. Admittedly, *pace* Eleanor Roosevelt, if the U.N. did not already exist, we would not now feel impelled to invent it. But since it does exist, and for as long as we choose to belong, it is better—to paraphrase Mrs. Roosevelt once again—to throw a few well-placed punches than to just to lick our wounds.

The figure of speech is all too apt. The U.N. is a combat zone, as well as a talking shop. In it, effectiveness depends on long- and middle-term strategic planning and deployment of seasoned forces to execute carefully calibrated defensive and offensive tactics. In the Puerto Rican debate, the United States responded defensively to an initiative taken by its enemies. In other instances, the U.S. delegation has successfully seized the initiative. Executing defensive or offensive strategy, alone or in concert with allies, the U.S. continues to win some victories, which, if not momentous, are at least indicative of the possibilities. These are not awesome victories. Perhaps they little alter the conduct of governments, at least in the short run. However, they do serve as salutary reminders that the United States and its allies, when they draw on the well-spring of their moral resources, can still command the attention of the world. We can discomfit regimes that oppress their populations and traumatize their neighbors. These small victories also demonstrate that, playing from our strengths, we can still, sporadically, evoke the powerful coalition of democratic forces that once moved the organization.

Those forces may be making a modest comeback. One way to measure trends in ideas is by listening to those who have recently overthrown a regime in a Third World state. The leaders of a coup, at least before they feel secure in power, are apt to be rather keen judges of what the people want most. By that test, some of America's traditional values seem once more to be in fashion. In April 1984, for example, the military junta that seized power in Guinea promised not "African socialism" or "death to the colonialists," as was customary hitherto, but rather, of all things, "democracy and free enterprise."

If a new ideological climate is evolving, the political organs of the U.N. will both have a role in bringing it about and also reflect it on the "big screen" that records Assembly votes. To prepare to accelerate this trend, small triumphs are worth studying, much as military victories are eagerly pondered by generals and admirals.

Bacteriological and Chemical Weapons

In 1980 the U.S. government charged that chemical weapons had been responsible for the death of at least 10,000 persons in Afghanistan and Southeast Asia. Washington characterized this as "a major humanitarian issue of our time"[1] and demanded an end to violations of the world's earliest arms-control agreement, the 1925 "Geneva" Protocol for the Prohibition of the Use in War of Asphyxiating, Poisonous or Other Gases, and of Bacteriological Methods of Warfare.[2] Since the Soviet Union is among the signatories of this treaty, our allegation raised issues both of respect for human life and respect for treaties.

These proved to be issues on which the West could rally strong support from the U.N.'s NAM majority, composed mostly of weak states heavily reliant for their safety on the net of humanitarian treaties. Moscow and its clients thus found themselves isolated. On December 12, 1980, by a large majority, but over the strenuous objection of the socialist bloc, the General Assembly decided to carry out an impartial investigation to ascertain the facts. It invited the Secretary-General to appoint qualified medical and technical experts to visit the affected areas.[3] To chair this group, the Secretary-General selected the head of scientific research of the Egyptian armed forces, Major General Dr. Esmat A. Ezz. To assist him, he chose the Chief Surgeon of the Kenyan Ministry of Health, the Philippine Deputy Surgeon General, and a professor of the Peruvian Institute of Tropical Medicine.[4]

These experts produced a preliminary report to the Assembly in 1981[5] and a final report in 1982.[6] They noted that the team had not been permitted to visit Afghanistan, Laos, or the parts of Kampuchea controlled by the Vietnamese-installed authority.[7] While this limited their investigation,[8] and despite indications that some samples gathered by them had been sabotaged,[9] they nevertheless found "circumstantial evidence suggestive of the possible use of some sort of toxic chemical substance in some instances."[10]

The report provoked intense controversy on all sides. U.S. deputy delegate Kenneth Adelman thought the investigators had been unduly pusillanimous in skirting the personal risks necessary to obtain first-hand evidence.[11] Washington therefore circulated its own field investigation, which came to far more damaging conclusions.[12] Ultimately, however, U.S. delegate Charles M. Lichenstein hailed the U.N. fact-finding mission as "a step forward," even though "less forceful than the U.S. had hoped."[13]

There was no such applause from the socialist bloc. Afghanistan's representative, Farid Zarif, accused the United States and, by implication, the Group of Experts, of the "technique of the 'big lie . . .' " that threatened to "eclipse" the "reputation of the Nazi minister of propaganda, Joseph Goebbels."[14] The Vietnamese delegate, Vo Anh Tuan, charged that Washington, through the experts, had "attempted to divert the attention of the international community from the United States' responsibility for its massive use of chemical weapons in South-East Asia."[15] Most, however, agreed with New Zealand's Richard J. Martin, who stated that the investigation had proceeded with "integrity, impartiality and objectivity," despite all efforts to hinder it.[16]

This intense controversy—reflected also in the U.S. academic and scientific community[17]—culminated in a 1982 Assembly resolution expressing "appreciation" to the experts and adopting their conclusions.[18] The resolution called for "strict observance" of the prohibition on the use of chemical and bacteriological weaponry.[19] Eighty-three members voted in its favor, while only the Soviets and a few Third World clients—Afghanistan, Angola, Congo, Cuba, Democratic Yemen, Ethiopia, Grenada, Laos, Libya, Mozambique, Syria, and Vietnam—voted against it. (There were also 33 abstentions.) Once again, the Soviets were isolated and their Third World clientele placed in a highly embarrassing and exposed position.

The Assembly, still in 1982, also asked the Secretary-General to compile a list of experts whose services would be available on short notice to undertake further field investigations, as well as a list of reliable laboratories able to weigh scientific evidence. He was also asked to devise procedures for the "timely and efficient investigation" of new charges[20]—procedures that could be activated whenever any member-state complained of a violation of the Geneva Protocol.[21] The Soviets were fiercely opposed and thoroughly defeated: 83 to 22, with 33 abstentions. While this outcome reflects widespread revulsion in the international community at the use of bacteriological and chemical weapons, it also results from diligent staff work by the New Zealand, French, American, and other like-minded missions.

In 1983 the Secretary-General reported that he had appointed the stand-by "group of qualified consultant experts" as required by the Assembly.[22] He was next asked to establish contingent procedures for their rapid deployment in an emergency.[23] Again, the proposal was supported by an overwhelming majority— the vote was 97 to 20, with 30 abstentions—thereby reminding Moscow that in this matter, the United States and its allies were in step with the preponderance of mankind. (India, however, stood with the Soviets, in almost complete isolation from the Non-Aligned bloc, which it was then chairing.)

The practical consequences of this initiative were not long in making themselves felt. On November 3, 1983, the government of Iran complained that Iraq was using chemical weapons against Iranian soldiers.[24] Further substantiation soon came from medical authorities in Western Europe where Iranian soldiers had been sent for treatment.[25] On March 8, 1984, Iran's U.N. ambassador, Said Rajaie Khorassani, addressed a letter to the Secretary-General invoking the Assembly's 1982 resolution and asking him to take "immediate" action[26] to investigate. On the next day, Friday, the Secretary-General announced that a team of experts would leave for Iran that weekend.[27] Faced with strenuous Soviet opposition to basing the fact-finding mission on the Assembly resolution,[28] his press officer took the position that the Secretary was dispatching the team "under his own authority" derived from the Charter.[29] There was no doubt in anyone's mind, however, that the Assembly's previous action in supporting exactly these procedures had significantly strengthened the Secretary-General's hand.

Despite vigorous Iraqi denials,[30] the four experts—one each from Australia, Spain, Sweden, and Switzerland—reported unanimously on March 21 that "chemical weapons in the form of aerial bombs have been used in the areas inspected in Iran by the specialists."[31] Nine days later, the Security Council, by consensus, declared "their grave concern" at these findings and strongly condemned the use of chemical weapons.[32] The speedy, efficient intervention by the Secretary-General had significantly, perhaps decisively, raised the costs to the user and appears to have caused Iraq to rethink its tactics.

The United States cannot claim sole credit for these accomplishments. The 1980 initiative establishing the mission headed by Major-General Ezz was led by New Zealand, while the 1982 effort to authorize the panel of experts and procedures for field investigation was spearheaded by France. In both instances, the U.S. quietly and efficiently did much to ensure victory, but was asked to stay behind the scenes lest its public involvement frighten away the NAMs. Both Washington and the U.S. delegation lobbied vigorously, but agreed not to be a sponsor of the relevant resolutions. In 1982, at one point, when U.S. delegate Adelman in a newspaper interview claimed public credit, several sponsors threatened to withdraw their support. For the most part, the U.S. delegation has learned the most difficult of political lessons: that it is more important to win than to be seen to be the winner.

"Massive Flows of Refugees"

Massive flows of refugees have become a tragic symptoms of deep disorders in the modern state system. The Federal Republic of Germany took the initiative to have the Assembly address the causes of this phenomenon, with the U.S. again working supportively behind the scenes. The problem, while universal, is one which is particularly embarrassing to Soviet clients: Afghanistan, Vietnam, and Cuba, whose policies and tactics are responsible for the largest exoduses of recent years. Yet so deep is the concern of the Non-Aligned that Moscow dared not oppose it openly. In 1981, by consensus, the General Assembly voted to "establish a group of governmental experts" with the task of improving "international co-operation to avert new massive flows of refugees."[33] This was no minor task. In effect, the Assembly by its resolution had determined that the policies of governments toward citizens cease to be purely domestic matters when those policies force neighboring states to absorb large numbers of persons fleeing their homes in terror.

The subject was one that attracted widespread interest. So many states wished to be represented on this Group of Experts that it took a year and an enlargement of the Group's numbers from seventeen to twenty-four[34] to get it organized. Meanwhile, another committee of the Assembly had begun to review a study by the Commission on Human Rights entitled "Human Rights and Mass Exoduses." By 1983, although no action had yet been taken, the governmental activities that generate flows of refugees had become a matter for regular debate in the Assembly,[35] as well as for study and negotiations between sessions. The Group of Experts has now begun to produce annual reports further spotlighting the policies that tend to create the problem.[36]

This provides the occasion for some hard-hitting exchanges. At the time of the adoption of the item in 1981, the U.S. representative expressed the hope that, "in investigating this subject the Group of Experts which the resolution creates will also take due note of the actions by which some Governments deliberately and cynically create refugee flows in order to rid themselves of political opponents or people they find in other ways undesirable." He named Cuba and Vietnam as "heinous examples" of a policy of "brutal expulsions of

the ideologically undesirable among their own population as a means of preserving totalitarian control."[37] This sort of plain talk apparently discomfitted its
intended targets, for the U.S. representative was constantly interrupted by the
Cuban and Soviet delegates. Once again, however, it was clear that the U.S.
was in harmony with the majority of members.

Medical Ethics
The General Assembly, on December 14, 1978, adopted a resolution that
requested the Commission on Human Rights to study the protection of those
detained on grounds of mental ill-health, with a view to formulating guidelines
and preparing a report for eventual adoption by the Assembly.[38] This initiative,
launched with strong U.S. support by the United Kingdom delegation, obviously pointed to the Soviet practice of dealing with dissidents by confining
them in psychiatric institutions. It was adopted by a vote of 83 to 0, with 48
abstentions.

A related initiative on "medical ethics relevant to . . . the protection of
prisoners," with special attention to the protection of those detained on grounds
of mental illness, led to consensus resolutions adopted by the Assembly in 1982
and 1983.[39] The 1982 resolution brands it "a contravention of medical ethics
for health personnel, particularly physicians, to be involved in any professional
relationship with prisoners or detainees the purpose of which is not solely to
evaluate, protect, or improve their physical and mental health."[40] The Soviets
did not vote against this resolution, only because to do so would have been
seen as an admission of guilt.

Totalitarianism
In 1981, as it has in several other years, the Assembly adopted by consensus a
resolution that "*condemns* all totalitarian or other ideologies and practices" that
involve "systematic denial of human rights and fundamental freedoms."[41] This
resolution began as a Soviet-bloc effort to condemn Nazism in the Federal
Republic of Germany. Seizing the initiative, the U.S. and its friends, including some in the Third World, have succeeded in revising the text so it echoes
the global aspiration for democracy. While the text may represent little but
hypocrisy, that, as the duc de la Rochefoucauld has observed, is the homage
vice pays to virtue.

Religious Tolerance
Another example of this homage is the Declaration on the Elimination of All
Forms of Intolerance and of Discrimination Based on Religion or Belief, which
was adopted by the General Assembly in 1981[42] after almost twenty years of
effort. As early as 1962 the General Assembly had proposed that the Commission on Human Rights prepare a set of draft principles, and eventually a
binding international convention, on the difficult subject.[43] In the intervening

years the U.S. encouraged Canada's ambassador, Yvon Beaulne, and Senegal's representative, Judge Abdoulaye Dieye, to take the lead in pushing the declaration of principles. Although the U.S. delegation again kept a low profile, the process could not have been brought to a successful conclusion without Washington's strenuous behind-the-scenes support.

The adoption of the Declaration by consensus should not obscure its remarkable and controversial content. Among other things, the Declaration recognizes everyone's right to freedom of thought, conscience, and religion, including freedom to choose and practice a religion or belief, individually or in community with others, in public or private.[44] It also avers that no one "shall be subject to discrimination by any State, institution, group of persons, or person on grounds of religion or other beliefs."[45] Far from couching its aspirations in vague generalities, the Declaration enumerates very specific rights: to assemble for the purpose of worshiping, make articles needed for worship, publish and disseminate religious writings, teach religion, solicit contributions, train clergy, observe holidays, and maintain communication across national boundaries with like-minded persons and institutions.

For many—perhaps a majority—of the members of the U.N. these principles are little short of revolutionary and bear no resemblance to actual practice of governments. The representative of Iran, for example, exempted his nation from compliance except insofar as the obligations were "in total conformity with Islamic Jurisprudence."[46] Still, as the delegate of the Netherlands observed, all "States Members of this great Organization have an obligation under the Charter to promote the observance of human rights, and by adopting the Declaration they have indicated their commitment to comply with that obligation. All individuals under the jurisdiction of the Member States have the right to remind their Governments of that obligation and may avail themselves of the rights set forth."[47] U.S. delegate Michael Novak added that the concept of "freedom of conscience" had "been discovered by millions of people in dramatic circumstances where freedom of thought and conscience had been outlawed in the name of the collective will. It was precisely that freedom of thought and conscience which lay at the root of human dignity and which made it wrong for human beings to be treated like cattle and imprisoned or sent to work camps in accordance with a doctrine of intolerance." The Assembly's adoption of the Declaration, Novak added, showed that failure to respect that dignity was "an offence not simply against the whole of humanity but also, for religious persons, against God."[48]

In the persistent campaign for the Declaration, the U.S. found both its true voice and a global echo. In a matter of fundamental importance, peer pressure had been used successfully, even on states which habitually compelled religious belief or disbelief. There had been a rallying of the majority in pursuit of what Novak referred to as "the universal dream."[49]

So powerful is this peer pressure and the force of the "universal dream" that

the representative of China felt obliged to state that "his Government's consistent policy" was one "of guaranteeing freedom of religion and religious
belief,"[50] even if the statement happened to be less than candid. As Ambassador
Jeane Kirkpatrick told a Congressional committee in 1984: "The decisions of
the United Nations are widely interpreted as reflecting 'world opinion' and are
endowed with substantial moral and intellectual force. The cumulative impact
of decisions of U.N. bodies is to influence opinions all over the world about
what is legitimate, what is acceptable, who is lawless and who is repressive,
what countries are and are not capable of protecting themselves and their
families [of states] in the world body."[51] And, one might add, what countries
are capable of protecting and projecting their fundamental values.

The United States is just beginning to reassert its role as part of a growing
coalition of countries harboring common values and aspirations. It is not now,
and may never become a bloc. It more resembles a single-issue coalition; but
there already are signs of its considerable potential for affecting the agenda of
the world organization. However, unlike the days when American leadership
was based on economic and military preponderance, any U.S. assertion of
leadership nowadays must be based on demonstrated and recognized moral
primacy, as well as on carefully planned and diligently executed diplomatic
strategy.

The Power of the Purse

In planning to win any victory in a political organ of the U.N., money is a key
ingredient. That the U.S. share in financing is very large (see below), does
provide a certain leverage, but one that is largely illusory so long as contributions are made automatically in deference to whatever the Assembly decides to
bill. But there is nothing sacred in the Assembly's system of assessments,
which, over the past forty years has become thoroughly politicized and inequit-
able. Some countries withhold payment for political reasons, and so can the
U.S. Although the U.S. share of the U.N. budget has declined over the forty
years, it still pays almost two-and-a-half times as much (25 percent of the total)
as the next largest contributor, the Soviet Union (10.5 percent). Consequently,
the mere threat to withhold is, for the U.S., a formidable weapon.

The Burgeoning Budget

As the membership of the U.N. has grown, practically tripling since its inception, so has the budget of the organization. Since 1963, it has expanded by 700
percent, and, in consequence, members' assessments have grown commensu-
rately, by 80 percent in the five year period, 1976 to 1981, alone. Of the
assessed contributions, 40 percent currently goes for economic, social, and
humanitarian undertakings, 40 percent for administration and support services,
and 20 percent for other purposes including legal and political activities.[52]

The organization's increasing expenditures are related to rapid growth in membership. The Assembly's Third World majority, which approves the budget,[53] has been responsible for initiating myriad new programs responsive to the new nations' virtually inexhaustible economic needs and political desires. Unfortunately, rapid growth in membership—except for the induction of wealthy capitalist West Germany and Japan—has done little to increase the funding available for expanded activity. For 1982 the assessed budget for the U.N. was $721,354,404.[54] Of this amount, the U.S. contributed $180,338,601 or 25 percent, plus an additional $60,398,000 for assessed peacekeeping operations.[55] A further $1.0 billion was budgeted for agencies, organizations, and operations supported by voluntary contributions,[56] of which the U.S. provided $236 million.[57] Altogether, the U.S. supplied 28.86 percent of all voluntary funds.[58]

While, in one sense, this may be regarded as "peanuts"[59] in comparison with the overall U.S. budget, nevertheless Washington's contribution makes a decisive difference to the U.N.'s ability to carry on most of its programs. Taken together with the Western European assessment, this fact becomes axiomatic. Without the Western nations' fiscal compliance, the U.N. could not maintain a balance between the few who pay the bills and those who run them up. U.S. delegate Senator J. Bennett Johnston recently pointed out that 80 percent of the United Nations' regular budget was financed by 10 percent of the members, and 90 percent, by one-quarter of the members. The Western (OECD) industrial states were assessed 73.6 percent of the organization's expenses for the period 1983–85.[60] On the other hand, 147 countries in the aggregate pay less than the United States share. Johnston predicted that financial disaster "awaits any international body that divorces the right to vote for programs from the necessity to pay for them. That simply invites and indulges waste."[61]

Echoing these sentiments, the Soviet delegate, Vladimir V. Shustov, pointed out that 93 members were being assessed at a level between 0.01 percent and 0.03 percent of the total budget. This meant that 60 percent of the members would be paying a sum representing little more than one percent of the organization's expenses.[62] Nearly half the members each contribute the minimum assessment which, in 1983, was slightly over $60,000.

On the one hand, this disproportion buys the U.S. potential influence. On the other, it creates problems with Congress and the American taxpayer. Washington has made a few fitful efforts to link voting power in the Assembly with financial contributions. In 1967 the U.S. tentatively raised the question of creating a new category of "associate membership" for the dozens of island mini-states, the flotsam and jetsam of empire, then moving to independence.[63] In 1970 the U.S., with Britain, proposed a form of non-voting membership that would cost nothing.[64] The Secretary-General in his 1969 annual report noted the dissatisfaction with the existing system.[65] Nevertheless, these proposals were non-starters. For one thing, they were introduced too late—after the Non-Aligned Movement (NAM) had already laid claim to a voting majority in the Assembly. Its members could not have been expected to react sympathetically to a proposal that would have halted that process. Besides, even the tiniest and most remote new nation knows that full membership is almost certainly going to be worth more than it must spend on the minimum annual fee, if only because its vote can be traded for promises of tangible assistance from more affluent members. It is not at all unusual, for example, for Japan to promise foreign aid to a micro-nation such as the Solomon Islands in explicit exchange for agreement to support Japan's perennial campaign for election to the Security Council.[66]

Allocating Costs

If the U.N. were truly a community, with a fair system for spreading its common expenditures among members, it could be argued that there existed a moral and legal obligation to pay, and that no nation was entitled to advance its own interests by withholding, or threatening to withhold, all or part of its assessed share of the common costs. As it happens, however, the U.N. is not a community, and the costs are not allocated fairly.

In addition to criticism of the disjuncture between the political power to incur expenses and the ability to bear the resultant financial burden, there is also much criticism from economically developed members at the way the financial burden is divided. Here, again, it is the Assembly, with its NAM majority, which sets the rules that determine who pays what. Those with the voting power use it to see that others pay.

Initially, the assessment process was geared to "capacity to pay."[67] This principle of fairness was laid down by the Preparatory Commission of the United Nations at its inception and has never been formally repudiated.[68] The main criterion for capacity to pay has always been gross national income.[69] Over the years, however, the principle has been reduced to a near-fiction.

Again, the U.S., when it controlled the Assembly, was the earliest transgressor. At the time the first scale of assessments was produced, in the fall of 1946, the Committee on Contributions proposed that 49.89 percent of the budget be paid by the United States.[70] Although this would have been in strict compliance with "capacity to pay" based on gross national income, it was vigorously opposed by Washington, which called for a ceiling of 25 percent[71] but eventually agreed to pay 39.89 percent.[72] In 1954, under insistent prodding by the American delegation, the Assembly reluctantly limited the top contribution, this time to 33.33 percent.[73] In 1972 the U.S. finally succeeded in bargaining the ceiling down to 25 percent.[74] That year, the U.S. contribution ought to have been 38.4 percent had it been based strictly on "capacity to pay" as determined by national income.[75] (Nowadays, however, thanks to our declining proportion of global productivity, there is only a 2 percent difference left between what Americans pay and what, by principle, we ought to.[76])

With the U.S. showing the way, other countries began to use political pressure to shift the fiscal burden. Canada, arguing that no nation ought to pay more *per capita* than the largest contributor, won support in 1948 for a "per capita ceiling,"[77] which persisted until abolished by the Assembly in 1974.[78] Even earlier, the Preparatory Commission itself had proposed several exceptions to the general principle. One set a minimum contribution of .04 percent of overall assessments. Another proposed to give the Assembly's Committee on Contributions "discretion to consider all data relevant to capacity to pay and all other pertinent factors in arriving at its recommendations."[79] This was intended to provide relief for countries whose gross national incomes were large, solely because of the size of their populations—India and China, in particular—but which had very low *per capita* incomes. In accordance with this directive, the first scale established a "low *per capita* income allowance," permitting a reduction of up to 40 percent in the assessment of any country having an income of less than $1000 per person.

The "low *per capita* income allowance" was a gesture by the rich nations to the poor. In recent years the NAMs have used their political muscle to gain other concessions. Thus, the floor has been lowered to 0.01 percent of total assessment.[80] Seventy-five members of the United Nations—roughly half— currently pay this nominal fee.[81] Resolutions committing the organization to spend tens of millions of dollars can be passed by the votes of members contributing only about one percent of the funds.

More significantly, the upper limit of the "low *per capita* income allowance" has been raised to $2100, and the gradient of relief has been raised to 85 percent.[82] The effect is that populous states with a quite high national income are able to shift part of their share of the costs to other high income states with smaller populations. This makes equitable sense in the context of a system based on the individual's ability to pay, rather than on the size of the economy of the state. But, rationally, such a system would also distribute its voting power very differently, in accordance with population.

More serious are recent NAM maneuvers to lengthen the "base period," which is the range of years over which the national income is averaged in order to arrive at an assessment. Since the agreed standard is "capacity to pay," it would be reasonable to assume that the statistics of national income used in calculating the annual assessment would try to reflect the most current state of each country's economy. For many years this was true, the assessment being based on the previous three years' national-income figures. Recently, however, the Third World majority has succeeded in stretching out the base period to seven years and, beginning in 1983, to ten years.[83] Since most Third World states pay at or near the floor level of 0.01 percent, it is not they who are the beneficiaries of this statistical finagling. Rather, they are being pulled along, in the name of Third World solidarity, by states that have become newly affluent but wish to postpone for as long as possible—preferably forever—the upward revision of their assessments. Representatives of these newly rich states actually have argued, quite successfully, that if they accepted a higher assessment they would be breaking NAM solidarity!

Besides making the "national income" standard virtually meaningless, the Third World majority has called for its burial, preferring a measure more favorable to their fiscal circumstances. Students of Henry George are familiar with efforts in the U.S. to adopt a tax base other than income. The obstacles are formidable. Asked to consider "the concept of accumulated wealth"[84] as a measure for setting assessments, the (U.N.) Committee on Contributions concluded that, as with many countries, alternative indicators were not available or were not comparable, for statistical or conceptual reasons.[85] Nevertheless, as recently as December 1982 the Assembly has continued to insist that its Committee on Contributions present "a thorough study on alternative methods to assess the real capacity of Member States to pay" that would be based on what a state has, rather than on what it earns: a property, rather than an income, tax. Further to protect "new money" at the expense of "old money," the Assembly proposed a "limit for increases between two successive scales of assessments."[86]

The assessments battle became particularly acrimonious during the Thirty-seventh Assembly, in the fall of 1982. After bitter haggling, the members adopted a new scale for the three-year period, 1983–85,[87] one Washington considers glaringly unfair. That Washington is right is easily demonstrated. For example, had assessments been based on 1980 gross-national-income figures, rather than on a ten-year base (and even if all other distortions were to remain untouched), the assessment of Iraq ought to have been higher by a factor of 3.5; that of Algeria, Bahrain, and Bolivia, by 2.5; and the assessments of Brazil, Costa Rica, Cyprus, Iran, Malaysia, Yugoslavia, Nigeria, Mexico, Trinidad, and Tunisia, doubled.[88] Many other nations were grossly underassessed as a deliberate consequence of stretching out the base period. The distortions are further magnified by other departures from the "capacity to pay" principle.

The Preparatory Commission, in 1946, had visualized the danger that some states might "desire to increase [contributions] unduly for reasons of prestige."[89] Rarely can a prognosis have been so wrong. Prestige, in Third World terms, appears to consist of "beating the fare." This was not always so. In 1946, of the ten largest contributors to the United Nations budget, three were developing countries. Currently, none are. China, when governed by the Nationalists, assumed a 5 percent scale of assessment purely as a matter of national pride, even though the size of the Chinese economy did not justify it. The People's Republic, when it succeeded the Nationalists, for a time accepted that level of contribution primarily in order not to have to make public its economic data. However, beginning in 1979, Peking launched a campaign which has succeeded in reducing its contribution to approximately 0.88 percent of the total. That has compelled others to take up the slack. In the words of a Canadian delegate to the Fifth Committee: "Most countries, apparently, no longer want to be among the largest contributors."[90] His sentiments were echoed by the

Soviet delegate who remarked that "because of the changes made in [the] statistical base period and in the low *per capita* income allowance formula," developing countries "were benefitting by an amount of some $68.5 million annually," an amount offset "by a corresponding increase in the assessments of developed countries."[91]

The U.S. attacked the 1983–85 scale as "artificial and discriminatory," and also pointed out that it is not the Third World alone that plays games with the system. The Soviets tend to produce "national statistics which helped skew the result," and to use "unrealistic exchange figures and purely arbitrary costs," to seek advantage.[92] The American spokesman noted that, until Moscow made slight corrections, the Soviets were to have been assessed less than Japan. He concluded that if Soviet statistics were to be believed, its economy would have to be such an "enormous failure . . . that its future eclipse was indicated."[93]

Withholding

It is, therefore, all too clear that the principle of "capacity to pay" based on "national income," while still rendered lip-service, has little to do with the actual outcome of the assessment process, which is primarily dictated by politics. In other words, there is nothing particularly moral or principled about the system of assessments, which produces results that reflect voting power—like everything else the Assembly does. It follows that there is nothing immoral or unprincipled about a state refusing to pay for cogent reasons of national self-interest.

Nor is such refusal illegal. Although the International Court in 1962 opined that there was a legal obligation to pay,[94] an opinion duly adopted as the view of the Assembly,[95] the norm fell into desuetude once the Assembly refused to discipline the defaulting Soviets. That refusal prompted U.S. Ambassador Arthur Goldberg to reserve the same option to withhold payments "if, in our view, strong and compelling reasons exist for doing so"[96] (see above, Chapter 5). Ambassador Jeane Kirkpatrick is fond of referring to this as the "Goldberg corollary."

It may fairly be concluded that the theoretical "obligation to pay" died on the floor of the Assembly in 1965. Since each U.N. organ is free to interpret the Charter, the Assembly was within its rights in refusing to apply the Court's advisory opinion. No formal resolution adopting the opinion can outweigh the actual practice. In effect, the Assembly has yielded to the Soviet Union's (and 29 other nations') stated refusal to pay for activities it opposed or regarded as violative of the Charter.[97] Therefore, it is now open to any state to refuse payment on the ground that a U.N. activity is beyond the powers of the organ that authorized it, and against that state's interest.

In recent years the United States has begun to make some use of its fiscal freedom, although not, to date, on anything like the scale practised by the Soviet Union, which, overall, owed $39 million by 1982.[98] Nor is it alone with the Soviets in practising selective withholding. By September 1982, some 58 members had not paid off their 1981 arrears.[99] In comparison, the U.S. has barely set a foot along that path. Since 1980, when Congress first required it to do so,[100] the State Department has withheld 25 percent, or $211,125.00,[101] of the amount the U.N. has budgeted for the Secretariat's Division on Palestinian Rights, and a like percentage of the budget for the Assembly's Committee on the Exercise of the Inalienable Rights of the Palestinian People. This withholding approximates the amount of the U.S. contribution which would otherwise have been allocated by the U.N. to these two activities. The Secretariat, in turn, treats these specific deductions as unallocated withholding, asserting that members may not, by earmarking, use their payments to "vote" for or against specific expenditures approved by the Assembly. Either way, the money is not forthcoming, and the effect is to exert a gentle squeeze that is a token of what might happen should confrontational tactics escalate.

A prognosis of such escalation is contained in an advisory resolution passed overwhelmingly by Congress in 1982 and made a mandatory law in 1983, which provides that, if the Assembly "or any specialized agency" of the U.N. were to deny participation to Israel, the United States should suspend its own participation and withhold its financial support for the U.N. or such agency.[102] Secretary of State George Shultz adopted this policy on behalf of the executive branch in October 1982.[103] It has already been invoked. At a 1982 meeting of the General Conference of the International Atomic Energy Agency (IAEA), Israel's credentials were rejected in the closing days of the meeting. The United States thereupon suspended its activities in the IAEA, withheld its financial contributions, and undertook to "reassess our participation."[104] The State Department's line was reinforced by Congress in the form of the "Kasten amendment" to a 1983 appropriations bill. It states that none of the appropriated funds may be used "for payment to the International Atomic Energy Agency unless the Board of Governors . . . certifies to the United States Government that the State of Israel is allowed to participate fully."[105] To everyone's relief— since the IAEA is one of the more useful and important international agencies—its Board of Governors did so certify,[106] and U.S. participation has resumed. The effect of this confrontation at IAEA was not lost on other U.N. agencies and organs. A subsequent challenge to Israel's participation in the International Telecommunications Union[107] was defeated, as were similar efforts in the General Assembly (see, above, Chapter 11).

In another, slightly different, demonstration of the uses of the power of the purse, the United States, in 1982, for a time withheld its voluntary contribution to the United Nations Relief and Works Agency for Palestine Refugees in the near East. UNRWA was established in 1949 by the General Assembly to provide "continued assistance for the relief of Palestine refugees" and "to further conditions of peace and stability."[108] Currently, the agency provides education and health programs and, until recently, distributed basic rations to

830,000 persons. It delivers schooling to 340,000 pupils and employs approximately 10,000 teachers.[109] As of June 30, 1982, there were 1,925,726 registered refugees eligible for the program, and the agency projected a 1983 budget of $271.4 million.[110]

UNRWA has been successful in the limited sense in which success is measured in many U.N. operations: it has helped to ameliorate a bad situation without eradicating it. As the Swedish Commissioner-General of UNRWA, Ambassador Olof Rydbeck, has noted, that without the amenities provided by the agency, "violence would certainly have been unleashed."[111] On the other hand, the agency has succeeded in perpetuating the problem by creating a constituency with a vested interest in being subsidized, thereby helping to delay the absorption of those people by the countries in which they currently reside. Although the agency was to establish industries ("works") offering the refugees employment and making them self-supporting, this has been resisted by the intended beneficiaries, who reject what they perceive as efforts to "bring about their integration into the host countries contrary to the commitments made to them."[112] Israel has also charged that in its occupied territories, as the more prosperous Palestinians moved out of camps, other poor people have moved in, in the hope of receiving aid. Thus, 23 percent of those now in the camps are allegedly not refugees at all.[113]

Congress has legislated that UNRWA shall receive no more U.S. aid—the total U.S. contribution already exceeds one billion dollars—"except on condition that [it] take all possible measures to assure that no part of the United States contribution shall be used to furnish assistance to any refugee who is receiving military training as a member of the so-called Palestine Liberation Army or any other guerilla type organization or who has engaged in any act of terrorism."[114] After the Israeli invasion of Lebanon, however, there was evidence that UNRWA's Siblin Training Center was being used for military training by the PLO.[115] This was at first denied, then subject to a rather cursory investigation.

Enforcing the 1969 law, the United States suspended a $15 million payment due in mid-1982 until UNRWA had undertaken a thorough self-investigation, and the U.S. refused to make a new pledge for 1983 until satisfied that the problem had been cleared up.

The UNRWA report, when finally completed, revealed that the school in which 781 trainees were enrolled for vocational and teacher training had been effectively taken over by the PLO, which used it to store arms, administer a basic military training program to the students, and operate a communications center. So complete was PLO authority that diplomas were routinely withheld until after students had served with the PLO for a minimum of twelve months. With most of its local services being performed by Palestinian employees. UNRWA had lost control. Ambassador Rydbeck later reported that, for some time prior to the "disclosure," he had not been allowed to visit UNRWA camps in southern Lebanon without prior notice to the PLO, and then only with an escort provided by that organization. He acknowledged that the problems at Siblin had probably become endemic throughout Southern Lebanon in the 1970s, while the area was effectively under PLO control.[116]

Although efforts by NAM and the socialist bloc to ostracize Israel have activated U.S. use of the power of the purse regarding this issue, the same tactic can be employed over a much broader spectrum of issues. In 1982 Congress prohibited any U.S. contribution to the United Nations Educational, Scientific and Cultural Organization (UNESCO) if it were to implement a mooted program for the global licensing of journalists or the control of press freedom.[117] More recently, Washington has withheld about $1 million,[118] the equivalent of its 25 percent share of the annual cost of the Preparatory Commission charged with drafting the rules for implementing the Law of the Sea treaty. Although the institutions established by that treaty are not organs of the U.N., the 1982 Assembly, by a vote of 135 to 2, with 8 abstentions, nevertheless decided to include the Commission's costs in the organization's general budget.[119] Washington has long objected to the tendency of the "automatic majority" in the General Assembly to use assessments to finance special interests that are not directly connected with the global organization and which serve the needs of only part of its membership.[120] (The United Nations Conference on Trade and Development (UNCTAD), with a large secretariat in Geneva, is another institution created by the U.N. primarily to serve Third World interests, but funded from the U.N.'s assessed contributions.) In the case of the Preparatory Commission, the practice was particularly galling because the U.S. had already indicated its unwillingness to sign the treaty or to join the institutions established by it. Even when the U.N. creates agencies to which the U.S. does belong, there is a strong preference on Washington's part that they be funded separately, preferably by voluntary contributions, as a way of better exercising the power of the purse over their rates of expansion and over the thrust of their activities.

The Secretary-General has complained that the U.S. decision not to pay for the Preparatory Commission is "of the utmost seriousness . . . since it affected the Organization's ability to carry out functions that had been determined by competent legislative organs."[121] The U.S. insists, however, that the new authority, established to regulate the use of the high seas, is a separate entity from the U.N. and one the American taxpayer cannot be forced to underwrite.

The Secretary-General, however, has acknowledged that the U.S. is still a minor defaulter in comparison with many others. In 1983 seventeen countries were withholding from the U.N. a total of $84.9 million for political reasons, almost half related to the repayment of bonds issued in 1962 as part of a "compromise" over the financing of the Middle East and Congo peacekeeping operations (see above, Chapter 5).

Consequences of Withholding

It could be argued that, while there is nothing unprincipled or illegal about selective withholding, nevertheless it has tactical risks. If carried far beyond its present limited use, the practice might eventually cause the U.S. to lose its vote in the Assembly. By article 19 of the Charter, a state in default for the equivalent of the previous two years' assessment may be disenfranchised. This provision has been invoked on occasion. When that happens, the president of the Assembly simply notes that, because of a nation's default, its vote is not being taken. However, only a few small states have found themselves in this position. When the Soviet and French defaults reached the article 19 level in 1964, instead of invoking article 19 the Assembly chose to operate without voting rather than risk a confrontation (see Chapter 5, above). Although the Assembly is a different place now from what it was then, it still seems unlikely that the majority would wish to proceed with a strategy likely to break up the organization. Nor is the U.S., even with much more extensive withholding, ever likely to reach a level of default equivalent to two years' assessment unless it had already deliberately decided to write off the Assembly as a place to pursue its interests. In any event, article 19 suspends voting rights only in the Assembly. Even were it applied, American delegates could continue to speak in the Assembly and to vote in the Security Council no matter how large the U.S. default.

In short, the dangers to the U.S. inherent in selective withholding, even at a relatively high level, are minimal. To the United Nations, however, the consequences could be far more serious. So severe is its perennial financial crisis that the Secretariat frequently borrows from funds contributed to the organization for other purposes in order to meet recurrent obligations. The Secretary-General reports that, in seven of the first nine months of 1982, he could not meet payments on the organization's legal commitments to member governments such as reimbursement for troops sent to a peacekeeping force.[122] Efforts to deal with this crisis produced little except proposals for the issuance of more commemorative postage stamps.[123] The Secretary-General has warned of "the steadily worsening rate of payment of contributions,"[124] particularly pertaining to peacekeeping activities.

To illustrate the so-far largely unused power of the purse and to help other members understand the implications of forcing its hand, the U.S. government has taken to delaying most of its annual contribution until late in the year. In this, too, it is far from alone. In 1982, of the 154 members in the organization, only fifty had paid their full assessed contribution by September 30 and only thirty more had paid any part of it. The Soviets, on that date, still owed $37 million on the current year's account. But it was the U.S. which had used delay to the most effect: it had paid only $30 million of its $180 million assessment.[125] While this could be explained in terms of prevailing domestic budgetary practices and constraints, it was widely perceived to have deeper significance.

Caveat

Withholding funds in certain contingencies is now a regular, if still minor, part of U.S. diplomatic strategy. But successful strategy requires a carefully calibrated choice of weapons. It is not achieved through random overkill, nor by substituting psychic gratification and vengeance for a thoughtful selection of goals and methods. Above all, as long as the U.S. has an interest in the U.N., it is better to reserve the power of the purse as a deterrent than actually to deploy and dissipate it in fiscal combat for ill-defined objectives. Yet, on September 22, 1983, the Senate, by a vote of 66 to 23, adopted a proposal by Senator Nancy Landon Kassebaum of Kansas that would have reduced the U.S. contribution by $500 million over four years. Senator Steven D. Symms of Idaho explained: "Taxpayers are sick and tired of playing host to our enemies and critics abroad."[126]

Such an exercise in nose-thumbing may be gratifying, but it serves no strategic purpose, the random use of the fiscal instrument only tends to blunt it. The State Department and White House were forced to bring strenuous pressure on the House-Senate conferees to get the amendment dropped.[127] Even so, Congress enacted an arbitrary ceiling which limits to the 1983 level the aggregate amount the U.S. can contribute in 1984 and 1985 to the U.N., UNESCO, WHO (World Health Organization), FAO (Food and Agriculture Organization) and ILO (International Labour Organisation).[128] As a way of enforcing "zero growth," this is a hammer-blow to kill a gnat. In its "power of the purse" the United States has a potent weapon, but, like any such ultimate device, it should be held in reserve to be used only to accomplish clearly specified objectives in an actual confrontation, not as a general means of communication.

Selective Withdrawal

Beyond the power of the purse is the option of selective withdrawal from U.N. agencies and organs. Like any ultimate weapon, its strategic use must be contemplated, especially by those who do not now advocate it, if the necessity for its use is to be avoided.

Contemplating withdrawal must include a realistic assessment of its price. In connection with the IAEA crisis over Israeli credentials, the State Department correctly took the position that, while such a move might become unavoidable, "the costs to the U.S. could be very great."[129] U.S. law makes all nuclear exports to foreign recipients subject to IAEA safeguards. If IAEA were to fail, a more costly—and probably less acceptable—bilateral inspection would have to be established and existing safeguards for exported U.S. nuclear materials in foreign consumers' hands might be vitiated.[130]

As for wider U.S. withdrawal from the entire U.N. system, the State Department has pointed out that the financial loss would constrain U.N. organizations drastically to cut back programs, including many regarded as especially important; refugee, health, and technical programs, for example. Moreover, "our departure from the U.N. would greatly weaken moderate elements in the Security Council and the General Assembly, strengthen the position of our enemies, and make it impossible for us to defend our interests when they are attacked in the U.N. Ideologically, it would give our enemies a free rein and encourage anti-U.S. and anti-democratic forces."[131]

Withdrawal, although an ultimate weapon, is not an indiscriminate one. It, too, can be calibrated. Current State Department contingency planning envisages a phased reduction in U.S. participation in specific objectionable activities. The U.S. already declines to take part in such Assembly committees as those on Palestinian rights and the Special Committee on Decolonization, and refused to take part in the 1983 U.N. conference on Palestine. There will be more of what one U.S. delegate earthily characterizes as "voting with the butt," the tactic of leaving the U.S. chair empty. But it is important to pick and choose with great care. As noted in Chapter 10, the U.S. boycott of the Decolonization Committee allowed Cuba to build a paper record on the Puerto Rican issue, which eventually amounted to a gratuitous strategic advantage for Havana. Certainly, nothing like a total withdrawal from the U.N. system is now contemplated under any conceivable circumstances. The U.S. has announced its intention to leave UNESCO, which is a move directed toward what, from the U.S. perspective, is the most expendable, inefficient, and corrupt part of the system.[132] In the words of Secretary of State Shultz to UNESCO Director-General Amadou Mahtar M'Bow, that decision had been made "inescapable" by the way the agency "is presently constituted and . . . governs itself." He added that "the management, policy, and budget of UNESCO were detracting from the Organization's effectiveness."[133]

The 1984 U.S. assessment for UNESCO is $46.8 million. Already in 1974, Congress had voted to prohibit U.S. payment of its share unless the President could certify that UNESCO "has taken concrete steps to correct its recent actions of a primarily political character."[134] President Ford did so certify in 1975, and U.S. payments resumed. Then, in 1983, Congress froze the level of U.S. contributions for 1984 and 1985 at the 1983 level and required the President to report annually on "the benefits derived by the United States from participation."[135] The notice of withdrawal was thus an incremental, not a sudden development. Among those applauding it were some, such as the editorial board of the *New York Times*, who are still basically supportive of the U.N..[136]

Even so, responsible voices in Congress and the U.S. scientific community have pointed out that withdrawal from UNESCO would have costs.[137] The organization is the focal point of various global cooperative networks[138] that benefit American scholars and researchers. By walking out, the U.S. leaves its allies in a weakened position to defend Western interests. Others have argued that what requires reexamination is not U.S. membership but rather "the way in which the U.S. participates in the organization, the way in which it collaborates with other governments and the ways in which we can help to bring about improvements in the organized intellectual and cultural cooperation that is so important to the world—including the U.S."[139] A staff report of the House of Representatives' Foreign Affairs Committee digs deeper, finding that the Department of State has failed to make multilateral diplomacy a high strategic planning priority or even an attractive career choice, thereby contributing to defeats in organizations like UNESCO.[140]

In the operation and direction of other multilateral organizations the U.S. government has used the threat of withdrawal and actual pullout as a tactical device to gain concessions from other member-states. But, even if successful, the maneuver could provoke an avalanche effect at home, as isolationist elements realize that withdrawal from international organizations has again become a thinkable alternative. It must therefore be used sparingly and precisely, accompanied by clear statements of the costs to U.S. interests, and by a careful delineation of the circumstances in which the decision to leave would be rescinded. Recently, Washington has let it be known that it is considering ending U.S. participation in the International Fund for Agricultural Development (IFAD) in circumstances that do not appear to meet this standard of prudence.[141]

Neither UNESCO nor IFAD is the first U.N. agency to become a candidate for U.S. withdrawal. On November 6, 1975, Secretary of State Henry Kissinger gave the requisite two years' notice to the Director-General of the International Labour Organisation,[142] charging it with a selective policy on human rights, disregard for due process and objectivity, and increasing politicization. At the time, the U.S. share (25 percent) of ILO financing was approximately $20 million.[143] When no noticeable improvement in ILO's performance occurred during the two-year notice period and the ILO continued to condemn Israel while granting observer status to the PLO, President Carter carried out the threatened U.S. withdrawal.[144] The move appears to have had a modestly salutary effect, even as it created a fiscal crisis in the agency that culminated in the staff taking a 10 percent pay cut.[145] The following year (1978), ILO defeated a move to censure Israel and later one of its committees took a critical stand on violations of trade union workers' rights in the Soviet Union.[146] In February 1980 the U.S. announced its willingness to resume participation.[147]

The U.S. is not alone in exercising the withdrawal option. Indonesia left the U.N. in 1965[148] (see above, Chapter 5), returning in September of the following year.[149] Vietnam withdrew "temporarily" from participation in the ILO in 1983 in protest against "ill-founded allegations" made there against it, and because of "economic and financial difficulties."[150] Poland also has withdrawn in 1984 from the ILO after that agency refused to halt an investigation of Warsaw's outlawing of the Solidarity trade union. While the Charter does not deal with withdrawal from the U.N., the Indonesian precedent shows that a state may cease both to contribute and to participate without adverse action by the organization. When Indonesia was ready to return, it simply resumed its seat in the Assembly. It did not reapply for membership.

Despite these precedents it seems very unlikely that any U.S. government in the foreseeable future would choose total withdrawal. Even in the worst circumstances, rational leaders would prefer to couple selective non-participation with the retention of a veto in the Security Council. The Soviet experience of withdrawing from that potentially potent political organ, prior to the beginning of the Korean War (see above, Chapter 2), argues strongly against any comparable move. However, it should not be assumed that strategy toward the U.N., which conjures up considerable passion among Americans, will forever be governed by rational strategic considerations unless these are carefully expounded by those in a position to lead. At present the leadership sometimes appears all too willing to allow the public to perceive it as indifferent to, or scornful of, the organization, without adequately distinguishing between a policy of playing hard-ball and quitting.

The Bilateral Option

While the U.S. was exerting its financial leverage to compel housecleaning in UNRWA, a debate was taking place in the State Department between Ambassador Jeane Kirkpatrick and the Assistant Secretary of State with operational responsibility for refugee programs. The Ambassador felt that U.S. aid to refugees could better be given on a bilateral basis to individual countries in which the refugees are located, while the Assistant Secretary favored resumption of U.S. funding for UNRWA, once the agency had controlled its problem of PLO penetration. Key members of Congress, as well as the several pro-Israeli lobbies, became involved in this debate, which some officials described as a "turf war" but which was really a disagreement over the proper relation of multilateral to bilateral diplomacy. This is an issue both of importance and complexity. Inside and outside the U.S. government there are voices urging the replacement of all multilateral with bilateral diplomacy, on the ground that Washington always fares better when it negotiates with states one at a time. Others argue that many issues cannot be handled bilaterally, but that U.S. bilateral relations do need to be harnessed to help achieve its objectives in a multilateral forum like the U.N.

In 1981, with the Reagan administration's blessing, Congress adopted an amendment to the Foreign Assistance Act which states that when considering assistance to countries belonging to the NAM, the President should take into account whether a potential recipient has dissociated itself from blatantly anti-American positions that bloc has taken. The State Department has confirmed that it takes this factor into account in the "determination of aid levels" and that "in nearly all cases" where a recipient has not repudiated an objectionable position "the proposed assistance levels . . . declined from levels provided in previous years."[151] More recently, Congress has required the head of the U.S. mission to the U.N. to provide it with country-by-country reports on voting patterns and practices, and on the policies each member pursues in international organizations of which the U.S. is a member.[152] The *Congressional Record* now bristles with tables of aid-levels to countries that vote against us in the Assembly on key resolutions.[153] The Department has approved these initiatives, stating that it views "the linkage of assistance with a country's U.N. votes as an important means of influencing that country's position."[154] To underscore this, Ambassador Kirkpatrick told the Foreign Operations Subcommittee of the Senate Appropriations Committee that "the conduct of other U.N. members with regard to [U.S. national goals] and interests . . . constitutes a significant dimension of our relations with other countries, to be considered with the utmost seriousness and gravity." Voting patterns provide "a reliable, systematic basis for assessing the attitudes, the policies" of members and constitutes "hard evidence" from which the U.S. "can make judgments concerning those whose values and views are harmonious with our own," are opposed, or are "in between." She deplored the "intermittent and inadequate efforts" to "integrate U.S. policies and relations with other nations inside the U.N." with "U.S. policies and relations with those same nations outside the U.N."[155]

Efforts to establish such a link are relatively new. Ambassador Daniel Patrick Moynihan publicly deplored the lack of linkage during his tenure on the East River. Sir Edward Heath, on becoming prime minister of Britain, had instructed the British mission to the U.N. to report on the voting behavior of states receiving substantial foreign aid from London. The U.S. has now borrowed this idea, but made the process public. Its potential utility was demonstrated during the General Assembly's consideration of the Puerto Rican status question in 1982. As one member of the U.S. delegation explained, when a state votes against us even on a "litmus" issue like Afghanistan we may file a diplomatic protest, but we rarely do anything to alter bilateral trade and aid relations. Trade, he explained, always seems to involve an exclusively bilateral balancing of "economic and security interests," while aid levels are usually based on "military sales, regional stability or military facilities. . . . Voting in New York has traditionally been extraneous to these considerations."[156]

It is not that the State Department officials responsible for relations with, say, Burma are not willing to play hard-ball. It is just that they may not see why, when there are a dozen other issues between the United States and Burma at a delicate stage of negotiation, a crisis must be precipitated over Burma's vote in the General Assembly on some resolution of dubious importance. Nevertheless, the argument for using bilateral relations to improve performance in the U.N. has gained ground in recent years. "Let the Tanzanians get their aid from the same capitals from which they got their politics," Senator Moynihan has written,[157] and more Americans have come to agree.

Since the U.S. government usually does not explain why a foreign assistance program is being reduced, or does so in terms which leave the specifics to the recipient's imagination, it is not simple to document, in individual instances, the implementation of linkage policy. Nevertheless, after Zimbabwe had abstained in the Security Council vote condemning the Soviet Union for shooting down the South Korean airliner in the fall of 1983,[158] its 1984 aid level was cut from $75 million to $40 million, a very hefty reduction. It has been reported that Ambassador Jeane Kirkpatrick lobbied for an even larger reduction, while the cut was vigorously resisted by the bilateral diplomats, led by Chester Crocker, the Assistant Secretary for African Affairs.[159] When the decision was made, a spokesman for the (U.S.) Agency for International Development noted that "Congress has directed us to consider a country's U.N. record when allocating assistance funds." He added, however, that this was only one of "a host of factors" involved in the decision.[160]

In assessing linkage strategy, the State Department has ruefully concluded that, while the weapon is useful, in a number of cases "levels of assistance are not large or enough to make linkage realistic."[161] Obviously, the less the U.S. gives, the less it can threaten to take away. Nor is this truism limited to bilateral relations. In the U.N., Washington is generally perceived as a Scrooge, a view abetted by its ideologically rigid, negative attitude toward multilateral efforts to improve the economic lot of the impoverished three-quarters of the world, efforts such as those to create a common fund to stabilize commodity prices, or to create a sea-bed authority to regulate the "common heritage of mankind" under the terms of the Law of the Seas Treaty. A distinction should also be preserved between playing hard-ball and being insensitive! Ambassador Kirkpatrick has been accused of both. She has won grudging admiration from her colleagues for telling the unvarnished truth as the U.S. sees it and not pandering in the double-faced style so widespread among diplomats. On the other hand, the Ambassador has displayed what may be a professorial penchant for gratuitous truculence, the personal put-down, and indifference to the feelings of others that has made her, by far, the most personally unpopular representative, ever, of the U.S. in the U.N. If a U.S. ambassador is to be effective, he or she must endeavor to balance the armory of sticks and carrots. Some carrots may be nothing more than common courtesy: for example, keeping a long-standing appointment with a Third World ambassador or a U.N. Under Secretary, rather than sending an underling, even if it means missing a TV opportunity. The U.S. mission, of late, is regarded as perilously short of carrots.

Conclusion

The United Nations has not brought the world to the hoped-for haven of pacific settlement and collective security. It was entirely unrealistic to expect that it would. Since its formation, twenty million persons have died in wars, a lugubrious fact attesting to the cost of that failure.[1]

To create an effective system of peaceful dispute-settlement and mutual defense against aggressors, the nations would have to institute fundamental structural changes in the international order. These changes, perforce, would reduce the independence of nations—the powerful, as well as the weak—subordinating them to a global political will made manifest in a political forum radically more effective than the Security Council and the General Assembly.

It is not difficult to create a design for such an alternative, but there is not the slightest prospect of its implementation. In 1945 there were only one-third as many sovereign states as now; the war had eroded faith in the ability of the traditional state system to provide security, peace, and progress; and there was a prevalent ethos—certainly among Americans—of globalism and the brotherhood of man. That would have been the time for nobler visions. Instead, there were grand illusions.

Still, in its forty-year journey from illusion to reality, the U.S., at first, came very close to transforming the U.N. into a more effective instrument. It was the U.S.'s penchant for institution-building and leadership that eroded the veto in the Security Council and increased the independence of the Secretary-General and the powers of the General Assembly. Even in 1945, however, calls by Americans for a stronger U.N. were mainly emanations of a misplaced confidence that the U.S., together with other liberal democracies, would continue to lead and that the new nations, when they joined, would follow the U.S.'s example and leadership.

By the mid-1960s, the U.S. stopped trying to shore up the system. Nowadays, most Americans are far less interested in strengthening it than in preventing whatever little power the U.N. has from being used to damage them. As the U.N. enters its fifth decade, this is the realistic starting point for seriously thinking about U.S. policy toward the organization.

If realism compels the U.S. to start from a scaled-down expectation of the U.N.'s potential, it also requires it to accept that the institution exists, and that it mirrors, even if in distorted fashion, some disagreeable but true aspects of the contemporary world: nationalism, avarice, racism, poverty, despotism and, yes, the politicization of almost *everything*. These will not go away if we ignore them, nor even if we leave the U.N..

More positively, the U.N. also manifests mankind's residual common concern for the survival of the species. Fortunately, the national self-interests of the superpowers and of the various blocs of members are not always in conflict. At times, these autonomous self-interests coincide, and, when that happens, the U.N. can be a useful forum for capitalizing on, or even institutionalizing, that coincidence. A treaty, or a peacekeeping force, demonstrates this utility. Occasionally the Secretary-General may even be instrumental in finding the elusive point on which disparate national interests can converge. Anger, frustration, and disappointment, should not cause Americans to ignore these more positive realities.

True, the U.N. is nowhere near as noble and efficacious as was once hoped; but, neither is it as venal or useless as some now claim. Both Moses and Jeremiah are wrong: the organization cannot point us to the promised land, but neither is it dispensable and ripe for destruction. Its political organs are likely to remain inhospitable to U.S. national interests. Yet the U.S. has shown, recently, that it can still win on issues ranging from Israel's right to participate in the system to respect for the status of Puerto Rico. The U.N. can still be used to marshall public opinion for religious freedom and against bacteriological warfare or the shooting down of civilian aircraft. Indeed, we could probably win more often, if we were willing to do the necessary long-range strategic planning and deploy seasoned personnel and equip them with sufficient carrots and sticks: in short, if we were to take the U.N. seriously as a place for politics.

There is even some evidence that the pendulum of political fashion is swinging away from enchantment with statist solutions toward a more positive reevaluation of our embattled liberal democratic values. If that is so, the U.N. will provide an opportunity to accelerate that swing, providing the U.S. is politically willing and intellectually able to manifest—in deed as well as word—a long-term, continuing commitment to those values with which it has been associated historically.

But what if the pendulum is not swinging in our favor? What if the rhetoric becomes even more inflammatory, the resolutions more polarizing, the Secretariat more politicized? Even while continuing, and upgrading, their participation, Americans should use the U.N.'s fortieth anniversary—in 1985—to begin to examine alternatives. At some point, the balance of U.S. national interest may well make it more prudent to leave than to stay. This is an alternative future to be contemplated, even—perhaps especially—if it is not desired.

Such contingency planning should encompass three imperatives:

First: The U.S. must not pull out of the U.N. unless there has been a full, informed public debate, at least on the order of the one which preceded entry in 1945, leading to something approaching a national consensus.

Second: The U.S. must not act alone, but only in concert with principal friends and allies, including non-Europeans. If the U.S. does leave, let it leave in good company.

Third: The U.S. must have ready at hand a credible plan for an alternative forum in which to conduct multilateral diplomacy, so that it does not become isolated or drift into isolationism. Such an alternative institution might take the form of an alliance of free nations, united to protect one another from increasingly common internal dangers: subversion, terrorism, and repression. It might constitute a sort of broader-based NATO for the defense not of boundaries but of democratic principles.

Even to suggest an alternative is to raise numerous questions. Is it the best alternative from the perspective of the U.S. national interest? Which states would qualify? How is the qualifying status to be defined in theory and in practice? What kinds of mutual assistance would be appropriate? Against what sort of threat? How are collective decisions to be made and implemented? If these are daunting questions, they are, at least, more interesting than those asked by the perennial committees and commissions on the reform of the U.N. system.

The U.N. system, except in the most marginal ways, is not about to be reformed, nor is it in the U.S. interest that it should be. It is what it is; the realistic choice presented to the U.S. is either to understand it and operate as effectively as possible within it, or to get out: in part, or altogether. For the present, the U.S. national interest is better served by a muscular strategy of staying in.

Notes

INTRODUCTION

1. Kurt Waldheim, *The Challenge of Peace* (New York, 1980), 3.

2. Report of the Secretary-General on the Work of the Organization, GAOR(XXXVI), Supp. No. 1 (A/36/1), Sept. 1981, p. 3 (hereafter: S.G. Report).

3. George L. Sherry, "Enhancing International Security—the Role of the United Nations," Proceedings of the Thirty-first Pugwash Conference on Science and World Affairs, 1981, p. 267.

4. S.G. Report, GAOR(XXXVII), Supp. No. 1 (A/37/1), Sept. 1982, p. 3.

5. In 1981, for example, he stated that the nations must learn "to take full advantage of the United Nations . . . to help solve, or at least to control, some of its intractable problems. To do so requires the steadfast application of political will." S.G. Report, 1981, p. 12. Also: "the prime reason we are facing so many difficulties today is because the leaders of the United Nations Member Governments do not always show the political will to solve the problems that confront us." Kurt Waldheim, *Building the Future Order: The Search for Peace in an Interdependent World* (New York, 1980), 236.

6. "It is one of the most important functions of the United Nations to foster such positive thinking." Waldheim, ibid., 240.

7. Kant believed that the "primary characteristic of the human species is the power as rational beings to acquire a character as such" and, by "character" meant that peculiar "property of the will according to which the subject binds himself to definite practical principles which he has unalterably prescribed through his own reason." I. Kant, *Anthropologie*, Vol. VII, Academy ed., pp. 292, 329, quoted and discussed in

John E. Smith, "The Question of Man," in Charles W. Hendel, ed., *The Philosophy of Kant and Our Modern World* (New York, 1957), 21.

    8. S.G. Report, GAOR(XXXIII), Supp. No. 1 (A/33/1), Sept. 1978, p. 10.

CHAPTER 1: Great Expectations

    1. *Congressional Record* (Senate), 91 (July 23, 1945): 7951.

    2. *New York Times*, April 12, 1945, p. 13.

    3. *New York Times*, March 25, 1945, p. 29.

    4. *New York Times*, June 27, 1945, p. 10.

    5. Boston, Cleveland, Detroit, Chicago, St. Louis, Shreveport, and New Orleans. *Department of State Bulletin*, 12 (April 8, 1945): 650.

    6. *Congressional Record* (Senate), 91 (May 3, 1945): 4125–26.

    7. Ibid. (July 23, 1945), 7953.

    8. *Congressional Record* (House), 91 (July 6, 1945): 7299.

    9. Ibid. (July 6, 1945), 7299–7300.

    10. Minutes, United Nations Charter, in the U.S. Senate, Saturday, June 30, 1945, Committee on Foreign Relations, Executive Session, verbatim transcript (unpub.), p. 3. National Archives, Washington, D.C. (hereafter: Minutes, U.N. Charter).

    11. *Congressional Record* (Senate), 91 (July 26, 1945): 8082.

    12. Ibid. (July 25, 1945), 8019.

    13. Ibid. (July 24, 1945), 7969.

    14. Ibid. (July 25, 1945), 8039.

    15. Ibid. (July 26, 1945), 8073.

    16. Ibid. (July 26, 1945), 8088.

    17. Ibid. (July 27, 1945), 8105.

    18. Ibid. (July 23, 1945), 7951.

    19. *The Charter of the United Nations*, Hearings, Senate Committee on Foreign Relations, Part 4, July 13, 1945 (Washington, 1945) (hereafter: *Charter of the U.N.*).

    20. *Congressional Record* (Senate), 91 (July 23, 1945): 7952.

    21. *New York Times*, June 30, 1945, p. 16.

    22. *Chicago Daily Tribune*, June 27, 1945. Reprinted in *Charter of the U.N.*, Part 5, p. 486.

    23. For better explanations of this failure see: "The Lessons of the League," in Evan Luard, *A History of the United Nations*, Vol. 1 (New York, 1982), 3ff.

    24. Ibid., 5.

    25. *Congressional Record* (Senate), 91 (June 28, 1945): 6874.

    26. Ibid. (July 27, 1945), 8130.

    27. Ibid. (July 25, 1945), 8019.

    28. Ibid. (July 26, 1945), 8083.

    29. Minutes, U.N. Charter, p. 5.

    30. Ibid., 19.

    31. Ibid., 5.

    32. Ibid., 14.

    33. *Congressional Record*, Appendix, 91 (April 16, 1945): A2198.

    34. Reprinted in *Charter of the U.N.*, Part 5, p. 484.

    35. Ibid., 483.

    36. *Department of State Bulletin*, 12 (April 8, 1945): 650

    37. Reprinted in *Charter of the U.N.*, Part 5, p. 484.

    38. *Congressional Record* (Senate), 91 (July 26, 1945): 8083.

39. Luard, A *History of the United Nations*, 18.

40. Ibid., 25.

41. Ibid., 26.

42. *Congressional Record* (Senate), 91 (July 25, 1945): 8033.

43. Ibid., 8036.

44. Ibid. (July 24, 1945), 8003.

45. Ibid. (June 29, 1945), 6985.

46. Ibid. (July 25, 1945), 8037.

47. Ibid. (July 24, 1945), 8002.

48. *New York Times*, June 26, 1945, p. 10.

49. *Department of State Bulletin*, 13 (July 15, 1945): 77.

50. Ibid. (July 1, 1945), 3.

51. Ibid., 5.

52. *Congressional Record* (Senate), 91 (July 26, 1945): 8081.

53. *Congressional Record* (House) 91 (July 6, 1945): 7298.

54. *Congressional Record* (Senate), 91 (July 26, 1945): 8083.

55. Ibid. (June 28, 1945), 6878.

56. Ibid. (June 29, 1945), 6981.

57. Ibid. (July 23, 1945), 7964.

58. Ibid. (July 27, 1945), 8107.

59. Ibid. (July 23, 1945), 7964–65.

60. Ibid. (July 23, 1945), 7957.

61. Reprinted in *Charter of the U.N.*, Part 5, p. 482.

62. Testimony of Mrs. Lillian T. Mowrer, Chairman, D.C. Chapter, Women's Action Committee for Victory and Lasting Peace. Printed in *Charter of the U.N.*, Part 4, p. 388.

63. *Department of State Bulletin*, 13 (July 1, 1945): 8.

64. Ibid., 12 (April 29, 1945): 789.

65. Ibid. (April 8, 1945), 605.

66. Testimony of William Green. Printed in *Charter of the U.N.*, Part 5, p. 401.

67. *Congressional Record* (Senate), 91 (June 28, 1945): 6878.

68. Ibid. (July 26, 1945), 8060.

69. Ibid. (July 24, 1945), 7972.

70. Reprinted in *Charter of the U.N.*, Part 5, p. 486.

71. *Congressional Record* (House), 91 (July 6, 1945): 7300.

72. *Congressional Record* (Senate), 91 (July 25, 1945): 8018.

73. See discussion of the hard-fought battles over these issues in Luard, A *History of the United Nations*, 27–54.

74. Ibid., 41–42.

75. Ibid., 42.

76. *Department of State Bulletin*, 13 (July 1, 1945): 3.

77. Reprinted in *Charter of the U.N.*, Part 5, p. 484.

78. *Congressional Record* (House), 91 (July 6, 1945): 7298.

79. *Congressional Record* (Senate), 91 (July 23, 1945): 7956.

80. *Department of State Bulletin*, 12 (June 3, 1945): 1010.

81. *Charter of the U.N.*, Part 1, p. 49.

82. *Congressional Record* (Senate), 91 (June 28, 1945): 6876.

83. Letter from Harold E. Stassen to Edward R. Stettinius, and attached "confidential preliminary memorandum," March 26, 1945 (unpub.), National Archives, Washington, D.C.

84. Clark M. Eichelberger, *Organizing for Peace* (New York, 1977), 237.
85. *Congressional Record* (Senate), 91 (July 24, 1945): 7992.
86. Ibid. (July 27, 1945), 8118.
87. Ibid., 8121.

CHAPTER 2: Happy and Misleading Auguries

1. SCOR, 1st Year, 1st Series, Supp. No. 1, 1945, p. 16.
2. Dean Acheson, *Present at the Creation* (New York, 1969), 197. Acheson's first meeting with Hussein Ala appears to have taken place in October. See also *Foreign Relations of the United States*, 1946, Vol. VII (Washington, 1969), 292–304, 313–14, 350–58, 418–19 (hereafter: F.R.U.S.).
3. Trygve Lie, *In the Cause of Peace* (New York, 1954), 75.
4. F.R.U.S., VII: 347.
5. Ibid., 389.
6. Ibid., 563.
7. Stephen S. Goodspeed, *The Nature and Function of International Organization*, 2nd ed. (New York, 1967), 184. See also Evan Luard, *A History of the United Nations*, Vol. 1 (New York, 1982), 106–12; Abraham Yeselson and Anthony Gaglione, *A Dangerous Place: The United Nations as a Weapon in World Politics* (New York, 1974), 129.
8. Acheson, *Present at the Creation*, 198.
9. Lie, *In the Cause of Peace*, 79–88.
10. F.R.U.S., VII: 417–42, 458–59, 480–82.
11. Leland M. Goodrich, *The United Nations in a Changing World* (New York, 1974), 140.
12. G.A. Res. 181A(II), 29 Nov. 1947.
13. S.C. Res. 48, 23 April 1948.
14. G.A. Res. 186(S-II), 14 May 1947.
15. S.C. Res. 50, 29 May 1948.
16. S.C. Res. 54, 15 July 1948.
17. S.C. Res. 62, 16 Nov. 1948.
18. S.C. Res. 73, 11 Aug. 1949. Ruth B. Russell, *The United Nations and United States Security Policy* (Washington, 1968), 165.
19. The accurate pun is the literary invention of Canada's distinguished jurist and professor, Maxwell Cohen, Q.C., Am. Society of Intl. Law, 55th Annual Mtg., 1959, pp. 100–101.
20. A concise summary of these events is to be found in *Present at the Creation*, 267–70.
21. G.A. Res. 190(III), 3 Nov. 1948.
22. Luard, *A History of the United Nations*, 220.
23. Lie, *In the Cause of Peace*, 218.
24. Acheson, *Present at the Creation*, 269.
25. Ibid., 269–75.
26. Trygve Lie's own account makes this clear. See, especially, *In the Cause of Peace*, 215.
27. Ibid., 217.
28. Yeselson and Gaglione, *A Dangerous Place*, 91.
29. Luard, *A History of the United Nations*, 221.
30. Ibid., 229–31.

31. G.A. Res. 195(III), 12 Dec. 1948.

32. Acheson, *Present at the Creation*, 402, 404.

33. SCOR, 5th Year, 473rd Mtg., 25 June 1950, p. 3.

34. Lie, *In the Cause of Peace*, 329.

35. SCOR, 5th Year, 473rd Mtg., 25 June 1950, p. 18.

36. S.C. Res. 82, 25 June 1950.

37. Lie, *In the Cause of Peace*, 332. See also: Harry S. Truman, *Years of Trial and Hope, Memoirs*, Vol. 2 (New York, 1956), 335–37 (hereafter: *Memoirs*).

38. S.C. Res. 83, 27 June 1950. For the Indian and Egyptian positions, see SCOR, 5th Year, 474th Mtg., 27 June 1950, pp. 14–16; SCOR, 5th Year, 475th Mtg., 30 June 1950, p. 2; U.N. Doc. S/1520, 29 June 1950, p. 2.

39. Lie, *In the Cause of Peace*, 332.

40. Ibid., 332–33.

41. Ibid., 346.

42. Acheson, *Present at the Creation*, 408.

43. S.C. Res. 84, 7 July 1950. As to its origins, President Truman wrote: "I had approved a proposal prepared jointly by the Departments of State and Defense to introduce in the U.N. a resolution creating a unified command in Korea, asking us to name a commander and authorizing the use of the blue U.N. flag in Korea." Truman, *Memoirs*, II:347.

44. Luard, *A History of the United Nations*, 242.

45. Cable of June 27, 1951. Ibid., 242–43.

46. Russell, *The U.N. and U.S. Security*, 125.

47. After Inchon, the North Korean army was left with only 30,000 of its original invading force of 400,000 troops. Acheson, *Present at the Creation*, 447.

48. Yeselson and Gaglione take this position. *A Dangerous Place*, 100–108.

49. Lie, *In the Cause of Peace*, 336.

50. Ibid., 334.

51. G.A. Res. 376(V), 7 Oct. 1950.

52. Acheson, *Present at the Creation*, 448.

53. Lie, *In the Cause of Peace*, 345–46.

54. The British government, under severe pressure to support the Acheson Plan—which they eventually felt compelled to do—told U.S. Ambassador Lewis Douglas, in London, that "safeguards provided by [the] veto are useful since at some future date [the] U.K. might need [the] veto to protect [its] own basic interests" against the potential "irresponsibility" of the General Assembly. F.R.U.S. (1950), II: 323; see also 320, 330.

55. Acheson, *Present at the Creation*, 450.

56. *Department of State Bulletin*, 23 (Oct. 2, 1950): 524–25. See also: Acheson, *Present at the Creation*, 450. F.R.U.S., II: 335–37.

57. Benjamin V. Cohen, *The United Nations, Constitutional Developments, Growth, Possibilities* (Cambridge, 1961), 18–19.

58. Ernest A. Gross, *The United Nations: Structure for Peace* (New York, 1962), 61.

59. *Certain Expenses of the United Nations*, Advisory Opinion of 20 July 1962, I.C.J. Reports, 1962, pp. 184–97.

60. G.A. Res. 39(I), 12 Dec. 1946.

61. G.A. Res. 288A(IV), 18 Nov. 1949.

62. McGeorge Bundy, ed., *The Pattern of Responsibility* (Boston, 1952), 256.

63. *New York Times*, Sept. 19, 1950, p. 30.

64. G.A. Res. 377(V), 3 Nov. 1950.

65. GAOR(V), 303rd Plenary Mtg., 3 Nov. 1950, p. 368.

66. *New York Times*, Oct. 20, 1950, p. 26.

67. SCOR, 11th Year, 749th Mtg., 30 Oct. 1956, p. 31. The vetoed U.S. resolution was U.N. Doc. S/3710, 30 Oct. 1956, p. 1. The vetoed Soviet resolution was U.N. Doc. S/3713/Rev. 1, 30 Oct. 1956, p. 1.

68. Texts of Five Messages Sent by Soviet Union on Fighting in the Middle East. *New York Times*, Nov. 6, 1956, p. 10.

69. *New York Times*, Nov. 7, 1956, p. 33; Nov. 11, 1956, p. 7. *The Times* (London), Nov. 13, 1956, p. 6.

70. *The Times* (London), Nov. 14, 1956, p. 10.

71. S.C. Res. 119, 31 Oct. 1956.

72. SCOR, 11th Year, 751st Mtg., 31 Oct. 1956, p. 22.

73. See John R. Beal, *Pearson of Canada* (New York, 1964), 108–20.

74. See Brian Urquhart, *Hammarskjold* (New York, 1972), 159–94.

75. G.A. Res. 998(ES-1), 4 Nov. 1956; G.A. Res. 1000(ES-1), 5 Nov. 1956; and G.A. Res. 1001(ES-1), 7 Nov. 1956.

76. G.A. Res. 1125(XI), 2 Feb. 1957.

77. U.N. Doc. A/3375, 20 Nov. 1956, p. 2.

78. G.A. Res. 1121(XI), 24 Nov. 1956.

79. Goodrich, *United Nations in a Changing World*, 143.

80. Urquhart. *Hammarskjold*, 194.

81. S.C. Res. 128, 11 June 1958.

82. G.A. Res. 1237(ES-III), 21 Aug. 1958.

83. Goodrich, *United Nations in a Changing World*, 145.

CHAPTER 3: Et Tu, Nehru

1. U.N. Charter, art. 51.

2. Art. 33.

3. Art. 39.

4. Art. 11(2).

5. Art. 41.

6. Art. 42.

7. Art. 43(1).

8. Francis Paul Walters, A *History of the League of Nations*, Vol. II (London, 1952), 479–83.

9. Lord Listowel in the House of Lords. Quoted in W.C. Smith, "Hyderabad: Muslim Tragedy," *Middle East Jour.*, 4 (1950): 35. Prime Minister Clement Attlee, while confirming the legal right of the Princely States to accede, or not, to either India or Pakistan, expressed the hope that they would not opt to go it alone. "If I were asked what would be the attitude of His Majesty's Government to any State which has decided to cut adrift from its neighbours and assert its independence, I would say to the ruler of that State, 'Take your time and think again. I hope that no irrevocable decision to stay out will be taken prematurely.' " Parliamentary Debates, House of Commons, 5th Ser., Vol. 439, col. 2451. Also, *Foreign Relations of the United States*, 1948, Vol. V (Washington, 1975), 361 (hereafter: F.R.U.S.).

10. Letter to Mountbatten, Sept. 26, 1947. *Hyderabad Relations with the Government of India*, Vol. 1, p. 17; Government of India, *White Paper on Hyderabad*, Supp., p. 8. In Smith, "Hyderabad," 36.

11. Smith, "Hyderabad," 37.

12. Ibid., 40–41.

13. SCOR, 3rd Year, Supp. for Sept. 1948, p. 5. F.R.U.S., V:370.
14. U.N. Doc. S/998, 12 Sept. 1948, p. 1.
15. F.R.U.S., V:392.
16. Ibid., 373.
17. Ibid., 387.
18. SCOR, 3rd Year, 357th Mtg., 16 Sept. 1948, p. 15.
19. SCOR, 3rd Year, 359th Mtg., 20 Sept. 1948, p. 3.
20. Smith, "Hyderabad," 46.
21. F.R.U.S., V:395.
22. Ibid., 400.
23. Ibid., 396.
24. Smith, "Hyderabad," 48.
25. S.C. Res. 39, 20 Jan. 1948.
26. S.C. Res. 47, 21 April 1948.
27. SCOR, 4th Year, Special Supp. No. 7 (S/1430), 1949, pp. 25–27.
28. U.N. Doc. S/5016, 8 Dec. 1961, p. 1.
29. U.N. Doc. S/5018, 11 Dec. 1961, p. 1.
30. U.N. Doc. S/5020, 13 Dec. 1961, p. 2.
31. Ibid.
32. U.N. Doc. S/5028, 18 Dec. 1961, p. 3.
33. Ibid., 4.
34. *New York Times*, Dec. 15, 1961, p. 1, and Dec. 17, 1961, p. 28.
35. Ibid., Dec. 18, 1961, p. 10.
36. U.N. Doc. S/5030, 18 Dec. 1961, p. 1.
37. SCOR, 16th Year, 987th Mtg., 18 Dec. 1961, p. 7.
38. Ibid., 15.
39. Ibid., 15–18.
40. Ibid., 16.
41. Ibid., 9.
42. Ibid., 10.
43. Ibid.
44. Ibid., 11.
45. Ibid., 14.
46. Ibid., 22–23.
47. SCOR, 16th Year, 988th Mtg., 18 Dec. 1961, p. 4.
48. Ibid., 6.
49. Ibid.
50. Ibid., 4.
51. Ibid., 18.
52. *New York Times*, Dec. 19, 1961, p. 17.
53. U.N. Doc. S/5033, 18 Dec. 1961, p. 1.
54. SCOR, 16th Year, 988th Mtg., 18 Dec. 1961, p. 27.
55. Ibid.
56. *New York Times*, Dec. 30, 1961, p. 2.
57. Ibid., Dec. 20, 1961, p. 1.
58. Ibid., Dec. 18, 1961, p. 34.
59. Ibid., Dec. 23, 1961, p. 22.
60. Ibid., Dec. 19, 1961, p. 32.
61. Ibid., Dec. 24, 1961, Sec. IV, p. 1.
62. Ibid., Dec. 19, 1961, p. 32.

63. Reprinted in *Congressional Record* (Senate), 108 (Jan. 15, 1962): 161.
64. Quoted in *New York Times*, Dec. 24, 1961, Sec. IV, p. 7.
65. Ibid.
66. Ibid.
67. Reprinted in *Congressional Record*, Appendix, Part 1, 108 (Jan. 15, 1962): A192.
68. *Congressional Record* (Senate), 108 (March 22, 1962): 4821.
69. *New York Times*, Dec. 31, 1961, Sec. IV, p. 9. The spokesman quoted is not identified.

CHAPTER 4: A Rather Good Document

1. Trygve Lie, *In the Cause of Peace* (New York, 1954), 230.
2. SCOR, 3rd Year, 268th Mtg., 17 March 1948, p. 1.
3. U.N. Doc. S/3232, 20 June 1954, p. 1. For a full account of "the American coup in Guatemala," see Stephen Schlesinger and Stephen Kinzer, *Bitter Fruit* (New York, 1982).
4. SCOR, 9th Year, 675th Mtg., 20 June 1954, p. 11.
5. S.C. Res. 104, 20 June 1954.
6. SCOR, 9th Year, 675th Mtg., 20 June 1954, p. 21.
7. Ibid., 22–23.
8. Ibid., 29–30.
9. SCOR, 9th Year, 676th Mtg., 25 June 1954, pp. 28–29.
10. SCOR, 9th Year, 675th Mtg., 20 June 1954, p. 32.
11. Foreign Relations of the United States, 1946, Vol. VII (Washington, 1969), 309 (hereafter F.R.U.S.).
12. SCOR, 9th Year, 676th Mtg., 25 June 1954, p. 34.
13. *The Charter of the United Nations*, Hearings, Senate Committee on Foreign Relations, Part 4, July 13, 1945 (Washington, 1945), 474.
14. SCOR, 1st year, 1st Series, Supp. No. 1, 1945, p. 18.
15. See Thomas M. Franck and Edward Weisband, *Word Politics: Verbal Strategy Among the Superpowers* (New York, 1972), 57–59, fn. 22.
16. U.N. Doc. S/3690, 27 Oct. 1956, p. 1.
17. SCOR, 11th Year, 752nd Mtg., 2 Nov. 1956, p. 24.
18. SCOR, 11th Year, 754th Mtg., 4 Nov. 1956, p. 1.
19. U.N. Doc. S/3726, 2 Nov. 1956, pp. 2–3.
20. U.N. Doc. A/3251, 1 Nov. 1956, pp. 1–2.
21. U.N. Doc. S/3730/Rev. 1, 4 Nov. 1956, pp. 1–2.
22. SCOR, 11th Year, 753rd Mtg., 3 Nov. 1956, p. 16.
23. Ibid., 20–21.
24. SCOR, 11th Year, 754th Mtg., 4 Nov. 1956, p. 2.
25. Ibid., 9–10.
26. Ibid., 12.
27. S.C. Res. 120, 4 Nov. 1956.
28. SCOR, 11th Year, 754th Mtg., 4 Nov. 1956, p. 14.
29. U.N. Doc. A/3286, 4 Nov. 1956, p. 1.
30. U.N. Doc. A/3311, 7 Nov. 1956, p. 1.
31. GAOR (ES-II), 564th Plenary Mtg., 4 Nov. 1956, p. 8.
32. Ibid., 13.
33. Ibid., 20.
34. GAOR (ES-II), 568th Plenary Mtg., 8 Nov. 1956, p. 31.

35. GAOR (ES-II), 569th Plenary Mtg., 8 Nov. 1956, p. 35.
36. Ibid., 40.
37. Ibid., 44.
38. *The Times* (London), Oct. 7, 1974, p. 14.
39. The author interviewed Foreign Minister Krishna Menon extensively on four occasions between 1954 and 1957, in Cambridge, Mass., New York, and New Delhi. These lines are based on those free-ranging discussions of contemporary issues, political ethics, and the role of ideology in international affairs. The author, however, is summarizing what he understood to be the implication of Krishna Menon's stated beliefs, not paraphrasing Menon.
40. GAOR (ES-II), 571st Plenary Mtg., 9 Nov. 1956, p. 67.
41. GAOR (ES-II), 564th Plenary Mtg., 4 Nov. 1956, p. 1.
42. GAOR (ES-II), 570th Plenary Mtg., 9 Nov. 1956, p. 56.
43. *New York Times*, July 16, 1957, p. 24.
44. Ibid., July 11, 1957, p. 9.
45. *Congressional Record* (House), 103 (June 21, 1957): 10024.
46. *New York Times*, Nov. 18, 1956, p. 9.
47. Brian Urquhart, *Hammarskjold* (New York, 1972), 244–45.
48. Emery Kelen, *Hammarskjold* (New York, 1966), 171–72.
49. "To have put their [the witnesses'] names in the secretariat files would have been tantamount to handing them to the Russians and Communist Hungarians." *Cleveland Plain Dealer*, July 8, 1958. Reprinted in *Congressional Record*, Appendix, 104 (July 11, 1958): A6248.
50. *New York Times*, June 21, 1957, p. 24.
51. Ibid., Aug. 3, 1957, p. 1.
52. Reprinted in *Congressional Record*, Appendix, 105 (Jan. 9, 1959): A23.
53. Reprinted in *Congressional Record* (Senate), 103 (March 19, 1957): S3913.
54. Ibid.
55. *New York Times*, Nov. 6, 1956, p. 46.
56. Ibid., Nov. 16, 1956, p. 26.
57. *Wall Street Journal*, Nov. 7, 1956, p. 14.
58. Ibid., Nov. 21, 1956, p. 12.
59. Ibid.
60. Ibid., Nov. 12, 1956, p. 10.
61. SCOR, 15th Year, 874th Mtg., 18 July 1960, p. 1.
62. SCOR, 20th Year, 1204th Mtg., 11 May 1965, p. 17.
63. Resolution VI of the Eighth Meeting of Consultation, Punta del Este, Uruguay, January 1962. U.N. Doc. S/5075, 3 Feb. 1962, p. 17.
64. L.C. Meeker, "Legal Basis for the United States Actions in the Dominican Republic," in 2 Chayes, Ehrlich and Lowenfeld, *International Legal Process: Materials for an Introductory Course* (New York, 1969), 1181–82.
65. S.C. Res. 203, 14 May 1965.
66. Ruth B. Russell, *The United Nations and United States Security Policy* (Washington, 1968), 183.
67. The observers were withdrawn at the end of 1966, after the Dominican Republic had held free and peaceful national elections. U.N. Press Release M-1709, 31 Dec. 1966, p. 7.
68. Franck and Weisband, *Word Politics*.
69. U.N. Doc. S/8758, 21 Aug. 1968, p. 1.
70. SCOR, 23rd Year, 1441st Mtg., 21 Aug. 1968, p. 13.

71. Ibid., 14.

72. Ibid., 24.

73. U.N. Doc. S/8761 and Add. 1, 22 Aug. 1968.

74. SCOR, 23rd Year, 1442nd Mtg., 22 Aug. 1968, p. 6.

75. Ibid.

76. Ibid., 11.

77. Ibid., 11–13.

78. SCOR, 23rd Year, 1443rd Mtg., 22 Aug. 1968, p. 2.

79. Ibid., 1.

80. Ibid., 7–8.

81. Ibid., 9.

82. Ibid., 14.

83. Ibid., 19.

84. Ibid., 22.

85. Ibid., 26.

86. See Thomas M. Franck and Nigel S. Rodley, "After Bangladesh: The Law of Humanitarian Intervention by Military Force," *Am. Jour. Intl. Law*, 67 (1973): 275.

87. SCOR, 23rd Year, 1443rd Mtg., 22 Aug. 1968, p. 29.

88. Ibid., 30.

89. Ibid., 31.

90. SCOR, 23rd Year, 1444th Mtg., 23 Aug. 1968, p. 8.

91. SCOR, 23rd Year, 1445th Mtg., 24 Aug. 1968, pp. 1–2.

92. Ibid., 9.

93. Ibid., 17.

94. *New York Times*, Aug. 22, 1968, p. 36.

95. Ibid.

96. Ibid., Sept. 24, 1968, p. 46.

97. Ibid., Sept. 29, 1968, Sec. IV, p. 11.

98. Introduction to the Annual Report of the Secretary-General on the Work of the Organization, GAOR(XXIII), Supp. No. 1A (A/7201/Add. 1), Sept. 1968, p. 21.

CHAPTER 5: The End of Innocence

1. U.N. Doc. S/1417, 10 Nov. 1949, p. 1.

2. Ibid., 24.

3. U.N. Doc. A/2694, 18 Aug. 1954, p. 1.

4. GAOR(IX), 477th Plenary Mtg., 24 Sept. 1954, pp. 43–47.

5. GAOR(IX), First Committee, 726th Mtg., 23 Nov. 1954, pp. 394–97.

6. U.N. Doc. A/L.354, 9 Oct. 1961, pp. 1–2. See also GAOR(XVI), 1055th Plenary Mtg., 15 Nov. 1961, pp. 665–69.

7. GAOR(XVI), 1065th Plenary Mtg., 27 Nov. 1961, pp. 840–41.

8. Ibid., 848.

9. G.A. Res. 1654(XVI), 27 Nov. 1961. It was voted upon at: GAOR(XVI), 1066th Plenary Mtg., 27 Nov. 1961, p. 875.

10. *New York Times*, Dec. 25, 1961, p. 22.

11. Ibid., Jan. 3, 1962, p. 1.

12. Ibid., Jan. 4, 1962, p. 1.

13. Ibid., Feb. 1, 1962, p. 8.

14. Ibid., March 28, 1962, p. 38.

15. Ibid., March 14, 1962, p. 11.

16. Ibid., April 14, 1962, p. 3, and April 15, 1962, p. 18.

17. Ibid., May 25, 1962, p. 32. U.N. Doc. S/5062, 18 Jan. 1962 and S/5123, 16 May 1962.

18. *New York Times*, May 25, 1962, p. 32.

19. Ibid., May 27, 1962, pp. 11, 14.

20. Ibid., Aug. 16, 1962, p. 7.

21. Ibid., Aug. 18, 1962, p. 2.

22. Ibid., Aug. 1, 1962, p. 1.

23. G.A. Res. 1752(XVII), 21 Sept. 1962.

24. Annual Report of the Secretary-General on the Work of the Organization, 16 June 1962–15 June 1963, GAOR(XVIII), Supp. No. 1 (A/5501), 1963, p. 36.

25. *New York Times*, Sept. 29, 1962, pp. 1, 3.

26. Ibid.

27. GAOR(XVII), 1127th Plenary Mtg., 21 Sept. 1962, pp. 56–57.

28. *Congressional Record* (Senate), 108 (Aug. 2, 1962): 15479.

29. Ibid.

30. Congressional Record (Senate), 108 (Aug. 20, 1962): 17093.

31. *Congressional Record*, Appendix, 108 (Aug. 23, 1962): A6615, and *Congressional Record* (Senate), 108 (May 3, 1962): 7653.

32. Ibid., (Aug. 17, 1962), 16952.

33. *New York Times*, Aug. 17, 1962, p. 22.

34. For typical comments from major columnists, see Thomas J. Hamilton in the *New York Times*, Aug. 19, 1962, Sec. IV, p. 9; also William S. White in the *Washington Evening Star*, May 25, 1962, reprinted in *Congressional Record*, Appendix, 108 (May 28, 1962): A3939-40.

35. GAOR(XVII), 1127th Plenary Mtg., 21 Sept. 1962, p. 51.

36. GAOR(XVIII), 1255th Plenary Mtg., 6 Nov. 1963, p. 4.

37. Report of the Secretary-General regarding the act of self-determination in West Irian. U.N. Doc. A/7723, 6 Nov. 1969, Annex I, pp. 58–60 (hereafter: West Irian Report).

38. *New York Times*, May 3, 1969, p. 7; May 16, 1969, p. 2; and July 7, 1969, p. 5.

39. West Irian Report, 29.

40. Ibid., 69.

41. Ibid., 41.

42. Ibid., 56.

43. Ibid., 70.

44. U.N. Doc. A/L.576, 19 Nov. 1969, pp. 1–2.

45. GAOR(XXIV), 1813th Plenary Mtg., 19 Nov. 1969, p. 17, adopting G.A. Res. 2504(XXIV), 19 Nov. 1969.

46. GAOR(XXIV), 1813th Plenary Mtg., 19 Nov. 1969, p. 17.

47. G.A. Res. 1731(XVI), 20 Dec. 1961.

48. *Certain Expenses of the United Nations*, Advisory Opinion of 20 July 1962, I.C.J. Reports, 1962, p. 163.

49. Ibid., 164.

50. Ibid.

51. Ibid., 168.

52. G.A. Res. 1854A(XVII), 19 Dec. 1962. See also G.A. Res. 1874(S-IV), 27 June 1963; G.A. Res. 1877 (S-IV), 27 June 1963.

53. Ernest Gross, *The United Nations: Structure for Peace* (New York, 1962), 103.

54. United Nations Yearbook, 1965, p. 14 (hereafter: U.N. Yearbook).

55. *New York Times*, Aug. 17, 1965, p. 6. U.N. Doc. A/5916/Add. 1, 30 Sept. 1965, p. 6.

56. U.N. Yearbook (1965), 15.

57. U.N. Doc. A/5916, 31 Aug. 1965, p. 1. *New York Times*, Aug. 17, 1965, p. 1.

58. Ibid., April 4, 1965, p. 10.

59. Ibid.

60. G.A. Res. 1125(XI), 2 Feb. 1957. See also G.A. Res. 1000(ES-I), 5 Nov. 1956 and G.A. Res. 1001 (ES-I), 7 Nov. 1956.

61. U.N. Doc. A/6672, 12 July 1967, p. 5.

62. A detailed survey of the issues, the relevant resolutions and reports, and the lego-political literature is found in: Nabil El-Araby, *N.Y.U. Jour. of Intl. Law and Politics* 1 (1968): 149.

63. U.N. Doc. A/6669, 18 May 1967, pp. 3–4.

64. Ibid., 4–5.

65. Ibid., 2.

66. Ibid., 1.

67. Ibid., 2.

68. El-Araby, survey in *N.Y.U. Jour. of Intl. Law,* 169–70. See also U.N. Doc. A/6730, 26 June 1967, pp. 7–8.

69. U.N. Doc. S/7896, 19 May 1967, p. 3.

70. U.N. Doc. A/6669, 18 May 1967, p. 9.

71. Ibid.

72. U.N. Doc. A/3375, Annex, 20 Nov. 1956, p. 1.

73. Letter of Ambassador Ernest Gross to the Editors, *New York Times*, May 26, 1967, p. 46.

74. Ibid.

75. Gross, *The United Nations*, 32.

76. El-Araby, survey in *N.Y.U. Jour. of Intl. Law,* 165.

77. Interview with Ambassador Nabil El-Araby (New York, Oct. 3, 1982).

78. U.N. Doc. S/7906, 26 May 1967, p. 2.

79. Ibid.

80. U.N. Doc. A/6672, 12 July 1967, p. 7.

81. SCOR, 22nd Year, 1343rd Mtg., 29 May 1967, p. 19.

82. Remarks of the President on the Near East situation, May 23, 1967. Reprinted in: *Congressional Record* (Senate), 113 (May 24, 1967): 13692.

83. Ibid. (May 19, 1967), 13279.

84. Ibid., 13280. ("U" serves the function of "Mr.")

85. Ibid., 13281.

86. Ibid., 113 (May 23, 1967): 13543–44.

87. Ibid., (May 24, 1967), 13693.

88. Ibid., 13804.

89. Ibid. (June 6, 1967), 14781.

90. *New York Times*, May 21, 1967, p. 8.

91. *Congressional Record* (Senate), 114 (Sept. 27, 1968): 28602.

92. *Congressional Record* (House), 113 (June 5, 1967): 14636.

93. *New York Times*, May 31, 1967, p. 42.

94. *Wall Street Journal*, July 18, 1967, p. 1.

95. Interview with June Bingham (New York, March 24, 1983).

96. *Wall Street Journal*, July 18, 1967, p. 1.

97. Ibid., Oct. 4, 1967, p. 16.

CHAPTER 6: His Sisters and His Cousins and His Aunts

1. Francis Paul Walters, *A History of the League of Nations*, Vol. 1 (London, 1952), 75–76.

2. Robert Rhodes James, "The Concept of the International Civil Service," in *International Administration: Its Evolution and Contemporary Applications*, Robert Jordan, ed. (New York, 1971), 57.

3. Walters, *A History of the League of Nations*, 75.

4. Stephen Roskill, *Hankey, Man of Secrets*, Vol. 1 (London, 1970), 276.

5. Walters, *A History of the League of Nations*, 75.

6. Ibid., 76.

7. Ibid.

8. In practice, the Secretary-General's exclusive power of appointment has been eroded by General Assembly resolutions creating semi-autonomous units whose chief officers are appointed with the consent of the Assembly. While this subject is beyond the scope of the present study, it is well documented in Theodor Meron, "Charter Powers of the United Nations' Secretary-General with regard to the Secretariat and the Role of General Assembly Resolutions," *Zeitschrift für ausländisches Recht und Volkerrecht*, Vol. 42, No. 4, Max Planck-Institut (1982), 734–53.

9. Ruth B. Russell, *A History of the United Nations Charter* (Washington, 1958), 861–63.

10. United Nations Conference on International Organization, Documents, Vol. 7, p. 507; see also pp. 854–62.

11. Theodor Meron, *The United Nations Secretariat* (Lexington, Mass., 1977), 4–7.

12. Dag Hammarskjold, "The International Civil Servant in Law and Fact," SG/1035, 30 May 1961, in Andrew W. Cordier and Wilder Foote, eds., *Public Papers of the Secretaries-General of the United Nations*, Vol. 5 (New York, 1975), 471.

13. Ibid., 489.

14. See, for example, *Introduction to the Annual Report of the Secretary-General on the Work of the Organization*, GAOR(XVI), Supp. No. 1A (A/4800/Add. 1), Aug. 1961, p. 6.

15. GAOR(XV), 869th Plenary Mtg., 23 Sept. 1960, pp. 71, 82.

16. U.N. Doc. A/4776, 14 June 1961, p. 1.

17. Ibid., 6.

18. Leon Gordenker, *The U.N. Secretary-General and the Maintenance of Peace* (New York, 1967), 93. The Secretary-General's views are set out in U.N. Doc. A/4794, 30 June 1961, p. 1.

19. *Reparations for Inquiries Suffered in the Service of the United Nations*, Advisory Opinion of April 11, 1949, I.C.J. Reports, 1949, p. 187.

20. Ibid.

21. Ibid., 179.

22. Ibid., 180–81.

23. Ibid., 182–84.

24. *Effect of Awards of Compensation Made by the United Nations Administrative Tribunal*, Advisory Opinion of 13 July 1954, I.C.J. Reports, 1954, p. 48.

25. Ibid., 62.

26. Ibid., 56–57.

27. Ibid., 59.

28. Ibid., 61.

29. Brian Urquhart, *Hammarskjold* (New York, 1972), 58.

30. *New York Times*, Dec. 3, 1952, p. 1.

31. Dean Acheson, *Present at the Creation* (New York, 1969), 698.

32. Ibid., 112.

33. *New York Times*, Jan. 2, 1953, pp. 1, 8.

34. Urquhart, *Hammarskjold*, 59.

35. U.N. Doc. A/2364, 30 Jan. 1953, pp. 2–3. The appointments were made on Oct. 22, 1952. These incidents are fully discussed in Urquhart, *Hammarskjold*, 58–68.

36. U.N. Doc. A/2364, 30 Jan. 1953, Annex III.

37. Urquhart, *Hammarskjold*, 59.

38. Decisions awarding compensation: *Gordon v. Secretary-General of the United Nations*, Judgement No. 29, p. 120; *Harris v. Secretary-General of the United Nations*, Judgement No. 31, p. 135; *Glassman v. Secretary-General of the United Nations*, Judgement No. 33, p. 151; *Older v. Secretary-General of the United Nations*, Judgement No. 34, p. 160; *Bancroft v. Secretary-General of the United Nations*, Judgement No. 35, p. 168; *Elveson v. Secretary-General of the United Nations*, Judgement No. 36, p. 176; *Reed v. Secretary-General of the United Nations*, Judgement No. 37, p. 184, Judgements of the United Nations Administrative Tribunal, U.N. Doc. AT/DEC 1 to 70. Decisions awarding reinstatement: *Crawford v. Secretary-General of the United Nations*, Judgement No. 18, p. 65; *Svenchansky v. Secretary-General of the United Nations*, Judgement No. 30, p. 128; *Eldridge v. Secretary-General of the United Nations*, Judgement No. 32, p. 151; *Glaser v. Secretary-General of the United Nations*, Judgement No. 38, p. 192, Judgements of the United Nations Administrative Tribunal, U.N. Doc. AT/DEC 1 to 70.

39. Ibid.

40. House Concurrent Resolution 262, *Congressional Record* (House), 100 (Aug. 10, 1954): 13949; (Senate) (Aug. 20, 1954): 15486; 68 Stat, B 114.

41. G.A. Res. 785(VIII), 9 Dec. 1953.

42. Urquhart, *Hammerskjold*, 70.

43. 22 U.S.C. 287, amended by Executive Order No. 11890 of Dec. 10, 1975, 40 Fed. Reg. 240 (1975).

44. Urquhart, *Hammarskjold*, 63. The Order was amended on June 2, 1953 (ibid.).

45. Meron, *The United Nations Secretariat*, 69.

46. Ibid.

47. Ibid., 70.

48. Shirley Hazzard, *The Defeat of an Ideal* (Boston, 1973), 58.

49. A recent publication of the Heritage Foundation notes that a "high official" of the U.S. Office of Personnel Management which used to handle the loyalty checks before President Ford reduced the degree of requisite investigation for Americans working at the U.N. is advocating a reversion to the 1953 system to alleviate the phenomenon of internationalization he perceives to be affecting U.S. personnel in the Secretariat. Juliana Geran Pilon, "Americans at the U.N.: An Endangered Species," United Nations Assessment Study of the Heritage Foundation, Washington, D.C., Feb. 14, 1983, p.16, n.22.

50. Urquhart, *Hammarskjold*, 63.

51. Ibid., 64.

52. Ibid., 73.

53. Ibid.

54. Acheson, *Present at the Creation*, 698.

55. Ibid.

56. Art. 100(1).

57. Art. 101(1).

58. Art. 101(3).

59. GAOR(XV), 882nd Plenary Mtg., 3 Oct. 1960, p. 319.

60. Urquhart, *Hammarskjold*, 459–65.

61. Meron, *The United Nations Secretariat*, 28.

62. Urquhart, *Hammarskjold*, 76–77.

63. These figures are found in Programme Budget for the Biennium 1982–83. U.N. Doc. A/37/790, 20 Dec. 1982, p. 33. See also: J.O.C. Jonah, "Independence and Integrity of the International Civil Service: The Role of Executive Heads and the Role of States." Paper prepared for the First Meller Conference, N.Y.U. Law School, Nov. 20, 1981, p. 38 (unpub.). The 50,000 figure for the overall system is cited in John P. Renninger, "Can the Comma System Be Maintained and Improved? The Role of the International Civil Service Commission," presentation prepared for Panel on "International Civil Servants: Neutrals or Politicians?" Annual Convention of the International Studies Assn., 1984 (unpub.).

64. U.N. Doc. A/4776, 14 June 1961, p. 11.

65. Jonah, "Independence and Integrity," 9.

66. Ibid. Jonah is paraphrasing "a view" not necessarily his own.

67. U.N. Doc. A/10184, 28 Aug. 1975, Annex, Table 9.

68. Ibid., Table 11. Meron, *The United Nations Secretariat*, 80. Meron points out, however, that it is now common practice to use fixed-term contracts as probationary employment, but, even so, only one out of five fixed-term contracts was converted to career appointments between 1958 and 1975.

69. Ibid., 34.

70. For a response of the Secretary-General to the systemic effects of this case, see Security, Safety and Independence of the International Civil Service, Secretary-General's Bulletin to Members of the Staff, U.N. Doc. ST/SGB/198, 10 Dec. 1982, pp. 1–3.

71. Report of the Staff Unions/Associations of the United Nations Secretariat on Personnel Questions, U.N. Doc. A/C.5/35/17, 30 Sept. 1980, p. 15.

72. Meron, *The United Nations Secretariat*, 34.

73. Jonah, "Independence and Integrity," 7.

74. Ibid., 14.

75. Ibid., 18.

76. Ibid., 26.

77. G.A. Res. 35/210, 17 Dec. 1980. For passage, see U.N. Doc. A/35/PV. 99, 19 Dec. 1980, p. 26.

78. G.A. Res. 33/143, 20 Dec. 1978.

79. Meron, *The United Nations Secretariat*, 11, citing: U.N. Doc. A/652, 2 Sept. 1948.

80. James, "The Concept of the International Civil Service," 60.

81. Meron, *The United Nations Secretariat*, 12. An upward deviation was only permitted for countries contributing 10 percent or less of the budget.

82. G.A. Res. 233(III), 8 Oct. 1948.

83. The figures exclude posts not subject to geographic distribution such as those requiring special language qualifications and certain technical services. U.N. Doc. A/5841, 23 Dec. 1964, p. 7.

84. The fixed-term staff that year constituted 29.7 percent of the total. U.N. Doc. A/6487, 26 Oct. 1966, p. 7.

85. GAOR(XVII), 1199th Plenary Mtg., 19 Dec. 1962, p. 1194, adopting the report of the 5th Committee on Personnel Questions; specifically paras. 16 and 40 of U.N. Doc. A/5377, 18 Dec. 1962, pp. 15, 29.

86. Meron, *The United Nations Secretariat*, 13.

87. U.N. Doc. A/7745, 5 Nov. 1969, p. 11.

88. U.N. Doc. A/8156, 12 Nov. 1970, Table D.

89. Meron, *The United Nations Secretariat*, 23.

90. Ibid.

91. G.A. Res. 35/210, 17 Dec. 1980.

92. Meron, *The United Nations Secretariat*, 25.

93. G.A. Res. 33/143, 20 Dec. 1978.

94. International Memorandum, June 4, 1979 (unpub.), in Meron, *The United Nations Secretariat*, 770–71.

95. Jonah, "Independence and Integrity," 41.

96. Chester Purves, *The International Administration of an International Secretariat* (London, 1945), 25.

97. Jonah, "Independence and Integrity," 42–43.

98. In a memorandum (unpub.) dated 28 April 1983, Louis P. Nègre, the Assistant-Secretary-General for Personnel Services, states that "the schedule for the [General Services] to [Professional] and external national examinations and occupations to be tested have now been determined" and "are scheduled for October 1983." The memorandum makes clear, however, that "the following distribution [of posts] has been made: administrative posts to be earmarked for Czechoslovakia, FRG, and UkSSR; economics for GDR, Japan, Norway and the USSR; finance for Japan; political affairs for FRG; social development for Venezuela." Success in such exams, moreover, does not guarantee a candidate that someone else will not be appointed to the post.

99. Report of the Joint Inspection Unit on personnel problems in the United Nations, JIU/REP/71/7 (Summary), 1972, pp. 7–8 (hereafter: Report of the JIU). Also recorded as: U.N. Doc. A/8826, 27 Sept. 1972.

100. U.N. Doc. A/9841, 8 Nov. 1974, p. 10. For the rather negative views on competitive examinations of the Secretary-General, see U.N. Doc. A/C.5/1601, 6 Sept. 1974, p. 7.

101. Report of the Staff Unions/Associations of the United Nations Secretariat on Personnel Questions (1980), p. 11.

102. Report of the Secretary-General on the Work of the Organization, GAOR(XXXIII), Supp. No. 1 (A/33/1), Sept. 1978, p. 10.

103. Seymour Maxwell Finger, "The Effect of Pressure by States or Groups of States on the Independence and Integrity of the U.N. Secretariat." Paper prepared for the First Meller Conference, N.Y.U. Law School, Nov. 20, 1981, p. 18 (unpub.).

104. Renninger, "Can the Comma System Be Maintained . . . ," 9, 12.

105. See Pilon, "Americans at the U.N.," 49.

106. Ibid., 1, 8. See also U.N. Doc. A/37/378/Add. 1, 28 Oct. 1982, p. 7.

107. Inis Claude, *Swords into Plowshares*, 3rd ed. (New York, 1964), 174.

108. Thomas M. Franck, John P. Renninger, Vladislav B. Tikhomirov, "Diplomats' Views on the United Nations System: An Attitude Survey," UNITAR Policy and Efficacy Study No. 7, 1982, p. 35.

109. Report of the JIU, p. 2.

CHAPTER 7: The Secretary-General Invents Himself

1. Kurt Waldheim, *The Challenge of Peace* (New York, 1980), Preface by Brian Urquhart, unpaginated.

2. League of Nations Covenant, art. 6.

3. U.N. Charter, art. 98.

4. Art. 99.

5. Art. 100.

6. Evan Luard, *A History of the United Nations*, Vol. 1 (New York, 1982), 343.

7. Trygve Lie, *In the Cause of Peace* (New York, 1954), 42.

8. GAOR(I), 22nd Plenary Mtg., 2 Feb. 1946, p. 325.

9. Andrew W. Cordier and Wilder Foote, eds., *Public Papers of the Secretaries-General of the United Nations*, Vol. 1: Trygve Lie (New York, 1969), 124.

10. Cited in Brian Urquhart, *Hammarskjold* (New York, 1972), 15.

11. Ibid.

12. Ibid.

13. Ibid.

14. GAOR(XII), 690th Plenary Mtg., 26 Sept. 1957, p. 175.

15. Brian Urquhart, "International Peace and Security: Thoughts on the Twentieth Anniversary of Dag Hammarskjold's Death," *Foreign Affairs*, Fall, 1981, pp. 3, 4.

16. U.N. Press Release SG/SM/567, 19 Sept. 1966, p. 4.

17. U.N. Press Release SG/SM/304, 21 May 1965, p. 3.

18. U.N. Press Release SG/1477, 30 April 1963, p. 5.

19. Arthur Rovine, *The First Fifty Years: The Secretary-General in World Politics, 1920–1970* (Leyden, 1970), 413–14.

20. Waldheim, *The Challenge of Peace*, 5.

21. Introduction to the Report of the Secretary-General on the Work of the Organization, GAOR(XXVII), Supp. No. 1A (A/8701/Add. 1), Aug. 1972, p. 4 (hereafter: Annual Report of S.G.).

22. Ibid.

23. Annual Report of S.G., GAOR(XXXI), Supp. No. 1A (A/31/1/Add. 1), Aug. 1976, p. 9.

24. Annual Report of S.G., GAOR(XXXIV), Supp. No. 1 (A/34/1), Sept., 1979, p. 7. See also Annual Report of S.G., GAOR(XXXV), Supp. No. 1 (A/35/1), Sept. 1980, pp. 9–10; Annual Report of S.G., GAOR(XXXVI), Supp. No. 1 (A/36/1), Sept. 1981, p. 9.

25. Kurt Waldheim, *Building the Future Order* (New York, 1980), xxi.

26. The avid reader may wish to pursue some or all of the following helpful works: Stephen M. Schwebel, *The Secretary-General of the United Nations—His Political Powers and Practice* (New York, 1952); Leon Gordenker, *The UN Secretary General and the Maintenance of Peace* (New York, 1967); Vratislav Pechota, *The Quiet Approach: A Study of the Good Offices Exercised by the United Nations Secretary-General in the Cause of Peace* (New York, 1972); Ruth B. Russell, *The United Nations and United States Security Policy* (Washington, 1968); Oran Young, *The Intermediaries* (Princeton, 1967); Rovine, *The First Fifty Years*; Marie-Claude Smouts, *Le Secretaire General des Nations Unies* (Paris, 1971); Waldheim, *Challenge of Peace* and *Building the Future Order*.

27. For a fuller discussion, see Rovine, *The First Fifty Years*, 214–16.

28. Schwebel, *The Secretary-General* . . . , 205.

29. Gordenker, *The UN Secretary-General*, 148–49.

30. Rovine, *The First Fifty Years*, 215.

31. SCOR, 5th Year, 473rd Mtg., 25 June 1950, p. 3.

32. Ibid. The first information relayed by the Commission actually came from U.S. intelligence sources. Gordenker, *The UN Secretary-General*, 143. Gordenker refers to

the "somnolent United Nations Commission on Korea." Elucidated in interview with
Gordenker (New York, May 31, 1983).

33. Rovine, *The First Fifty Years*, 287.

34. Urquhart, *Hammarskjold*, 172.

35. SCOR, 11th Year, 748th Mtg., 30 Oct. 1956, pp. 3–4.

36. SCOR, 11th Year, 751st Mtg., 31 Oct. 1956, pp. 1–2.

37. Gordenker, *The UN Secretary-General*, 146.

38. Quoted from unpublished sources by Urquhart, *Hammarskjold*, 335.

39. Ibid., 339–40.

40. Ibid., 340.

41. Ibid., 345.

42. Ibid., 393.

43. Ibid., 396–97.

44. SCOR, 15th Year, 873rd Mtg., 14 July 1960, pp. 41–42. The resolution
adopted was S.C. Res. 143, 14 July 1960.

45. SCOR, 15th Year, 873rd Mtg., 14 July 1960, p. 42.

46. SCOR, 21st year, 1329th Mtg., 2 Dec. 1966, pp. 1–2.

47. Waldheim, *The Challenge of Peace*, 45.

48. Ibid., 65–66. Waldheim states that the Council was "convened at my initiative . . ." (ibid., 66).

49. U.N. Doc. S/13646, 25 Nov. 1979, p. 1.

50. S.C. Res. 457, 4 Dec. 1979. The call for the Secretary-General to use his good
offices was later reiterated in S.C. Res. 461, 31 Dec. 1979.

51. SCOR, 1st Year, 33rd Mtg., 16 April 1946, pp. 142–46.

52. U.N. Doc. S/39, 16 April 1946, pp. 2–4.

53. U.N. Doc. S/1466, 9 March 1950, p. 6.

54. SCOR, 5th Year, 473rd Mtg., 25 June 1950, p. 3.

55. Rovine, *The First Fifty Years*, 242.

56. Harry S. Truman, *Memoirs*, Vol. 2 (New York, 1956), 455–56. See also Lie, *In
the Cause of Peace*, 363–66.

57. Brian Urquhart, "Dag Hammarskjold: The Private Person in a Very Public
Office," in Robert S. Jordan, *Dag Hammarskjold Revisited* (Durham, 1983), 139.

58. U.N. Doc. A/8160, 11 Nov. 1970, pp. 1–3.

59. U.N. Doc. A/SPC/37/L.24, 29 Nov. 1982, p. 2.

60. U.N. Press Release U.N. Doc. GA/SPC/1691, 3 Dec. 1982, p. 1.

61. Luard, *A History of the United Nations*, 350.

62. Rovine, *The First Fifty Years*, 299.

63. S.C. Res. 128, 11 June 1958.

64. GAOR(ES-III), 732nd Plenary Mtg., 8 Aug. 1958, p. 4.

65. Urquhart, *Hammarskjold*, 290.

66. Lie, *In the Cause of Peace*, 162.

67. Luard, *A History of the United Nations*, 344.

68. Ibid., 350.

69. G.A. Res. 1237(ES-III), 21 Aug. 1958. For the vote, see GAOR(ES-III), 746th
Plenary Mtg., 21 Aug. 1958, p. 182.

70. S.C. Res. 143, 14 July 1960.

71. S.C. Res. 146, 9 Aug. 1960. Urquhart simply states that the resolution closely
corresponded with Hammarskjold's "requirements." Urquhart, *Hammarskjold*, 423.

72. S.C. Res. 215, 5 Nov. 1965. Rovine, *The First Fifty Years*, 388. See also U Thant,
"The Role of the Secretary-General," *U.N. Monthly Chronicle*, 8 (Oct. 1971): 178.

73. Waldheim, *The Challenge of Peace*, 45–46.

74. Luard, *A History of the United Nations*, 348.

75. This concept is advanced in: Annual Report of S.G., GAOR(XV), Supp. No. 1A (A/4390/Add. 1), Aug. 1960, p. 3.

76. Quoted by Urquhart, *Hammarskjold*, 255, citing Gunnar Jarring.

77. GAOR(XVI), 1046th Plenary Mtg., 3 Nov. 1961, p. 551.

78. Waldheim, *The Challenge of Peace*, 5; Waldheim, *Building the Future Order*, 223–24. See also Annual Report of S.G., Aug. 1972, p. 3; Annual Report of S.G., GAOR(XXVIII), Supp. No. 1A (A/9001/Add. 1), Aug. 1973, p. 2.

79. Annual Report of S.G., Aug. 1976, p. 4.

80. Annual Report of S.G., GAOR(XXX), Supp. No. 1A (A/1001/Add. 1), Aug. 1975, p. 2.

81. Waldheim, *The Challenge of Peace*, 37.

82. Waldheim, *Building the Future Order*, xxiii and 241.

83. Ibid., 241.

84. Ibid. See also on this theme Annual Report of S.G., Aug. 1976, pp. 8–9.

85. Ibid., GAOR(XXXIII), Supp. No. 1 (A/33/1), Sept. 1978, pp. 8–9. See also ibid., Sept. 1979, pp. 8–9.

86. Ibid., Aug. 1976, pp. 5–6.

87. Ibid., Sept. 1979, p. 11.

88. Ibid., Aug. 1972, p. 1.

89. Ibid.

90. Ibid., Aug. 1973, p. 1.

91. Ibid., Aug. 1975, p. 3.

92. Ibid., 5–6.

93. Ibid., GAOR(XXXIII), Supp. No. 1 (A/33/1), Sept. 1977, p. 2.

94. Ibid.

95. Ibid., Sept. 1980, p. 10.

96. Ibid., GAOR(XXXVII), Supp. No. 1 (A/37/1), Sept. 1982, p. 1.

97. Ibid., 3.

98. Ibid., 9.

CHAPTER 8: Filling the Void

1. M. Gerner, "The Brain and Behavior: Casting Light into the Black Box," *Psychological Reports*, 49 (1981): 511.

2. G.A. Res. 906(IX), 10 Dec. 1954.

3. Arthur W. Rovine, *The First Fifty Years: The Secretary-General in World Politics, 1920–1970* (Leyden, 1970), 244.

4. Trygve Lie, *In the Cause of Peace* (New York, 1954), 353.

5. Brian Urquhart, *Hammarskjold* (New York, 1972), 98.

6. Ibid.

7. Ibid., 101.

8. The six established organs are: the Security Council, General Assembly, Economic and Social Council, Trusteeship Council, International Court of Justice and Secretariat. U.N. Charter, art. 7(1).

9. The substance of these talks is set out in fascinating detail in Urquhart, *Hammarskjold*, 104–13.

10. Private letter of Dag Hammarskjold to Uno Willers, quoted, ibid., 117.

11. The first four releases were announced on May 30, 1955. The release of the remainder was announced on Aug. 1, 1955 (ibid., 122, 126).

12. Ibid., 131.

13. Unpublished. Quoted, ibid., 124.

14. Ibid., 96.

15. S.C. Res. 113, 4 April 1956.

16. Rovine, *The First Fifty Years*, 285.

17. G.A. Res. 998(ES-I), 4 Nov. 1956.

18. Rovine, *The First Fifty Years*, 289.

19. U.N. Doc. A/3289, 4 Nov. 1956.

20. U.N. Doc. A/3302, 6 Nov. 1956.

21. Rovine, *The First Fifty Years*, 291.

22. S.C. Res. 128, 11 June 1958.

23. Urquhart, *Hammarskjold*, 264.

24. Cited, ibid., 265.

25. Ibid., 268.

26. G.A. Res. 1752(XVII), 21 Dec. 1962. The resolution authorized the Secretary-General to carry out the agreement between the Republic of Indonesia and the Kingdom of the Netherlands concerning West New Guinea (West Irian). This agreement provided for a temporary U.N. government (see Chapter 5).

27. S.C. Res. 186, 4 March 1964.

28. Ibid., 7.

29. S.C. Res. 210, 6 Sept. 1965.

30. Rovine, *The First Fifty Years*, 387. The United Nations India-Pakistan Observation Mission (UNIPOM) was disbanded by the Secretary-General in March 1966 (p. 389).

31. S.C. Res. 340, 25 Oct. 1973. In that instance, however, the Security Council did approve specifically the selection of UNEF II interim commander, General Siilasvuo. Decision of S.C., 1750th Mtg., 25 Oct. 1973, p. 15; however, the approving measures proposed by the Secretary-General in U.N. Doc. S/11049, 25 Oct. 1973. See further decision of S.C., 1751st Mtg., 26 Oct. 1973, p. 23, on transfer of additional troops from Cyprus. The Council also limited its authorization of UNEF II to six months, in S.C. Res. 341, 27 Oct. 1973.

32. Kurt Waldheim, *The Challenge of Peace* (New York, 1980), 60–61. The Security Council Resolution urging Waldheim to intervene personally in the stalled negotiations is S.C. Res. 367, 12 March 1975. The guidelines are found in U.N. Doc. S/12323, 30 April 1977.

33. See para. 6 of S.C. Res. 367, 12 March 1975.

34. See Report of the Secretary-General on the Work of the Organization, Sept. 1977, GAOR(XXXII), Supp. No. 1 (A/32/1), p. 4 (hereafter: Annual Report of S.G.).

35. Annual Report of S.G., Sept. 1981, GAOR(XXXVI), Supp. No. 1(A/36/1), p. 4.

36. G.A. Res. 1004(ES-II), 4 Nov. 1956.

37. GAOR(XI), 586th Plenary Mtg., 21 Nov. 1956, p. 170.

38. G.A. Res. 1131(XI), 12 Dec. 1956.

39. G.A. Res. 3458A(XXX), 10 Dec. 1975.

40. G.A. Res. 3458B(XXX), 10 Dec. 1975.

41. G.A. Res. 3458A(XXX), 10 Dec. 1975.

42. For a fuller account, see Thomas M. Franck, "The Stealing of the Sahara," 70 *Am. Jour. Intl. Law*, 70 (Oct. 1976): 694.

43. S.C. Res. 384, 22 Dec. 1975. See also para. 5 of G.A. Res. 3485(XXX), 12 Dec. 1975.

44. Annual Report of S.G., Aug. 1976, GAOR(XXXI), Supp. No. 1A (A/31/1/Add. 1), p. 3.

45. S.C. Res. 457, 4 Dec. 1979.

46. U.N. Doc. S/13646, 25 Nov. 1979.

47. S.C. Res. 457, 4 Dec. 1979.

48. Kurt Waldheim, *Building the Future Order* (New York, 1980), 37.

49. U.N. Doc. S/13704, 22 Dec. 1979.

50. S.C. Res. 461, 31 Dec. 1979. The resolution threatened in para. 6 that "in the event of non-compliance . . . effective measures under Articles 39 and 41 of the Charter" would be adopted. Articles 39 and 41 provide for collective economic sanctions.

51. *New York Times*, Dec. 31, 1979, p. A5.

52. Ibid.

53. *New York Times*, Jan. 1, 1980, p. 6.

54. Ibid., Dec. 31, 1979, p. A1.

55. Annual Report of S.G., GAOR(XXXV), Supp. No. 1(A/35/1), Sept. 1980, p. 3.

56. *New York Times*, Jan. 5, 1980, p. 4.

57. Ibid.

58. Waldheim, *The Challenge of Peace*, 47–48.

59. Annual Report of S.G., Sept. 1981, pp. 3–4.

60. See, for example, his speech to the Non-aligned Summit Conference in New Delhi, 8 March 1983. U.N. Press Release SG/SM/3388, 8 March 1983.

61. *New York Times*, May 13, 1983, p. A11.

62. Ibid., June 22, 1983, p. A12.

63. Ibid.

64. Paras. 10 and 11 of G.A. Res. 34/22(XXXIV), 14 Nov. 1979.

65. Annual Report of S.G., Sept. 1981, p. 4.

66. U.N. Press Release, 8 March 1983.

67. G.A. Res. ES-6/2, 14 Jan. 1980.

68. G.A. Res. 35/37, 20 Nov. 1980.

69. Annual Report of S.G., Sept. 1980, p. 3.

70. Ibid., Sept. 1981, p. 4.

71. U.N. Press Release SG/SM/3372, 17 Jan. 1983.

72. U.N. Press Release SG/1823, 3 Feb. 1983, p. 1.

73. U.N. Press Release SG/1824, 9 Feb. 1983, p. 1.

74. Ibid. See also U.N. Press Release WS/1114, 11 Feb. 1983, p. 2.

75. U.N. Press Release SG/SM/3382/Rev. 1, 15 Feb. 1983, p. 1.

76. *New York Times*, April 24, 1983, p. 10.

77. Ibid.

78. Selig S. Harrison, "Nearing a Pullout from Afghanistan," *New York Times*, June 7, 1983, p. A23.

79. Sabah Kushkaki, "Afghans Will Fight On," *New York Times*, June 22, 1983, p. A27.

80. Ibid., June 25, 1983, p. 3.

81. Wilder Foote, ed., *Dag Hammarskjold—Servant of Peace: A Selection of His Speeches and Statements* (New York, 1962), 264.

82. Joseph P. Lash, "Dag Hammarskjold's Conception of His Office," *International Organization*, 16 (1962): 551, 553.

83. SCOR, 1st Year, 70th Mtg., 20 Sept. 1946, p. 404.

84. Rovine, *The First Fifty Years*, 227; Evan Luard, *A History of the United Nations*, Vol. 1 (New York, 1982), 347.

85. Rovine, *The First Fifty Years*, 227–28.
86. Luard, A *History of the United Nations*, 347.
87. Rovine, *The First Fifty Years*, 244–45.
88. Urquhart, *Hammarskjold*, 166–73.
89. Ibid., 174.
90. Ibid.
91. SCOR, 13th Year, 835th Mtg., 21 July 1958, pp. 6–9. Sobolev had tried to amend the resolution to provide for immediate U.S. withdrawal but including provision for increasing the size of UNOGIL; SCOR, 13th Year, 837th Mtg., 22 July 1958, pp. 2–3.
92. SCOR, 13th Year, 837th Mtg., 22 July 1958, p. 4.
93. Ibid.
94. Ibid.
95. Urquhart, *Hammarskjold*, 286.
96. The report is U.N. Doc. S/4236, 5 Nov. 1959, pp. 1–32.
97. Urquhart, *Hammarskjold*, 351.
98. Ibid., 352.
99. Unpublished. Quoted, ibid.
100. Ibid., 352–53.
101. Foote, *Dag Hammarskjold*, 264.
102. SCOR, 16th Year, 962nd Mtg., 22 July 1961, pp. 1–4.
103. S.C. Res. 164, 22 July 1961.
104. Urquhart, *Hammarskjold*, 533.
105. Ibid., 534.
106. Charles deGaulle, *Mémoires d'Espoir—Le Renouveau 1958-1962* (Paris, 1970), 118.
107. U.N. Doc. S/4894 and Add. 1, 27 July 1961.
108. U.N. Doc. S/5298, 29 April 1963, pp. 1–3.
109. S.C. Res. 179, 11 June 1963.
110. Rovine, *The First Fifty Years*, 376.
111. *United Nations Review*, Oct. 1963, pp. 14–15.
112. U.N. Doc. S/5182, 22 Oct. 1962.
113. U.N. Doc. S/5187, 23 Oct. 1962.
114. U.N.Doc. S/5190, 24 Oct. 1962.
115. Rovine, *The First Fifty Years*, 370.
116. U.N. Doc. S/5195, 25 Oct. 1962.
117. SCOR, 17th Year, 1024th Mtg., 24 Oct. 1962, p. 20.
118. Ibid., 21.
119. U.N. Press Release SG/1357, 26 Oct. 1962, p. 1.
120. U.N. Press Release SG/1358, 26 Oct. 1962, p. 2.
121. U.N. Press Release SG/1357, 26 Oct. 1962, p. 2.
122. David L. Larson, ed., *The "Cuban Crisis" of 1962, Selected Documents and Chronology* (Boston, 1963), 155–207.
123. U.N. Press Release SG/1360, 28 Oct. 1962.
124. *New York Times*, Oct. 28, 1962, p. 31. See also: Rovine, *The First Fifty Years*, 374.
125. U.N. Doc. S/5227, 7 Jan. 1963.
126. S.C. Res. 211, 20 Sept. 1965.
127. SCOR, 20th Year, 1247th Mtg., 28 Oct. 1965.
128. Remark made off the record to the author.

129. For an account of this exercise of "good offices" see Vratislav Pechota, *The Quiet Approach: A Study of the Good Offices Exercised by the United Nations Secretary-General in the Cause of Peace* (New York, 1972), 45.

130. S.C. Res. 278, 11 May 1970.

131. U.N. Doc. S/9737, 4 April 1970, p. 1.

132. Waldheim, *The Challenge of Peace*, 1–2; see the *New York Times*, Nov. 13, 1977, p. A3; Dec. 16, 1977, p. A7; *The Times* (London), Dec. 21, 1977, p. 5; *New York Times*, Dec. 24, 1977, p. 2; U.N. Press Release SG/SM/2521/Rev. 1, 14 Dec. 1977, p. 1.

133. T. T. B. Koh, "The United Nations: Perception and Reality." Speech to a meeting of Asian mass media, sponsored by the U.N. Department of Public Information, Manila, 12–14 May 1983, p. 14 (mimeo). *New York Times*, July 22, 1979, p. 1. See Memorandum of understanding, 30 May 1979, between the Government of the Socialist Republic of Viet Nam and the United Nations High Commissioner for Refugees (UNHCR) concerning the departure of persons from the Socialist Republic of Viet Nam. U.N. Doc. A/C.3/34/7, 2 Nov. 1979, Annex; the announcement of the moratorium on expulsions—two-thirds of which were ethnic Chinese—by sea was made by Waldheim in a press conference at the end of the Geneva meeting, U.N. Press Release SG/REF/8, 23 July 1979, p. 1. In a dissonant note, officials of the U.N. High Commission for Refugees were quoted as dissociating themselves from the agreement and expressing distaste for its provisions limiting the right of Vietnamese to flee their country (ibid.).

134. Koh, "The United Nations," 1.

135. Annual Report of S.G., Sept. 1981, pp. 3–4.

136. *New York Times*, Oct. 24, 1982, Sec. IV, p. E3.

137. G.A. Res. 492(V), 1 Nov. 1950. The resolution was adopted by a vote of 46 to 5, with 8 abstentions, see GAOR(V), 298th Plenary Mtg., 1 Nov. 1950, p. 289

138. Ibid., 290.

139. *New York Times*, May 27, 1964, p. 1.

140. Ibid., July 9, 1964, p. 1.

141. Ibid., July 26, 1964, p. 9.

142. Ibid., Aug. 7, 1964, p. 1.

143. Chester L. Cooper, *The Lost Crusade, America in Vietnam* (New York, 1970), 326.

144. Ibid.

145. Ibid., 328.

146. *New York Times*, Feb. 25, 1965, p. 1.

147. Ibid.

148. Ibid., Feb. 26, 1965, p. 1.

149. Ibid., 2.

150. Ibid., 2.

151. Cooper, *The Lost Crusade*, 328.

152. Ibid.

153. *New York Times*, March 9, 1965, pp. 1, 4.

154. Ibid., 4.

155. Ibid., March 10, 1965, p. 40.

156. Ibid., March 11, 1965, p. 2.

157. Eric Sevareid, "The Final Troubled Hours of Adlai Stevenson," *Look*, Nov. 30, 1965, p. 81.

158. Ibid., 84.

159. *New York Review of Books*, Nov. 17, 1966, p. 8.
160. David Kraslow and Stuart H. Loory, *The Secret Search for Peace in Vietnam* (New York, 1968), esp. 91ff.
161. *New York Times*, April 12, 1965, p. 1.
162. Ibid.
163. Ibid., April 27, 1965, p. 6.
164. Joseph P. Lash, *Dag Hammarskjold: Custodian of the Brush-Fire Peace* (New York, 1961), 143. See also Urquhart, *Hammarskjold*, 353.
165. Lash, *Dag Hammarskjold*, 143.
166. For an eloquent example, see Annual Report of S.G., GAOR(XXXIV), Supp. No. 1 (A/34/1), Sept. 1979, p. 1.
167. Ibid.
168. *New York Times*, July 13, 1983, p. A7; U.N. Press Release SG/SM/3446, 14 July 1983, p. 1, renders the second sentence: "I mean, if you want to ask others for help, you have to start by helping yourself . . . We have to start by putting order in our own house before we ask for help from the developed countries."
169. U.N. Press Release SG/1307, 30 Aug. 1962, p. 1.
170. Rovine, *The First Fifty Years*, 349.

CHAPTER 9: Unfulfilled by UNIFIL

1. U.N. Charter, art. 33(1).
2. Art. 34.
3. Art. 39.
4. Art. 33(1).
5. Art. 34.
6. Art. 36(1).
7. Art. 37(2).
8. Art. 41.
9. Art. 42.
10. Art. 43(1) and (2).
11. Art. 45.
12. Art. 47(1) and (2).
13. Art. 48(1).
14. See Ruth B. Russell, *A History of the United Nations Charter* (Washington, 1958), 464–72, 646–50, 657–78, 713–49.
15. Ibid., 663–64.
16. Ibid.
17. The Five-Power San Francisco Declaration on the veto power. Statement of the Delegations to the San Francisco Conference of the Governments of the United States, the United Kingdom, the Soviet Union and the Republic of China, with which the Delegation of France associated itself. San Francisco, 7 June 1945, UNCIO Doc. 852, III/1/37(1), to be found in United Nations Conference on International Organizations, Vol. 11, pp. 711–14.
18. U.N. Charter, art. 27(3).
19. For further discussion, see: Evan Luard, *A History of the United Nations*, Vol. 1 (New York, 1982), 47–48.
20. San Francisco Declaration, para. 4.
21. Luard, *A History of the United Nations*, 193.

22. S.C. Res. 54, 15 July 1948.

23. S.C. Res. 84, 7 July 1950.

24. S.C. Res. 253, 29 May 1968; S.C. Res. 277, 18 March 1970.

25. S.C. Res. 418, 4 Nov. 1977.

26. The Amendments were adopted as G.A. Res. 1992(XVIII), 17 Dec. 1963. Ratification by a sufficient number of states occurred on 31 Aug. 1965, see U.N. Doc. A/6019, 27 Sept. 1965, Annex, pp. 1–3.

27. For an interesting discussion of this event, and Secretary-General Dag Hammarskjold's disapproval of the tactic, see Brian Urquhart, *Hammarskjold* (New York, 1972), 344–45.

28. SCOR, 5th Year, 507th Mtg., 29 Sept. 1950, pp. 6–7.

29. S.C. Res. 502, 3 April 1982.

30. U.N. Yearbook, 1971, p. 144. The memorandum was not recorded in the documents of the Security Council.

31. Ibid., 146–50.

32. S.C. Res. 303, 6 Dec. 1971.

33. S.C. Res. 307, 21 Dec. 1971.

34. *New York Times*, Aug. 10, 1971, p. 1.

35. UNYOM was established by S.C. Res. 179, 11 June 1963; UNIPOM was authorized by S.C. Res. 211, 20 Sept. 1965; UNDOF was established by S.C. Res. 350, 31 May 1974.

36. SCOR, 28th Year, 1743rd Mtg., 8 Oct. 1973, p. 15.

37. *New York Times*, Oct. 8, 1973, p. 15.

38. Henry A. Kissinger, *Years of Upheaval* (Boston, 1982), 471.

39. *New York Times*, Oct. 10, 1973, p. 46.

40. Ibid., Oct. 11, 1973, p. 19.

41. U.N. Doc. S/11021, 11 Oct. 1973, p. 2. See also SCOR, 28th Year, 1745th Mtg., 11 Oct. 1973, p. 1.

42. *The Times* (London), Oct. 15, 1973, p. 10.

43. *New York Times*, Oct. 20, 1973, p. 12; see also Oct. 22, 1973, pp. 1, 21.

44. S.C. Res. 338, 22 Oct. 1973.

45. Ibid.; see also SCOR, 28th Year, 1747th Mtg., 21 Oct. 1973, pp. 1–2.

46. SCOR, 28th Year, 1747th Mtg., 21 Oct. 1973, p. 12.

47. Ibid., 2.

48. Kissinger, *Years of Upheaval*, 570.

49. S.C. Res. 339, 23 Oct. 1973.

50. Kissinger, *Years of Upheaval*, 572.

51. *New York Times*, Oct. 25, 1973, p. 1.

52. Kissinger, *Years of Upheaval*, 578.

53. Ibid., 580.

54. *New York Times*, Oct. 25, 1973, p. 1.

55. Kissinger, *Years of Upheaval*, 584–89.

56. Ibid., 592. See also Marvin Kalb and Bernard Kalb, "Twenty Days in October," *New York Times Magazine*, June 23, 1974, pp. 62–64; SCOR, 28th Year, 1749th Mtg., 24 Oct. 1973, pp. 1–18.

57. SCOR, 28th Year, 1750th Mtg., 25 Oct. 1973, p. 11.

58. S.C. Res. 340, 25 Oct. 1973.

59. U.N. Doc. S/11049, 25 Oct. 1973, p. 1.

60. SCOR, 28th Year, 1750th Mtg., 25 Oct. 1973, p. 15.

61. *New York Times*, Oct. 26, 1973, p. 19.

62. SCOR, 28th Year, Supp. (S/11052/Rev. 1), 1973, p. 91.

63. Ibid., 92.

64. *New York Times*, Oct. 27, 1973, p. 30.

65. U.N. Doc. S/11198, 18 Jan. 1974, Annex, pp. 2–3.

66. Ibid., p. 2, arts. 2–5.

67. *New York Times*, Dec. 23, 1973, p. 5.

68. The materials in this abbreviated account of the United Nations Operation in the Congo are taken from: Thomas M. Franck and John Carey, *The Legal Aspects of the United Nations Action in the Congo*, Hammarskjold Forum Papers, Lyman Tondel, Jr., ed. (Dobbs Ferry, N.Y., 1963), 11–43.

69. Keesing's Contemporary Archives, p. 18193A.

70. U.N. Doc. S/4382, 13 July 1960, p. 1.

71. U.N. Doc. S/4381, 13 July 1960, p. 1.

72. SCOR, 15th Year, 873rd Mtg., 13 July 1960, p. 5.

73. Ibid., 42.

74. S.C. Res. 143, 14 July 1960.

75. S.C. Res. 157, 17 Sept. 1960.

76. S.C. Res. 143, 14 July 1960.

77. S.C. Res. 426, 19 March 1978. For the vote, see SCOR, 33rd Year, 2075th Mtg., 19 March 1978, p. 2.

78. U.N. Doc. S/12611, 19 March 1978, p. 3. This set of guidelines was adopted by the Council in S.C. Res. 426, 19 March 1978.

79. Ibid.

80. SCOR, 33rd Year, 2075th Mtg., 19 March 1978, pp. 1, 2.

81. *New York Times*, March 21, 1978, p. 16.

82. U.N. Doc. S/12620/Add. 5, 13 June 1978, pp. 4–5.

83. See, for example, S.C. Res. 429, 31 May 1978.

84. Ibid.

85. *New York Times*, July 19, 1983, p. B3.

86. Interview with Mr. Y.Z. Qiu, Press Officer of the Mission of China to the U.N., conducted by Mr. J. Lehrman, August 3, 1983 (telephone).

87. The resolution establishing the Force and calling for negotiations is S.C. Res. 186, 4 March 1964. The report criticizing lack of negotiations is Report of the Secretary-General on UNFICYP, 12 June 1967, U.N. Doc. S/7969, 13 June 1967, p. 1.

88. Ibid.

89. U.N. Doc. S/11353/Add. 7, 25 July 1974, p. 3.

90. U.N. Doc. S/11353/Add. 12, 31 July 1974, p. 2.

91. S.C. Res. 357, 14 Aug. 1974; S.C. Res. 358, 15 Aug. 1974; S.C. Res. 359, 15 Aug. 1974.

92. S.C. Res. 360, 16 Aug. 1974.

93. G.A. Res. 34/65B, 29 Nov. 1979.

94. Peace Treaty between the Arab Republic of Egypt and the State of Israel, Annex I, Protocol Concerning Israeli Withdrawal and Security Arrangements, Article VI.

95. Quoted in Annual Report of the Director General, Multinational Force and Observers, Rome, April 25, 1983, p. 5.

96. Ibid.

97. Ibid., 6.

98. Ibid., 12.

99. U.N. Doc. S/9835, 12 June 1970, p. 1.

100. U.N. Doc. S/PV. 1555, 21 Oct. 1970, p. 1.

101. The Independent Commission on Disarmament and Security Issues, *Common Security, A Blueprint for Survival* (New York, 1982), 161–64.

102. Interview with Ambassador Nabil El-Araby of Egypt (New York, Nov. 3, 1982).

103. Interview with Ambassador William C. Sherman of the United States (New York, Nov. 9, 1982).

CHAPTER 10: The General Assembly and the U.S. National Interest

1. The reference is to the first part of the session only, which dealt with all but a few items (e.g., Cyprus) left to the second session convened the following year.

2. "The United Nations' Campaign Against Israel," The Heritage Foundation Backgrounder, UN Assessment Project (Washington, 1983), 1.

3. For example, G.A. Res. 37/40, 3 Dec. 1982; G.A. Res. 37/46, 3 Dec. 1982. For the votes thereon, see, respectively, U.N. Doc. A/37/PV.90, 3 Dec. 1982, pp. 13–15, and U.N. Doc. A/37/PV.90, 6 Dec. 1982, pp. 23–24.

4. Compiled from: Resolutions and Decisions Adopted by the General Assembly During the First Part of Its Thirty-seventh Session, 21 Sept. to 21 Dec. 1982, U.N. Press Release GA/6787, 4 Jan. 1983.

5. G.A. Res. 37/98A, 13 Dec. 1982.

6. G.A. Res. 37/94B, 10 Dec. 1982.

7. G.A. Res. 37/137, 17 Dec. 1982.

8. G.A. Res. 37/6, 28 Oct. 1982.

9. G.A. Res. 37/37, 29 Nov. 1982. For the vote, see U.N. Doc. A/37/PV.82, 30 Nov. 1982, pp. 38–40. The same resolution was passed by an even larger majority—116 to 20, with 17 abstentions—in 1983 as G.A. Res. 38/29, 23 Nov. 1984. For the vote, see U.N. Doc. A/38/PV.69, 1 Dec. 1983, p. 22.

10. G.A. Res. 36/148, 16 Dec. 1981. For passage, see U.N. Doc. A/36/PV.100, 19 Dec. 1981, pp. 57–60. See also G.A. Res. 37/121, 16 Dec. 1982; for passage, see U.N. Doc. A/37/PV.108, 4 Jan 1983, p. 28.

11. G.A. Res. 35/124, 11 Dec. 1980; G.A. Res. 36/148, 16 Dec. 1981; G.A. Res. 37/186, 17 Dec. 1982. For passage, see, respectively: U.N. Doc. A/35/PV.92, 13 Dec. 1980, pp. 172–75; U.N. Doc. A/36/PV.100, 19 Dec. 1981, pp. 57–60; U.N. Doc. A/37/PV.110, 8 Jan. 1983, p. 161.

12. G.A. Res. 34/180, 18 Dec. 1979; G.A. Res. 37/61, 3 Dec. 1982. For passage, see, respectively, U.N. Doc. A/34/PV.107, 29 Dec. 1979, pp. 24–30; and U.N. Doc. A/37/PV.90, 6 Dec. 1982, p. 46.

13. G.A. Res. 37/168, 17 Dec. 1982.

14. G.A. Res. 3452(XXX), 9 Dec. 1975; G.A. Res. 37/193, 18 Dec. 1982. For passage, see, respectively, U.N. Doc. A/PV.2433, 9 Dec. 1975, p. 77; and U.N. Doc. A/37/PV111, 8 Jan. 1983, p. 12.

15. Where a resolution groups separate resolutions by headings (A, B, C, etc.), these are counted separately.

16. Interview with the author (Sept. 1983).

17. W.A. Mozart, "Abduction from the Seraglio," Act III, scene 4.

18. U.N. Yearbook, 1968, p. 714. See also G.A. Res. 2430(XXIII), 18 Dec. 1968, para. 4.

19. U.N. Doc. A/37/23 (Part II), 9 Sept. 1982 (Appendix).

20. U.N. Doc. A/37/501, 11 Oct. 1982 (Annex).

21. U.N. Press Release GA/6738, 22 Nov. 1982.

22. GAOR(XXXII), Supp. No. 23(A/32/23/Rev. 1), Vol. IV, ch. XXVII, Annex.

23. U.N. Doc. A/33/23/Add. 5, 16 Oct. 1978, pp. 122–23.

24. G.A. Res. 37/26, 23 Nov. 1982. Draft Res. proposed by the Special Committee to the 38th General Assembly, U.N. Doc. A/38/23 (Part VI), 10 Oct. 1983, p. 62.

25. U.N. Doc. A/AC.109/639, 23 Oct. 1980.

26. U.N. Doc. A/33/23/Add. 4, 23 Oct. 1978, p. 94.

27. U.N. Doc. A/AC.109/679, 16 Oct. 1981 and Add. 1, 30 Oct. 1981.

28. Ibid., 13, 15, 17, 25, 35.

29. Ibid., 35.

30. Interview with the author.

31. G.A. Res. 37/20, 23 Nov. 1982; for the 1983 draft resolution, see U.N. Doc. A/38/23 (Part VI), 10 Oct. 1983, p. 22.

32. U.N. Yearbook, 1977, pp. 873–74.

33. G.A. Res. 32/28, 28 Nov. 1977.

34. G.A. Res. 33/33, 13 Dec. 1978.

35. G.A. Res. 35/22, 11 Nov. 1980.

36. U.N. Doc. A/36/23/Rev. 1, 30 Oct. 1981, ch. XVI, p. 134.

37. U.N. Doc. A/C.4/36/L.22, 9 Nov. 1981.

38. GAOR(XXXVI), Fourth Committee, 24th Mtg., 18 Nov. 1981.

39. Ibid.

40. U.N. Doc. A/36/677/Add. 2, 24 Nov. 1981.

41. G.A. Res. 36/63, 25 Nov. 1981.

42. G.A. Res. 37/21, 23 Nov. 1982.

43. Draft contained in U.N. Doc. A/38/23 (Part VI), 10 Oct. 1983, p. 29.

44. Para. 6 of G.A. Res. 37/21, 23 Nov. 1982.

45. G.A. Res. 37/35, 23 Nov. 1982, paras. 4, 10.

46. Ibid., para. 12. See also draft resolution presented by the Special Committee to the 38th General Assembly. U.N. Doc. A/38/23 (Part III), ch. IV, 23 Sept. 1983, p. 7.

47. Text of the Agreement is in U.N. Yearbook, 1946-47, p. 398. It was adopted unanimously by the Security Council on 12 April 1947, SCOR, 2nd Year, S/318.

48. Trusteeship Agreement, art. 5.

49. Compact of Free Association, Office for Micronesian Status Negotiations (Washington, 1983). The Compact is intended to be applicable, albeit somewhat differently, to the three associated states. The provisions for termination are in Title Four, Article IV of the Compact and in other articles enumerated therein.

50. See, for example, SCOR, 37th Year, Special Supp. No. 1 (S/15705), 1982. Also, Report of the United Nations Visiting Mission To Observe the Plebiscite in Palau, Trust Territory of the Pacific Islands, Feb. 1983, TCOR, 50th Sess., Supp. No. 3 (T/1851), 1983.

51. U.S.S.R. Letter to the President of the Security Council, U.N. Doc. S/13871, 21 Feb. 1980. See also Bulgarian Note Verbale, U.N. Doc. S/13913, 28 April 1980 and German Democratic Republic Letter, U.N. Doc. S/13914, 28 April 1980.

52. SCOR, 37th Year, Special Supp. No. 1 (S/13705), 1982.

53. The Trusteeship Council consists of China, France, the U.K., the U.S.A., the U.S.S.R. China has consistently refused to participate.

54. For a discussion of causes of delay, see the *New York Times*, Feb. 18, 1983, p. A16; Feb. 19, 1983, p. 5. For evidence that the Council regards the process of devolution as an "eminently satisfactory spectacle," see the remarks of the British, French, and U.S. members at the May 27, 1983, meeting of the Trusteeship Council. U.N. Press

Release WS/1129, 27 May 1983, p. 7. For the Soviet dissent, see U.N. Press Release WS/1132, 17 June 1983, p. 4.

55. Interview with a member of the U.S. delegation to the U.N. (Nov. 9, 1982, New York).

56. See, for example, U.N. Doc. A/AC.109/661, 28 Aug. 1970.

57. See, for example, U.N. Doc. A/37/23 (Part V), 23 Sept. 1982, p. 22.

58. U.N. Doc. A/36/23/Rev. 1, 30 Oct. 1981.

59. U.N. Doc. A/C.4/36/SR.25, 23 Nov. 1981, p. 15.

60. Ibid., 16.

61. Ibid., 17.

62. Ibid., 18.

63. U.N. Doc. A/37/23 (Part V), Add. 2, 11 Oct. 1982.

64. U.N. Doc. A/37/621, and Corr. 1, 18 Nov. 1982.

65. U.N. Doc. A/37/PV.77, 26 Nov. 1982, p. 46.

66. See, for example, U.N. Doc. A/AC.109/L.1493, 10 Oct. 1983.

67. GAOR(VIII), Supp. No. 15 (A/2465), pp. 2–8.

68. G.A. Res. 748(VIII), 27 Nov. 1953.

69. U.N. Yearbook, 1967, p. 622.

70. Ibid., 622–23. The report of the Special Committee to the General Assembly for that year is silent on the subject.

71. GAOR(XXVII), Supp. No. 23 (A/8723/Rev. 1), Vol. 1, ch. 1.

72. Ibid. The Chilean request was dated 25 March 1972.

73. Ibid. The resolution of the Committee is in U.N. Doc. A/AC.109/419, 28 Aug. 1972.

74. G.A. Res. 2908(XXVII), 2 Nov. 1972.

75. U.N. Doc. A/AC.109/L.900, 29 Aug. 1973; GAOR(XXVIII), Supp. No. 23 (A/9023/Rev. 1), Vol. 1 ch. 1.

76. U.N. Doc. A/AC.109/L.1276, 30 Aug. 1978. See also GAOR(XXXIII), Supp. No. 23 (A/33/23/Rev. 1), Vol. 1, ch. 1, pp. 24–36.

77. Ibid.

78. Ibid.

79. Ibid. The same language was adopted the following year (1979): GAOR(XXXIV), Supp. No. 23 (A/34/23/Rev. 1), Vol. 1, ch. 1, pp. 23–26.

80. U.N. Doc. A/34/PV.101, 21 Dec. 1979, pp. 81–83.

81. U.N. Doc. A/34/PV.102, 27 Dec. 1979, pp. 13–15.

82. U.N. Doc. A/AC.109/628, 26 Aug. 1980, pp. 1–3.

83. Ibid.

84. Ibid.

85. U.N. Doc. A/AC.109/PV.1178, 21 Aug. 1980, p. 36.

86. U.N. Doc. A/AC.109/677, 20 Aug. 1981.

87. U.N. Doc. A/AC.109/PV.1200, 1 Sept. 1981, pp. 6–7.

88. U.N. Doc. A/AC.109/PV. 1201, 1 Sept. 1981, pp. 20–21.

89. U.N. Doc. A/36/23 and G.A., A/36/PV.72, 28 Nov. 1981, p. 7.

90. Interview with a senior member of the U.S. delegation to the U.N. (Nov. 9, 1982, New York).

91. U.N. Doc. A/36/L.30, 28 Nov. 1981.

92. U.N. Doc. A/36/PV.79, 3 Dec. 1981, pp. 3–4

93. Interview with Ambassador Sherman, U.S. Mission to the U.N. (Nov. 9, 1982, New York).

94. Statement by Mr. Acevedo, Member, Puerto Rico House of Representatives, A/AC.109/PV.1196, 19 Aug. 1981, p. 36.

95. Statement by Mr. Lopez Pacheco, Gran Oriente Nacional de Puerto Rico, A/AC.109/PV.1196, 19 Aug. 1981, p. 41.

96. U.N. Doc. A/AC.109/PV.1197, 24 Aug. 1981, p. 86.

97. U.N. Doc. A/AC.109/PV. 1198, 25 Aug. 1981, pp. 14–15.

98. U.N. Doc. A/AC.109/PV.1200, 1 Sept. 1981, pp. 23–25.

99. U.N. Doc. A/37/194, 18 Aug. 1982.

100. U.N. Doc. A/37/250, 22 Sept. 1982, p. 7.

101. A/37/PV.4, 24 Sept. 1982, pp. 56-57.

102. Interview with a senior member of the U.S. delegation to the U.N. (Nov. 9, 1982, New York).

103. Interview with a member of the U.S. delegation to the U.N. (Nov. 9, 1982, New York).

104. Ibid.

105. Ibid.

106. U.N. Doc. A/37/PV.4, 25 Sept. 1982, p. 22.

107. U.S. Mission to the U.N. Press Release, USUN 83(82), Oct. 15, 1982.

108. A. Lincoln, *First Inaugural Address* (March 4, 1861), in *Famous Speeches of Abraham Lincoln*, Introduction by William H. Townsend (New Rochelle, N.Y., 1935), 88.

CHAPTER 11: "A Place Where Lies Are Told"

1. G.A. Res. 3379(XXX), 10 Nov. 1975.

2. Albania, Bulgaria, Byelorussia, Cambodia, China, Cuba, Czechoslovakia, German Democratic Republic, Hungary, Laos, Mongolia, Poland, Ukraine, U.S.S.R. U.N. Doc. A/PV.2400, 10 Nov. 1975, p. 146.

3. Afghanistan, Algeria, Bahrain, Bangladesh, Chad, Democratic Yemen, Egypt, Gambia, Guinea, Indonesia, Iran, Iraq, Jordan, Kuwait, Libya, Malaysia, Maldives, Mali, Mauritania, Morocco, Niger, Nigeria, Oman, Pakistan, Qatar, Saudi Arabia, Senegal, Somalia, Sudan, Syria, Tunisia, Turkey, United Arab Emirates, Cameroon, Tanzania, Yemen (ibid.).

4. SCOR, 23rd Year, 1443rd Mtg., 22 Aug. 1968, p. 26.

5. U.N. Doc. A/PV.2400, 10 Nov. 1975, pp. 19–20.

6. Ibid., 27.

7. Ibid., 162.

8. Ibid., 164–65.

9. The quotation is attributed to Ambassador Chaim Herzog, Daniel Patrick Moynihan, *A Dangerous Place* (Boston, 1978), 176.

10. Lima Programme for Mutual Assistance and Solidarity, Lima, Peru, 25 Aug.–30 Aug. 1975. U.N. Doc. NAC/FM/CONF. 5/15, 30 Aug. 1975, p. 4.

11. Report of the Women's Conference of the International Women's Year, Mexico City, 19 June–2 July 1975. E/Conf./66/34, ch. 1, p. 7.

12. U.N. Yearbook, 1975, p. 650.

13. Moynihan, *A Dangerous Place*, 30.

14. U.N. Doc. A/*V.2370, 1 Oct. 1975, pp. 71–72.

15. Moynihan, *A Dangerous Place*, 159.

16. Ibid.

17. Ibid., 161.

18. Ibid. (See also Rules of Procedure of the Assembly of Heads of State and Government, OAU, rule 9.)

19. Ibid., 162.

20. U.N. Doc. A/PV.2400, 10 Nov. 1975, pp. 162–63.

21. Quoted in Moynihan, *A Dangerous Place*, 195–96.

22. See Chapter 2, above.

23. SCOR, 1st Year, Supp. No. 10, Annex 16, pp. 169–90. For an excellent analysis, see Van Coufoudakis, "The United States, the United Nations, and the Greek Question, 1946–1952," in *Greece in the 1940's: A Nation in Crisis*, John O. Iatrides, ed. (Hanover, N.H., 1981), 275ff.

24. S.C. Res. 15, 19 Dec. 1946.

25. U.N. Doc. S/360, 27 May 1947, p. 15. See also the relevant report of the Security Council to the General Assembly, 16 July 1946–15 July 1947, UN Doc. A/366, 21 Aug. 1947, pp. 24–32.

26. *Foreign Relations of the United States*, 1947, Vol. V (Washington, 1972), 238–42.

27. G.A. Res. 109(II), 21 Oct. 1947. (For the vote, see GAOR(II), 100th Plenary Mtg., 21 Oct. 1947, 461–62.)

28. Ibid., para. 4.

29. Ibid., para. 9(I).

30. Ibid., paras. 6 and 8, respectively.

31. G.A. Res. 193(III), 27 Nov. 1948.

32. Ibid., para. 3.

33. Coufoudakis, "The United States, . . . ," 285.

34. G.A. Res. 508(VI), 7 Dec. 1951. The Greek request for UNSCOB's discontinuance is U.N. Doc. A/CN.7/SC.1/52, 27 Nov. 1953, p. 1, and U.N. Doc. A/CN.7/SC.1/55, 17 May 1954, p. 1.

35. G.A. Res. 181(II), 29 Nov. 1947.

36. Paras. 8 and 11, respectively. G.A. Res. 194(III), 11 Dec. 1948. See also para. 1 of G.A. Res. 303(IV), 9 Dec. 1949.

37. Para. 11 of G.A. Res. 194(III), 11 Dec. 1948.

38. G.A. Res. 997(ES-I), 2 Nov. 1956.

39. S.C. Res. 242, 22 Nov. 1967. Para. 1 reads as follows: "1. *Affirms* that fulfillment of Charter principles requires the establishment of just and lasting peace in the Middle East which should include the application of both the following principles: (i) Withdrawal of Israel armed forces from territories occupied in the recent armed conflict; (ii) Termination of all claims or states of belligerency and respect for and acknowledgment of the sovereignty, territorial integrity and political independence of every state in the area and their right to live in peace within secure and recognized boundaries free from threats or acts of force."

40. G.A. Res. 2443(XXIII), 19 Dec. 1968. For an elucidation of this prejudgment, see paras. A, B, and C (ibid.).

41. Para. 3 of G.A. Res. 33/29, 7 Dec. 1978.

42. G.A. Res. 32/20, 25 Nov. 1977.

43. *See* GAOR(XXV), 1,915th Plenary Mtg., 30 Nov. 1970, p. 3, adopting G.A. Res. 2649(XXV), 30 Nov. 1970.

44. For example, G.A. Res. 33/183D, 24 Jan. 1979.

45. The representative of Israel has frequently stated publicly, without being refuted, that his country's trade with South Africa amounts to two-fifths of one percent of South Africa's foreign trade. He has unreservedly denied the charge of Israeli military and

nuclear collaboration with the Republic. He observed that one need only consult the 1977 edition of *African Abstract of Trade Statistics*, published by the government of South Africa, to see the extent of Eastern Europe's trade with South Africa.

46. Sometimes the U.S., France, West Germany, and Japan are linked to Israel in these accusations. G.A. Res. 32/35, 28 Nov. 1977.

47. G.A. Res. 3237(XXIX), 22 Nov. 1974.

48. G.A. Res. 3236(XXIX), 22 Nov. 1974.

49. Ibid., para. 1.

50. G.A. Res. 3376(XXX), 10 Nov. 1975.

51. G.A. decision 31/318, 22 Dec. 1976.

52. Para. 3 of G.A. Res. 34/70, 6 Dec. 1979. This resolution had its origins in an earlier version—passed by the Assembly after Egypt's President Anwar Sadat had visited Jerusalem—which said "that peace is indivisible," in a thinly veiled effort to preclude Israeli-Egyptian peace negotiations. G.A. Res. 32/20, 25 Nov. 1977. Egypt also voted in favor of that resolution.

53. U.N. Doc. A/34/PV.92, 12 Dec. 1979, p. 46.

54. G.A. Res. 2949(XXVII), 8 Dec. 1972.

55. United Nations Treaty Series, Vol. 75, pp. 970–73.

56. G.A. Res. 3092B(XXVIII), 7 Dec. 1973.

57. G.A. Res. 3414(XXX), 5 Dec. 1975. This has been confirmed annually, for example, G.A. Res. 31/61, 9 Dec. 1976.

58. G.A. Res. 3525A(XXX), 15 Dec. 1975.

59. G.A. Res. 36/226A, 17 Dec. 1981.

60. Para. 10 of G.A. Res. 4(ES-VII), 30 April 1982.

61. Preamble of G.A. Res. 34/44, 23 Nov. 1979.

62. Para. 11 of G.A. Res. 4(ES-VII), 30 April 1982.

63. U.N. Doc. A/38/PV.34, 24 Oct. 1983, p. 12.

64. Ibid., 13–15.

65. The vote is cited in *Congressional Record* (April 3, 1984), S3659. See also U.S. Dept. of State, *Report to Congress on Voting Practices in the United Nations*, Feb. 24, 1984, Table 9, Appendix; Table 10, however, lists 35 abstainers.

66. U.N. Doc. A/37/PV.99, 16 Dec. 1982, p. 34.

67. Interview with a member of the U.S. delegation (New York, Oct. 14, 1982).

68. G.A. Res. 37/40, 3 Dec. 1982.

69. U.N. Press Release GA/SPC/1691, 3 Dec. 1982, p. 4.

70. Ibid. For evidence of U.S. reaction to the Golan Heights issue, see *New York Times*, Jan. 5, 1982, p. 45. The U.S. also supported a Security Council resolution that declared illegal the extension of Israeli law to Golan. S.C. Res. 497, 17 Dec. 1981.

71. G.A. Res. 3210(XXIX), 14 Oct. 1974.

72. For a discussion, see Julius Stone, *Israel and Palestine: Assault on the Law of Nations* (Baltimore, 1981), 76–77.

73. G.A. Res. 32/40B, 2 Dec. 1977.

74. These studies include: W. Thomas Mallison and Sally V. Mallison, *An International Law Analysis of the Major United Nations Resolutions Concerning the Palestine Question*, U.N. Doc. ST/SG/SER. F/4, 1979, and studies prepared by the Unit's staff: ST/SG/SER. F/1, 2 and 3. Also "prepared for, and under the guidance of, the Committee on the Exercise of the Inalienable Rights of the Palestinian People" are the following titles which do not bear U.N. document numbers: *The Question of the Observance of the Fourth Geneva Convention of 1949 in Gaza and the West Bank Including Jerusalem Occupied by Israel in June 1967* (New York, 1979); *The Status of Jerusalem* (New York,

1979); *The Palestine Question: A Brief History* (New York, 1980); *The International Status of the Palestinian People* (New York, 1981); *The Question of Palestine* (New York, 1981); *The Legal Status of the West Bank and Gaza* (New York, 1982); *Israeli Settlements in Gaza and the West Bank Including Jerusalem: Their Nature and Purpose* (New York, 1982).

75. Typical instances of its partisan propaganda activities in the United States and abroad are to be found in GAOR(XXXVII), Supp. No. 23 (A/37/23/Rev. 1), 1983, pp. 66–79.

76. Stone, *Israel and Palestine*, 79.

77. G.A. Res. 33/28C, 7 Dec. 1978.

78. Charles W. Maynes, "US Power and Influence in the UN of the 80s," in Toby T. Gati, *The US, the UN, and the Management of Global Change* (New York, 1983), 336.

79. Ibid., 338.

80. For example, Dept. of State Authorization Act, F.Y. 1980 and 1981, s.102(a) (2) and 102 (c) (1) and (2).

81. U.N. Doc. A/37/PV.99, 16 Dec. 1982, p. 22.

82. G.A. Res. 34/65D, 12 Dec. 1979.

83. Ibid.

84. U.N. Doc. A/37/485, 20 Oct. 1982, p. 12.

85. Ibid., 13.

86. G.A. Res. 36/146G, 16 Dec. 1981.

87. U.N. Doc. A/37/599, 5 Nov. 1982, p. 2.

88. Ibid., 3.

89. See, for example, U.N. Doc. A/36/648, 10 Nov. 1981, p. 19.

90. *New York Times*, June 20, 1984, p. A4.

91. U.N. Doc. A/37/723, 10 Dec. 1982, p. 20.

92. Ibid.

93. U.N. Doc. A/SPC/37/L.40, 2 Dec. 1982, p. 1.

94. The Geneva Convention Relative to the Protection of Civilian Persons in Time of War.

95. GAOR(XXXVII), Special Political Committee, 44th Mtg., 3 Dec. 1982 (A/SPC/SR.44, 10 Dec. 1982), pp. 11–12.

96. U.N. Doc. A/37/PV.108, 16 Dec. 1982.

97. Moynihan, *A Dangerous Place*, 86.

98. Juliana Geran Pilon, "The United Nations' Campaign Against Israel," Heritage Foundation Backgrounder, UN Assessment Project (Washington, 1983), 9.

99. U.N. Doc. A/37/601, 9 Nov. 1982, pp. 2–4.

100. Telephone interview with Press Assistant to Ambassador Yehuda Z. Blum (Feb. 8, 1983).

101. *New York Times*, Oct. 2, 1983, p. 19.

CHAPTER 12: The Double Standard

1. *New York Times*, Feb. 10, 1984, p. A27.

2. Quoted in Burton Y. Pines, "The U.S. and the U.N.: Time for Reappraisal," The Heritage Foundation Backgrounder, September 29, 1983, p. 10.

3. The motion to close debate passed by 60 in favor with 54 against and 24 abstentions. U.N. Doc. A/38/PV. 43, 5 Nov. 1983, pp. 12–15.

4. G.A. Res. A/RES/38/7, 2 Nov. 1983.

5. U.N. Doc. A/38/PV. 43, 5 Nov. 1983, pp. 45–50.

6. G.A. Res. A/RES/38/7, 2 Nov. 1983.

7. Ibid.

8. U.N. Doc. A/38/PV. 43, 5 Nov. 1983, pp. 98–99.

9. Ibid., 102–3.

10. G.A. Res. 34/22, 14 Nov. 1979.

11. Ibid. For the vote on this resolution, see GAOR(XXXIV), Supp. No. 46 (A/34/46), 1980, p. 294.

12. U.N. Doc. A/34/PV. 67, 14 Nov. 1979, pp. 78–79.

13. G.A. Res. 34/22, 14 Nov. 1979; 35/6, 22 Oct. 1980; 36/5, 21 Oct. 1981; 37/6, 28 Oct. 1982; and 38/3, 27 Oct. 1983.

14. Ibid. For the votes, see, respectively: GAOR(XXXIV), Supp. No. 46 (A/34/46), 1979, p. 294; GAOR(XXXV), Supp. No. 48 (A/35/48), 1980, p. 309; GAOR(XXVI), Supp. No. 51 (A/36/51), 1981, p. 283; GAOR(XXXVII), Supp. No. 51 (A/37/51), 1982, p. 315; U.N. Doc. A/38/PV. 38, 29 Oct. 1983, p. 78.

15. U.N. Doc. A/38/PV. 43, 5 Nov. 1983, p. 45 (Grenada); U.N. Doc. A/38/PV. 38, 29 Oct. 1983, p. 78 (Kampuchea).

16. The Uniting for Peace resolution is G.A. Res. 377(V), 3 Nov. 1950. The Special Session debates are to be found in GAOR, ES-VI, Part I.

17. GAOR (ES-VI), 5th Plenary Mtg., 12 Jan. 1980, p. 78.

18. G.A. Res. (ES-VI), 14 Jan. 1980.

19. GAOR (ES-IV), 7th Plenary Mtg., 14 Jan. 1980, p. 111.

20. Ibid.

21. Ibid.

22. GAOR (ES-IV), 1st Plenary Mtg., 10 Jan. 1980, pp. 8–9.

23. GAOR (ES-IV), 5th Plenary Mtg., 11 Jan. 1980, p. 26.

24. GAOR (ES-IV), 5th Plenary Mtg., 12 Jan. 1980, p. 78.

25. GAOR (ES-IV), 7th Plenary Mtg., 14 Jan. 1980, p. 99.

26. GAOR (ES-IV), 5th Plenary Mtg., 12 Jan. 1980, p. 67.

27. G.A. Res. 35/37, 20 Nov. 1980, passed by a vote of 111 to 22, with 12 abstentions. See GAOR(XXXV), Supp. No. 48 (A/35/48), 1980, p. 310. G.A. Res. 36/34, 22 Nov. 1981, passed by 116 to 23, with 12 abstentions. See GAOR(XXXVI), Supp. No. 51 (A/36/51), 1981, p. 284. G.A. Res. 37/37, 30 Nov. 1982, passed by 114 to 21, with 13 abstentions. See GAOR(XXXVII), Supp. No. 51 (A/37/51), 1982, p. 316. G.A. Res. 38/29, 23 Nov. 1983, passed by 116 to 20, with 17 abstentions. See U.N. Doc. A/38/PV. 69, 1 Dec. 1983, p. 22.

28. U.N. Doc. A/38/PV. 69, 1 Dec. 1983, p. 22.

29. Resolutions on Political and Information Affairs Adopted by the Twelfth Islamic Conference of Foreign Ministers, 1-5 June 1981, Baghdad. U.N. Doc. A/36/421, 12 Aug. 1981, p. 52.

30. In 1983, according to the calculations of the U.S. Mission, 39 countries which voted to condemn the U.S. action in Grenada had failed to vote to condemn the Soviet role in Afghanistan. This includes those who failed to vote, or abstained, on the Afghan resolution. Specifically, it includes Afghanistan, the three nations of Indochina, the three Marxist states of the Caribbean (Cuba, Grenada, and Nicaragua), and eight Marxist states of Eastern Europe. U.S. Dept. of State, *Report to Congress on Voting Practices in the United Nations*, Feb. 24, 1984, Table 14.

31. For a discussion of this assertion of principle over politics, see Thomas M. Franck, "Dulce et Decorum Est: The Strategic Role of Legal Principles in the Falklands War," *Am. Jour. Intl. Law*, 77 (1983): 109. The resolution is S.C. Res. 502, 3 April 1982.

32. For example, Ambassador Javier Chamorro Mora of Nicaragua, who was particularly strident in denunciation of British colonialism. U.N. Doc. S/PV. 2363, 23 May 1982, pp. 16–25.

33. U.N. Doc. S/PV. 2362, 22 May 1982, pp. 41, 46.

34. U.N. Doc. S/PV. 2364, 24 May 1982, pp. 21, 23–26.

35. The resolution was addressed to both India and Pakistan, but since Pakistani troops were not on Indian soil it was obviously aimed at New Delhi. G.A. Res. 2793(XXVI), 7 Dec. 1971.

36. U.N. Doc. A/PV. 2003 and Corr. 1, 7 Dec. 1971, pp. 44–45.

37. G.A. Res. 3292(XXIX), 13 Dec. 1974.

38. G.A. Res. 3458A(XXX), 10 Dec. 1975.

39. U.N. Doc. A/PV. 2435, 10 Dec. 1975, pp. 112–15.

40. The effect, however, was undermined by another resolution passed by the same session, albeit with the narrowest margin of 56 to 42, with 34 abstentions, which *"Takes note"* of the agreement made on Nov. 14, 1975, between Spain, Morocco, and Mauritania, by which Madrid ceded the territory to the two invading African nations. G.A. Res. 3458B(XXX), 10 Dec. 1975.

41. See, for example, Report of the Special Committee on the Situation with Regard to the Implementation of the Declaration on the Granting of Independence to Colonial Countries and Peoples. U.N. Doc. A/38/23 (Part VI), 10 Oct. 1983, p. 5.

42. G.A. Res. 37/28, 23 Nov. 1982, was adopted by 78 to 15, with 50 abstentions. See GAOR(XXXVII), Supp. No. 51 (A/37/51), 1982, p. 316. See also G.A. Res. 38/40, 7 Dec. 1983, adopted without a vote. For passage, see U.N. Doc. A/38/PV. 86, 7 Dec. 1983, p. 7.

43. U.N. Doc. A/PV. 2439, 12 Dec. 1975, p. 38.

44. G.A. Res. 3485(XXX), 12 Dec. 1975.

45. G.A. Res. 31/53, 1 Dec. 1976. For the vote, see GAOR(XXXI), 85th Plenary Mtg., 1 Dec. 1976, p. 1298.

46. The term was used by Senator Kasten of Wisconsin. *Congressional Record* (Senate), 130 (April 5, 1984): S13842.

47. In recent years, the conflict appears to have died down (although it is claimed by Freitlin sources that the continuing civil war in Timor has cost 100,000 lives—a figure which the Indonesians call grossly exaggerated). With a decline in actual fighting, the Assembly's interest has waned. The 1976 majority of 68 to 20, with 49 abstentions (G.A. Res. 31/53, 1 Dec. 1976) had by 1982 withered to a mere 50 to 46, with 50 abstentions (G.A. Res. 37/30, 23 November 1982). For the votes, see, respectively: GAOR(XXXI), Supp. No. 39, Vol. 1 (A/31/39), 1976, p. 219; GAOR(XXXVII), Supp. No. 51 (A/37/51), 1982, p. 316. There was no resolution on Timor in 1983, although the Assembly's Special Committee on Decolonization continued to hold hearings on the situation. GAOR(XXXVII), Supp. No. 23 (A/37/23/Rev. 1), 1983, ch. X. By then, most states, including many in the Third World, no longer saw much point in incurring the wrath of oil-rich Indonesia solely to affirm a principle which, at least in this instance, evidently could not be applied.

48. G.A. Res. 38/10, 11 Nov. 1983.

49. G.A. Res. 38/180E, 19 Dec. 1983.

50. Ibid.

51. U.N. Charter, arts. 13(1), 55, 62, 68, 76.

52. Art. 13(1) (b).

53. Art. 55(c).

54. Art. 60. See also Chapter X, below.

55. *Reform of the United Nations: An Analysis of the President's Proposals and Their Comparison with Proposals of Other Countries*, Prepared for the Committee on Foreign Relations, Congressional Research Service, Oct. 1979 (Washington, 1979), p. 63.

56. Nigel S. Rodley, "The Development of United Nations Activities in the Field of Human Rights and the Role of Non-Governmental Organizations," in Toby T. Gati, ed., *The U.S., the U.N., and the Management of Global Change* (New York, 1983), 263.

57. *Reform of the United Nations*, 63.

58. Ibid., 65.

59. G.A. Res. 217(III), 10 Dec. 1948.

60. Rodley, "The Development of United Nations Activities . . . ," 264.

61. The Covenants were adopted by G.A. Res. 2200A(XXI), 16 Dec. 1966.

62. See arts. 12, 18, 19, 21, and 22 of International Covenant on Civil and Political Rights, GAOR(XXI), Supp. No. 16 (A/6316), 1967, pp. 54–55. The Covenant entered into force on 23 March 1976.

63. See, ibid., art. 4, p. 53.

64. Prevention and punishment of the crime of genocide. G.A. Res. 260(III), 9 Dec. 1975. "Convention on the Prevention and Punishment of the Crime of Genocide," United Nations Treaty Series, Vol. 78, p. 277.

65. Declaration on the Elimination of All Forms of Racial Discrimination. G.A. Res. 1904(XVIII), 20 Nov. 1963. "Convention on the Elimination of All Forms of Racial Discrimination," United Nations Treaty Series, Vol. 660, p. 195.

66. International Convention on Suppression and Punishment of the Crime of Apartheid, G.A. Res. 3068(XVIII), 30 Nov. 1973.

67. G.A. Res. 3059(XVIII), 2 Nov. 1973.

68. G.A. Res. 3452(XXX), 9 Dec. 1975.

69. G.A. Res. 34/169, 17 Dec. 1979.

70. G.A. Res. 37/194, 18 Dec. 1982.

71. For proposals along these lines, see: L.B. Sohn, "Human Rights: Their Implementation and Supervision by the United Nations," in T. Meron, *Human Rights in International Law: Legal and Policy Issues*, Vol. II (Oxford, 1984), 369; T. Meron, *Remarks*, 1983 Proceedings of the Annual Mtg. of the Am. Soc. of Intl. Law (to be published).

72. Report of the Human Rights Committee, GAOR(XXXVIII), Supp. No. 40 (A/38/40), 1983, p. 91.

73. Rodley, "The Development of United Nations Activities," 267.

74. Francis Wolf, "Human Rights and the International Labour Organisation," in Meron, *Human Rights in International Law*, II: 273.

75. ECOSOC Res. 1503(XLVIII), 27 May 1970.

76. Ibid., art. 6(a) and (b).

77. Ibid., arts. 7(c) and 8. For the relevant subsidiary documentation and practice, see M.E. Tardu, *Human Rights: The International Petition System* (New York, 1979).

78. U.N. Doc. E/CN.4/1371 (1980), 12 Feb. 1980.

79. Commission on Human Rights (hereafter: CHR) Report on the Thirty-sixth Session, ESCOR(XXXVI), Supp. No. 3 (E/1980/13; E/CN.4/1408), 1980, p. 85.

80. Rodley, "The Development of the United Nations," 281 n.28.

81. Ibid.

82. Ibid., 275.

83. CHR Res. 1983/5, 15 Feb. 1983, CHR Report on the 39th Session,

ESCOR(XXXIX), Supp. No. 3 (E/1983/13; E/CN.4/1983/60), 1983, pp. 123–25. G.A. Res. 38/3, 27 Oct. 1983.

84. CHR Report, 1983, p. 123.

85. CHR Res. 1983/5, 15 Feb. 1983, arts. 1, 6, 9; ibid., 124–25.

86. U.N. Doc. A/38/PV. 38, 29 Oct. 1983, p. 78.

87. G.A. Res. 38/3, 27 Oct. 1983, preamble.

88. CHR Res. 1983/7, 16 Feb. 1983, art. 1; CHR Report, 1983, p. 128.

89. CHR Report, 1983, p. 127.

90. G.A. Res. 38/29, 23 Nov. 1983. For vote, see U.N. Doc. A/38/PV. 69, 1 Dec. 1983, p. 22.

91. G.A. Res. 38/29, 23 Nov. 1983, preamble and arts. 1, 3.

92. Ibid., art. 8.

93. CHR Res. 1983/30, 8 March 1983. This resolution was passed by a vote of 19 to 14, with 10 abstentions. CHR Report, 1983, p. 160.

94. Ibid., preamble and arts. 1, 2, 3, 4, 5.

95. CHR Res. 1983/34, 8 March 1983, arts. 1, 4; CHR Report, 1983, pp. 164–65.

96. CHR Report, 1983, p. 164.

97. CHR Res. 1983/8, 16 Feb. 1983; ibid., 129.

98. CHR Res. 1983/6, 16 Feb. 1983; ibid., 126.

99. G.A. Res. 38/40, 7 Dec. 1983.

100. CHR Res. 1983/37, 8 March 1983; CHR Report, 1983, pp. 168–69.

101. CHR Res. 1983/38, 8 March 1983; ibid., 169–71.

102. CHR Res. 1983/29, 8 March 1983; ibid., 157–60.

103. CHR Res. 1983/1, 15 Feb. 1983; ibid., pp. 112–16; CHR Res. 1983/2, 15 Feb. 1983; ibid., pp. 116–18; CHR Res. 1983/3, 15 Feb. 1983; ibid., pp. 118–20; CHR Res. 1983/27, 7 March 1983; ibid., pp. 154–55.

104. CHR Report on the 40th Session, ESCOR(XXXX), Supp. No. 4 (E/1984/14; E/CN.4/1984/77), 1984, p. 151.

105. Ibid., 153.

106. G.A. Res. 38/100, 16 Dec. 1983; Res. 38/102, 16 Dec. 1983; Res. 38/101, 16 Dec. 1983.

107. CHR Res. 1983/1, 15 Feb. 1983; CHR Report, 1983, pp. 112–16.

108. Ibid., arts. 3, 5.

109. Ibid., art. 6.

110. Ibid.

111. Thomas M. Franck and H. Scott Fairley, "Procedural Due Process in Human Rights Fact-finding by International Agencies," *Am. Jour. Intl. Law*, 74 (April 1980): 327.

112. CHR Res. 1983/2, 15 Feb. 1983; CHR Report, 1983, pp. 116–18.

113. CHR Res. 1983/27, 7 March 1983; CHR Report, 1983, pp. 154–55.

114. G.A. Res. 38/180A, 19 Dec. 1983. See also G.A. Res. 38/180B, C, D, E, 19 Dec. 1983.

115. U.N. Doc. A/34/PV. 14, 29 Sept. 1979, pp. 4–6.

116. See Meron, *Remarks*.

117. ESCOR, 56th Sess., Supp. No. 5 (E/5464), 1974, pp. 56–57.

118. ECOSOC Res. 1873(LVI), 17 May 1974.

119. Sub-Commission on Prevention of Discrimination and Protection of Minorities, Res. 8(XXVII), 21 Aug. 1974, at p. 53 of U.N. Doc. E/CN.4/1160, 18 Oct. 1974.

120. G.A. Res. 3219(XXIX), 6 Nov. 1974.

121. ESCOR, 58th Sess., Supp. No. 4 (E/5635), 1975, p. 4.

122. U.N. Doc. A/10285, 7 Oct. 1975.

123. G.A. Res. 3448(XXX), 9 Dec. 1975.

124. Ibid.

125. U.N. Doc. A/PV. 2433, 9 Dec. 1975, pp. 41–42.

126. See chapters IB (draft decision number 1), VI and XXA (Res. 3(XXXII)) and XXB (decision No. 1 (XXXII)) and annex of ESCOR, 60th Sess., Supp. No. 3 (E/5768), 1976, p. 1. See also: ECOSOC Res. 1994(LX), 12 May 1976; G.A. Res. 31/124, 16 Dec. 1976 and Letter of 30 Sept. 1976 from Chile transmitting 16 communications between Chile and the Human Rights Commission, U.N. Doc. A/C.3/31/4, 4 Oct. 1976, p. 1.

127. CHR Res. 9(XXXIII), 9 March 1977. For the resolution and the vote, see, respectively, ESCOR, 62nd Sess., Supp. No. 6 (E/5927), 1977, pp. 82, 35–36.

128. U.N. Doc. A/32/227, 29 Sept. 1977, p. 1.

129. G.A. Res. 32/118, 16 Dec. 1977.

130. U.N. Doc. A/32/PV. 105, 16 Dec. 1977, pp. 29–30.

131. U.N. Doc. A/33/331, 25 Oct. 1978, pp. 224–29.

132. G.A. Res. 33/175, 20 Dec. 1978.

133. Ibid., para. 7.

134. U.N. Doc. A/34/583, and Add. 1, 21 Nov. 1979, p. 1 in both documents.

135. G.A. Res. 34/179, 17 Dec. 1979.

136. G.A. Res. 37/183, 17 Dec. 1983; G.A. Res. 38/102, 16 Dec. 1983.

137. U.N. Doc. A/38/PV. 100, 26 Dec. 1983, pp. 22–23.

138. Address at the opening of the 38th Session of the Commission on Human Rights, Geneva, 1 Feb. 1982. Reprinted in Theo von Boven, *People Matter: Views on International Human Rights Policy* (Amsterdam, 1982), 83.

139. U.N. Doc. A/37/564, 4 Nov. 1982, p. 2.

140. Ibid., 3.

141. Ibid., 123.

142. Ibid., 123–26.

143. Ibid., 127.

144. Ibid., 128.

145. Ibid.

146. Ibid., 129.

147. Ibid., 123.

148. U.N. Doc. E/CN.4/1983/18, 21 Feb. 1983, p. 1.

149. Ibid., 15.

150. Ibid.

151. Ibid., 12–15.

152. Ibid., 15.

153. Ibid., 16.

154. Ibid.

155. Ibid. It should be noted that the International Labour Organisation has appointed a commission of inquiry, under the chairmanship of Dr. Valticos, to investigate the non-compliance of Poland with its legal obligations under ILO covenants. Those familiar with the ILO's performance in fact-finding expect better things of this examination than have so far been produced by the office of the Secretary-General. See the *New York Times*, March 8, 1984, p. A14.

156. U.N. Doc. E/CN.4/1984/26, 1 March 1984, p. 12.

157. *Regents of the University of California v. Bakke*, 438 U.S. 265 (1978).

158. *Morton v. Mancari*, 417 U.S. 535 (1974).

CHAPTER 13: Playing Hard-Ball

1. U.S. delegate Kenneth L. Adelman in the G.A.'s First Committee, 57th Mtg., 8 Dec. 1982. U.N. Press Release GA/PS/2388, 8 Dec. 1982, p. 2.

2. League of Nations Treaty Series, Vol. XCIV (1929), no. 2138, p. 65.

3. G.A. Res. 35/144C, 12 Dec. 1980.

4. The three ordinary members listed by titles in the text are: Dr. Edward E. Ambeva, Col. Hugo B. Javier, and Dr. Humberto Guerra. U.N. Doc. A/37/259, 1 Dec. 1982, p. 5.

5. U.N. Doc. A/36/613 (Annex), 20 Nov. 1981, p. 1.

6. U.N. Doc. A/37/259, 1 Dec. 1982, p. 1.

7. Although the Group made an effort to visit those parts of Kampuchea that were under the control of the Sihanouk regime recognized by the U.N., it proved impossible to make the necessary travel and security arrangements to their satisfaction, thereby dissipating the only possible on-site inspection (ibid., 30–31).

8. Ibid., 49.

9. On one occasion, when the Group did obtain some reliable samples, they were sent to a "neutral country" for analysis. What follows is described in the Group's report: "Upon arrival, they were met by a representative of one of the laboratories. In accordance with prior arrangements, the representative accepted the box of samples and took it to the laboratory. A few hours later, the Chairman [of the Group of Experts] received a message from the head of the laboratory to the effect that official authorization had not been forthcoming and, hence, the laboratory was no longer in a position to carry out the analysis. However, since authorization had been anticipated the box had been opened. The Group, therefore, decided not to use those samples for analysis, with a view to preserving the impartiality of the process" (ibid., 45).

10. Ibid., 50.

11. *New York Times*, Nov. 25, 1982, p. A17.

12. "Chemical Warfare in Southeast Asia and Afghanistan: An Update," U.N. Doc. A/C.1/37/10, 1 Dec. 1982.

13. *New York Times*, Dec. 5, 1982, pp. 1, 23.

14. GAOR(XXXVII), First Committee, 58th Mtg., 8 Dec. 1982. U.N. Press Release GA/PS/2389, 8 Dec. 1982, p. 1.

15. U.N. Press Release GA/PS/2388, p. 13.

16. Ibid, 8.

17. See the *New York Times*, June 2, 1983, p. A16; June 3, 1983, p. A30; June 13, 1983, p. A14; June 21, 1983, p. C1; Nov. 28, 1983, p. A22; Dec. 14, 1983, p. A34; Feb. 14, 1984, p. A26.

18. G.A. Res. 37/98E, 13 Dec. 1982.

19. Ibid.

20. G.A. Res. 37/98D, 13 Dec. 1982.

21. Ibid.

22. U.N. Doc. A/38/435, 19 Oct. 1983, p. 2.

23. G.A. Res. 38/187C, 20 Dec. 1983.

24. U.N. Doc. S/16128, 7 Nov. 1983, p. 1. See also U.N. Doc. S/16104, 31 Oct. 1983, p. 1.

25. U.N. Doc. S/16433, 26 March 1984, pp. 20–26.

26. U.N. Doc. S/16397, 8 March 1984, p. 1.

27. U.N. Daily Press Briefing (Mr. Giuliani), 9 March 1984. Summary for U.N. Secretariat.

28. Soviet Press Briefing (Mr. Ovinnikov), 12 March 1984. Summary for U.N. Secretariat.

29. U.N. Daily Press Briefing (Mr. Giuliani), 9 March 1984. Summary for U.N. Secretariat.

30. U.N. Doc. S/16438, 27 March 1984, p. 1.

31. U.N. Doc. S/16433, 26 March 1984, p. 11.

32. U.N. Doc. S/16454, 30 March 1984, p. 1.

33. G.A. Res. 36/148, 16 Dec. 1981.

34. G.A. Res. 37/121, 16 Dec. 1982.

35. See, for example, G.A. Res. 38/84, 15 Dec. 1983.

36. See Report of the Group of Governmental Experts, U.N. Doc. A/38/273 (Annex), 6 July 1983.

37. U.N. Doc. A/36/PV.100, 19 Dec. 1981, pp. 62–70.

38. G.A. Res. 33/53, 14 Dec. 1978.

39. G.A. Res. 37/194, 18 Dec. 1982. G.A. Res. 38/118, 16 Dec. 1983.

40. G.A. Res. 37/194 (Annex), 18 Dec. 1982.

41. G.A. Res. 36/162, 16 Dec. 1981.

42. G.A. Res. 36/55, 25 Nov. 1981.

43. G.A. Res. 17/1843, 19 Dec. 1962.

44. Ibid., art. 1, para. 1.

45. Ibid., art. 2, para. 1.

46. U.N. Doc. A/36/PV.73, 28 Nov. 1981, p. 13.

47. Ibid., p. 11.

48. U.N. Doc. A/C.3/36/SR.36, 30 Oct. 1981, p. 6.

49. Ibid.

50. U.N. Doc. A/C.3/36/SR.43, 9 Nov. 1981, p. 7.

51. Testimony of Ambassador Jeane J. Kirkpatrick, before the Senate Appropriations Committee, Foreign Operations Subcommittee, March 2, 1984, p. 6 (mimeo).

52. Richard L. Jackson, *The Non-Aligned, the U.N. and the Superpowers* (New York, 1983), 153.

53. U.N. Charter, art. 17(1).

54. U.S. Dept. of State, *31st Annual Report: United States Contribution to International Organizations, Report to the Congress for Fiscal Year 1982*, Dept. of State Publ. 9368, 1983, p. 3.

55. Ibid., 3–4.

56. Proposed Programme Budget of the Biennium 1982–1983, GAOR(XXXVI), Supp. No. 6 (A/36/6), p. 65.

57. U.S. Dept. of State, *31st Annual Report*, 119–22.

58. Ibid., xi.

59. John P. Renninger et al., *Assessing the United Nations Scale of Assessments: Is it Fair? Is It Equitable?* Policy and Efficacy Study No. 9, UNITAR, 1982, pp. 41–42.

60. U.N. Doc. A/C.5/37/SR.8, 8 Oct. 1982, pp. 8–9.

61. Ibid., 9. The summary record has been corrected by actual quote from the mimeo of Senator Johnston's speech.

62. Ibid., 6.

63. U.N. Doc. S/8296, 13 Dec. 1967, p. 1.

64. See Interim Report, Committee of Experts. U.N. Doc. S/9836, 15 June 1970.

65. GAOR(XXIV), Supp. No. 1A (A/7601/Add. 1), Sept. 1969, p. 2.

66. The author cast those votes for the Solomon Islands as *pro bono* delegate.

67. Renninger, *Assessing the United Nations . . .* , 3.

68. *Report of the Preparatory Commission of the United Nations.* (PC/20), ch. IX, s.2, para. 13.

69. Renninger, *Assessing the United Nations . . . ,* 3.

70. U.N. Doc. A/80, 11 Oct. 1946, p. 11.

71. Renninger, *Assessing the United Nations,* 16–17.

72. G.A. Res. 1/69, 14 Dec. 1946.

73. G.A. Res. 9/876, 4 Dec. 1954.

74. G.A. Res. 27/2961B, 13 Dec. 1972.

75. U.N. Yearbook, 1972, p. 713.

76. Interview with Mr. Theodore Papendorp (March 2, 1983, New York).

77. Renninger, *Assessing the United Nations . . . ,* 17. G.A. Res. 3/238, 18 Nov. 1948.

78. G.A. Res. 3228(XXIX), 12 Nov. 1974.

79. *Report of the Preparatory Commission of the United Nations.*

80. GAOR(XXXII), Supp. No. 11 (A/32/11), 26 Aug. 1977, p. 22; as adopted in G.A. Res. 32/39, 2 Dec. 1977.

81. Report of the Committee on Contributions, GAOR(XXXVII), Supp. No. 11 (A/37/11), p. 12.

82. G.A. Res. 36/231A, 18 Dec. 1981.

83. GAOR(XXVII), Supp. No. 11 (A/38/11), 30 Aug. 1983, p. 13.

84. G.A. Res. 34/6B, 25 Oct. 1979.

85. Renninger, *Assessing the United Nations,* 9.

86. G.A. Res. 36/231A, 18 Dec. 1981.

87. G.A. Res. 37/125, 17 Dec. 1982.

88. The statistics for these calculations are available in: GAOR(XXXVII), Supp. No. 11 (A/37/11), Annex III, Table I; and in A/37/11/Add. 1, 29 Nov. 1982, pp. 6–9.

89. *Report of the Preparatory Commission of the United Nations.*

90. Mr. Petersen. U.N. Doc. A/C.5/37/SR.7, 8 Oct. 1982, p. 7.

91. U.N. Doc. A/C.5/37/SR.8, 8 Oct. 1982, p. 6.

92. Ibid., 7–8.

93. Ibid.

94. *Certain Expenses of the United Nations,* Advisory Opinion, 20 July 1962, ICJ Reports, 1962, p. 164.

95. G.A. Res. 1854(XVII), 19 Dec. 1962.

96. U.N. Doc. A/5916, 31 Aug. 1965 and Add. 1, 30 Sept. 1965, p. 6. See also *New York Times,* Aug. 17, 1965, pp. 1, 6.

97. "The U.S. Role in the United Nations," Hearings before the Subcommittee on Human Rights and International Organizations, Committee on Foreign Affairs, House of Representatives, Sept. 27 and Oct. 3, 1983, p. 61 (Appendix B).

98. *Financial Emergency of the United Nations,* Report of the Secretary-General, U.N. Doc. A/C.5/37/15, 13 Oct. 1982, p. 12.

99. Ibid., 3.

100. Department of State Authorization Act, FY 1980 and 1981, PL 96–60, s.102(a) (2) and 102(c) (1) and (2), 93 Stat. 395, Aug. 15, 1979.

101. Jackson, *The Non-Aligned,* 157.

102. H. Cong. Res. 322, S. Cong. Res. 68, 97th Cong., 2d sess.: *Congressional Record,* (House), 128: H1943 (May 10, 1982). For more recent statutory version, see: Department of State Authorization Act, FY 1984 and 1985, PL 98–164, s.115, 97 Stat. 1021, Nov. 22, 1983.

103. Cited in speech by Gregory J. Newell, Assistant Secretary of State for Interna-

tional Organization Affairs, U.S. Dept. of State, at the 24th Annual Conference of the International Studies Assn., April 8, 1983 (mimeo).

104. Ibid.

105. Further continuing appropriation, 1983, PL 97–377, s.159, 96 Stat. 1923, Dec. 21, 1982.

106. *Congressional Record* (Senate), 129 (March 14, 1983): S2792.

107. See statement by the Secretary of State, Oct. 16, 1982, made available to news correspondents by acting Department officer Susan Pittman. *U.S. Dept. of State Bulletin*, 82 (Dec. 1982): 63.

108. G.A. Res. 302(IV), 8 Dec. 1949.

109. Report of the Commissioner-General UNRWA, 1 July 1981–30 June 1982. GAOR(XXXVII), Supp. No. 13 (A/37/13), 16 Sept. 1982, pp. 49, 50, 55.

110. Ibid., 47, 70.

111. GAOR(XXXVI), A/SPC/36/SR.21, 2 Nov. 1981, p. 3.

112. Ibid., 2.

113. Mr. Lavin. GAOR(XXXVII), A/SPC/37/SR.26, 10 Nov. 1982.

114. Foreign Assistance Act of 1969, PL 91–175, s.108(a), 83 Stat. 819, Dec. 30, 1969.

115. Report on UNRWA Inquiry into Allegations of Misuse of Its Training Center at Siblin, Lebanon, 18 Oct. 1982. See also Special report of the Commissioner-General UNRWA, G.A.(XXXVII), A/37/479, 28 Sept. 1982, pp. 12–13. *New York Times*, Oct. 27, 1982, pp. A1, 9.

116. Interview with Ambassador Olof Rydbeck (Nov. 23, 1982, New York).

117. Department of State Authorization Act, FY 1982 and 1983, PL 97–241, s.109(a), Aug. 24, 1982.

118. *New York Times*, Dec. 31, 1982, p. A1.

119. G.A. Res. 37/66, para. 9, 3 Dec. 1982.

120. *New York Times*, Dec. 31, 1982, p. A1.

121. U.N. Press Release WS/1109, 7 Jan. 1983.

122. *Financial Emergency of the United Nations*, 3.

123. Ibid., 2.

124. Ibid., 4.

125. Ibid., 3, 12–13.

126. *New York Times*, Sept. 23, 1983, p. A7.

127. Ibid., Oct. 21, 1983, p. A11.

128. PL 98–164, s.113.

129. *U.S. Participation in the U.N.*, Hearings and Markup before the Committee on Foreign Affairs etc. of the House of Representatives, 97th Cong., 2d Sess., April 22, 27; May 4, 1982, p. 170.

130. Ibid.

131. Ibid., 159.

132. The decision, in the form of a letter from Secretary of State George P. Shultz was communicated to UNESCO Director-General Amadou Mahtar M'Bow in Paris on Dec. 28, 1983, to become effective on Dec. 31, 1984.

133. *Los Angeles Times*, Dec. 29, 1983, p. 1. The Letter of Notification by Secretary George P. Shultz to Director-General Amadou Mahtar M'Bow is in "U.S. Withdrawal from UNESCO," Committee on Foreign Affairs, House of Representatives, April 1984, p. 50.

134. Foreign Assistance Act of 1974, PL 93–559, s.9(a) (2) (h) (2).

135. PL 98–164, s.113, s.116(b) (1) (c). For a discussion, see Richard Bernstein,

"The U.N. versus the U.S.," *New York Times Magazine*, Jan. 22, 1984, p. 18, and esp. 68.

136. *New York Times*, Feb. 25, 1984, p. 22. For the view of more committed anti-U.N. forces, see "The U.S. and UNESCO: Time for Decision," Executive Memorandum, The Heritage Foundation, No. 40, Dec. 5, 1983.

137. "U.S. Withdrawal from UNESCO," a study by the staff of the House of Representatives' Foreign Affairs Committee, is essentially opposed to withdrawal now.

138. A.K. Solomon, "Stay in UNESCO," Op-Ed, *New York Times*, Jan. 2, 1984, p. 23.

139. John E. Fobes, "U.S. and UNESCO: The Folly of 'Copping Out,' " Letters, *New York Times*, Jan. 1, 1984, p. 12E. This view is shared by the staff of the Foreign Affairs Committee. See "U.S. Withdrawal from UNESCO."

140. Ibid., 12.

141. *New York Times*, Jan. 22, 1984, p. 7.

142. Reprinted in Second Supplemental Appropriations Bill, 1976, Hearings before the Subcommittee of the Committee on Appropriations, House of Representatives, 94th Cong., 2d Sess., Part 2, 1976, p. 11.

143. Ibid., 8.

144. *New York Times*, Nov. 2, 1979, pp. A1, 13.

145. Ibid., Jan. 28, 1978, p. 42.

146. Ibid., June 28, 1978, p. 4; February 28, 1979, p. 7.

147. Ibid., April 16, 1980, p. 5.

148. U.N. Doc. A/5857, 1 Jan. 1965, p. 1.

149. U.N. Doc. A/6419, 19 Sept. 1966, p. 1.

150. U.N. Press Release WS/1131, 10 June 1983.

151. *U.S. Participation in the U.N.*, 154.

152. Continuing Res. of Nov. 14, 1983, s.101(b), 97 Stat. 964, and State Department Authorization Act FY 1984 and 1985, PL 98-164, s.117, 97 Stat. 1022, Nov. 22, 1983. See, for example, U.S. Department of State, Report to Congress on Voting Practices in the United Nations, Feb. 24, 1984.

153. For example, *Congressional Record* (Senate), 130 (April 3, 1984): S3660; (April 9, 1984); S4087; (April 10, 1984): S4191.

154. *U.S. Participation in the U.N.*, 154.

155. Testimony of Ambassador Jeane J. Kirkpatrick, pp. 2-3 (mimeo).

156. Jackson, *The Non-Aligned*, 107.

157. Daniel Patrick Moynihan, *A Dangerous Place* (Boston, 1978), 259; see also 106–8.

158. *New York Times*, Oct. 21, 1983, p. A20; Dec. 20, 1983, p. A5.

159. *New York Times*, Oct. 21, 1983, p. A20.

160. Frank J. Donatelli, Assistant Administrator for Africa, Letters, *New York Times*, Jan. 16, 1984, p. A14.

161. *U.S. Participation in the U.N.*, 154.

CONCLUSION

1. The figure is contained in a statement by Secretary-General Pérez de Cuéllar at a meeting of the Brookings Institution and U.N. Association of U.S.A., Washington, D.C., 25 May 1984. SG/SM/3558, 25 May 1984.

Index

New York Times (continued)
  on UN's peacekeeping role, 173
  on UN's role in Yom Kippur war, 170
  on U Thant, 93
  and U Thant's efforts to mediate Viet-
    nam War, 155–157
New Zealand, 251
Ngo Dinh Diem, 156
Nicaragua, 60, 167, 226, 230, 235, 246
Niger, 78
Nigeria, 208, 227, 258
Nixon, Richard M., 172
Nkrumah, Kwame, 124, 176
Non-Aligned Movement, 117
  and chemical warfare question, 248–
    251
  and Cuban missile crisis, 149
  disaggregation, 208–209
  in Dominican Republic crisis, 71
  double standard for aggression, 226
  efforts to lower budgetary assessments,
    257–258
  and fiscal crisis, 84–85
  fragility of coalition, 212
  in Goa crisis, 56–58
  and human rights, 237–238
  importance of non-intervention to, 230
  on Indonesian independence, 80, 82
  linkage of Israel and South Africa,
    218–219
  neutralist views, 159
  proposed consensus on Guam, 189–190
  and Puerto Rico question, 201
  and refugee question, 251
  response to Soviet invasion of Afgha-
    nistan, 226–227
  Soviet surrogates in, 189–192
  US criteria for aid to, 267–268
Non-intervention, 65
North Atlantic Alliance, 4
North Atlantic Treaty Organization, 181
North Borneo, 81, 228
North Borneo-Sarawak, 148–149
Norway, 35
Novak, Michael, 253
Nyerere, Julius, 214

Olivieri, Anibal, 64
Omaha World Herald
  on Goa crisis, 57

support of US joining UN, 10
  on UN Charter, 20
ONUC. *See* United Nations Congo
    Operation
Organization of African Unity, 207–208
Organization of American States, 60–61,
    70–71, 127
Ortona, Egidio, 124, 165

Pacific Islands Strategic Trust. *See* Pacific
    Trust Territory
Pacific Trust Territory, 187, 191–195
Padilla, Hernan, 202
Pakistan, 72–75, 150, 169, 211, 229,
    236. *See also* Hyderabad
  civil war, 166–167
  independence, 47
  in Kashmir crisis, 51
  support of Afghan resistance, 143–144
Pakistani Bengal, 237
Palau, 192
Palestine, 169
  1983 UN conference, US boycott, 265
  linkage to South Africa, 214–215
  partition, 28–29, 128
Palestine Liberation Organization. *See*
    PLO
Palestine National Covenant, 219
Palme, Olof, 142, 152, 182
Papanek, Jan, 60
Paraguay, 71
Parthasarathi, Gopalaswami, 73, 91
Peace criminals, 9
Peacekeeping
  interpositional, 168–170
  non-UN institutions, 180, 181
Peacekeeping forces, 28, 42, 92. *See also*
    specific force
  on Cyprus, 125–126
  Secretary-General's power of initiating,
    125
Peacekeeping operations
  financing, 84–85, 172, 173, 263
  in India-Pakistan, 150
  in Mid-East (1956), 137–138
Pearson, Lester, 42, 64, 137
Pe Kin, U, 65
Peking formula, 136, 151
Pepper, Claude, 9
Pereira, Pedro Theotonio, 56